Laissez-faire banking

Foundations of the market economy series

Edited by Mario J. Rizzo, *New York University* and
Lawrence H. White, *University of Georgia*

A central theme of this series is the importance of understanding
and assessing the market economy from a perspective broader than
the static economics of perfect competition and Pareto optimality.
Such a perspective sees markets as causal processes generated by
the preferences, expectations and beliefs of economic agents. The
creative acts of entrepreneurship that uncover new information
about preferences, prices and technology are central to these processes. Accordingly, institutional arrangements will be assessed
with respect to their ability to promote the discovery and use of
knowledge in society.

The market economy consists of a set of institutions that facilitate
voluntary cooperation and exchange among individuals. These
institutions include the legal and ethical framework as well as
more narrowly 'economic' patterns of social interaction. Thus the
law, legal institutions and cultural or ethical norms, as well as
ordinary business practices and monetary phenomena, fall within
the analytical domain of the economist.

Other titles in the series

The meaning of market process
Essays in the development of modern Austrian economics
Israel M. Kirzner

Prices and knowledge
A market-process perspective
Esteban F. Thomsen

Keynes' general theory of interest
A reconsideration
Fiona C. Maclachlan

Laissez-faire banking

Kevin Dowd

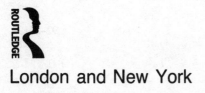

London and New York

First published 1993
by Routledge
11 New Fetter Lane, London EC4P 4EE

Simultaneously published in the USA and Canada
by Routledge
29 West 35th Street, New York, NY 10001

© 1993 Kevin Dowd

Phototypeset in Baskerville by Intype, London
Printed and bound in Great Britain by
Mackays of Chatham PLC, Chatham, Kent

British Library Cataloguing in Publication Data

A catalogue record for this title is available from the British Library

Library of Congress Cataloging in Publication Data
Dowd, Kevin.
  Laissez-faire banking / Kevin Dowd.
      p.   cm. — (Foundations of the market economy series)
  Includes bibliographical references and index.
  ISBN 0–415–08584–5
  1. Free banking—History. 2. Monetary policy—History.
I. Title. II. Series.
HG1588.D68   1993
332.1—dc20   92–26123
                                                        CIP

Contents

Figures and tables

Acknowledgements

I should like to thank the Cato Institute for permission to reprint chapters 2, 4 and 14; the Durell Foundation for permission to reprint chapters 9 and 16; Forrest Capie and Geoffrey Wood for permission to reprint chapter 11; and the Australian Institute for Policy Analysis for permission to reprint chapter 13. I should also like to thank the editors of the *Journal of Financial Services Research*, *Kyklos*, the *Journal of Economic Surveys*, the Scottish Economic Society and Blackwell's for permission to reprint chapters 3, 5, 6, 10 and 15 respectively. I am also indebted to the Cato Institute, the Durell Foundation and the Wincott Foundation for financial support for much of this work.

Last, and most important of all, I should also like to thank all those who have contributed in one way or another to the essays. I am indebted to George Selgin, Lawrence H. White and Charles Goodhart for valuable feedback, and to Alan Jarvis and an anonymous referee for their help on the volume itself. I am also grateful to friends at the Universities of Sheffield and Nottingham and outside for their support, and I would particularly like to thank Mark Billings, Dave Chappell, Alec Chrystal, David Greenaway, Duncan Kitchin, Mervyn Lewis, Tony McGuiness, Tony and Sue Sampson, and Basil Zafiriou for that and much else besides. My biggest debt, as always, is to my parents and brothers, Brian and Victor, and most of all to my wife Mahjabeen and (even though she does not yet know it) to my daughter Raadhiyah. I would therefore like to dedicate the book to them.

Chapter 1

Introduction

The idea of free (or *laissez-faire*) banking has enjoyed a remarkable renaissance in recent times, and there are few economists by now who are still unaware of it. Yet it was not so long ago that 'respectable' economists would have dismissed it as more or less obvious nonsense – many did – and most people today still seem to find the idea of free banking somewhat mystifying. It is a novel idea that challenges too much of what most people still take for granted – that banking is inherently unstable, that the banking system needs a lender of last resort or deposit insurance to defend it in a crisis, and that the government has to protect the value of the currency, to mention only the most obvious of such beliefs. Many economists have invested a great deal of human capital getting to grips with the theory that lies behind these claims, and they are understandably reluctant to throw that capital away and rethink their views on money and banking over again from scratch. Yet, as Lawrence H. White has aptly observed, free banking itself is 'an obvious and simple idea' (1989: 1), and one would have thought it intuitively appealing to economists who believe that markets are better able to allocate scarce resources than politicians and government officials.[1]

The argument for free banking is also very simple. If markets are generally better at allocating resources than governments are, then what is 'different' about 'money' and the industry that provides it, the banking industry, to lead one to conclude that money and banking are an exception to the general rule? Each industry is different, of course, but the fact that the clothing industry differs in some ways from the footwear industry does not lead me to believe that a different public policy stance is appropriate to each, or that either is an exception to the general rule that free trade and *laissez-faire* are best. It may be, however, that the industries are 'different' in some ways because public policy has made them so, but that still does not tell us that the industries are intrinsically different, or that the intervention that makes them 'different' is justified. So it is, I believe, with money and banking. Banking is 'different' from other industries, but not in a way that is relevant to public policy, except perhaps in so far as the banking industry is itself the product of that policy.

FREE BANKING THEORY

This book contains a collection of essays on free banking and related subjects written between 1987 and 1991. Broadly speaking, the chapters fall into three categories, the first of which deals primarily with the theoretical issues raised in the free banking controversy. Chapter 2, 'Automatic stabilizing mechanisms under free banking', was originally published in the winter 1988 issue of the *Cato Journal*. It uses the Mengerian 'invisible hand' process to describe how a free banking system might evolve from a primitive economy, and argues that this free banking system would have three distinct features: (1) multiple note issuers who issued convertible currency, (2) a regular note exchange between those issuers, and (3) the insertion of 'option clauses' into banknote contracts that would give the issuer the right to postpone demands for redemption provided they later paid compensation to those whose redemption demands had been deferred. It argues that each of these features helps to stabilize the banking system – convertibility and the note exchange help to discipline over-issues, ensuring that excess notes are returned rapidly to their issuers, and the option clause helps ensure that banks can meet sudden large demands for redemption (and in the process makes such events less likely to occur anyway). The chapter goes on to compare the stability of the free banking system with that of the highly regulated, interventionist systems we have today. Generally speaking, governments first intervened to raise revenue by suppressing banking competition and forcing bank customers to accept a quality of service they would otherwise have rejected. The usual pattern was then to establish a monopoly bank of issue (and thus, incidentally, to eliminate the note-clearing process). With the currency monopolized, the link between the currency and gold was severed and the price level made a hostage of the political process. These interventions were associated with restrictions on banking activity that weakened the banks more, and the weakness of the banks in turn put pressure on the government to intervene further to 'support' the banking system (e.g. by deposit insurance), but in so doing the government weakened the banks even more. A vicious circle was set up in which bank weakness appeared to justify government intervention to cure it, but progressive doses of that medicine only made the underlying disease worse – and therefore apparently even more necessary – and the patient went from bad to worse.

Chapter 3, 'Option clauses and the stability of a *laissez-faire* monetary system', was originally published in the *Journal of Financial Services Research* in 1988 and develops the option clause idea further. It had two primary aims. First, it set out to explain why the insertion of option clauses into banknote contracts might be in the mutual interest of both banks and their customers – an important point which earlier work on the option clause tended to gloss over – and, second, it sought to examine further the stabilizing features of option clauses. The option clause would be invoked by a bank if market interest rates rose beyond a critical point, but we would expect this critical point to be well above normal interest rates. The prices of bills would consequently be well below normal, and a speculator in the bill market could expect to make a medium-term profit by buying bills. Speculative purchases would therefore tend to restore bill prices and interest rates to normal. They would also reward those who helped to reverse the rise in interest rates, and penalize those who 'panicked' and pushed interest rates up. Rational speculators would usually be able to anticipate the exercise of the option clause, however, so it would seldom if ever be the case that interest rates actually reached the trigger point. The threat of the exercise of the option clause would usually suffice to reverse the rise in interest rates, so option clauses could be stabilizing even if they were never actually exercised. The chapter ends with an examination of Scottish experience of option clauses over the period 1730–65 which suggests that the Scottish evidence was broadly consistent with what this theory would lead us to expect. The chapter suggests, therefore, that the option clause idea might be a useful direction for further free banking research.[2]

Chapter 4 was prepared for the seventh annual Cato monetary conference 'Alternatives to Government Fiat Money' in Washington in February 1989. The single most important argument underpinning the modern apparatus of central banking is that it is there to counteract the alleged inherent instability of monetary *laissez-faire*, and the position of the central banking school collapses without it. If this argument were correct, a stable *laissez-faire* monetary system would be self-contradictory, and a viable example of such a monetary system would suffice to refute it. The chapter therefore sets out to provide such an example and explore its properties. Starting from an initial primitive state, the chapter uses the 'invisible hand' story to trace the development of an anarchic monetary system driven entirely by the self-interest of those who operate within it. The early part of the story is very familiar, but the later part is not. The exchange media issued by the banks are initially denominated and redeemable in gold dollars, but the banks eventually drop the pledge to redeem in gold and switch to redeeming with financial instruments instead, which are more efficient for the purpose and which, it turns out, also help to stabilize the banking system against shocks to the gold market. By this stage gold is no longer used as a medium of exchange or as the banks' medium of redemption, but the monetary system is still tied to gold by virtue of the nominal price of gold being fixed, and the price level is determined by the factors that determine the relative price of gold against goods and services in general. An increase in the supply of gold, for example, leads to a decrease in its relative price and therefore, since its nominal price is fixed, to a rise in the general price level. The price level is vulnerable to shocks from changes in the factors determining the demand and supply of gold. If agents demand price-level stability, as they presumably do, then the gold anchor is unlikely to provide them with the amount of price-level stability they desire, and the banks would be prompted by public demand (as well as their own interest) to change the gold anchor for one that would generate a more stable price level. The chapter suggests as an example that they should switch to bricks but, whatever it was they switched to, it would have to have a stable relative price against goods and services generally in order to generate a stable price level. This anarchic monetary system is thus both stable and efficient. It is stable because the agents operating in it demand stability and have the means to make those demands effective. It is efficient because there are no restrictions against mutually beneficial trades. It is driven purely by the self-interest of the private agents operating 'within' it, and it has no guardian – no government, no central bank or lender of last resort, and no deposit insurance corporation – to look after it. It has no need of such a guardian, however, and is perfectly capable of protecting itself.

A secondary aim of the chapter was to explain how we got the much less desirable monetary systems we actually have. It turns out to be relatively straightforward, and all one needs to do is introduce a government into our hypothetical anarchy and see what happens. The new government is driven by its own 'private' interests, but it differs from other agents in having a legal monopoly of the use of force. The process of government intervention argument is then similar to that described in chapter 2, but described here in more detail. Governments intervene initially for revenue reasons – taxing the banks in politically less costly than other forms of taxation, and so on – but these interventions create problems of their own, and the political process then requires further intervention (supposedly) intended to straighten out the mess caused by earlier interventions. The first-best solution – removing the earlier intervention – is usually ruled out for political reasons, and we end up caught in a vicious circle in which one mess leads to another and the health of the monetary and banking system is weakened further at each stage. The only solution is to roll back the interventions and allow market forces free rein to establish the stable and efficient system that people want.

Chapter 5 considers a different issue. Many people still appear to believe that banking is a natural monopoly and, moreover, that the monopolization of the currency and other aspects of present-day central banking can be justified on natural monopoly grounds. There have been a number of good discussions of natural monopoly in recent free banking literature,[3] but it seemed to me that all of them looked only at one or more aspect of natural monopoly, and no single treatment had examined the issue in each of its different guises. Natural monopoly occurs where there are economies of scale so large that the competitive equilibrium has room for only one firm. There are two main sources of economies of scale in banking – economies in reserve-holding and economies from diversification – but once one examines them closely there is no reason to expect any of these scale economies to be sufficiently strong to produce a natural monopoly. There are also some other arguments for natural monopoly, but they turn out to be spurious. There is the well known argument that competitive note issue leads to hyperinflation (e.g. Friedman 1960: 8), but this argument is an argument about externalities and not really a natural monopoly argument at all. Remember that a natural monopoly argument maintains that one firm can produce at less cost than two or more, and this particular argument makes no such claim. The competitive hyperinflation argument is also dubious as an externalities argument, but that is another issue. The second argument is that banking is a natural monopoly because everyone in the same economy (typically) uses the same unit of account, but this argument is invalid because it confuses economies of standardization (or economies in use) and economies of production. Economies of standardization arise because we find it convenient to use certain social conventions, but they do not involve production *per se*. The fact that I might use a particular unit of account implies nothing about the production of 'money' or anything else, but a natural monopoly argument is an argument about production and therefore cannot apply to a situation where production is absent. The third argument is that banking is a natural monopoly because of economies of scale in building public 'confidence'. This type of argument usually maintains that there are certain fixed costs to building confidence, and that the government usually has an advantage providing currency because of its power to tax. This line of reasoning runs into various problems – it seems to presuppose that competitive banks would issue inconvertible notes, which they would not; it would appear to imply that deposit banking is a natural monopoly, which it does not appear to be; it is not clear why the power to tax should promote confidence; and it is very difficult to claim seriously that the history of banking supports the notion that governments have helped promote confidence. The chapter ends by taking a brief look at the evidence on economies of scale in banking, which comes from a large number of empirical studies and the experience of (relatively) free banking systems in the past. The evidence would appear to be clear – there are economies of scale in banking, but not a single empirical study or historical instance of free banking suggests that banking is a natural monopoly. The argument that banking is a natural monopoly is decisively rejected.

Chapter 6 tries to grapple with certain other issues raised in recent theoretical work. I had been deeply suspicious of the alleged 'necessity' for government deposit insurance (or, for that matter, a government-sponsored 'lender of last resort') for years, but my early attempts to argue against deposit insurance usually met with the response that Diamond and Dybvig (1983) had established a sound case for it, and, though I was not convinced, it embarrassed me that I had no adequate response. After a certain amount of work on the issue I eventually concluded that the basic problem with their model is that it ignores any role for equity capital. Their intermediary takes in deposits which it invests in projects in the 'real' economy, and depositors are issued with liabilities which they can redeem in either of two periods, but the intermediary's resources are limited to whatever the public deposit with it, and there is no outside (i.e. 'equity') capital. The Diamond–Dybvig intermediaries offer depositors who withdraw in the first period a greater return than that which the underlying 'real' investment process has yet generated – underlying investments have to be liquidated prematurely to meet such depositors' demands, and yet the intermediary had to make some such promise to early withdrawers in order to attract business – and the problem is that there is a limit to how many such demands it can meet without running out of assets. This weakness can lead depositors who do not have to withdraw for consumption purposes to lose confidence and run themselves, and Diamond and Dybvig argue that government deposit insurance is needed to reassure them and thereby prevent a run. The underlying theme of the chapter is that this sort of analysis of bank runs properly applies only to the peculiar intermediary that exists in Diamond and Dybvig's model, and it applies because it has no other capital to cushion its early withdrawal losses; but it does not apply to real-world banks, which can use such capital to guarantee the value of their deposits. This chapter was written over 1989 and 1990 and attempts to provide a perspective on the large literature that has followed the initial Diamond–Dybvig paper and demonstrate what I believe is wrong with it. It makes three main points:

Virtually all this literature follows Diamond and Dybvig in dealing with intermediaries that issue only one class of liability – a peculiar kind of debt–equity hybrid that looks like debt to those who redeem in the first period but which looks like equity to those who redeem afterwards. The fact that we do not observe such liabilities strikes me as a major problem with this work, but an even bigger problem is the fact that most real-world financial intermediaries issue more than one class of liability – they issue both claims that are fixed in value outside bankruptcy (i.e. debt, properly speaking) and residual claims which constitute ownership of the intermediary (i.e. equity). This distinction between different types of liability is very important, and corresponding to it is the difference between different types of institution – between mutual funds, which issue only one class of liability, and banks in the normal sense of the term, which issue both. Diamond and Dybvig explain the instability that can arise from a particular kind of mutual fund, but it is banking instability as such that we are really interested in.

The chapter develops further the point that whether an intermediary distinguishes between its liabilities or not has a critical bearing on its exposure to runs. A mutual fund is exposed to Diamond–Dybvig-type runs, but a bank need not be, provided that it keeps an adequate capital base. We thus arrive at a strong theoretical rationale for why capital adequacy matters, and it is reassuring to recall that the practical bankers at least have long understood its importance in shoring up confidence in a bank and discouraging depositors from running. The fact that the theoretical literature on banking instability seems to have little or no place for it simply suggests to me that that literature has little to say on the real-world problems that we wish to address.

Finally, it seems to me that the arguments for deposit insurance made in most of this literature come close to assuming what they set out to prove. In order to explain why there should be any financial intermediation in the first place, it is necessary to explain what is 'wrong' with an unintermediated market that the intermediary can improve. In the Diamond–Dybvig world this requirement translates into the existence of 'frictions' in the operation of a credit market between the first and second periods. (Wallace 1989, refers to agents being 'isolated' from each other in the first period.) The problem then arises that a government deposit insurance guarantee would violate this 'isolation' condition. In order to provide a credible guarantee, the government needs the means to be able to 'find' agents in the first period after they have made their withdrawals, and that implies that it must be able to overcome their 'isolation'. The argument for deposit insurance thus runs into a dilemma: if the technology exists to overcome isolation, then that technology means that financial intermediation serves no purpose, and therefore financial intermediaries should not exist and there would be no need for deposit insurance to protect them; but if the technology does not exist, then the government cannot physically provide (credible) deposit insurance and it makes no sense for it to try. Arguments for deposit insurance must implicitly suppose that the government has access to a technology that the private sector lacks – and one, incidentally, that the private sector cannot (for some unspecified reason) 'rent out' from the government. As far as I can see, the argument for deposit insurance thus virtually assumes what it purports to prove.

HISTORICAL EXPERIENCE

We then turn to the second part of the book, which looks at the historical evidence on free banking. History can make an important contribution to our understanding of monetary and banking theory because it provides a kind of laboratory in which we can test some of the predictions of our theories, and the information that comes from these 'tests' is valuable even though none of the 'experiments' was conducted under 'pure' laboratory conditions. Chapter 7 examines one of the most interesting historical experiences of free banking – Australian free banking in the nineteenth century. The Australian episode is of unique interest because the Australian banking system experienced a major crisis in 1893 which many have blamed on free banking, and many Australian economists apparently still do. The chapter attempts to assess the overall Australian experience of free banking, but it focuses particularly on the extent to which free banking contributed to the debacle of the 1890s. It turns out that the banking 'crash' was not the systemic banking collapse that it might superficially appear to have been. The strong banks were never in serious danger – indeed, several of them received more (re-)deposits than they really knew what to do with – and almost every note-issuing bank that suspended was afterwards able to reopen successfully. The bank suspensions were also encouraged by government intervention. This intervention included certain recent legislative changes – some of them not necessarily bad in themselves – which had allowed banks to suspend without being forced into liquidation, and the government of Victoria introduced a banking holiday and tried (unsuccessfully) to close all its banks down. The banks' capital and liquidity ratios also provide little support for the view that the banks as a whole had overreached themselves – though some individual banks certainly did – and many Australian bankers had seen the crisis coming a long time before and pulled in their horns before it hit them. Nor is there any evidence that the banking system delivered a major negative shock to the real economy, as we might have expected had the banking system collapsed in the way sometimes portrayed. The economy actually reached its nadir at around the same time as the bank 'crash', and it was already beginning to recover just when the systemic collapse hypothesis predicts it ought to have fallen further. The general picture suggests that the banking system was for the most part dragged down by the 'real' factors that were the true impetus behind the depression, and the evidence seems to point to the conclusion that the idea that Australia experienced a systemic banking collapse caused by free competition should be rejected as a myth.

The next chapter looks at US banking in the (so-called) 'free banking' period – the quarter-century before the Civil War. Anyone who has looked at the literature on this period will be painfully aware of how overwhelming it is. The federal government effectively withdrew from the banking scene in 1837 when the charter of the Bank of the United States expired, and for the next generation the field was left free for the individual states to pass whatever banking legislation they wished. The result was a staggering diversity of experience as states went off in all sorts of different directions. Some adopted (so called) 'free banking' laws – laws which allowed free entry into the banking industry provided banks observed certain (by no means innocuous) collateral requirements – modelled after the New York 'free banking' law of 1838. Others experimented with state monopoly banks or with various forms of state chartering systems, some of which had been in existence for decades already, and some states even prohibited banking altogether. These experiments took place against a very varied background of financial crisis and suspension in the late 1830s and on occasion afterwards, of severe recession in the early 1840s, of severe fiscal instability in the same states in the early 1840s and in the run-up to the Civil War, and of strong economic growth in the 1850s. To make matters more complicated, many later historians have had a tendency to see in that period what they expected to see, and many accounts are effectively corrupted by their (often dubious) theoretical prejudices, and nowhere is this tendency more obvious than in the myths of the 'wildcat' banker and the monetary 'chaos' that allegedly characterized the period.

This chapter is an attempt to step back and form a reasonably sensible overview of the banking experiences of the period as a whole. By and large, it seems to confirm the revisionist view of

Rockoff, Rolnick and Weber, and others, that New York-style 'free banking' was much more successful than earlier historians and economists had realized. It goes beyond their interpretations, however, in emphasizing the role of fiscal factors in accounting for many of the 'free bank' failures that did occur – the eligible bonds that 'free banks' were required to hold were primarily state bonds, and fiscal instability sometimes led to holders of state bonds suffering large losses when the price of those bonds fell. My interpretation of these experiences also goes beyond earlier ones in another respect which is perhaps even more important. It draws an explicit distinction between free banking – which is what we are really interested in – and 'free banking' as the term is normally used in this literature (i.e. to refer to the 'free banking' laws of the period modelled on that of New York). It seems to me that there has been too much tendency to focus on the latter, and then transfer conclusions about the latter into inferences about the former. Such a procedure is sometimes valid, but it can be misleading or at least controversial on other occasions (e.g. when one concludes from the failure of 'free banks' that (genuinely) free banks would have failed as well). I suspect that the tendency to think this way is due in part simply to the 'free banking' label attached to the New York-style law, and I find it hard to believe that modern economists would be so interested in these particular experiences if they had come in less suggestive packaging. The excessive tendency to focus on 'free banking' also distracts economists from the most natural approach to examining the banking experiences of this period, and that is to examine the extent to which each state approximated *de facto* free banking regardless of whether it had something called a 'free banking' law. A number of states – North and South Carolina and Massachusetts are notable examples – either never had 'free banking' laws or had little banking done under them, but had relatively liberal chartering policies which effectively granted free entry to the industry anyway, and, moreover, allowed entry without the potentially onerous restrictions of formal 'free banking'. Other states – Michigan in 1837 is the best example – enacted 'free banking' laws, but these laws operated under such unusual circumstances that the legal framework could not be considered as approximating genuine free banking. It is therefore crucial to distinguish (reasonable approximations to) genuine free banking from banking under 'free banking' laws, and once one does so a quite different picture emerges. Instead of the generally good, but occasionally marred, performance of banking under 'free banking' laws one gets a much clearer picture that is also much more favourable to free banking than has hitherto been appreciated. Genuine (approximately) free banking was apparently always successful, in some cases spectacularly so, and I was surprised myself at how strong the overall performance of *de facto* free banking actually turned out to be. As if to reinforce the point, state monopoly banks and state probibitions on banks in this period all appear to have failed, and there was a pronounced tendency towards the end of the period towards increasing financial liberalization as a result.

If free banking theory is the application of market economics to money and banking, then it ought to be able to do more than just explain how a free banking system might work. It ought also to be able to explain how we arrived at the monetary and banking institutions we have today, and the next four chapters attempt to use it towards that end. The first, 'Money and banking: the American experience', was prepared for the Durell Foundation conference on that theme in Washington in May 1990, and provides a very general overview of US monetary and banking history and the main lessons to be drawn from it. The US constitution originally allowed virtually no federal involvement in money and banking, and left the regulation of banking to the individual states. To set up a bank one had to acquire a charter from the local legislature, and the charter normally imposed restrictions on where one could do business. These restrictions severely limited the growth of branch banking and consequently made the American banking system much weaker than it would otherwise have been. The charter system also gave rise to a powerful lobby – the unit bankers – who not only had a vested interest in maintaining the restrictions against branch banking but who lobbied – sometimes successfully – for state protection of the artificially weakened banks in the form of note deposit insurance schemes, and these schemes usually weakened the banks even further by eroding the discipline of the market and encouraging excessive risk-taking. Despite the constitution, the federal government tried early on to charter its own national banks, but opponents of the banks were able to prevent their charters being renewed in each case, and the federal government effectively withdrew from banking after the lapse of the federal charter of the Second Bank of the United States. The following generation saw the banking experimentation of the 'free banking' period which was discussed in more detail in the previous chapter. Considerable progress in American banking had been made by the time of the outbreak of the Civil War, but the federal government then introduced the National Banking System as a wartime measure. This system was a version of the bond collateral system at the federal level, but the restrictions it involved exposed it to considerable instability, and dissatisfaction with it led eventually to the passing of the Federal Reserve Act in 1913. The Federal Reserve took over control of the provision of emergency currency – such currency had been provided earlier by the private clearing-house associations – but its failure to provide sufficient emergency currency when it was required in the early 1930s led to the banking collapses. Congress responded by extending the Fed's powers and establishing federal deposit insurance, and the consequences of the latter policy can be seen today in the collapse of much of the industry and its *de facto* nationalization by the federal government. Over the course of the century the Congress also weakened the convertibility of the currency into gold, and eventually abolished it altogether in the early 1970s. In so doing it destroyed the discipline the gold standard provided against over-expansion of the money supply and paved the way for the inflation of the last thirty years or more. The American experience of money and banking has not been particularly happy.

Chapter 10 is a review essay, first published in the February 1990 issue of the *Scottish Journal of Political Economy*, on Charles Goodhart's book *The Evolution of Central Banks* (1988). The gist of Professor Goodhart's thesis is that central banking is a 'natural' phenomenon which evolved as a response to the problems caused by market failings, and Goodhart suggests three failings in particular: he claims that free banking would not provide the information necessary for it to work properly; he questions the claims made by free bankers that the clearing system would provide a sufficient check against over-issue; and he argues that free banking would be more likely than central banking to lead to general economic fluctuations. This chapter was my attempt to respond to Goodhart's claim that he had refuted the argument for free banking, and it rejects both his theoretical analysis and his interpretation of history. It argues that information is generally scarce, like most other goods, and, though one can usually choose to describe it as 'imperfect' if one wishes, this 'imperfection' in no way constitutes a market 'failure' that can be corrected with the appropriate governmental policy response; it also argues that the clearing house argument put forward by free bankers was meant only to show how the clearing house disciplines an individual bank, but it is convertibility that disciplines the system as a whole; Goodhart's third argument, about free banking producing economic fluctuations, presupposes either that banking is a natural monopoly or that competitive banks would expand past the point where they could expect to maximize their profits, and it seems to me that the former is empirically rejected and the latter is unreasonable. As for the historical evidence, the theory that free banking is inherently unsound has a very strong empirical prediction – it predicts that free banking would not work if put into practice – which runs up against the evidence that free banking (or something like it) *was* tried and apparently *did* work in countries such as Scotland and Canada (and many others).[4] The supporters of central banking have never managed to explain the apparent success of Scottish free banking (or of other cases, either, as far as I know) which their own theory predicts could not occur. As far as I can see, the case against free banking must therefore be considered empirically refuted.

Chapters 11 and 12 then look at the evolution of English central banking over its formative period in the nineteenth century. Chapter 11, 'The evolution of central banking in England, 1819–90', was prepared for the conference 'Unregulated Banking: Chaos or Order?' held at City University Business School in May 1989 and subsequently published in Capie and Wood (1991). England had experienced relatively 'advanced' central banking while specie payments were suspended during the Napoleonic Wars, but the Bank of England reverted to a much more modest role when convertibility was restored in 1821. The chapter tries to explain how the Bank of England of the 1820s evolved into the recognizable central bank that it had become by 1890. The Bank enjoyed various privileges in the early part of this period which weakened its competitors, and the weakness of English banks gave rise to considerable public controversy. A free banking school arose which wanted to abolish the bank's privileges and establish a free banking system modelled after Scotland's, but it was the currency school that won the legislative war and saw its programme of an automatic note monopoly – one that left no room for discretionary management – implemented in the Bank Charter Act of 1844. (It was also the currency school that was responsible for the abolition

of Scottish free banking in 1845.) Having won the war, the currency school then lost the peace as it became apparent that the
restrictions on the note issue imposed by the Bank Charter Act
were themselves destabilizing and that the Bank of England could
not avoid some responsibility for the safety of the rest of the
banking system. Thomas Hankey fought a rearguard action in the
1860s to argue that the Bank should maximize its shareholders'
profits and leave other institutions to look after themselves, but
most economists – and, eventually, the Bank itself – came to accept
that its privileges imposed on it a responsibility for the welfare of
the broader banking system, and the question then was how the
Bank should best discharge that duty. The Baring crisis of 1890
illustrated the Bank's willingness to accept this responsibility as
well as the acceptance of its financial hegemony by the rest of the
financial community, and yet no Act had been passed since 1844
to confer formal central banking powers on it. Professor Goodhart
is right when he says that English central banking *evolved*, but the
Bank's early privileges and the legislation of the period 1826–45
had a decisive bearing on the course that that evolution took.[5]

Chapter 12 is a reply to my discussants at the City University
conference – Dr Michael Collins of the University of Leeds and
Mr Bill Allen of the Bank of England. I am grateful to them both
for the chance to debate these issues in public, but, while I certainly did not expect them to agree with the main themes of the
paper, I was frankly amazed at their reactions, which had no
significant bearing on the substantive points I made. Neither
of them really picked up the main themes of the paper, and both
for the most part were content to set up and shoot down straw
men that I had actually repudiated myself. Such substantive points
as they did make simply presupposed the very position I was
criticizing, and they made no attempt to defend the position on
which their assertions depended – and that despite the fact that
I had criticized that very position myself at various points throughout my paper. The two chapters and the discussants' comments[6]
are all relatively self-explanatory, and the reader can judge for
himself.

MONETARY AND BANKING REFORM

The next chapters are attempts to apply the insights of free banking theory as I understand it to current monetary and banking

issues. The point of studying the world, after all, is to see how we should try to change it, and it is important to see what guidance our theory can give us. Chapter 13, 'Stopping inflation', was originally written for circulation in Australia in 1990 and is loosely based on Sargent (1981). It sets out a proposal to reconvert the currency and tie it to a basket of goods and services, and it also reviews some potential objections to the proposal and considers the historical evidence on related monetary reforms. The basic idea is that the law should be amended to require the issuer of (what is now) base money to peg its price against a basket of goods and services, and that basket would be chosen to ensure that the price level would be relatively stable. The main objection I met with in Australia was that the cure might be worse than the disease because it might involve unpleasant side effects on output or unemployment. Such effects cannot be entirely ruled out, but rational expectations theory indicates that a credible monetary reform (i.e. one that the private sector can rationally believe) should involve lower output and unemployment costs than a disinflationary monetary policy that the public rationally disbelieve, and the standard examples of costly disinflation (e.g. the UK in 1979–81) were all cases where the public had good reason to doubt that the government was as serious about bringing inflation down as it claimed to be. The government then found itself moving south-east along an expectations-augmented Phillips curve, but the Phillips curve itself showed little sign of moving down because the government policy had little immediate impact on inflationary expectations. Had the policy been credible, on the other hand, the Phillips curve would have moved down and the costs of disinflation should have been substantially less. The chapter then considers some of the historical evidence from the monetary reforms of the 1920s. In Germany, Austria, Hungary and Poland monetary reforms to establish a convertible currency cured hyperinflation virtually immediately, and these monetary reforms apparently involved no large losses in output or employment. The 1920s also saw two moderate inflations cured in much the same way – Czechoslovakia in 1919 and France in 1926 – so the lessons from the earlier cases should apply to the elimination of moderate inflations as well as to the elimination of very rapid ones.

The next two chapters turn to western Europe and consider different aspects of the monetary unification debate. Chapter 14, 'Does Europe need a Federal Reserve system?', was prepared for the Cato/IEA conference '1992 and Beyond' held in London in February 1990. The tempo and urgency of the debate on European monetary union have accelerated considerably in recent years, much of it spurred by the Delors report (1989) and its plan to establish a European central bank and a single European currency. In my opinion this sort of approach suffers from two fundamental drawbacks. The first is that it gets its priorities mixed up. What really matters is monetary stability, not monetary union as such, and it is not even obvious that union would be a good thing anyway. What disturbs me is the prospect that the attempt to establish monetary union could lead to the sacrifice of whatever monetary stability we already have, and I am not reassured by Delors's claim that the new central bank would be 'committed to the objective of price stability'. After all, aren't most central banks already? But, even if we accept that monetary union is desirable, I very much doubt whether the Delors approach is the best way to achieve it, anyway. The historical record of central banks is hardly encouraging, and the Delors report is inconsistent on the question of the new central bank's independence from the European political authorities. (The report proposes that the bank should be independent, but the bank is also to be accountable to the political authorities, who would have overall responsibility for macro-economic policy.) The biggest danger is that the bank would fall under the influence of a European central authority that is apparently incapable of controlling its own expenditure, and I have no confidence whatever that it could resist the temptation to lean on the bank for cheap 'loans' to keep itself afloat financially. Banking history provides a lot of worrying examples where this sort of thing has happened before, and I see no reason to believe that we could expect it not to happen again here. We might also expect inflation to rise, because the new central bank would reflect some kind of average view about the appropriate rate of monetary expansion, while inflation in the EMS is determined by the views of the most conservative central bankers, the Germans. Dissatisfaction with German monetary 'conservatism' seems to me to be one of the forces behind the drive to replace the EMS with a Continental central bank in the first place. If the European monetary authorities were really committed to price stability, which I very much doubt, they would reform the value of the currency along the sort of lines suggested in chapter 13.

Chapter 15 considers another aspect of the debate on European monetary reform – the UK government's proposal for a new parallel currency, the 'hard ecu', as an alternative to the Delors plan. The UK government has never got its act together over European monetary union. It sensed the inadequacies of the Delors plan but never managed to come up with a viable alternative. Their first reaction to Delors was to suggest that the appropriate way forward was 'competing currencies', whatever that meant, but no one ever seemed to understand what the 'proposal' actually involved, government included. It was then tacitly dropped the next year when the new Chancellor, John Major, decided that the 'hard ecu' was now the way forward, and few people appear to understand that much better, either. It seems to me that the hard ecu proposal is a particularly unconvincing variant of the old parallel currency theme. The problem with a parallel currency is to show what incentive people have to switch over to it, and the empirical evidence suggests that a sufficient incentive exists only when the initial currency perfoms very badly relative to the alternative, and that usually means the old one has to hyperinflate. Since we do not (yet) have hyperinflation in western Europe, it must therefore be extremely doubtful whether Europeans would voluntarily switch over to a new currency. Yet the proposal envisages the new currency, the hard ecu, as being effectively tied to the strongest ERM currency, at present the mark. There is therefore no incentive to switch over from marks to hard ecus, and, given the exchange rate margins implied by EMS membership, precious little incentive to switch over from any other currency either. The irony is that if sufficient incentive did exist, as the proposal requires, then many of us would already have switched to the deutschmark, and the mark would be well on the way to becoming a common European currency. The very fact that it has not yet happened seems to indicate that the incentive is not there. The hard ecu would therefore appear to be a non-starter, and the fact that it was not even mentioned in the Maastricht treaty in December 1991 suggests that the British government has already given up on it.

The last chapter, 'The US banking crisis: the way out', returns to the United States. It was written for the Durell Foundation conference 'Financial Fitness in the 1990s?' in Scottsdale, Arizona, in May 1991, and it set out to provide both an explanation of the causes of the crisis in the US banking and thrift industries as well as a suggested way out of the crisis. The approach I took was to adopt a benchmark free banking model and explain how market forces there would provide the public with the banking stability they required, and this time I particularly emphasized the role of capital adequacy. The public would avoid banks they perceived as weak and withdraw their deposits from them, so weak banks would be unable to maintain their market share. Their business would go to those banks the public perceived as strong, judging primarily by their capital adequacy. Competition for business would therefore lead the banks to provide the public with the capital adequacy standards they demanded, and, since the public desire strong banks, strong banks would be what they would get. Now introduce deposit insurance into the picture. Deposit insurance weakens the industry in two principal ways. First, it undermines the incentive to maintain capital adequacy. With its deposits insured, a bank no longer has to reassure its depositors about its soundness, and the marginal value of maintaining decent capital standards falls. The cost of capital remains unaffected, so a bank's rational response to deposit insurance is to drive its capital ratio down, and one can easily imagine situations where the privately (but not socially) optimal capital ratio was just a little above zero. (The discrepancy between private and social optima arises because the depositors no longer care about bank risk, but someone – in this case, the taxpayer – still has to bear it. Under free banking, by contrast, market forces ensure that private and social benefits are appropriately aligned.) The other consequence is that deposit insurance would encourage banks to take more lending risks. It creates a discrepancy between upside and downside lending risks which allows a bank to keep all the benefits of any risks it takes that pay off but to pass off to the insurance company at least some of the losses it would have suffered on risks that did not pay off. Even a bank with a sound capital position would be tempted to take more risks to exploit this discrepancy, but what is really damaging is that the discrepancy worsens as the bank's capital position deteriorates. The worse its capital position the less of the downside risk it bears itself and the greater is the incentive to take (socially) irresponsible lending risks. Deposit insurance thus creates a dynamically unstable process which eventually transforms an initially safe and sound banking industry into a group of zombies artificially kept alive by policies that suspend the normal mechanism by which weak firms are eliminated from the market, and the perversity of the whole process is aggravated by the incentives that individual deposit insurance officials have to hide the true state of affairs from Congress, because Congress would hold them responsible, and by the incentives to the individual politicians themselves to turn a blind eye or hide what they do know from the electorate who would hold them responsible.

The chapter outlines a plan to resolve the crisis, on the (heroic?) assumption that some group in power eventually decides to take it seriously. If the cause of the crisis is a perverse incentive structure that rewards anti-social behaviour, the key to resolving it is to restore reasonable incentives. The various peculiarly American restrictions on banking – branch banking laws, Glass–Steagall, and so on – need to be swept away, but the most important reform is the abolition of deposit insurance itself, and deposit insurance must go because it is the cause of the worst of the perverse incentives that destroy the banking system.[7] The problem is how to dismantle the whole apparatus in a way that does not bring down the whole house of cards in the process. There *is* a way to do it, but a viable reform programme would have to satisfy three conditions. First, it would have to set out a date for the abolition of deposit insurance. This announcement would concentrate minds in the banking and thrift industries, and all those engaged in it (and those thinking about entry, like foreign banks) would have to decide whether they wished to continue under the new post-insurance regime. Those who decided to carry on would have to restore their financial health in order to be able to withstand the impact of competition without the crutch of insurance to lean on, and the others would simply continue to sink. As the date approached for the abolition of deposit insurance, the difference between the two types of institution would become increasingly apparent, and any zombies that were still undead when the date arrived would be finished off then. The second principle is that Congress should honour its debts. That requires that it should avoid such tempting but counterproductive options as trying to make the sound banks bear the cost of the clean-up operation, which would only cripple the good banks and delay recovery. It should also avoid cutting back the deposit insurance guarantee before the banking system had been weaned off its dependence on it, which might provoke a nationwide bank run. Congress should bear the costs up-front and avoid short cuts. Last, but by no means least, the financial system should be deregulated to establish free trade in the financial services industry. This last plank of the reform package is essential if the industry is ever to reach full financial health and be able to compete effectively with foreign competitors.

Part I

Free banking theory

Chapter 2

Automatic stabilizing mechanisms under free banking

One objective of this chapter is to explain the automatic stabilizing mechanisms inherent in a free banking system. Starting from an initial primitive state of society, I suggest how a banking system would evolve in the absence of state intervention. The state is assumed only to enforce contracts freely entered into by private individuals. Government expenses are paid through taxation, but there is no taxation specific to the monetary system. (In other words, there is no seigniorage.) The evolutionary process is driven by individuals' pursuit of their own private interests, and no one consciously attempts to promote any wider 'social interest'. At each stage individuals seek to reduce their exchange or operating costs, and these attempts lead to the growth of new institutions that reduce the costs of co-ordinating economic activity.[1] With no state interference to hinder it, this evolutionary process would lead to the development of a highly sophisticated 'free banking system' with several distinctive features, including: (1) multiple note issuers who would guarantee to redeem their notes in a commodity that the community recognized as valuable; (2) a regular note exchange between these notes issuers; and (3) the insertion of 'option clauses' into the convertibility contracts to protect the note issuers against sudden excessive demands for liquidity. Each of these would contribute significantly to the stability of the monetary system, making the resulting monetary equilibrium a highly stable one.

The second objective of this chapter is to compare the stability of the free banking system with that of the highly regulated central banking monetary regimes we have today. Showing how the monetary system would have evolved in the absence of state interference provides a benchmark against which to assess the effects

of that interference. The essential difference between free banking
and central banking is that the latter involves the suppression of
stabilizing mechanisms that would arise spontaneously without
government interference. This strongly suggests that central banking is a destabilizing form of state intervention.

THE EVOLUTION OF A FREE BANKING SYSTEM

The development of coins

In a relatively primitive society in which individuals are just beginning to trade with each other, 'coincidence of wants' problems
would arise frequently if market participants were restricted to
barter. Some goods would be more in demand than others, however, and at some stage individuals would realize that they had a
better chance of getting the goods they wanted if they first accepted
some popular intermediate good and then swapped it for the good
they wanted to consume. This resort to 'indirect exchange', which
employs a certain class (or classes) of intermediate goods, would
allow individuals to avoid the 'coincidence of wants' problem, but
their transaction costs would remain high. In particular, they
would still need to measure the quantity of the goods they were
offered and assess their quality. They would therefore prefer intermediate goods whose quantity was easily measured and whose
quality was relatively uniform. To minimize transport and storage
costs, market participants would also want goods that were sufficiently scarce for small amounts to have a high exchange value.
Historically, people have tended to converge on the precious metals
as desirable intermediate goods and to abandon alternatives as the
advantages of precious metals become more apparent.

The use of precious metals as intermediate goods would still
leave individuals with the inconvenience of weighing lumps of
metal and assessing their purity. This would create an opportunity
for some individuals to act as intermediaries and make their living
assessing the purity of the metal brought to them and recasting it
into pieces of more convenient size. As such practices spread,
the fineness and sizes of metal pieces would gradually become
standardized, and the private intermediaries would mark the pieces
to show their weight and quality. The profits made by the earliest
of these intermediaries would attract others, and they would compete with each other for business. It would not take long for them

to realize that they could attract more business by using distinctive marks on the metal pieces they issued. The intermediaries would thus become private mints and their metal pieces privately issued coins.

Each of these private mints would exist primarily to maximize its own profits, which could be generated in several ways. One would be by offering competitive minting fees. Another would be by developing a reputation for probity to reassure prospective customers that they would not be cheated. A third would be by innovation: mints would experiment with coins of new denominations, alternative metals, and so on. Any successful innovations would be imitated by other mints and would become widely adopted. It bears stressing that these mints would have no incentive to cheat by overstating the weight of their coins, because such deception would be easy to detect, and this would harm the mint's reputation and hence its business. Furthermore, the law would classify such activity as fraud.[2]

As an aside, it is exactly at this stage that the state historically has intervened in the monetary system. Governments realized they could use their coercive powers to create a legal monopoly that would make the minting business very profitable. Even if the government's service was inferior to that of private mints, the public could be forced to accept it, as the state would prohibit its subjects from using the coins of other mints.[3] The government could then impose high minting charges or misrepresent the weight of the coins it issued. Note that it is only the state's monopoly over the means of legal coercion that enables the state mint to stay in business. A private mint could not provide an inferior service and survive because it would have no way of compelling people to use its services.

The development of banks issuing convertible notes

The use of coins would still involve considerable costs, particularly the cost of storage (including the costs of ensuring that one's coins were safe), and the cost of moving coins around. To avoid storage costs, some people would be prepared to pay others who already had the facilities to keep gold safe – those with strongboxes – to store their gold for them. In practice, this would mean that metalsmiths ('goldsmiths') or merchants who regularly kept large amounts of gold or silver would be asked to look after other people's gold for a fee, and they would probably do so, because the marginal cost would be quite low. Depositors would obtain receipts from those holding their gold of silver attesting to the value of each deposit.

As the practice spread it would increasingly happen that, when two people agreed on an exchange, one would go and withdraw his coins and hand them over to the other, who would deposit them again. Provided that the party accepting payment was satisfied that the goldsmith was likely to honour his commitment, it would be more convenient for him simply to accept the goldsmith's receipt and save both parties the bother of visiting their goldsmiths. Goldsmiths' receipts would thus begin to circulate as a medium of exchange in their own right. At the same time, the goldsmiths would begin to notice that only a small proportion of their deposits of gold would be demanded in redemption over any given period, and they would realize that they could lend out some of the gold deposited with them and face little danger of being unable to meet their liabilities. This lending activity would give them an opportunity to earn an additional profit.

The goldsmiths would thus become bankers and begin to compete with each other for deposits. One way of doing this would be to offer interest on deposits, replacing the earlier fees charged depositors for the safe keeping of their money. More important, the goldsmith–bankers would also compete for deposits by offering guarantees to prospective depositors that the receipt notes issued by them would retain their value. Perhaps the most persuasive guarantee they could offer would be to make their notes 'convertible', that is, to promise to convert their notes back into specie. The goldsmith-bankers would in fact have offered such promises right from the start, of course, because no one would have placed deposits with them unless they were assured that they could withdraw them. These guarantees would have the status of legally binding contracts, and the violation of such a contract would therefore expose the banker to the legal penalty for default, which we will assume to be sufficiently high to make a banker careful to avoid it.

This commitment to convertibility is one of the most important features of a free banking system, and it has several major implications. First, it would help ensure that banknotes remained relatively stable in value. The value of convertible notes would be tied to the value of gold. It follows that the exchange value of notes against goods in general would fluctuate only with changes in the relative price of gold – that is, the exchange rate between gold and other goods – and we would not normally expect this to be particularly volatile. We might therefore expect the price level to be reasonably stable.

Second, the commitment to convertibility would provide an effective discipline against goldsmith-bankers who issued an excess of notes. When banks issued convertible notes, their circulation would be limited by the demand to hold them. That demand would depend on such factors as the precise features of the convertibility contract (for example, whether the depositor had to give notice when he wanted to withdraw his deposit), the bank's reputation, the familiarity of its notes, the number of branches it maintained, and so on. Any notes issued beyond the demand to hold them would be returned for redemption. A bank would not deliberately choose to issue an excess of notes, because they would not remain in circulation long enough to justify the expense of putting them into circulation and then taking them back again. If a bank sought to increase its note issue, it might attempt to improve its reputation, advertise its notes more, or open more branches. But it could not increase its note issue simply by putting more notes into circulation. It is one thing to *put* more notes into circulation, but quite another to *keep* them there.

The development of note-clearing

The next stage in the evolution of the banking system would be the development of a note clearing system that would arise out of bankers' attempts to raise their profits by increasing the demand for their notes. In the beginning, no banker would accept the notes of other banks when such notes were submitted by the public because to do so would make rivals' notes more acceptable and raise his competitors' profits. But any two banks could make themselves jointly better-off by agreeing to accept each other's notes. Each bank would benefit, because the public would more readily accept the notes of either of the two banks, given the knowledge that the other bank would accept the notes as par as well. The notes of those two banks would thus become slightly more attractive than alternative media of exchange such as gold or the notes of other banks. Thus additional bank pairs would be formed, and it would become increasingly apparent that the easiest way to organize the note exchange system would be to meet regularly at a central clearing session where the banks would hand back each others' notes and settle the differences.[4] In this way a central clearing system would evolve out of the banks' own private self-interest.[5]

The clearing system is important because it would provide a further restraint on the ability of any one bank to overissue its notes. Without the clearing system a bank that overissued would face a reserve drain only from the general public's returning its notes for specie, and it might take some time for this to force the bank to restrain its issues. Once the clearing system was in operation, however, a bank issuing more notes than the public wanted would also face reserve losses at the central clearing sessions. These losses would occur as the public deposited the extra notes at other banks and those banks returned them to the issuing bank. A bank that over-issued notes would thus lose reserves through two channels – through direct redemption by the public, and through indirect redemption via the clearing system – but the latter channel would be likely to operate more quickly.

The development of a liquidity market

We have seen that the bankers' self-interest would lead to note convertibility and to a central clearing system, and both of these would discipline any bank that overissued its notes. They would therefore contribute significantly to the stability of the monetary system. However, if a bank was committed to redeeming all its note liabilities on demand, it would still face a problem of potential illiquidity, given its ability to redeem only a fraction of its liabilities at any given time. With sufficient advance notice a sound bank would be able to meet demands for redemption by liquidating assets,[6] but a problem could arise if it failed to receive the notice it needed. It is this lack of notice that gives rise to the possibility that an otherwise sound bank might become illiquid and unable to honour its obligations.

Two institutions would develop to deal with the problem. The first would be the growth of a market in short-term liquidity. This would arise because bankers' holdings of liquidity would be subject to random short-term fluctuations that were difficult to predict accurately. At any given time some banks would find themselves with more liquidity than they had anticipated and others with less. Those with 'excess' reserves would be willing to lend them out on a short-term basis, while those that were short of reserves would be willing to borrow them, making both groups better-off. Experience would teach the lending banks what kind of collateral policy to adopt, what information they needed from prospective borrowers, and so on.

The development of option clauses

However, a bank could borrow only if others were ready to lend to it. This is an important qualification, because it means that the banking system as a whole might not be able to obtain the reserves needed from the liquidity market, even though any individual bank could.[7] This constraint could pose a problem if an unexpectedly high demand for cash caused the short-term liquidity market to dry up temporarily as everyone demanded more reserves and no one was willing to supply them.[8] In principle, this could cause the banking system to collapse. Since the danger is caused by the banks' commitment to redeem their notes on demand without notice, the banks might try to avoid it by modifying the convertibility contract on their notes. Instead of guaranteeing to redeem their notes for specie on demand, the banks could reserve the right to defer redemption for some pre-specified period on the condition that noteholders would be paid pre-specified compensation when the notes were finally redeemed. In other words, the bankers could insert clauses into the convertibility contract that would give them the option of deferring redemption.

These 'option clauses' would need to be carefully designed.[9] To remain in business, a bank that introduced option clauses would need to reassure the public that its notes were still safe. It would want to make a credible promise that it would use the option only in exceptional circumstances and that noteholders would suffer no losses even then. To be convincing the bank would need to set the compensation paid to noteholders at a level high enough for it never to be in the bank's interest to exercise the option except in an emergency. The bank might also stress the advantages of the option clause to the risk-averse noteholder.[10] Those noteholders slow to react to a run on specie would lose little or nothing by their failure to be first in line, and indeed would gain from the compensation the bank would have to pay for suspending convertibility. And even if the bank should turn out to be insolvent as well as illiquid, then losses would be shared on a *pro rata* basis among noteholders and other bank creditors rather than falling disproportionately on those who were not quick enough to demand redemption before the bank suspended. It would thus be clear to the public that the bank would have recourse to the option only as a last resort, and that the option, if anything, would probably make individuals better-off.

Trial and error in the market place would determine the period over which redemption could be deferred and the interest to be paid on notes whose redemption had been suspended. The exact form of the option clause is therefore difficult to predict before-hand. The compensatory interest rate would presumably be linked to the interest rate in the short-term liquidity market. A plausible formula would be 'x points above the average rate prevailing in the short-term market over the past y months'. With such a for-mula, the option would never be exercised in 'normal' times because a bank could always obtain liquidity more cheaply in the short-term market. If a liquidity crisis were to develop, however, the short-term interest rate would rise sharply, and once it rose beyond a certain threshold level it would be cheaper for the bank to obtain – or, strictly speaking, to retain – liquidity by invoking its option of deferring payment. For simplicity we assume that all banks face the same threshold level,[11] leading all banks to invoke their options simultaneously.

This would set in motion a chain of events that would break the crisis, send interest rates downward again and alleviate the shortage of liquidity. In the period immediately after the banks started to exercise their options, market interest rates would remain above the penalty rates the banks were paying through the use of their options, making it worthwhile for banks to borrow by invoking their options and to lend on the short-term liquidity market. The banks would thereby channel liquidity to where the demand for it was greatest, thus beginning to alleviate the shortage of liquidity and causing market interest rates to begin to fall. The banks would continue these arbitrage activities until the market interest rate had come down to the penalty level. Once it reached that level the banks would no longer derive any benefit from exercising their option to defer redemption, and they would be ready to resume redemption on demand. By the time interest rates had fallen to that level, the public's panic over liquidity would have abated. As the demand for liquidity continued to fall interest rates would return to pre-panic levels. The introduction of option clauses would thus protect the liquidity of the banking system and break the panic. The knowledge of this would itself make the banking system considerably more stable by eliminating the possibility of a bank run starting because of the public's self-fulfilling expectations of a run.[12]

This completes our discussion of the evolution of a *laissez-faire* banking system. Note, in particular, how institutions like convertibility, a clearing system, a market for short-term liquidity and option clauses would develop and protect the banking system against shocks. The sole driving force behind these stabilizing mechanisms would be individuals' self-interested attempts to protect themselves against adverse conditions. A free market monetary system would thus be highly stable.

THE EFFECTS OF STATE INTERVENTION INTO THE MONETARY SYSTEM

We have seen how an ideal monetary system would have evolved had only two conditions been satisfied: (1) that individuals should promote their own private interests, and (2) that the state should adopt a policy of benign neglect and do nothing except enforce contracts freely entered into by private agents. Of these two conditions, the first appears to occur regularly while the second is much more difficult to achieve. A casual glance at monetary history will confirm that states have interfered in the monetary system on an almost continuous basis. Recent monetary history also confirms that the current monetary system is frequently unstable and very different from the system that would have evolved in the absence of state interference.

But why did a less stable monetary system come to replace a more stable one? The process begins when the state intervenes in the monetary system to raise revenue by suppressing competition and forcing its subjects to accept a quality of service they would reject if they had wider freedom of choice. At first this intervention takes the form of establishing a government-sponsored bank with a monopoly over note issues. Regulations are also imposed on other banks. Such intervention prevents a clearing system from developing and makes the private-sector banks more vulnerable to shocks, thus undermining the stability of the banking system. The state also frequently turns to the private banking system for forced

loans when there is a fiscal crisis (such as a war), and such
pressure further weakens and destabilizes it. By this stage public
concern about the instability of the banking system has become
acute, and the state feels obliged to intervene further to try to
stabilize the monetary system. Banks' activities are then regulated
and supervised to improve their 'safety and soundness'. This intervention increases the instability even more, and we end up with
the monetary system we have today.

The effects of a monopoly note issue

Establishing a monopoly bank of issue serves to destabilize the
monetary system in several ways. The absence of competition and
alternative currency choices makes it more difficult for the public
to get rid of an over-issue of notes, creating more economic disruption in the presence of a currency monopoly than with multiple
competing note issuers. With multiple banks of issue a bank that
over-issues its notes will be checked relatively quickly by clearing
losses. If there is only one bank of issue, however, there cannot
be a clearing system, so the only check on over-issue will be direct
redemption of the notes by the general public, and this will take
somewhat longer. (Assuming that is, that it is allowed to occur in
the first place. With an inconvertible currency, such as we have
at present, there is no automatic check at all against over-issue.)
Another way of looking at the difference is to see a monopoly
bank's over-issue as similar to what would happen if multiple
banks of issue were able to form a cartel and expand in tandem,
so that none suffered clearing losses. The banks would still be
disciplined when the public brought in notes for redemption, but
the process of correcting the over-issue would obviously take
longer. A larger over-issue could take place than would have
occurred otherwise, and the economic disruption it caused would
obviously be greater.

The lack of competitors thus gives a monopoly bank of issue
greater discretion than any competitive bank would have. But it
then has to face the problem of how to use that discretion. The
government-sponsored monopoly bank would have extreme difficulty judging the likely effects of its actions, and it would frequently
have to fall back on its judgement and manage as best it could.
To avoid this and make its actions consistent, the monopoly bank
would try to develop rules-of-thumb to guide it on a day-to-day

basis, but what should such rules be? In practice there are a wide range of policies to choose from, and it would be very difficult to choose one.[13]

This problem of finding the right policy would soon become even more difficult, because the private banking system would adapt to the monopoly note issuer and gradually force the monopoly bank into the role of 'guardian' of the monetary system. This would occur as private banks increasingly used the monopoly bank's notes as reserves. Paper would replace gold as the other bank's reserve medium because paper is easier to store and less expensive to transport than gold, and because the public would generally prefer to withdraw their deposits in notes rather than in gold. As notes replaced gold in circulation and in banks' vaults, the country's gold reserves would tend to become centralized in the vaults of the monopoly bank of issue. This would force on it the role of lender of last resort in a liquidity crisis. Even if it wanted to, the bank would find it difficult to ignore requests for assistance in a crisis because of the danger that the crisis would spread further and destroy it as well. Whether intended or not, the monopoly bank of issue would become responsible for protecting the country's liquidity, and this would force it to take an increasingly broad view of the effects of its policies. The pressure to find the right policy would increase, but the right policy would be increasingly difficult to find.

The effects of restrictions on bank organization

A second source of instability is the regulation of the monetary system. In the early days of state intervention, regulations would be imposed to reinforce the monopoly of the note issuer. A good example was the 'six partner rule' embodied in an Act of Parliament of 1708. This Act restricted all banks in England and Wales to partnerships of no more than six persons. The intention was to reinforce the Bank of England's privileges (in return for which the bank granted the government a subsidized loan). The Act effectively prohibited reliable (that is, large) aggregations of capital in banking, as those partnerships that were allowed to enter the industry were too small to withstand any substantial shock. People knew how vulnerable the banks were and, whenever there was any disturbance, rushed to withdraw their gold. As a result, scores and sometimes hundreds of these banks failed. The 'six partner rule' thus made English banking extremely unstable. Restrictions on branch banking have had a somewhat similar effect in the United States. Many examples of this kind of regulation exist. What they all have in common is that they destabilize the banking system by hindering the attempts of banks to protect themselves against shocks.

The effects of further government demands for revenue

It soon became apparent that the state could not always obtain the revenue it wanted by simply establishing or strengthening a currency monopoly. Each time war broke out the state would experience considerable – and often extreme – financial difficulties. Government expenditure would rise steeply, but it would be difficult (or at least awkward) to cover the additional expenditure by taxation or borrowing. The government would therefore press the banking system for subsidized loans instead. These loans would drain the banks' reserves and thereby expose the banking system to a liquidity crisis. This in turn would weaken the ability of the banking system to maintain convertibility and hence threaten not only the stability of the banking system but also the stability of the value of the paper currency. The threat posed by these loans obviously depended on their size, but in some cases they led to the suspension of convertibility. In more extreme cases they also led to inflation.

Two historical examples will illustrate the point. In 1793 the government of William Pitt suddenly found itself at war with France. It had made no provision for war and was reluctant to raise taxes or to borrow enough to cover its additional expenditure. As its expenditure mounted, the government repeatedly applied to the Bank of England for loans. The bank protested but dared not refuse, and in granting the loans its reserves were seriously depleted. The threat of French invasion in 1797 was then enough to trigger a major liquidity crisis which the bank had not the reserves to meet. It was saved from insolvency only by the government stepping in to abolish its commitment to redeem its notes.[14] Convertibility was thus wrecked, in large part by the demands the government had made on the Bank of England.

Something similar happened at the outbreak of the US Civil War in 1861. When war broke out, the federal government found it difficult to obtain the revenue it wanted by borrowing from the general public. The Secretary of the Treasury drew up a plan to borrow from the banks by compulsion. At the same time he started to issue US notes which he obliged the banks to redeem in specie. This put the banks' reserves under a great deal of pressure, and they were forced to suspend convertibility at the end of 1861. The federal government resorted to a series of issues of inconvertible paper money that produced substantial inflation.[15]

In both these cases the pressure put on the banking system was enough to destroy convertibility. In each case, however, public opinion was sufficiently in favour of the principle of convertibility for convertibility to be restored once peace had returned. The public were prepared to accept inconvertible paper currency in an emergency like a war, but they were not prepared to accept it on a permanent basis. This antipathy to inconvertible currency lasted throughout the nineteenth century and was reinforced by experience in France during the *assignat* period, in England during the Restriction period (1797–1821), and in the United States during the Civil War suspension period (1861–79).

This support for convertible currencies lasted until the 1920s. Support for convertibility then fell as economies tried to readjust after the shock of the First World War and people became increasingly attracted to the idea that further state intervention in the economy was the only way to solve the major economic problems of the day. Supporters of this view were opposed to convertibility because it limited the government's freedom to act. They argued that the commitment to convertibility was nothing more than a needless restraint on the ability of the government to conduct what was euphemistically described as a 'rational' monetary policy. By the end of the 1920s this view had won many adherents, and the commitment to convertibility was abandoned soon afterwards by one country after another.

There was no longer any guarantee that the currency would retain its value. The value of the currency was henceforth to be determined by the amount of it issued by the government. The proponents of inconvertible currency were not particularly concerned because they believed that the extra leeway this gave the government would be used to promote the social good. Even if that meant a certain amount of inflation, they argued, it would still be in the public interest if it helped to achieve a 'higher' social good than price stability – such as lower unemployment. The price level had thus changed from something the private sector could depend upon in making plans for the future to a policy tool for the government to manipulate as it pleased.

The argument for managed currencies was based on the premise that the government could be expected to promote the social good, provided only that it was given sufficient power. But this requires that the interests of the state should coincide with those of the rest of society, and proponents of governments' economic intervention have failed to recognize a serious conflict of interest between the two. This conflict is particularly acute on the question of price stability. The private sector needs a stable framework in which to go about its business and make plans for the future. It therefore has a strong vested interest in the maintenance of price stability. The state has no such interest. Its interest, in fact, is usually to create inflation to reduce the real value of its debt to the private sector. For the state, inflation is simply a form of taxation, and a form of taxation that has the political advantage of being heavily disguised. Whatever harm it might do to the private sector, it enables the state to raise revenue without most of the electorate even realizing that they are being taxed. The new fiduciary monetary regime thus has an in-built inflationary bias with consequences we all know.

Demands for further state intervention

The kinds of intervention in the monetary system we have examined so far were motivated principally by governments' desire for more revenue. But each of these interventions destabilized the monetary system in its own way: the monopolization of the note issue prevented a clearing system's arising and thus made over-issues of notes longer-lasting and more harmful; the restrictions placed on deposit banks weakened them and made them vulnerable to shocks; the state's persistent demands for revenue from the banking system weakened and eventually destroyed the guarantee of price stability provided by convertibility, and so paved the way for inflation.

These problems of monetary instability gave rise to a great deal of public debate, and there were countless proposals of measures to deal with them. Most of the proposals advocated further state intervention, oblivious of the fact that state intervention was the cause of the problem in the first place. The state thus intervened further to correct the instability it caused, and generally made it even worse.

One such intervention was the introduction of a legal requirement that banks of issue must redeem their notes on demand, that is, the prohibition of option clauses.[16] This measure was motivated by two beliefs, one true and the other false. It is true that convertibility is a guarantee that notes will retain their value, but it is not true that failure to force redemption on demand would lead banks to issue notes of inferior value. As the earlier discussion of free banking pointed out, all that is needed to ensure that notes keep their value is a legal system to enforce convertibility contracts. Because of the greater stability of the issuing banks, both the public and the banks stand to gain when banks have the option of deferring the redemption of their notes. Enforcing convertibility on demand deprived the banking system of the benefits of option clauses, and thereby exposed it to an increased danger of bank runs.

There are many other regulations imposed on the banking system that, while designed to make it more stable, have the opposite effect. Two others will suffice here. The first was the Bank Charter Act of 1844 which separated the Bank of England into an Issue Department, which issued notes against a 100 per cent marginal reserve requirement, and a Banking Department, which took in deposits and carried on the rest of the bank's business. The Act was motivated by the currency school's belief that monetary crises were caused principally by the bank's over-expanding its note issues. The aim of the legislation was to restore monetary stability by ensuring that the bank was forced to maintain sufficient reserves to be able to redeem its notes at any time. Unfortunately, the Act also prohibited the Issue Department from lending to the Banking Department, and this exposed the bank to a serious danger. If depositors withdrew sufficient deposits the Banking Department, which operated with fractional reserves, might default. If that happened the bank itself would default, despite the fact that it still has plenty of reserves in the Issue Department. This nearly happened on three occasions, and the bank was saved only by the government intervening to suspend the Act and allow the Issue Department to lend gold to the Banking Department.

The other example was the institution of compulsory, government-controlled deposit insurance in the United States after the bank failures of the early 1930s. Federal deposit insurance was introduced in the belief that the banking system would be more stable if banks were free of the danger of sudden runs for liquidity. Unfortunately, proponents of deposit insurance failed to take account of how the banking system would respond to the incentive structure implied by the deposit insurance regime.[17] The new regime encouraged banks to take risks they would otherwise have avoided. The banks that took greater risks could offer shareholders higher expected returns, and the depositors were no longer particularly concerned about the risks because they were insured. At the same time, there was no attempt by the Federal Deposit Insurance Corporation to charge risk-related premiums. As a result, the system had the effect of subsidizing risk-taking. In time the banks responded to these incentives and adopted policies that were more likely to lead to failure. Thus the FDIC regime had a stabilizing effect in the short run but a destabilizing one in the longer run.

CONCLUSION

This chapter has argued that the free market would have provided a stable monetary system had it been left alone to do so. Its stability would have arisen from the attempts of private individuals to protect themselves against shocks. There is, as it were, no 'public good' aspect of stability that requires the state to intervene to provide more of it than the free market would provide on its own. Indeed, state intervention often has just the opposite effect because it suppresses the automatic stabilizing mechanisms that would have evolved under *laissez-faire*.

This argument suggests that the free market would still be capable of providing a stable monetary system if the appropriate conditions were established. The problem is then to find the safest way to dismantle the apparatus of state intervention and establish those conditions. We must bear in mind that private agents have grown used to intervention and have adapted to it. Some of them are dependent on it (as some banks are dependent on the FDIC). We must also bear in mind that people will not adapt to *laissez-faire* overnight, and the automatic stabilizing mechanisms it would provide would take time to evolve. Our task is therefore to design a programme that will take us to *laissez-faire* but avoid destabilizing the monetary system before we get there.

Chapter 3

Option clauses and the stability of a *laissez-faire* monetary system

This chapter further explores option clauses on convertible notes issued by competitive banks. These give banks the option of deferring redemption of their notes provided that they later pay compensation to the noteholders whose demands for redemption are deferred. They therefore allow banks to protect their liquidity if they are faced with an unexpected increase in demands for redemption. In addition, the knowledge that the banks had this protection would reassure the public that the banks were not likely to become illiquid, and this knowledge would reduce the likelihood of a bank run occurring in the first place. Option clauses are therefore a potentially important form of protection for banks that have redeemable liabilities and operate on a fractional reserve.

Despite these potential benefits, option clauses have received very little attention from economists, and most of that has been unfavourable. Adam Smith condemned them in *The Wealth of Nations* (1776: 290–1), and most succeeding economists who have discussed the issue have agreed with him (e.g. Graham 1886: 65; Kerr 1918: 74; MacLeod 1896: 188–9 and Whittick 1896: 67–9, to mention only four). Significantly, though, the only writer to examine the issue in any detail at all was Meulen (1934),[1] and he was unequivocally in favour of them. He argued that option clauses would stabilize a free banking system as well as promote the replacement of gold by paper and thereby encourage the further spread of credit. This chapter takes up where Meulen left off and analyses further the potential of option clauses to stabilize the banking system. The chapter first outlines how a *laissez-faire* banking system driven purely by private interest might develop the option clause to deal with the problem of potential illiquidity to which fractional reserve banking is otherwise subject. It then suggests reasons why individual noteholders would be prepared to accept option-clause notes in preference to notes convertible on demand – an important point which Meulen glossed over – and discusses how option clauses would both protect the banking system against liquidity crises and reduce the probability of such crises occurring in the first place. It then goes on to consider the historical experience of option clauses in Scotland in the period 1730–65. This clearly confirms the claim that option clauses would be acceptable to the public and is not obviously inconsistent with the claim that option clauses would help to stabilize the monetary system.

THE DEVELOPMENT OF A FREE BANKING SYSTEM WITH CONVERTIBLE NOTES

To discuss the theory of option-clause notes we consider the evolution of a free banking system from the following hypothetical primitive economy. Let us suppose that people originally use gold as their medium of exchange, but the use of gold is attended by various costs of storage and portability (e.g. it is expensive to keep it safe, and its weight wears holes in pockets). Now suppose that there exist individuals ('goldsmiths') who already have the means of keeping gold safe (i.e. they have strongrooms). Members of the public and the goldsmiths are both assumed to be concerned only with their own private self-interest and not at all with any broader notions of 'social interest'. Let us also suppose that there is a legal system capable of enforcing any contracts entered into by private agents, and that people wish to avoid the penalty for default, which involves having one's assets sold off to pay one's debts.

A banking system starts to evolve from this initial state of society when members of the public begin to pay goldsmiths to store their gold for them. Individuals will be ready to deposit their gold with a goldsmith provided that the fee is not too high and they are sufficiently confident that the goldsmith will not default while he has their gold. The goldsmiths will be prepared to accept the gold provided that the fee is above their marginal costs, which we would expect to be low anyway. Hence there is some potential for mutually beneficial gains from trade. The practice of making gold deposits then gradually spreads, and the goldsmiths start to notice that withdrawals and deposits will be closely matched over time, and that over a given period the net loss in gold is likely to be quite small. They will realize that they could lend out some of the gold deposited with them and earn interest on it. They will then start competing with each other for deposits to lend out. The practice of charging depositors fees will die out, and goldsmiths will start offering depositors interest payments to attract them. At the same time, it will increasingly be the case in private trade that when one person withdraws gold to pay a debt the payee will simply deposit the gold again. Provided that both parties 'trust' the goldsmith, they would both save time and trouble if the goldsmith's receipt were simply handed over instead. In this way these receipts/banknotes would start to circulate as a medium of exchange in their own right. This would reduce demands for redemption even more, and enable the goldsmith/bankers to expand their lending further.

We therefore arrive at a situation where competitive banks issue their own redeemable notes. Let us suppose that it is not feasible to pay interest on notes.[2] Let us also suppose that a market evolves in which agents can borrow gold on a short-term basis. If one likes, one could view this market as arising originally from agents' inability to predict their future cash needs with certainty. Over any given period some agents will find themselves with more cash than they anticipated, and some with less. It would then be mutually beneficial for the former to lend to the latter, and a short-term liquidity market would develop.

CONVERTIBILITY ON DEMAND AND POTENTIAL ILLIQUIDITY

To stay in business, a bank would have to persuade people to accept its notes. (For simplicity, we shall ignore deposit banking throughout). To do that, it will try to reassure people that its notes will retain their value. The most effective way to do that would probably be for the bank to offer a legally binding commitment to redeem its notes under certain specified conditions. The question then arises as to what those conditions might be. An 'obvious' commitment the bank could make would be to redeem on demand without notice, that is, to make its notes 'fully convertible'. If the banks developed originally from goldsmiths it is quite likely that they started off by offering this kind of guarantee. Such a guarantee would give the public more flexibility and cost the goldsmiths little because they would operate with a 100 per cent reserve ratio, to begin with at least. Once they started to lend out, however, they would not be able to honour more than a fraction of their note liabilities over any given (short) period, and this would expose them to the danger of defaulting on their legal obligations. This danger arises from the combination of a typical bank earning much of its income from borrowing short to lend long and its legally enforceable obligation to redeem any notes presented to it. Given sufficient time, it could liquidate enough assets to meet any demand for redemption – assuming it was solvent – but the danger of default arises because it would not get the notice it might need.

The demands for redemption could come from various sources. One source is the general public, members of which might want to redeem their notes if they believed that the bank was insolvent (i.e. if its net value was negative). They might also demand redemption if they believed – rightly or wrongly – that there was some danger of the bank becoming illiquid. They might want to avoid holding the notes of a potentially illiquid bank because they might fear that other people would be reluctant to accept the notes of a bank that suspended, or because they thought that such notes would be accepted only at a discount. Such fears might lead to noteholders demanding redemption 'just in case', and this would give rise to the possibility that the public's expectations of a run on the banks could become 'self-fulfilling' in the sense that any intrinsically irrelevant event could trigger off a bank run if it made enough noteholders apprehensive about one (see, for example, Diamond and Dybvig 1983). Demands for redemption might also come from other banks: if a bank were committed to redemption on demand, a competitor might be tempted to collect a large amount of notes and present them without warning for redemption, to make it default. These 'note duels' were a significant feature of early banking in Scotland, for instance, and we shall return to them below.

A possible solution to this potential illiquidity problem would be to modify the convertibility contract. Instead of promising to redeem on demand without notice, the bank might insert clauses into its notes giving it the option to defer redemption provided it later paid compensation to the noteholders. These 'option clauses' would have two distinctive features: a period over which redemption could be deferred, and a compensatory (or penalty) interest rate, both of which would be specified in the contract.

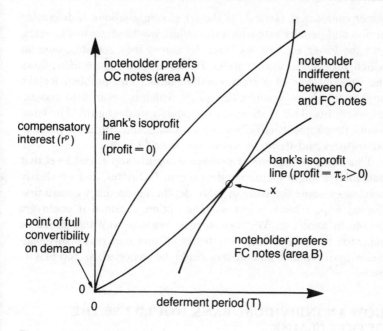

Figure 3.1 The (*ex ante*) benefits of option clauses

Other things being equal, the bank would generally prefer a longer deferment period, to give it more time to replenish reserves (which it could then do more cheaply), and it would obviously prefer a low penalty rate of interest to a higher one. In designing an option clause, however, a bank would have to make sure that it did not lose its noteholders to other banks. The first bank to introduce them would have to make sure that its new option clause (OC) notes were at least as attractive as the fully convertible (FC) notes issued by the other banks. If it failed to do so it would be overtaken by its rivals. The bank might reason that noteholders would prefer low deferment periods (because they would presumably prefer assets that could be redeemed more quickly) and high penalty rates (since a higher penalty rate would imply a larger claim to compensation if the option were invoked). Assuming appropriate convexity conditions, these preferences can be represented as in figure 3.1. The diagram shows those combinations of higher deferment periods and higher penalty interest rates that define the indifference map of the representative noteholder. The upper contour set (area A) is the set of combinations of deferment period and penalty rate which the public would prefer to FC notes, and the lower contour set (area B) shows those combinations at which the public would prefer FC notes. The figure also shows the isoprofit line of a representative bank. The problem for the bank is to select a combination (T, r^p) which is not in B to maximize its profits. This is shown at the point x in the figure. The bank would then replace its FC notes with OC notes with these particular features and its profit would rise from O to π_1.

This analysis suggests at perhaps a slightly superficial level that noteholders might be prepared to accept OC notes, and we clearly need to examine the issue in more depth. To do this we shall first discuss how a bank might use the option clause if it could get people to accept it. We then suggest reasons why this could be expected to make noteholders better-off and can reasonably conclude that rational noteholders could be expected to accept OC notes.

HOW AN INDIVIDUAL BANK WOULD USE THE OPTION CLAUSE

Let us suppose that an individual bank has managed to persuade its noteholders to accept notes with option clauses on them. Since the bank is concerned purely with its own private interest, it would invoke the option whenever that provided a cheaper way to remain liquid than borrowing liquidity in the short-term market. There seem to be three situations in which this might be the case:

The first is if the bank were suddenly presented by a rival bank with a large amount of notes for redemption. In that case the demand might be so large and unexpected that it might not be feasible to borrow in the short-term market and the bank would have to suspend. One should add, however, that much of the temptation to engage in these duels comes from the prospect of forcing a rival to default, and a bank contemplating such an attack would not expect to destroy its rival if it were protected by an option clause. It would also appreciate that an attempt to collect notes and present them for redemption would invite the other bank to retaliate at a later date. A bank might thus choose to exercise its option clause if it found itself under attack from another bank, but the chances of that happening would be likely to be reduced precisely because it had that option.

The second case is where a bank could not borrow on the market because of its poor credit rating. A bank in such circumstances would presumably have exhausted its own supply of liquid assets, and it would have difficulty using its illiquid assets for the collateral that potential lenders would require from it. In this case its borrowing difficulties would reflect the suspicions of potential lenders about its solvency. The bank could then remain liquid only by selling off illiquid assets at an increasing loss or by invoking the option clause. It would presumably liquidate assets until the effective borrowing rate was equal to the penalty rate and then it would suspend. This would give the management a chance to put the bank's affairs in order without suffering increasing capital losses, and this would help to preserve what was left of the bank's net worth. It would also protect the bank against a run which might otherwise have forced it to liquidate more of its remaining assets or even pushed it to default, either of which could inflict large losses on its creditors.[3]

The third case is where the bank can continue to borrow at the market rate, but where the market rate itself rises so far that it is cheaper for the bank to obtain (or retain) liquidity by using its option. This would happen if there was a system-wide liquidity crisis. A bank would continue to redeem on demand for as long as it was cheaper to do so. Once interest rates reached a threshold level, however, it would exercise its option and suspend convertibility. It would do so because it could make arbitrage profits by lending its reserves on the short-term markets and realize the difference between market interest rates and the penalty rate it was paying on its funds. In doing so it would not only be acting to preserve its own liquidity but it would also be channelling liquidity to where the demand for it was greatest, and thereby would help to alleviate the rise in interest rates.

WOULD NOTEHOLDERS ACCEPT OC NOTES?

We can now address the question we raised earlier: would noteholders accept OC notes, given their expectations of how they would be used? There are several reasons why noteholders might expect to be at least as well off accepting these notes as they would be with FC notes:

The first stems from the fact that a bank protected by option clauses would face little if any danger from either note duels or self-fulfilling bank runs. With FC notes, as we have seen, there is always the danger that a rival might try to destroy it in a note duel, or that an intrinsically irrelevant event might trigger off a bank run which would be fuelled by the public's knowledge that the bank could not redeem all its notes on demand. These sudden demands for redemption would harm noteholders in so far as notes that would normally be widely acceptable might be accepted only at a discount, or they might be refused outright. They would also harm noteholders if they led to capital losses on notes as a result of the bank defaulting. The prospect of a note duel or a 'self-fulfilling' bank run thus increases the probability of noteholders suffering losses, and noteholders might prefer OC notes because they would help substantially to avoid these dangers.

OC notes would offer noteholders an additional potential advantage. A bank that introduced option clauses would effectively relax the liquidity constraint under which it operated. This would make certain lending opportunities profitable that would not otherwise be worth while. The bank's prospective profits would rise and increase the valuation of its stock. Other things being equal, this would reduce the probability of bankruptcy and hence make the notes safer. The higher expected profits of the bank would therefore indirectly help the noteholders even if the bank could not pass on some of that profit by paying them direct pecuniary returns.

There is, however, a possible drawback of OC notes that noteholders would have to take into consideration. It is possible that an insolvent bank might invoke the option clause to 'buy time' and take risks in the hope of salvaging an otherwise bankrupt organization. If that happened the bank would be able to take gambles at the expense of its noteholders, and they would be deprived of the normal recourse of demanding instant redemption. We must bear in mind, however, that the bank would be aware of this, and it would have a clear incentive to provide noteholders with credible reassurance that it would not happen. The bank could do this by 'bonding' shareholders' capital. In Scotland, for instance, the shareholders of some banks assumed unlimited liability, while in the early United States the custom was for shareholders to assume 'double liability'. Provided shareholders still had something to lose, they would have an incentive to avoid wild risks even if the bank had a negative net worth. Knowing this, rational noteholders would presumably discount the likelihood of the bank becoming insolvent and taking wild risks at their expense.

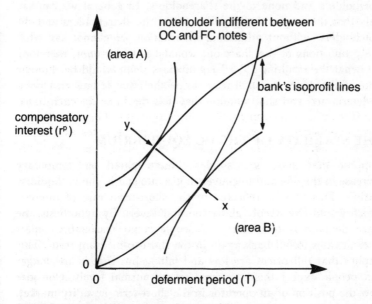

Figure 3.2 The option clause equilibrium

THE BANKING SYSTEM WITH OC NOTES

I have given some reasons why it might be in the private interest of a bank to introduce option clauses on its notes, and why it might be in the private interest of its customers to prefer them to FC notes. If this is so, a bank which introduced OC notes would have a competitive advantage over others. In the context of figure 3.1, such a bank would only have to choose a point (T, r^p) in the set A to outcompete its rivals. The latter would be forced to introduce option clauses of their own to stay in business. The banks that introduced successful option clauses first would make higher profits, but when equilibrium was restored all banks would make zero profits again. The situation is illustrated in figure 3.2. The set of possible long-run equilibrium points is given by the line xy; x would be an equilibrium point if the banks' shares were traded on the stock market and their price rose to capitalize the expected future profits. In that case the people who owned the shares initially would get the economic surplus. The opposite polar extreme is illustrated by y, at which all the surplus goes to the noteholders and none to the shareholders. In general we can say only that the surplus is divided between the shareholders and the noteholders; without additional information we cannot say what the proportions of the share-out would be. We cannot, therefore, say what the resulting (T, r^p) equilibrium point would be. For the sake of simplicity we shall leave aside the issue of how this point is determined and shall assume that it is the same for each bank.

THE STABILITY OF THE OC EQUILIBRIUM

Suppose that there is a sudden, unanticipated but temporary increase in the demand to convert notes into specie (i.e. a 'liquidity crisis'). This will be reflected in the short-term rate of interest, which would rise steeply above 'normal' levels. By hypothesis, the extra demand is temporary, so people could reasonably expect interest rates to fall back again in the short-to-medium term. This implies that bill prices are low and falling but that in the longer run people expect them to rise back to normal levels. Consider now the position of an operator in the short-term liquidity market. He can be reasonably sure that in the longer run he should buy bills, but in the very short run it might be worth while to sell them instead. He might therefore sell bills and thereby bid up interest rates even further. As this continues, other people would be encouraged to enter the market and bet on the prospects of medium-term capital gains by buying bills. These people would therefore run down their stocks of gold, demand reproduction of their notes, and import gold with the intention of lending it out in the short-term market. This bullish activity might be enough to satisfy the demand for liquidity and bring interest rates down, but there is no telling just when the market will turn round.

This situation could be dangerous for the banks if they were obliged to redeem on demand. Noteholders might be tempted to demand redemption either because they wished to make a profit by lending the gold or because they feared that the banks would default. If the demand for liquidity continued unabated the banks might eventually default and the banking system could collapse. This would not happen if the banks were protected by option clauses. In that case, if interest rates continued to rise, they would eventually reach a 'threshold' level at which it would be cheaper for banks to remain liquid by exercising their options than by borrowing on the short-term market. As this point would be the same for all banks they would invoke their options simultaneously and immediately stop the liquidity 'drain' they were facing from noteholders demanding redemption. Once the interest rate passed this threshold level it would become worth while for the banks to lend their reserves on the short-term market. These arbitrage activities would continue to be profitable for as long as market interest rates remained above the penalty rate, and so the banks' intervention would bring market rates down to that level. The demand for liquidity would be satisfied, the panic would subside, and interest rates would return to normal levels. In this way the panic would be corrected by the banks acting to maximize their profits with no thought at all of any wider 'social interest'. It is also worth noting that there would be no need at all for any 'lender of last resort' to stand above the banking system to protect it against a liquidity crisis – an argument which suggests that the lender of last resort function would be redundant in a *laissez-faire* monetary system.

This is still not the whole story. The discussion so far has ignored the possibility that the banks' intervention might have been anticipated. However, it seems reasonable to suppose that their intervention would be anticipated, because the public could calculate the threshold level of the short-term interest rate at which the banks would suspend and intervene. It follows that as interest rates continued to rise a rational bear speculator would estimate that the chances of it going significantly above that threshold rate would be very low. He would therefore appreciate that the threshold put an effective floor on expected bill prices. As bill prices approached that floor our speculator would estimate that his chances of making further profits by selling bills would diminish considerably while the probability of capital loss would increase. At some point before the threshold was reached he would almost certainly decide that further risks were not worth taking, and buy instead to take his capital gains. He would be further encouraged to do so by the knowledge that other people were making the same calculation, and he would be anxious to avoid being short on bills when their prices started to rise. The demand for liquidity would therefore almost certainly 'break' before interest rates hit the threshold level because of the banks' anticipated intervention. Option clauses can thus be effective even if they are never actually invoked. In most cases one would expect the mere prospect that they might be invoked to suffice to stabilize the panic and protect the banking system from collapse.

OPTION CLAUSES IN SCOTLAND, 1730–65

It would be interesting to compare the speculations above with an empirical example of OC notes under free banking. Unfortunately, such examples are hard to find. Historical instances of 'free banking' are rare, but instances of option clauses being tolerated under free banking are rarer still, and the only recorded case seems to be in Scotland during the period 1730–65.

Option clauses were introduced by the Bank of Scotland in 1730 after it had fought a note duel with a newly established rival, the Royal Bank of Scotland, and been forced to suspend convertibility. The bank inserted option clauses on its notes to protect itself when it later reopened. These clauses gave the bank the option of deferring redemption for six months provided it paid compensation of sixpence in the pound on redemption (i.e. 5 per cent per annum).[4] The bank announced the reason for the innovation, and its notes continued to circulate at par afterwards. The Royal Bank refused to imitate it and advertised the fact that its notes were redeemable on demand at all times, but this attempt to persuade the bank's noteholders to abandon it was not successful, and the two notes circulated side by side at par. The episode shows that option clauses can be acceptable to the public even when FC notes are also available.

The next thirty years saw a rapid growth of banking in Scotland. The Bank of Scotland and the Royal Bank continued to wage war on each other for most of the period, as well as on new banks that were set up in the meantime. The business of banking was new to everyone, so it took the banks a long time to develop appropriate rules of thumb to guide them. They had to learn by trial and error the reserve ratios to observe, how to respond to specie shortages, how to deal with each other, and so on. Despite all this, the banking system was relatively stable during these years, and the option clause was apparently never invoked.

Things changed in the early 1760s. As Checkland (1975: 109) explains:

> A good deal of money from England had been lent in Scotland at 4% between 1748 and 1757; much of this was now with-

drawn, for under war conditions it could be more profitably placed at home ... The Edinburgh exchange on London became very adverse. Bills on London rose to a premium of 4½% or 5%. It was well known that when this rate reached 2–3% specie would be carried south ... The banks were faced with a major liquidity crisis.

This crisis had two main effects on the Scottish banking system. The first was that banks started looking for ways to protect their liquidity. By June 1762 all of them had adopted option clauses. In addition they resorted to a number of other expedients. One such was to borrow gold from London at a heavy loss. This involved heavy costs of both exchange and conversion which together amounted to over 5 per cent of the value of the specie (Checkland 1975: 109). It was also pointless because the gold simply found its way south again, where returns were higher: 'while in this state, bringing gold into the country was like pouring water into a sieve' (MacLeod 1896: 189). One must bear in mind, however, that this was the first time the Scottish banks had experienced a major drain on their resources, and the banks presumably had to learn through experience which measures were effective and which were not. The banks also contracted credit and raised deposit interest rates to cut gold outflows. The Bank of Scotland and the Royal Bank began doing so in January 1762, but at the cost of some public criticism (Checkland 1975: 109–10). In contracting credit the banks were particularly careful to refuse credit to 'badly disposed people' like specie exporters and those who aided them. The banks also discouraged people from demanding redemption by offering to grant requests for redemption in part only, and by threatening to invoke the option clause and give them no gold at all if noteholders insisted on more gold than the banks were willing to part with. Measures like these were effective, but they were resented and helped make the option clause unpopular. Fortunately for the banks, the measures appeared to work, and normality seemed to be returning in the early part of 1763.

The second effect of the shortage of specie was an increase in the demand for small-denomination notes to replace coins. For reasons that remain unclear, the major banks refused to satisfy this demand. Many private individuals therefore began to issue notes of their own. Clapham (1970: 241) talks of a 'grotesque multitude of small notes, not issued by regular bankers' for different sums, to be redeemable into various goods, while Checkland (1975: 105) talks of the provision of substitutes for coin being left to 'petty tradesmen'. The public accepted these notes for lack of any alternative in the same way that they used to accept similar substitutes in the past whenever coin was scarce. None the less, the dubious status of the issuers gave small notes a bad name and paved the way for their later suppression.

The pressure on reserves started to mount again in August 1763. It was occasioned by the failure of an Amsterdam bank which had been engaged in speculation towards the end of the Seven Years' War. This failure triggered off a general collapse of banks across the Continent and a flight towards specie. The increased demand for specie again pushed interest rates up in London, and all the banks experienced a renewed shortage of liquidity. The pressure became so intense that the Bank of Scotland and the Royal Bank were obliged to exercise their option clauses in March 1764. They also cut back credit and increased deposit rates (Checkland 1975: 121–2).

In the meantime there was much public dissatisfaction with small notes, the contraction of credit, and the way the banks were threatening and sometimes using option clauses. Public meetings up and down the country in 1763–64 petitioned Parliament to legislate. The government indicated that it was sympathetic to the requests, so the banks lobbied to influence the legislation. The two big Edinburgh banks had been reconciled with each other since 1752 and lobbied for a legislated duopoly to eliminate their opposition. In return they were prepared to pay an annual sum of £1,500 each and surrender their right to the option clause. The main Glasgow banks lobbied instead for free banking to protect their right to issue notes. The government would have none of the Edinburgh banks' attempts to do away with the opposition and was also concerned to protect people from what it perceived as the abuse of small notes and option clauses. The result was an Act of 1765 which guaranteed freedom of entry to the Scottish banking industry but prohibited option clauses and Scottish notes of less than £1. And so the Scottish experiment with option clauses was suppressed only thirty-five years after it had begun.

IS THE SCOTTISH EXPERIENCE CONSISTENT WITH OUR PRIOR EXPECTATIONS?

Our discussion of the theory of option clauses suggested two main 'empirical predictions'. The first was that there would be some conditions under which option clauses would be accepted by the public, and the second was that the adoption of option clauses promotes monetary stability. Are these consistent with the Scottish experience?

The first prediction obviously is. Noteholders in Scotland were clearly prepared to accept OC notes even when they could have chosen FC notes instead. As Meulen (1934: 132) states, 'The one fact which is firmly established . . . is that option-clause notes were issued by the foremost banks in Scotland, and in these cases were freely circulated, at par.'

The second prediction is much more difficult to assess. Part of the problem is that the Scottish banking system was developing rapidly throughout the brief option-clause period. Banking was a new business which the bankers were still trying to learn and the public were trying to become used to. Mistakes were frequent, and it took time for bankers to realize where their true interests lay. This is well illustrated by the length of time it took them to agree to a note exchange. A note exchange was in each bank's own interest because it promoted the demand for its notes, and yet the note exchange was established only in 1771. Another example seems to have been the regular banks' reluctance to meet the demand for small notes. If private individuals found it worth while to issue notes, the regular banks would certainly have, and they would have had a comparative advantage at it. Why they failed even to try is a mystery. Considerations like these suggest that the Scottish banking system of the early 1760s had not yet settled into the 'OC equilibrium' discussed earlier, and so any inferences drawn from a comparison of the two must be very cautious.

Several inferences can, however, be drawn. Opponents of option clauses made much of the depreciation of the OC notes relative to FC notes or gold when the option was exercised, and used this to suggest that OC notes destabilized the value of money. Adam Smith (1776: 290–1), for example, cited the example of a Dumfries bank whose notes were at a considerable discount in Carlisle relative to FC notes. However, as Meulen (1934: 132) points out:

. . . the option clause was introduced only in order to stave off outside demands for gold. The ordinary customers of banks needed only an exchange medium, not necessarily gold, and they were quite content to accept the option-clause notes of a reliable bank. Those who desired to obtain gold for export, however, would undoubtedly differentiate between option-clause notes and those which were redeemable in gold on demand, and this would undoubtedly be twisted . . . into an evidence of 'depreciation' of Scottish paper . . .

One might extend this argument further. During a crisis interest rates rise because of the increased demand for gold relative to notes and other goods, and the exercise of the option clause temporarily breaks the link between the value of the notes and gold. This helps to stabilize the value of the notes in terms of goods, and thus to insulate day-to-day trade from the monetary shock. The exercise of the option also stabilizes trade by protecting the banks' liquidity, thus reducing the danger of a run, as we discussed earlier. In this context it is worth noting that there was apparently no major public concern about the danger of bank runs in Scotland during this period. It is also possible that the exercise of the option helped to stabilize interest rates, although we have very little evidence about this. In short, the very fact that OC notes fell to a discount against gold when the option was used may well have helped to stabilize the economy because it was an essential part of the mechanism through which the domestic economy was insulated from the external shock. If this is what happened, it would lend further support to our second prediction that option clauses would help to stabilize the banking system. Given the tenuous nature of the evidence, however, it would be safer to conclude that this prediction is not obviously at variance with the Scottish experience.

SOME LIMITATIONS AND CONCLUSIONS

Our discussion of option clauses has left a number of issues unresolved. Some of these centre on the option clause itself. We have not discussed how banks would choose a penalty rate and deferment period, for example. One possibility is that banks might choose these using the formula 'x per cent above the short-term market rate of interest prevailing over the last y months', but even if the banks used this formula, we would still have to explain how

x and y would be chosen. A related issue is how banks would 'compete' with different option clauses. If the option clause is used only rarely, or possibly never, then one has to explain the process whereby the public and the banks settle on a particular kind (or kinds) of option clause contract. Also, we have considered only 'simple' option clauses which give the bank two options only. It might be worth their while for the banks to introduce more 'sophisticated' option clauses which would give them more options. It is interesting to note that White (1984b: 29) reports an instance of a 'triple' option clause in Scotland in the early 1760s. The idea did not catch on, but that may have been because option clauses were banned so soon after.

Option clauses also have important implications for the lender of last resort and our perception of the 'inherent' instability of a fractional reserve banking system. Our discussion indicates that private profit-maximizing banks can and will protect themselves adequately against shocks that threaten their liquidity. All they appear to need is a legal framework that allows them to do so, and this suggests that the lender of last resort function is redundant in a *laissez-faire* monetary system.

Another issue is how option clauses relate to current commercial banking arrangements. We have examined option clauses on notes, but option clauses could also be inserted into the contracts governing deposits as well. In the recent past banks in both the United States and the United Kingdom frequently inserted 'notice of withdrawal' clauses into deposit contracts but seldom if ever invoked them. It is not clear why banks do not write these clauses into their deposit contracts more than they appear to do. Perhaps it is because they believe they can get the reserve media they might need from other banks or the central bank.

Chapter 4

Monetary freedom and monetary stability

The single most important argument in favour of government intervention in the monetary system is that intervention is required to counteract the inherent instability of monetary *laissez-faire*. In one form or another this belief lies behind the justifications usually given for the need for a monopoly over the supply of base money, the lender of last resort function of the central bank and government deposit insurance. As these are the principal pillars of modern central banking, it is probably fair to say that the case for central banking stands or falls with it.

This chapter argues that it is false. If it were correct, a stable *laissez-faire* monetary system would be self-contradictory. A counter-example of a stable *laissez-faire* monetary system therefore suffices to refute it. The chapter outlines such a monetary system and explains why it is stable.[1] The underlying reason for its stability is that the agents operating within it demand stability and have the means to make those demands effective. Besides being stable, monetary *laissez-faire* is also efficient because all agents look after their self-interest and all mutually beneficial trades are carried out. These features make the *laissez-faire* system a very attractive one, far superior to our current monetary systems, which are obviously neither stable nor optimal.

The question then arises how we managed to end up with monetary systems that are so patently unsatisfactory. The answer suggested is that our monetary systems are unstable and inferior precisely because they are not based on *laissez-faire*. This answer is confirmed by considering what would happen if we introduced an interventionist state into a previously *laissez-faire* system. Taking into account how and why the state would intervene, the outcome of the interventionist regime is a monetary system not unlike those we have already. This strongly suggests that the intervenionist regime is the underlying cause of our monetary difficulties.

THE EVOLUTION OF A *LAISSEZ-FAIRE* MONETARY SYSTEM

To examine these issues, let us consider a hypothetical anarchist society. People have well defined preferences and advanced division of labour. All property is private, trades are decentralized and contracts are enforced by an efficient private legal system.[2] There is no government, and everyone is motivated purely by his own private self-interest.

Its origins

The society's monetary system originated from a primitive system of barter exchange. Indirect trades were found to be more convenient than barter, and gold displaced other intermediary goods to become the dominant medium of exchange. After this private mints evolved which converted lumps of gold into coins. Coins were minted in standardized units ('dollars') and the public found them a more convenient exchange medium than heterogeneous lumps of gold.[3] Competitive pressures then led traders to post prices in terms of gold dollars. (Traders who posted prices in terms of other commodities imposed additional reckoning costs on potential trading partners, and therefore lost business (for example, see, eg, White 1984a: 704).) The gold dollar thus became both the medium of exchange and the unit of account.

The development of banks issuing convertible media of exchange

In time, individuals came to use exchange media issued by banks. These exchange media evolved from the receipts issued by earlier goldsmiths who used to accept deposits of gold for safe keeping. Because they were less expensive to move and store than gold, these exchange media eventually displaced gold entirely as a medium of exchange. They continued, however, to be convertible into gold as the old goldsmiths' receipts had been. This meant that the holder of a liability with a face value of $1 had the right to demand at any time that the issuing bank should exchange it for $1 in gold.[4] Banks that had announced in the past that they intended to make their liabilities inconvertible had found that the public distrusted them – not unreasonably, since these banks had proposed to dispense with the legally binding commitment to maintain their value against gold – and the banks lost their market share to competitors who promised to maintain convertibility. Nor could the banks as a whole form an effective cartel and jointly abandon convertibility: they had no means of keeping out potential entrants who would undercut them by offering the public convertible media of exchange. Competition among the banks forced them to maintain convertibility because the public wanted it.

The convertibility of their note and deposit liabilities implied that banks would contract their issues on demand by the public at a given 'price' in terms of gold. At the same time the banks were always ready to issue new liabilities on demand, at the same fixed price, because they would make additional profits by doing so. In other words, the supply of liabilities was perfectly elastic, and the amount and composition of liabilities in circulation were determined entirely by the demand to hold them. The banks realized that their profits depended on their note and deposit issues, and they could increase their issues only if they increased the public's demand for them.

The banks also appreciated that the public would be more willing to accept a particular bank's notes if other banks were also willing to accept them. They therefore entered into clearing arrangements by which each bank accepted every other bank's liabilities at par. A central clearing house was set up to organize the regular clearing sessions at which the banks returned each other's liabilities and settled up the differences in an agreed-upon medium. The establishment of the clearing system meant that a member of the public could redeem an unwanted note (or deposit) at any bank, not just at the bank that issued it. Whenever note issues exceeded demand, the excess issues were now returned more quickly to the banking system. The more rapid redemption process in turn reduced the disruptions of economic activity caused by occasional over-issues. The banks' attempts to increase the demand for their issues thus led them to create a clearing system that had the side-effect of stabilizing the monetary system by returning excess issues more rapidly.

Bank solvency and the threat of bank 'runs'

While gold was still the dominant medium of exchange each bank would make a profit by lending out some of the gold deposited with it. It would hold gold to be able to honour demands for redemption, but it would economize its gold holdings because they represented forgone lending opportunities. Once gold had been replaced as a medium of exchange, a bank would create and lend out its own liabilities instead of gold, but it would continue to optimize its reserve ratio, because it would still need to hold gold to meet demands for redemption. However, by issuing more liabilities than it kept in gold reserves a bank over any short period could redeem only a fraction of the liabilities that might be presented for redemption. It then faced the problem of how to avoid a situation where it ran out of gold and defaulted on its promise to redeem its issues.

There are various ways in which the banks would protect themselves against this danger. A bank would supplement its stock of gold by holding assets which could be sold relatively quickly and at little loss if it needed to obtain more gold. It would also cultivate a reputation for soundness to reassure liability holders and potential creditors that they had no reason to fear losses. One way of doing this would be to maintain a high capital ratio to demonstrate that it had the capital to withstand unexpected losses. To reassure customers further, a bank's shareholders might also adopt extended liability, or perhaps allow their management to extend their liability if that was a condition of a loan. A bank might also open its books or employ independent monitors to verify its soundness.[5]

If a bank were faced with large unanticipated demands for gold, it would meet them by running down its reserves, and if necessary by borrowing gold or selling assets to buy gold from those who had it. In most cases where this happened those redeeming the bank's liabilities would have no wish to hold gold, but would convert the gold into other assets instead. Much of the gold would therefore be rapidly redeposited in the banking system. Other banks would then be flush with gold. Provided they were satisfied about the soundness of the bank wanting the loan, it would be in their interest to lend the gold to it, and it would be in the bank's interest to satisfy them. A sound bank should normally be able to demonstrate its soundness and thereby ensure that it could obtain whatever loans it required. It could then meet any drain on its reserves from the public. Of course, once they appreciated its soundness, the public would have far less reason to start a run on the bank in the first place. If a bank could not reassure creditors, on the other hand, they would have good reason to refuse to lend to it, and the bank might not be able to meet a 'run' on it from the public. A 'run' would then be much more likely to happen anyway, and such a run might well force the bank to default. In short, a sound bank would be unlikely to face a run, and could meet one at relatively little cost even if it did occur, but an unsound bank would be more likely to face a run and would have much more to lose from it. The threat of a run would therefore be a useful discipline against excessive risk-taking by bank managements.

Financial instruments replace gold as banks' reserves

While banks clearly want to protect themselves against demands for redemption, they also have an incentive to reduce the cost of the reserves they hold to meet such demands. These costs will fall anyway as the banking system develops, because public demands for redemption will fall as confidence in the banking system increases, and the lower demands for redemption imply that the banks can operate on lower reserve ratios.[6] The banks will reduce the cost of holding reserves further by offering financial instruments as alternative redemption media. The costs of storing and protecting financial instruments are considerably lower than for gold, and many financial instruments have the benefit that they bear explicit returns. The banks would usually have little difficulty in persuading the public to accept financial instruments rather than gold when they demand redemption. The public would normally prefer them because of their lower storage, protection and moving costs. To qualify as a suitable redemption medium, an asset must have a value substantially independent of the bank that is using the asset to redeem its issues (i.e. it must not use its own debt). Obvious examples are the debt or equity of other firms. Note that there is nothing to stop an individual bank using the debt of another bank to redeem its own liabilities – indeed, banks will often find it particularly convenient to redeem their liabilities by giving out other banks' notes or by drawing cheques on other banks – but the banking system as a whole cannot redeem all its liabilities by drawing cheques on itself – there must be some 'outside' redemption medium at the aggregate level. Of course, if the banks give out financial assets instead of gold there is a danger that the original issuers may default, the assets may fall in value, and so on, but they could always refuse a particular instrument and the banks would have to provide them with something else instead. If the public accept a particular redemption medium, on the other hand, that implies that they consider it at least 'as good as gold' and that they are willing to accept any risk it entails.

A further attractive feature of financial instruments is that the banks can be confident of obtaining additional supplies at short notice. The large trading volume in many financial markets would reassure banks that they could obtain any quantities they desired. Also, the supply of assets is often highly elastic, and it makes relatively little difference anyway if a bank has to pay more to obtain greater quantities of a particular asset. The bank makes a loss only when it buys an asset at a high price and holds on to it while its price can fall. A bank that bought an asset for redemption purposes would normally intend to 'sell' it reasonably rapidly. Its 'loss' when it bought an asset whose price had risen would be matched by the 'gain' it made when it 'sold' the asset at the new higher price to the person who was demanding redemption. In any case, a bank would seldom be forced to buy a particular asset that might have risen in price because there would normally be plenty of substitutes to choose from. If the banks use gold as redemption medium, on the other hand, they have to cope with a thinner market, a lack of substitutes and a potentially inelastic supply made worse by their inability to pay more for gold even though they would willingly do so. They are prevented from paying more for gold by their commitment to maintaining its price. Just when they most need additional gold, this restriction prevents them from being able to induce more holders of gold to part with it. It is not therefore surprising that banks have had redemption difficulties in the past when they simultaneously pegged the price of gold and used gold to redeem their issues. The use of financial instruments as a medium of redemption means that the banks can be more confident about obtaining further supplies, and they can safely hold less of them than they would gold.

The banks' ability to obtain additional redemption securities in the market has the side effect of protecting the monetary system from the disruptions that would otherwise occur when there were

large-scale demands for redemption. Had they continued to redeem
in gold, the banks could have met a large loss of reserves only by
raising the interest rate they paid on deposits of gold, and arbitrage
would then have forced interest rates up across the board. The
banks would also have tried to maintain their solvency by recalling
loans and cutting back lending. Many firms would then have
responded to the credit squeeze by dumping assets on the market,
and asset prices would have fallen further and reinforced the rise
in interest rates. Falling asset prices would have inflicted capital
losses on many firms, the banks included, and business failures
would have risen. Firms would also have responded to the credit
squeeze by curtailing production, laying workers off and dumping
commodities at basement prices, and the falling commodity prices
would have increased business failures further. On the other hand,
when the banks use financial instruments as reserves, they no
longer have to raise interest rates and cut back their own lending
to meet a reserve drain. They simply obtain reserves on the
market. The prices of some reserve assets may rise, but that would
cause no particular problems, and interest rates, lending and so
on would be substantially unaffected. The replacement of gold by
financial instruments as banks' reserves therefore helps to insulate
interest rates, bank lending and economic activity generally from
the effects of fluctuations in the demand for gold. This is a very
important stabilizing feature of the *laissez-faire* monetary system.

The public's principal concern is that the exchange medium
they accept should maintain its purchasing power and general
acceptability, and for this purpose it generally suffices if the banks
guarantee to take their notes back in exchange for something of
the same nominal value. This commitment 'pegs' the nominal
value of bank issues and forms the basis of the public's confidence
in them. When demands for redemption do occur, the public will
usually want to convert bank liabilities from one form into another
(e.g. when they write cheques against deposits), and the banking
system as a whole will not lose reserves. Demands for bank liabilities to be converted into 'outside' media will be unimportant by
comparison, and in most such cases the public would prefer to
accept financial instruments in order to avoid the relatively heavy
cost of handling gold. It will be relatively rarely that a member
of the public will specifically want gold, and these occasional
demands will have little significance. The commitment to redeem
specifically in gold thus becomes more or less redundant, and the

banks can easily replace it with a commitment to redeem their issues with alternative instruments of the same value as gold.[7]

The fixed price of gold

It bears stressing that the abandonment of the commitment to redeem in gold does not mean that the price of gold would float. The banks would still be committed (for the time being) to maintaining the price of gold at par. Given the high cost of handling gold, however, the banks would probably find it cheaper to peg the (spot) price of gold by intervening in the futures market. They would manipulate the future price of gold to keep the spot price at par. To avoid having to take delivery of gold, they would sell all futures contracts before they expired. Similarly, they would avoid having to deliver gold by buying back any contracts they had sold before they expired. Since operating in the futures market would relieve the banks of any need to handle physical amounts of gold, they could then dispense entirely with their stocks of it. Any remaining 'resource costs' would be completely eliminated.

The commitment to maintaining the price of gold is of the utmost importance. It provides the 'anchor' that ties nominal prices down. To see this, suppose that the banks as a whole over-issue their liabilities. If there is a commitment to maintain the price of gold, then the over-issue can have no lasting effect on the price level, and the whole of the over-issue must be returned to the issuing banks. Without that commitment, however, the over-issue can permanently change the price level. In that case, some of the 'excess' notes will stay in circulation to satisfy the higher nominal demand for notes at the higher price level. How many notes stay out and how many are returned to the banks depends on how rapidly the note reflux mechanism works and how flexible individual prices are. The more rapid the reflux, and the more 'sticky' individual prices, the less the price level will rise. To modify Wicksell's analogy (1907), the price level would behave rather like a cylinder on a flat surface. Each over- (or under-) issue of bank liabilities would give the cylinder a push. The weight of the cylinder would correspond to the rapidity of the reflux mechanism, and the flexibility of prices would correspond to the smoothness of the surface. The lighter the cylinder, and the smoother the surface, the more the cylinder would move, and once it had moved there would be no tendency for it to move back.

Prices therefore drift from one period to another, and what give the system whatever price stability it has are the rapidity of the reflux and the inertia of individual prices. Short-run inertia notwithstanding, prices in the long run are indeterminate. Fortunately, however, the commitment to peg a nominal price is not something the banks can just abandon. If a bank announced that it intended to let the price of gold float it would suffer the same fate as the earlier banks that tried to abandon convertibility – with no guarantee of their value, the public would distrust its notes, and it would lose its market share. The public desire the protection that a nominal peg gives them, and competition among the banks forces them to provide it.

The replacement of the gold peg

There is one last stage in the evolution of the monetary system. The system is still vulnerable to disturbances arising from changes in the relative price of gold. Since the price of gold is 'fixed' at unity by the banks, the relative price of gold can change only if the prices of other goods change. This makes nominal prices dependent on conditions in the gold market. An improvement in the technology of extracting gold, for instance, would decrease the relative price of gold, and since the nominal price of gold is fixed its relative price can fall only if other (nominal) prices rise. The more variable the relative price of gold the less stable prices generally will be. This instability imposes costs on the general public – they find it hard to distinguish between true price signals and irrelevant price noise, and therefore make 'mistakes' they would otherwise have avoided; they have less peace of mind about the future, and so on. The banks also have to live with these problems, but they have the additional problem that changes in the relative price of gold affect their net value. A bank's liabilities are indexed to the price of gold, but the value of its assets will depend to a considerable extent on prices generally. If the relative price of gold starts to rise, therefore, banks will find that the nominal value of their assets will fall while their liabilities remain fixed in value. Changes in the relative price of gold can undermine the banks' capital value.

To rectify these problems the banks will switch to a nominal anchor whose relative price is more stable. They will select an appropriate commodity (or commodity bundle) and announce that, from a certain date on, they will intervene to maintain its price instead of the price of gold. The price of gold would then be free to float and it would have no more monetary significance. Since both the banks and the public prefer more price stability to less, the new commodity (bundle) would be chosen to maximise (*ex ante*) price stability. Apart from unnecessarily exposing themselves to fluctuations in the relative price of gold, any banks that continued with the old peg would lose their deposit and note market share because of the public's preference for a medium of exchange with more stable purchasing power. The same would apply to banks that adopted other commodity pegs that were considered to generate less price stability. Competition among the banks therefore leads not just to a commodity peg that generates price stability, but to one that generates the maximum possible price stability.

The banks could peg the price of a single commodity (or a small set of commodities) whose relative price was stable, or else they could choose a large commodity bundle whose relative price was stable because the movements of the individual commodity prices tended to cancel each other out.[8] As they did previously with gold, the banks would avoid any physical handling costs by intervening in the futures market to maintain the spot price. On the date the new regime came into force the banks would peg the dollar price of the new commodity (bundle) at a rate given, say, by its previous day's market value. This would avoid any 'jumps' in the purchasing power of exchange media (and hence in prices) as the change took effect.

The simplest case would be where the banks selected a single commodity whose supply was perfectly elastic. Its relative price would then be constant, and price stability would be maximized. A good example of a commodity that might satisfy this condition is bricks. Bricks have a very high elasticity of supply because they are produced under competitive conditions at a more or less constant marginal cost. If banks decided that the spot supply of bricks was insufficiently elastic, and therefore that the relative price of current bricks was insufficiently stable, the banks might adopt a modified form of the 'brick standard' and peg the price of future bricks (e.g. bricks four months ahead) instead. Since factors are more mobile in the longer run, future bricks will have a higher supply elasticity than current bricks and, therefore, a more stable relative price.[9] Bricks are suggested purely for illustration. What matters is that the commodity whose price is pegged has a stable relative price. Bricks, however, might be as good as anything else.[10]

THE MATURE FREE BANKING SYSTEM

Its stability

This completes our account of the evolution of the free banking system. We can now assess its main features, and begin with its stability. There are three main senses in which we can talk of the stability of a monetary system. The first is whether it is self-sustaining. To be stable in this sense, the system must leave no group able and willing to overturn it. The free banking system satisfies this condition because everyone already maximizes his own private utility (conditional on the external environment), and so no one has any incentive to change his behaviour. The free banking system fares better on this criterion than current monetary systems because it does not rely on an outside 'guardian' to protect it who may be inclined to undermine it instead. It also fares better because it does not try to foist responsibility for any 'social interest' on some institution that will not look after the 'social interest' because it has insufficient private incentive to do so.

The second sense in which we can talk of the stability of a monetary system concerns its ability to respond to exogenous events while maintaining its integrity. In particular, there is the question of the ability of the banks to meet demands by the public to be able to convert bank liabilities into other bank liabilities or into 'outside' redemption media. Measured by this criterion, the *laissez-faire* monetary system performs extremely well. The supply of bank liabilities is perfectly elastic, and so their extent is determined by demand. If the public wish to convert one form of bank liability into another, the banking system contracts the issue of one and expands that of the other. The banking system accommodates public demands in the same automatic way that current banking systems convert one form of bank deposit into another. With the *laissez-faire* banking system, however, it makes no difference what kind of liabilities the public wish to convert. Deposits can be converted into notes as easily as into another form of deposit, or vice versa. Nor do the banks have any difficulty accommodating demands for the conversion of liabilities into outside redemption media. The banks simply run down their reserves and if necessary obtain more on the market, and there are no major disturbances of interest rates, credit markets or economic activity. The only exception is that banks which are judged to be unsound may not be able to meet a run on them, but the threat of a run will discourage bank managements from taking risks that could make their banks unsound.

The other sense in which we usually talk of the stability of a monetary system refers to the stability of nominal prices. The *laissez-faire* system gets high marks on this account as well. Since both the public and the banks benefit from price stability, the banks will peg their issues to a commodity chosen to maximize price stability. The old argument about competition in money leading people to print it until it becomes worthless could not be more misleading. Competition will eliminate every money *but* the one that generates the most price stability.

Its optimality

The mature free banking system is optimal by virtually any criterion. All feasible and mutually beneficial trades take place because there are no barriers to prevent them. The banks provide the public with exactly the exchange media they want, and deposit interest rates, bank charges and other contract provisions (e.g. regarding liability) are competitively determined. The rent from issuing exchange media is therefore competed away to the public. Similarly the banks' competition for loan business passes the rent from lending to their loan customers. The banks have an incentive to keep their reserves costs low but not to reduce them to a level that would threaten their solvency. A bank will use financial instruments rather than physical commodities to redeem its liabilities, and there will be no 'resource costs' as such even though the currency is a convertible one. The cost of intervening to maintain the price of the pegged commodity (bundle) will be minimal. There are no 'free rider' or externality problems, and therefore no discrepancies between 'private' and 'social' interests.[11] The problem of guarding guardians does not arise because there are no 'outside' guardians to be watched. We do not have to worry about the incentives faced by the monetary authorities, the time consistency of their policies, and so on, because there are no authorities. There is no 'policy' as conventionally understood, and therefore no 'optimal policy problem'. Everyone pursues his own self-interest, and all interests are harmonized by the market.

THE EVOLUTION OF OUR CURRENT MONETARY SYSTEMS

We have suggested that unfettered private interest would have produced a highly stable and attractive monetary system. To be complete, however, we must also explain why such a monetary system did not evolve, and why we ended up instead with the monetary systems we have. The easiest way to do this is to introduce the state into our hypothetical anarchist society and see what happens. Once we introduce the state, we have to consider the rewards and penalties faced by the individuals who operate it (i.e. the politicians and civil servants). They differ from other individuals in that they have unique power to coerce other agents and to rewrite the rules under which other agents operate. We must presume that this power will be used to further their own interests, selfish or altruistic as they may be.

This new state will intervene in the monetary system for two main reasons. The first, and most basic, is to raise revenue from it. From a political point of view, the monetary system is often a very attractive source of tax revenue. The costs are usually heavily disguised and, more often than not, the tax is not even perceived as such by those who pay it (e.g. inflation). Also, the public often fail to distinguish between nominal and effective tax burdens, and are quite ready to acquiesce in taxes on the banks without realizing that much of the burden will be passed on to them. In addition, governments sometimes intervene in the monetary system to seize economic rents and transfer them to groups that have the political power to lobby successfully for them. This explains much of the regulation imposed on the banking system. An example is the separation of commercial and investment banking by the Banking Act of 1933. This cartelized the banking industry by preventing commercial and investment banks from encroaching on each other's territory. Finally, politicians are drawn to raise revenue from the monetary system because in that way they can by-pass the usual constitutional constraints against raising taxes. The inflation tax is perhaps the most conspicuous example, but subsidized loans are another.

The other principal reason for government intervention is to stabilize the monetary system. One of the state's primary responsibilities is to maintain (a semblance of) social order, and perceived monetary instability usually leads to political pressure on the government to do something about it. The irony is that the instability can almost always be traced to earlier intervention, but the 'first-best' solution – to remove the earlier intervention – is usually ruled out as 'politically unrealistic'. The government therefore intervenes to correct the unintended consequences of its own earlier intervention. The new intervention later turn out to have unexpected side effects of its own, and further intervention seems to be required to deal with them, and so it goes on. On top of which, the government may continue to intervene now and them to raise more revenue from the monetary system. A good example of this 'logic of intervention' is provided by US monetary history. The United States had a reasonably adequate monetary system when the Civil War broke out, but during the war the federal government intervened to impose the regulations of the National Banking System. The principal motive was to raise revenue, but the consequence was to destabilize the banking system. Rather than abolish the restrictions that had caused the instability, however, Congress instead established the Federal Reserve System to act as lender of last resort. Unfortunately, in the early 1930s the Fed refused to function as lender of last resort and much of the US banking system collapsed. Instead of abolishing the Fed and at least going back to the National Banking System, Congress responded to the crisis by establishing a system of federal deposit insurance which subsidized risk-taking and prepared the way for the present banking crisis. It also relaxed and eventually abolished the Fed's commitment to maintain the gold standard, and in the process converted the Fed into an engine of inflation. Each intervention probably made the monetary system even less stable than it was before.

We will now examine in more detail some specific types of intervention and the effects they have.

The creation of a fiat currency

A very common form of intervention is to create a fiat currency. The process usually begins when the state intervenes to give privileges to one bank (e.g. it may establish a monopoly over the note issue). The motive behind such intervention is usually to raise revenue by selling the privileges. Since the privileged bank has the 'protection' of the state, the other banks typically view its liabilities as being 'as good as gold' but cheaper to hold. The banks therefore start to use them as redemption media instead of gold, and in time they come to replace gold more or less entirely.[12] They continue for a while to be convertible into gold at the issuing bank, but in the end the state intervenes to suspend that commitment. It does so because it enables the state to extract more revenue out of the banking system. The banks thus find themselves using inconvertible redemption media issued monopolistically by a central bank (i.e. there is a fiat currency).

Once convertibility has been abandoned, the value of the central bank's liabilities – and hence the price level – depend on the amount of them it creates, that is, on central bank policy. We therefore have to examine what the central bank and its political masters have to gain and lose from price-level changes. A perceptive analysis of this issue is provided by Barro and Gordon (1983a). They suggest that unexpected inflation gives certain benefits to the central bank but also imposes certain costs on it. One benefit is the reduction in the real value of the government's fixed-interest nominal debt. Other benefits include greater tax revenue and lower unemployment payments when the 'surprise' inflation increases output. The costs include the higher interest rates the government must pay if inflationary expectations rise, and the erosion of the central bank's 'reputation' for monetary 'good behaviour'. Barro and Gordon suggest that the central bank will aim to create that rate of inflation which equalizes the marginal costs and benefits to it of surprise inflation. Starting from a low rate of inflation (e.g. zero), the benefits from a surprise inflation are likely to be quite high and the costs quite low. Consequently the public will not rationally expect low inflation and the central bank will not deliver it. The public will instead expect that higher rate of inflation at which the central bank's marginal benefits and costs from inflationary surprises are equal. On average, this will also be the inflation rate that the central bank actually delivers. This inflation rate will change (usually unpredictably) as the costs and benefits of surprise inflation vary. A fiat money issuer will therefore produce a rate of inflation that is high relative to what the public want (i.e. presumably zero) and which will tend to vary unpredictably. There will be no price stability because the central bank has no incentive to provide it.

Restrictions on banks' issues

Governments also intervene to restrict the issue of bank liabilities. These measures are often motivated by the intention of stabilizing the monetary system. A good example is the 1844 Bank Charter Act in the UK, which gave the Bank of England an effective monopoly of the note issue but required that the bank should issue further notes only if it kept the equivalent value of gold in its vaults. At the time Bank of England notes (and deposits) formed the principal reserve medium of the other banks, and Bank notes were also used by the public as hand-to-hand currency. The motivation behind the measure was largely to stem the disturbances perceived to result from 'reckless' over-issues of notes in the past. The solution proposed was to make the supply of notes behave as if it were a metallic currency – this was the 'currency principle'. The consequence, however, was to make it impossible for the banking system to satisfy large-scale public demand for notes to be converted into deposits. The knowledge that the banking system could satisfy only a limited demand for notes encouraged people to 'play safe' and demand notes if they felt notes might become difficult to obtain. These 'pre-emptive' demands for notes then sometimes provoked the very crisis that everyone was anxious to avoid. Such crises occurred in 1847, 1857 and 1866, and they subsided only when the government intervened to allow the Bank to issue more notes.

Another type of restriction on the note issue is to lay down the redemption assets that banks must use when they issue notes. The classic example is where banks are compelled to redeem their issues for gold at a fixed price. This type of restriction is usually motivated by the fear that banknotes might otherwise somehow lose their value. This was certainly the case when such a restriction was imposed on UK banks by Act of Parliament in 1765. The consequences have been discussed already on p. 39. When faced with a large demand for redemption of their issues the banks need to obtain gold, but they are not allowed to pay more for it. They are therefore forced to raise interest rates and cut back their lending to protect their solvency, and economic activity falls. The restriction makes interest rates, bank credit and economic activity generally hostages to the vagaries of the demand for gold.

The lender of last resort and deposit insurance

A third common sort of intervention is to establish an agency to 'protect' the banks. The classic examples are a lender of last resort and a system of liability (e.g. deposit) insurance. As our earlier discussion suggested, the 'need' for a lender of last resort arises from the imposition of restrictions on the liabilities a bank may create. The usual case is where the public want to convert deposits into currency but the banks are not allowed to create the additional currency the public want. The 'first-best' solution is simply to abolish the restrictions on the note issue and let the banks issue the additional currency. Often, however, this option is dismissed – or not even considered – for political reasons. The only alternative is to establish a lender of last resort to print the additional currency and lend it to the banks that need it. Once the lender of last resort has been created, it must resolve a variety of problems: it must know when to 'intervene' and issue emergency money; it must resolve the tension between its commitment to behave conservatively in normal times and its obligations to create money freely during a crisis; and it needs a rule to tell it how much emergency money to create and on what terms to lend it. Most basic of all, perhaps, some means has to be found to make the lender of last resort responsive to the desires of the banks. One would also like to be reassured that the lender of last resort would actually function in a crisis. As the Fed demonstrated in the 1930s, having a lender of last resort that refuses to lend can be worse than having no lender of last resort at all.[13]

The other example is deposit insurance. The principal justification for this is to protect banks against runs by removing the public's incentive to participate in them. The problem with this is that it mistakes the symptom (i.e. the bank run) with the underlying disease (i.e. banking instability) and applies a remedy that makes the disease worse. People run on a bank because they fear losses, and they have reason to fear losses when they hold deposits in banks of questionable soundness. The public have no reason to run on banks of obvious soundness, and such banks have no need for deposit insurance. Deposit insurance makes banks unstable in the longer run because it encourages them to take risks they would otherwise have avoided. Banks' managements take more risks because they no longer have to worry about a bank run. If they need more funds they can simply raise deposit rates.

They know that depositors will no longer need to monitor banks because their deposits are insured. Depositors will therefore tend to deposit their funds with the banks which promise them the highest return, regardless of the risks that such a bank may take. More cautious banks will have to raise their deposit rates to keep their deposits, and they may feel obliged to take more risks to cover their higher expenses. Banks thus take more risks, and more of them will eventually become unsound. To make matters worse, inadequate failure resolution policies will often enable an unsound bank to fend off its creditors and remain solvent for a long time. During that time it has little left to lose and its management will be tempted to take extravagant risks at the expense of the deposit insurance agencies. Even though this may massively increase their losses,[14] the insurance agencies sometimes allow such behaviour because their main concern is to put off the evil day when they have to reveal to the government the extent of their own bankruptcy.

CONCLUSION

Contrary to widespread belief, monetary *laissez-faire* is highly stable. For that reason, as well as for others, it is also highly desirable. Our current monetary problems arise not because of 'free markets' but because markets are not free enough. They arise because of state meddling with the monetary system. The implications for reform are clear and unambiguous: if we really wish to put these problems right, we should be thinking about how to roll back the apparatus of state intervention to allow market forces to establish a stable and efficient monetary system.

Chapter 5

Is banking a natural monopoly?

A perennial issue in the banking literature is whether banking is a natural monopoly – are there economies of scale in banking such that only one firm can survive in the competitive equilibrium? In one way or another natural monopoly issues underlie many discussions of banking, and it is important to clarify them, because many people still believe, not only that banking is a natural monopoly, but that the monopolization of the currency supply and other aspects of present-day central banking can be justified on natural monopoly grounds.[1] An industry can be said to be a natural monopoly if the average production cost is lower for one firm than it would be for two or more firms, and this condition requires that the production technology exhibits increasing returns to scale, to the point where all market demand is satisfied. There is nothing to prevent a second firm entering an industry characterized by natural monopoly, but average costs would be higher while both firms continued to supply the market, and these higher costs would presumably indicate scope for one firm to 'eliminate' the other in a mutually profitable way – bribing it to leave the market, for instance, or taking it over and then closing down its production facilities. It follows that while we might observe more than one firm in the industry over some short period, we would not expect that state of affairs to persist in the long run.

RETURNS TO SCALE IN BANKING

Economies of scale in reserve holding

There are several reasons why banks might face increasing returns to scale that could conceivably lead to natural monopoly. One factor is economies from reserve holdings. The underlying idea goes back to Edgeworth (1888) and it has been developed since in a number of places (e.g. Porter 1961; Niehans 1978: 182–4; Baltensperger 1980: 4–9; Sprenkle 1985, 1987; Selgin 1989b: 6–12; Glasner 1989a). These economies are based on a well known result that subject to certain plausible conditions a bank's optimal reserves rise with the square root of its liabilities, implying that the bank's optimal reserve ratio falls as the bank gets bigger. Given that reserves are costly to hold, a larger bank therefore faces lower average reserve costs. Following Baltensperger (1980: 4–9), these economies can be illustrated as follows.

Suppose that a bank has N £1 notes outstanding. Each note indexed by i is either held or presented for redemption during a given planning period. In the former case, X_i realizes a value 0; in the latter case it realizes a value 1. Each X_i is assumed to be independent, and total withdrawals

$$X = \sum_{i=1}^{N} X_i$$

The bank holds a level of reserves R at the start of the planning period, and it has to pay a penalty p for each £1 more than R which is withdrawn. Each £1 held in reserve bears an opportunity cost r. The bank's decision problem is then to choose R to minimize the sum of its reserve opportunity costs (i.e. rR) and the expected penalty costs if withdrawals exceed R (i.e.

$$\int_R^N p(X-R) \, f(X) \, dX$$

where $f(X)$ is the density function for X). Optimization with respect to R yields the first-order condition

$$r = p \int_R^N f(X) \, dX \tag{1}$$

Assuming that $f(X)$ is approximately normal,[2] we can derive the following optimal reserve condition:

$$R = b \, \sigma_x \tag{2}$$

where $b = r/p$. Noting that $\sigma_x^2 = N \, \sigma_{xi}^2$, equation (2) can then be rewritten[3] as

$$R = b \, \sigma_{xi} \sqrt{N} \tag{3}$$

and so optimal reserve holdings rise with the square root of the bank's liabilities.[4] This means that the average reserve/liability ratio falls as the bank gets bigger, and that increasing scale reduces the average reserve cost for each outstanding £1 liability. It follows that any two banks can always economize on their reserves by combining to form a larger bank, but it should also be apparent that these gains tend to diminish with size.[5] Returns to scale are always increasing, but they increase at a decreasing rate, and the marginal return to scale diminishes in the limit to zero.

While these economies might at first be thought to provide a reason for banking to be a natural monopoly, they actually seem to diminish rapidly with scale. As Glasner (1989a: 7) writes:

> A simple numerical example will demonstrate how trivial savings on reserve costs are as a source of natural monopoly. Suppose the rate of interest is 10% on short-term liquid securities that are the alternative to holding non-interest-bearing reserves. And suppose that if a bank issued just $1 of money, its optimal reserve would be exactly $1 of non-interest-bearing reserves [i.e., in terms of equation (3), Glasner is assuming that $b \sigma_{Xi} = (r/p) \sigma_{Xi} = 1$], which would imply a yearly interest cost of 10 cents per dollar issued. If the bank increased its deposits or notes a hundredfold, the square-root rule tells us that the bank would have to increase its holdings of non-interest-bearing reserves only tenfold. The annual interest cost would be only 1 cent per dollar – a reduction of 90 percent in reserve costs. If it increased its deposits or notes another hundredfold, the bank would reduce its interest cost to only .1 cent per dollar – a reduction of 99 percent of its original cost. In other words, a bank with only $10,000 of liabilities would exhaust 99 percent of the possible savings in holding reserves. . . . there are virtually no further economies of scale in holding reserves.

This is a very plausible argument, yet there are several reasons to believe that Glasner exaggerates the potential gains from banks' merging by overstating the costs of holding reserves:

1. His example implicitly assumes that redemption media are non-interest-bearing. If we relax this assumption – and banks have an obvious interest in holding reserves that bear a return instead of 'sterile' ones that do not – then the opportunity cost of holding reserves will be less than the interest rate and the gain from merger will be less than his example indicates. This qualification, of course, only reinforces the point he is making.

2. Glasner's example also overstates the advantage of a large firm over a smaller one because of the possibility that smaller firms might be able to appropriate some of the benefits of scalar economies without explicitly merging. For example, two banks might agree to pool their reserves (and thereby economize on them) but continue to operate as otherwise separate institutions. Such an arrangement is not without its difficulties – reserves would presumably need to be monitored, and there might be a moral hazard problem which would be costly to keep under control – but the point is that the existence of these options implies that we need to distinguish between the benefits of scalar economies *per se* and the benefits of merger as a means of obtaining those scalar economies, and it consequently means that the benefits of merger are usually less than the economies of scale. Once again, we have a qualification that only strengthens his main argument further.[6]

So, while there are always increasing marginal returns to scale in reserve holding, these returns diminish rapidly and once a certain point is passed the gains from further expansion become more or less negligible. In any case, as Selgin (1988: 151) argues:

> For a single bank to gain a monopoly of note [or deposit] issue it is not sufficient that banking involve substantial fixed costs, with relatively small marginal costs, from *issuing* additional notes [or deposits]. The bank must also take steps to improve the popularity of its notes relative to [substitutes], or it must suffer the expense of redeeming them soon after their issue. If the costs to the bank of extending the market or of redemption rise rapidly enough at the margin, its average costs per unit of outstanding currency will rise above the minimum level long before the point at which it would saturate the demand for currency. In this case the industry cannot be considered a natural monopoly . . .

Economies of scale from diversification

A second source of a possible natural monopoly is economies of scale from a bank's increased diversification of its assets. There are various factors that might make diversification more costly for a smaller bank than for a larger one. Transaction costs have a fixed element, for example, and Diamond (1984) shows that a larger bank will also be able to reduce average delegation costs if monitoring each project involves a fixed cost. His argument is that as the bank increases the number of loans it makes to projects whose returns are independent (or, more generally, are not perfectly correlated) the probability that it will incur the deadweight penalties implied by very low average returns (i.e. bankruptcy) will fall, and this lower probability of bankruptcy implies a lower average delegation cost. Diamond (1984: 401) writes that:

> for all projects with less than perfect correlation, the delegation cost for N projects monitored by a single intermediary is less than the sum of the delegation costs for monitoring proper subsets of them by several intermediaries. *Increasing returns to scale from delegation cost savings is a very general result.* The assumption of independence allows a stronger result. The expected delegation cost per entrepreneur monitored by the intermediary gets arbitrarily small as (the number of entrepreneurs involved) . . . grows without bound. This implies that the total cost (per entrepreneur) of providing monitoring services converges to . . . the physical cost of monitoring. [Emphasis added]

These reductions in transaction and delegation costs mean that larger banks will be safer – and perceived to be safer – than smaller ones, *ceteris paribus*. This greater safety enables a large bank to obtain certain other benefits for itself and its customers, and, hence, outcompete smaller competitors:

1. A large bank can economize on confidence-building expenditure and still be safer than a smaller bank. For example, it can reduce its capital ratio and increase its expected rate of return on capital. A large bank can thus convert some of its greater safety into a higher rate of return for shareholders.

2. There will be less pressure on liability-holders to monitor a larger bank, and so they can reduce their monitoring expenditure. If it wanted to, the bank might also capitalize on the greater public confidence in its liabilities by reducing the interest it pays on its deposits.

3. A large bank can provide borrowers with more assurance that their credit will not be curtailed in the future, provided they honour their present commitments, and this greater likelihood of future credit will increase the value to them of their relationships with the bank. The bank, in turn, can then increase its loan rates or its charges for associated services.

4. A large bank will be under less pressure to reveal its books

to outsiders, and so be better placed to honour the confidentiality of its clients. They in turn will then 'trust' the bank more readily with sensitive information, and this increased 'trust' will translate into lower monitoring costs for the bank. This increased client protection might also be an additional reason why a large bank could charge more for credit.

The problem is how large these gains might be, and whether they produce a natural monopoly. While the marginal returns to scale are always positive, these gains are based on limit theorems and (apparently) disappear in the limit to zero, so there is no compelling reason to expect them to be sufficiently 'extreme' to produce a natural monopoly. One must also bear in mind, as with the reserve economies, that there are other ways to realize them than merger. Banks could form 'correspondent' relationships, loan syndicates, and so on, which also allow them to share fixed costs and reap the benefits of economies of scale, and these alternative means of appropriating scalar economies need to be ruled out before we could really expect banking to be a natural monopoly.

SOME SPURIOUS ARGUMENTS FOR NATURAL MONOPOLY

There are also some common but spurious arguments for natural monopoly:

The argument that competitive note issue leads to hyperinflation

One argument is based on the gap between the marginal private cost of printing notes and the marginal social cost of putting those notes into circulation (see, for example, Friedman 1960: 8). The argument goes as follows. The private marginal cost of issuing a note is just the cost of the paper and ink needed to print it, and that cost is virtually nothing. Under conditions of private competition, issuers of banknotes will therefore find it worthwhile to keep on issuing additional notes until the marginal revenue is brought down to the marginal cost, and this can only mean that so many notes are issued that they become virtually worthless (i.e. there would be hyperinflation). The problem with private competition is that each issuer of notes fails to take into account the effect of his notes on the value of the notes issued by others –

that is, the private cost of a banknote is less than the social cost – and it is this discrepancy between private and social costs that leads to the excess of notes and the resulting hyperinflation. The 'solution', supposedly, is to make the issue of notes a monopoly which is usually entrusted to the government.

Perhaps the main problem with this argument is that it is not really a natural monopoly argument at all, although it is often presented as such. A natural monopoly argument maintains that an industry can produce at lower cost with a single firm, and the argument here cannot be a natural monopoly argument (at least in any conventional sense) because it relies on no such claim. It is more accurately described as an 'externalities argument' based on a distinction between private and social costs, and the substantive question is whether it is a valid externalities argument or not. Yet even as an externalities argument it suffers from the weakness that it identifies the costs of issuing a note and keeping it in circulation with the cost of printing it, and these costs are the same only if notes are inconvertible.[7] Under competitive conditions, however, market forces would force banks to make their notes convertible (see, for example, Selgin 1988: chapter 10 or Dowd 1989a: chapter 1) and the cost of issuing a convertible note and keeping it in circulation is much more than the cost of printing it. A convertible note is evidence of debt, and a large part of the cost of issuing any debt is the obligation to repay – a cost that dwarfs the cost of printing the document itself. There is then no longer any obvious gap between the private and social costs of issuing notes, and no reason for competitive banks to issue virtually unlimited quantities of them. The argument that competitive note (or deposit) issue would lead to hyperinflation is valid only if there is already an inconvertible currency, which in turn presupposes that competition has already been suppressed.

Economies of standardization and natural monopoly

A second argument claims that banking is a natural monopoly because everyone in a community (typically) uses the same unit of account. This argument is invalid because it is based on a confusion between economies of standardization (or economies in use) and economies of production. Economies of standardization arise where we find it convenient to adopt certain social conventions. We usually find it convenient to use the same language, drive on the same side of the road, post prices in terms of the same unit of account, and so on. A convention simply exists, and it is (usually) meaningless to say that the user of it produces more of it merely by the act of using it. The English language exists, and I can use it or not as I choose, but if I use it I will not (normally) be described as producing more of it in the process. The fact that an individual uses a convention does not imply that he produces more of it, and our use of a common unit of account implies nothing about the production of 'money' or anything else. A natural monopoly argument is, however, an argument about production and therefore it cannot apply to a situation where production is absent. The production of banknotes may or may not be a natural monopoly, but at least it makes sense to discuss whether it might be; the use of an existing social convention like a unit of account does not involve production in any relevant sense, and so arguments about production cannot apply to it.

'Confidence' as a natural monopoly

A third spurious argument is that banking is a natural monopoly because of economies of scale in building public 'confidence'. We met a superficially similar argument already when we discussed earlier why bigger banks might be considered safer than smaller ones, but we found no compelling reason to expect confidence-building economies to produce a natural monopoly. What we are dealing with here is a somewhat different argument which maintains that public confidence in the value of a currency depends on confidence-building expenditures which involve certain fixed costs, and these fixed costs imply that one bank could always produce confidence more cheaply than two or more could (Klein and Melvin 1982). Klein and Melvin suggest that the government would have an advantage in providing this confidence because its ability to tax implies that it does not need to hold reserves to maintain confidence as private banks would. There are a number of problems with this argument:

1. It depends on the assumption that competitive banks would issue inconvertible currencies, but, as mentioned already, competitive issues would be convertible and convertibility undermines the whole trust of the Klein–Melvin analysis. If competition leads to a convertibility guarantee, and that guarantee is reasonably credible, there should be no lack of public confidence regarding the value

of the currency, and the problem that Klein and Melvin discuss does not even arise.

2. If their argument is valid, it proves too much (Selgin 1988: 153). The logic of the Klein–Melvin argument applies to deposit banking as well as to the note issue. Why therefore do they restrict the monopoly to the note issue only, and not include deposit banking as well? And why restrict the monopoly to banking? Many other industries (e.g. insurance) also exhibit similar features, so the Klein–Melvin argument would appear to imply that they should be monopolized too.

3. To put it mildly, it is difficult to make out a serious case that government intervention in the monetary system has helped promote confidence in the currency. The very problem that Klein and Melvin discuss – the question of confidence in an inconvertible currency – arises in the first place only because governments have suppressed the convertibility 'guarantee' of the value of the currency that private competition would have provided. Far from providing the public with currencies in which they can have confidence, or promoting confidence in their own currencies, the policy of governments has often been designed to compel the public to use currencies in which they had little or no confidence. As Selgin (1988: 152) writes:

> government monopolies in money production have everywhere been achieved by coercion: governments have outlawed private coinage, passed forced-tender laws, restricted private and incorporated banking, prohibited branch-banking and note exchange, taxed bank notes out of existence, passed bond-deposit legislation, refused to enforce redemption contracts, and imposed exchange controls. All of these measures discouraged private, competitive production of money while encouraging production by governments. Most were undertaken to aid the monetization of government debt, which means they were undertaken precisely because confidence in governments was too *low* to allow them to obtain funds through normal channels.

Far from supporting the claim that governments promote confidence, the historical record suggests, on the contrary, that they tend to destroy it.

4. It is doubtful anyway that the government's power to raise taxes promotes confidence.[8] Klein and Melvin suggest that the power to raise taxes enables the government to dispense with

reserves that private issuers would need to hold by them, but the counter is that it is not reserves as such that maintain confidence but the performance bonds that private issuers pledge when they enter into contracts with note and deposit holders. A bank holds reserves only to satisfy relatively immediate demands for redemption – as would a government bank, if it issued a convertible currency – but it is factors like the bank's capital buffer and the knowledge that the bank can obtain more reserves if it needs them that form the basis of public confidence in the bank.[9]

THE EMPIRICAL EVIDENCE ON RETURNS TO SCALE AND NATURAL MONOPOLY IN BANKING

We turn now to the empirical evidence. One source of evidence is the experience of relatively 'free' banking in the past. These experiences all suggest that there are some economies of scale in banking but no tendency towards natural monopoly. White's assessment (1984b: 36) of Scottish 'free banking' is typical:

> The rise of nationally branched joint-stock banks and the decline of local banks in Scotland during the heyday of free banking (1775–1844) indicates that there emerged substantial economies of scale in producing banknote services . . . But these economies were always limited. Thomas Kinnear, an Edinburgh private banker who also served as director of the Bank of Scotland, testified [. . .] that the Bank of Scotland had been forced to abandon some of its branch offices due to competition from local banks. No one bank could serve the entire market so cheaply as to exclude others. Scottish experience offers no reason to suppose that there exist 'natural monopoly' characteristics in the production of convertible currency.

Studies of relatively free banking in various countries – among them Australia (Dowd 1992a; Pope 1989), Canada (Schuler 1992), China (Selgin 1992), Switzerland (Weber 1988, 1992) and the United States (e.g. King 1983 for New York or Dowd (1992b) – all suggest that the experience of other countries is broadly consistent with that of Scotland: in every case there were some economies of scale but there was no natural monopoly. Nor is this conclusion contradicted by the fact that in one country after another a single bank was able to secure for itself a monopoly of the national note issue. In every case, without exception, the establishment of a single note issue was due to state intervention which gave one bank monopoly privileges over the note issue – see, for example, White (1984b, 1992), Selgin (1988), Glasner (1989b) or Dowd (1989a) – and there is no reason to suppose that any of these banks would have been able to establish itself as a natural monopoly in the absence of restrictions on its competition.

The conclusion that there are economies of scale but there is no natural monopoly is also supported by the extensive empirical literature on returns to scale in modern banking.[10] There are three recent surveys of this literature and they come to similar conclusions. Gilbert (1984) and Lewis and Davis (1987: 202–7) between them surveyed twenty-four studies of varying age and methodology. The general finding is that banking does exhibit increasing returns to scale, and the more recent (and presumably more sophisticated and more reliable) studies also emphasized that these economies are limited. The third survey (Clark 1988) covered an additional nine studies and concluded that the 'empirical evidence appears to support a conclusion of significant overall economies of scale only for depository institutions of relatively small size – less than $100 million in total deposits (p. 26). Clark's conclusion is robust to the types of institution covered (i.e. commercial banks, savings and loan institutions and credit unions), the data sets used, the product and cost definitions and the general methodology. The conclusion is that returns to scale exist but are limited, and, significantly, not a single study finds evidence that banking is a natural monopoly. Given the weakness of the theoretical arguments for it, and the lack of any evidence to support it, it is strange that the belief that banking is a natural monopoly persists as it does.

Chapter 6

Models of banking instability

After lying dormant for decades, the problem of banking instability has once again become the focus of wide-ranging controversy. World banking systems appeared to be relatively stable from the late 1930s to the late 1970s, and most economists during that period had lost interest in the earlier controversies on banking stability of the nineteenth and early twentieth centuries. A combination of factors then led to renewed interest in the subject in the early 1980s. The world debt crisis and the crisis in the US banking and thrift industries reopened old questions about the stability of banking competition and the role of the authorities in preventing – or aggravating – banking crises. In addition, the process of financial deregulation served to undermine traditional tools of central banking control, and the renewed interest in unregulated or 'free' banking led economists to ask again what, if anything, was wrong with *laissez-faire* in banking, and what purpose was served by central banking and financial regulation.

The new literature on banking instability differs noticeably from previous work in placing considerable emphasis on formal analysis in place of the informal, discursive treatments that are to be found in the traditional literature. Earlier treatments never developed a theory of banking instability or even a satisfactory explanation of why banks exist, and formal attempts to model banking instability only really began during the last decade. A key paper in this new literature is Diamond and Dybvig (1983), which sets out an analytical framework that has since become more or less standard. Diamond and Dybvig attempt to explain why banks are subject to potentially damaging runs, and what the government could do to protect them, and one can view much of the rest of the literature as attempting to sort out the issues raised by their work. Two

general issues dominate this literature. Why is there banking instability and, as a subsidiary question, why is it damaging? And what,
if anything, should the government or the banking authorities do
about it? Diamond and Dybvig suggest that banking instability
arises because depositors' liquidity demands are uncertain and
banks' assets are less liquid than their liabilities, and they suggest
that banking instability is harmful because it ruins risk-sharing
arrangements and harms production. They also argue that this
instability creates a need for government deposit insurance or a
lender of last resort to provide emergency loans to banks. Later
literature in the Diamond and Dybvig tradition develops these
answers further and has been used to justify additional policies
such as interest rate ceilings (e.g. Anderlini 1986b; Smith 1984)
and reserve requirements (e.g. Freeman 1988). If one wishes, one
can therefore view this literature as attempting to provide a rigorous theoretical underpinning to some of the key features of modern
central banking.

This chapter provides an overview of this literature and an
assessment of it. To this end, we need first to establish criteria by
which the literature can be assessed. As it has evolved this literature has gradually developed the yardstick that, if it is to explain
banking instability and motivate a role for the government in the
banking system, the models involved must also explain why financial intermediaries exist in the first place. Financial intermediation
should therefore be 'properly motivated' in the sense that the
agents involved prefer the intermediated outcome to the unintermediated one (i.e. the intermediated outcome is superior).[1] One
reason for using this criterion is to weed out explanations of banking instability or analyses of government intervention in the banking industry that are unconvincing[2] because they come from
models that also predict that there should be no financial intermediaries to be unstable or in which the government could
intervene. In addition to explaining the mere existence of
intermediation, it would also seem reasonable to expect (or at least
hope) that our models could say something about the characteristics of observed financial intermediation, and the most basic
characteristics to be explained would seem to be the types of
claims that financial intermediaries issue and hold. The most
common forms of claims are debt-type claims and equity. Debt
instruments promise the holder a pre-specified return in 'normal',
non-default states, and first claim to (and control of) the issuer's

assets in the event of his default. In addition, the debt claims issued by banks typically grant the holder the right to redeem any time he chooses without giving prior notice (i.e. they are redeemable on demand), so our theory ought to be able to explain the demandability of bank-issued debt as well. Equity claims, by contrast, promise the holder a fixed proportion of a firm's residual income and give him certain rights of control over the firm's management. Most real-world financial intermediation is done by two types of institution – banks, which issue both equity and (mostly demandable) debt, and mutual funds, which issue only equity – and our theory should be able to predict at least the main features of these types of financial intermediary.

One should also be clear how the papers considered here fit in with other recent literature. The focus of the present chapter is on the instability of financial intermediation, and the literature in which we are interested needs to be distinguished from a large amount of related work that none the less has little to say on this particular issue. There is, for example, a sizeable literature on why financial intermediaries exist (see, for example, Diamond 1984 or Chant 1992), but this existence literature says little about the instability of intermediation *per se*. There is also a large amount of work on why agents use particular financial instruments such as debt or equity – overviews of it are provided by Harris and Raviv (1991) and Dowd (1992c) – but this literature too has relatively little to say on bank runs or related aspects of financial intermediary instability. Much work has also been done on the behaviour of financial intermediaries – why they engage in credit rationing, what determines their collateral policies, and so on (see, for example, Stiglitz and Weiss 1981; Bester 1985; Williamson 1986) – and on the instability of financial markets – how collateral requirements and credit rationing can change in response to other factors, how financial factors can influence the real economy (e.g. Bernanke and Gertler 1990; Calomiris and Hubbard 1990), and how financial markets can collapse (Mankiw 1987) – but none of this literature has much to say on the instability of financial intermediaries as such. There is, finally, a large amount of other banking literature which does address some of the issues considered here (e.g. Benston *et al.* 1986), and most of this other literature is older, but, for reasons that should become apparent later, the new literature makes relatively little reference to it. How these literatures relate to each other should also become apparent by the end of the chapter.

THE DIAMOND–DYBVIG MODEL WITH NO AGGREGATE CONSUMPTION RISK

We now begin with a benchmark model suggested by Diamond and Dybvig (1983). This model is based on the following assumptions.

1. There are three periods ($T = 0, 1, 2$) and a single good.

2. Everyone has access to an identical production technology which converts each unit invested in period 0 to one unit output if liquidated in period 1, and $R > 1$ units of output if left until period 2. These assumptions are meant to capture the idea that interrupting the production process is costly, and these costs can be interpreted as the costs of physical interruptions to the production process[3] or (as in Freeman 1988: 47–8) as resale costs.[4] All investments are perfectly divisible, and R is assumed to be certain.

3. Agents have access to a private storage technology which enables them to store the good without being observed, and the storage technology yields a zero net return.

4. There is a continuum of agents whom we can think of as distributed along a unit line. They are identical in period $T = 0$, when each agent is endowed with one unit of the good.

5. In period $T = 1$ each agent is revealed to be one of two types. Type 1 agents die at the end of $T = 1$ and type 2 agents die at the end of $T = 2$. The probability of being type 1 is t, and t is initially assumed to be known as $T = 0$. These assumptions are meant to capture the idea that agents have unpredictable consumption 'shocks' which may lead them to want to liquidate their investments before they have matured. Their preferences are assumed to take the form

$$\mu(c_1, c_2, \theta) = \theta\, u(c_1) + (1-\theta)\, \rho\, u(c_2) \tag{1}$$

where c_T indicates consumption in period T, θ is a random variable taking the value 1 if the agent is type 1 and 0 if he is type 2, and ρ represents the time preference rate which satisfies $1 \geqslant \rho > 1/R$. These assumptions imply that type 1 agents will consume only in period 1, and type 2 agents will consume only in period 2 (i.e. agents have 'corner preferences'[5]). We also assume that the utility function satisfies the Inada conditions, and the coefficient of relative risk aversion is greater than one.

6. At $T = 0$ agents are assumed to maximize the expectation of their (state-dependent) utility function

$$E(\mu(c_1, c_2, \theta)) = t\, u(c_1) + (1-t)\, \rho\, u(c_2) \tag{2}$$

since $E(\theta) \equiv t$.

7. At $T = 1$ each agent learns his own type only. He has no credible way of directly revealing his type, and he does not know what type others are.

These assumptions imply that all agents will make investments in $T = 0$, but type 1 agents will want to liquidate their investments in $T = 1$ while type 2 agents will consume their investments when they mature in $T = 2$. If agents decide to invest autarkically, they are guaranteed returns of 1 if they turn out to be type 1 and choose to liquidate their investments in $T = 1$, and R if they turn out to be type 2 and keep their investments until $T = 2$. However, since they are risk-averse and know the proportion of types, there is presumably some scope for mutually beneficial risk-sharing against the 'unlucky' event of turning out to be type 1. If we let $c_{j,i}$ represent the consumption of a type i agent in period j, this 'insurance' would involve $c_{1,1} > 1$ and $c_{2,2} < R$, and Diamond and Dybvig show that an optimal insurance contract exists and satisfies

$$c_{1,2}{}^* = c_{2,1}{}^* = 0,\ u'(c_{1,1}{}^*) = \rho\, R\, u'(c_{2,2}{}^*)$$
$$tc_{1,1}{}^* + [(1-t)\, c_{2,2}{}^*/R] = 1 \tag{3}$$

(where the * denotes optimality). The first condition comes from noting that type 1 households derive no utility from consumption in period 2, and vice versa; the second indicates that marginal utility is in line with marginal productivity, and the third is the resource constraint. Note that $\rho R > 1$ and the second condition in (3) imply that $c_{1,1}{}^* < c_{2,2}{}^*$. It follows, then, that the optimal outcome satisfies the self-selection constraint that no agent has an incentive to misrepresent his type – type 1s have no incentive to represent themselves as type 2s, since $c_{1,1}{}^* > 1 > c_{1,2}{}^* = 0$, and type 2s have no incentive to misrepresent themselves, since $c_{2,2}{}^* > c_{1,1}{}^*$.

The Diamond–Dybvig intermediary

The problem is to find a way to implement this contract. A conventional mutual insurance scheme (i.e. one where agents just announce their types) is ruled out because each agent would claim to be type 1 to get the insurance hand-out and there would be no way of distinguishing truthful claims from false ones. Diamond and Dybvig suggest that agents might be able to implement the optimal contract by establishing an intermediary which would take in deposits and invest them in the production process but promise depositors a reasonable return if they withdrew their deposits in period 1.[6] They therefore suppose that this intermediary would offer a contract that promises to pay r_1 $(=c_{1,1}) > 1$ for each deposit withdrawn in period 1 provided that the intermediary still has assets to liquidate. Demands for withdrawals arrive at random times at the intermediary, which deals with them as they come until it runs out of assets. If it has any assets left, they are liquidated in period 2 and divided *pro rata* among remaining deposit holders. More formally, if V_i is the pay-off in period i for each unit deposited, f_j is the number of withdrawers' deposits serviced before agent j as a fraction of total deposits, and f is the proportion of deposits withdrawn in $T = 1$, then the return to a depositor is given by

$$V_1(f_j, r_1) = r_1 \text{ (if } f_j < 1/r_1) \text{ or } 0 \text{ (if } f_j \geq 1/r_1) \tag{4}$$

and

$$V_2(f, r_1) = \max \left[R(1 - r_1 f)/(1 - f), 0 \right]$$
(see Diamond and Dybvig 1983: 408).[7]

The assumption that demands arrive randomly and are dealt with sequentially is meant to capture the notion that depositors withdraw at different times through period 1, and Diamond and Dybvig justify it as allowing them to 'capture the flavor of continuous time' in a discrete model (1983: 408) and to represent intermediary services that they do not explicitly model (1983: 414). This sequential service constraint means that the intermediary does not – and, for reasons that are not spelt out, presumably cannot – simply cumulate requests for withdrawal and then make payments contingent on the total number of withdrawal requests, and it also means that an agent's return can depend on his place in a queue. The sequential service constraint turns out to be very significant and we shall return to it later.

One should also note the form of the contract between the intermediary and its depositors. Diamond and Dybvig (and much of the subsequent literature) refer to it as a 'demand deposit contract', which suggests that it is some sort of debt, but this description is misleading because the contract does not specify a fixed return for deposits withdrawn in non-bankruptcy states. Those who withdraw in $T = 1$ are promised a fixed return provided the intermediary still has funds, but those who withdraw in $T = 2$ are residual (or equity-like) claimants rather than debt–holders *per se*. As noted already, the term 'debt' is normally understood to refer to an asset whose promised return is pre-specified outside default by the issuer. The contract is thus a kind of debt–equity hybrid which looks like debt to those who withdraw in $T = 1$ and looks like equity to those who withdraw later, but there is no debt–equity distinction as such because all claims issued by the intermediary are identical. Note too that the identical nature of its liabilities means that the intermediary is more like a mutual fund than a bank as such, since banks as we know them issue *both* debt *and* equity, whereas a mutual fund normally issues only one type of liability. Note, however, that the debt–equity 'hybrid' liabilities issued by the Diamond–Dybvig mutual fund differ from the equity usually issued by conventional mutual funds, so the Diamond–Dybvig intermediary is something of an unconventional mutual fund. We shall come back to these points later as well.

The problem of 'runs' and the Diamond–Dybvig solution

Diamond and Dybvig show that their contract can support the optimal insurance contract as a Nash equilibrium, but the equilibrium is not unique and there exists an alternative 'run' equilibrium in which all the intermediary's assets are liquidated in period 1. This equilibrium occurs when type 2 depositors 'panic' and withdraw their deposits because they anticipate that the intermediary will run out of assets, and this possibility exists because the intermediary's potential liability in $T = 1$ is r_1, which is greater than what it could recover from its assets if they were all liquidated then (i.e. unity). It is a worse outcome for both types of agent than the initial 'autarky' equilibrium because certain returns of 1 and R for each type are replaced by uncertain returns of mean unity. Runs are damaging because they 'ruin the risk sharing between agents and take a toll on the efficiency of production because all production is interrupted at $T = 1$ when it is optimal for some to continue until $T = 2$' (1983: 409).[8]

The occurrence of the run equilibrium hinges on the beliefs type 2 agents have about each other. If a type 2 agent believes that others will not demand redemption, then he has no reason to demand redemption either, because his investment would yield him a greater return if it were liquidated the next period. But if he believed, for whatever reason, that others would demand redemption, then he would demand redemption as well because he would expect the intermediary to have no assets left the next period. There is therefore a sense in which runs are self-fulfilling: 'once they have deposited, anything that causes [depositors] to anticipate a run will lead to a run' regardless of whether it has anything fundamentally to do with the soundness of the institution's condition or not (Diamond and Dybvig 1983: 410; see also Azariadis 1981; Waldo 1985: 273, n. 7). The implication drawn by Diamond and Dybvig is that the 'good' equilibrium is very fragile and the intermediary will be acutely concerned with maintaining depositor confidence.

Having established that runs are possible, Diamond and Dybvig none the less have difficulty explaining why they should occur. The problem of determining which equilibrium actually results when there are possible multiple equilibria is common in forward-looking rational expectations models, and it is questionable whether Diamond and Dybvig provide the kind of plausible story that is needed to reduce the possibility of multiple equilibria to a single determinate outcome. They suggest that a run could occur:

> if the selection between the bank run equilibrium and the good equilibrium depended on some commonly observed random variable in the economy. This could be a bad earnings report, a commonly observed run at some other bank, a negative government forecast, or even sunspots.
>
> (1983: 410)

But the problem is that none of these factors is in their model. They cannot rely on a bad earnings report because their model has no uncertainty regarding the returns to production; they cannot rely on a run on another institution because they would then have to explain how that started; and they cannot rely on a report by the government or anyone else because it is not clear what there is in the model that they could report on. Diamond and Dybvig end up relying on extraneous uncertainty (i.e. sunspots) to generate expectations, but this explanation is also incomplete because they fail to explain why rational agents should form their expectations in this way (see also Webb 1986: 180). The Diamond–Dybvig story thus explains that runs might occur, but in the absence of any theory of expectations formation it is not clear whether they would occur or not.[9]

Be that as it may, Diamond and Dybvig then show that the 'bad' equilibrium can be eliminated by a simple modification of their contract. Since it knows what t is, the intermediary can predict exactly how many type 1 agents there will be, so it promises to redeem on demand in $T = 1$ until that number of agents has been dealt with and then refuses to redeem any more deposits until $T = 2$. This 'suspension of convertibility' version of the Diamond–Dybvig contract specifies the following returns to type 1 and type 2 agents:

$$V_1(f_j, r_1) = r_1 \text{ (if } f_j \leq t) \text{ or } 0 \text{ (if } f_j > t)$$

$$V_2(f, r_1) = \max \ [R(1 - r_1 f)/(1 - f), \ R(1 - r_1 t)/(1 - f)] \tag{5}$$

The $T = 1$ payments are set so that type 1 agents get their optimal return, and no type 2 agent will wish to withdraw in that period because he is confident of getting his optimal return if he leaves his investment until $T = 2$. The 'suspension of convertibility' contract thus guarantees optimal returns and eliminates the possibility of a run.[10]

Equity contracts, agents' 'isolation', and the sequential service constraint

A problem with this analysis is that the Diamond–Dybvig contract is not the only one that can deliver the optimal outcome. An alternative, suggested by Jacklin (1987: 30–1), is for agents to invest in a mutual fund that invests its deposits in the production process and issues investors with equity claims in $T = 0$. The intermediary also promises in $T = 0$ to pay a fixed dividend D at $T = 1$ – the intermediary has to announce the dividend in $T = 0$ since individuals would no longer be able to agree on dividend policy if they waited till $T = 1$ when they knew their types (Jacklin

1987: 31) – and the residual (i.e. $R(1-D)$) to those shareholders who remain at $T = 2$. When $T = 1$ arrives, individuals receive their dividend D and learn their types, and the type 1s sell their shares to type 2s for additional period 1 goods. If D is set at tr_1 and the market clears, then the price of shares in $T = 1$ is $(1-t)r_1$ and the optimal outcome results. Type 2s will buy at this price because the return they would get from those shares is greater than the market price (i.e. $R(1-D) = R(1-tr_1) > r_1(1-t)$). The type 1s will sell at this price because future dividend payments are no use to them. The total return to type 1s is then equal to their $T = 1$ dividend (i.e. tr_1) plus what they get for their shares (i.e. $(1-t)\,r_1$). Their return is therefore equal to r_1, which is optimal if r_1 is set to $c_{1,1}{}^*$. It is then easy to show that the return to type 2s is equal to $R(1-c_{1,1}{}^*t)/(1-t)$, which is the social optimum by (3). The Jacklin equity contract thus delivers the same (optimal) outcome as the Diamond–Dybvig contract, but it relies on a market in shares instead of a suspension mechanism to do it.[11]

A more serious problem is that the assumptions so far imply that an intermediary is not even necessary to achieve the social optimum. Each individual could issue shares in his own 'back yard' investment project, and everyone could buy shares in all the other projects. All shares would be identical because the underlying projects are identical, and each share contract would have the conditions specified in the Jacklin equity contract just outlined. In this case, however, there would be no intermediary. Individuals would then trade shares that were 'direct' claims to project outcomes instead of 'indirect' claims on an intermediary, but there would be no essential difference, and the earlier Jacklin argument can be adapted to show that this investment process would yield the same social optimum. It follows, then, that far from being able to say what intermediaries would do, and what problems they would face, we have no reason yet for them even to exist in the first place.

If we are to have a properly motivated intermediary, there must therefore be some credit market 'frictions' that the intermediary can overcome. Wallace (1989: 9) suggests that we assume that agents in period $T = 1$ cannot trade because they are 'isolated' from each other. He writes that:

> Although this isolation assumption may seem extreme, it is consistent with the notion that people hold liquid assets because

they may find themselves impatient to spend when they do not have access to asset markets, in which they can sell any asset at its usual market price.

(1989: 9)

The important point is not that trade between $T = 1$ and $T = 2$ is prohibited, but that it is sufficiently costly for agents to prefer to deal with an intermediary instead, and the prohibition of trade between these periods is only an extreme means towards that end. Wallace also notes that this isolation assumption is consistent with the notion that 'liquid' assets 'provide the holder with the possibility of spending at any time, if not also at any place, a notion which implicitly assumes that not all people are together' (1989: 9). Since the isolation assumption prevents agents meeting together in $T = 1$, it effectively rules out both the Jacklin intermediary share market and the 'private' credit market in $T = 1$. Apart from 'pure' autarky, the only remaining option is then an intermediary such as the one originally suggested by Diamond and Dybvig, but with the difference that the sequential service constraint now plays a much more explicit role than it did in their original formulation.

THE DIAMOND–DYBVIG MODEL WITH STOCHASTIC AGGREGATE CONSUMPTION

Stochastic aggregate consumption makes Diamond–Dybvig contracts sub-optimal

Suppose that we now relax the assumption that t is determinate and known, and suppose that it is random instead, with a known density function. No one can now predict how many agents will turn out to be type 1s, and none of the earlier Diamond–Dybvig contracts can be relied on to achieve the previous optimum. Since the optimal payment is contingent on t but t itself is no longer known, the intermediary will not know what to pay out until all requests for withdrawals have been dealt with. If the intermediary is to ensure that the optimum is to be attained, it will need some way of contacting those who have already withdrawn to top up the earlier payments it made to them if the earlier payments were too low, or to recover part of the earlier payments if they were too high. If the intermediary had the means to do that, however, it would effectively nullify any 'isolation' between agents at $T = 1$, and if there is no isolation, as we have just seen, the intermediary itself would have no reason to exist in the first place. If we are to take isolation seriously, it would also seem to follow that the intermediary cannot offer contracts contingent on actual, as opposed to expected, t. The optimal feasible contract must take this constraint into account and the Diamond–Dybvig optimal contract does not. A stochastic t also exposes the Diamond–Dybvig contracts to an additional problem. As we have seen, the contract must have a suspension clause if it is to prevent runs, and a suspension clause requires that the intermediary should select as part of its contract (and, therefore, before t is realized) a threshold level of withdrawals at which it will suspend payments. But if the suspension threshold is set too low (i.e. if f' is less than the maximum possible realization of t), then outcomes are possible which would be inefficient *ex post* because some type 1 agents would be unable to withdraw when they wanted to. The only way to avoid such an outcome would be to set f' at the upper bound of t's distribution (i.e. unity), but in that case the intermediary would only suspend when it had nothing left, and the suspension would serve no purpose. A threshold as high as that would thus be tantamount to having no suspension facility at all, and the contract would be vulnerable to runs again. If there is to be an effective suspension facility, type 1 agents must therefore run the risk that they might be unable to withdraw in $T = 1$. A final problem, noted by Anderlini (1986c) and Engineer (1989), is that if agents have a longer time horizon than two periods and they discover their types over time, then the Diamond–Dybvig-type suspension contract might not be able to rule out runs anyway.[12]

A case for government intervention?

The question then is whether the outcome could be improved if some outside agency (i.e. the state) were to intervene to 'improve' it, and Diamond and Dybvig suggest that it could. Suppose that there exists a state that could tax (or subsidize) those agents who withdraw in $T = 1$. Suppose also that it could assess taxes after all withdrawals have taken place in $T = 1$, so it could base the amount taxed on the realized total withdrawals and hence, in the absence of panic, on the realized value of t. Diamond and Dybvig then show that a tax subsidy policy exists which enables the earlier socially optimal outcome to be achieved (proposition 2, pp. 414–15). One can think of this policy as a deposit insurance scheme or as a central bank bail-out rule to help illiquid intermediaries, and it operates as follows.[13] When $T = 1$ arrives, those who wish to withdraw queue up at the financial intermediary which redeems their deposits on the basis of some expected value of t. (Remember that the intermediary does not yet know the true realization of t.) Assuming that only type 1s desire to withdraw in $T = 1$, the government infers the realized value of t after all requests for withdrawal have come in and then implements a tax subsidy policy to ensure that type 1s receive their optimal consumption bundle contingent on the realization of t, as given by (3).[14] This policy means that type 1s receive a subsidy or tax assessment after withdrawals have taken place but before they have consumed in $T = 1$. The tax subsidy is assumed to be costless to operate, so a Diamond–Dybvig contract would give the type 2s their optimal consumption as well (again, see (3) above). Since the returns are guaranteed contingent on t, the earlier self-selection constraint is satisfied, and there is no incentive for type 2s to withdraw in $T = 1$. The 'bad' run equilibrium is then eliminated and the only equilibrium left is the 'good' one where agents receive their optimal bundles.

The state intervention might, however, create moral hazard problems that can only be dealt with by further intervention. Since the expected value of the bail-out to any individual banker rises with the probability of default, and the probability of default rises with the promised return to withdrawals in $T = 1$, the latter would rise as each individual banker attempted to maximize the value of his bail-out subsidy, so the bail-out facility might encourage competitive intermediaries to bid more aggressively for deposits by raising the deposit rates paid to those who withdraw in $T = 1$. $T = 1$ deposit rates would then rise indefinitely, and a point would come where the anticipated returns on $T = 2$ withdrawals had fallen so low that there was no point keeping deposits beyond $T = 1$. Type 2 depositors would then run and trigger off the bail-out mechanism (Anderlini proposition 4, 1986b: 25); see also Smith 1984: 305–8 and Freeman 1988: 61–2). Anderlini draws the conclusion that the bail-out rule needs to be supplemented with 'regulation' – in this case, a deposit interest ceiling – and proves (proposition 5, 1986b: 28) that an appropriate combination of bail-out facility and interest rate ceiling can eliminate the bankers' moral hazard and achieve the optimal outcome.[15] If production is irreversible (e.g. as in Freeman 1988), moral hazard might also manifest itself in a tendency to hold too few reserves, so reserve requirements might be necessary as well.[16]

These 'improvements' to the *laissez-faire* outcome, however, turn out to violate the 'isolation' assumption made earlier (see also Wallace 1989: 13). The private sector is assumed to lack the means to overcome isolation in $T = 1$, and this isolation is the reason why a private intermediary cannot 'get back' to agents after they have withdrawn in $T = 1$ to top up their payments or retrieve what it has already paid out. The problem is that the assumption that the government has the means to tax or subsidize agents in $T = 1$ after agents have withdrawn (i.e. when it is in a position to infer what the realization of t was) is tantamount to *assuming that the government has access to the very technology the private sector is assumed to lack.*[17] If the technology exists, one ought to explain why the private sector does not have access to it. In addition to explaining why the government has a technology that the private sector has not, one would also want to explain why the private sector cannot simply hire the government's technology as it might hire any other service. And, if the technology exists to overcome isolation, one must also explain why intermediaries exist at all, given that the absence of isolation implies that the intermediary contract is undermined by arbitrage at $T = 1$. If the technology does not exist, on the other hand, then the government tax subsidy scheme is not feasible because the government has no way of 'getting back' later to those who have already withdrawn in $T = 1$. In the context of the model itself, the government scheme would therefore appear to be either unnecessary or infeasible, and neither way would it generate a superior outcome to *laissez-faire* (see also McCulloch and Yu 1989).

Many economists none the less reject this conclusion and argue that the government's unique legal powers do give it the necessary 'technological superiority' over the private sector to justify at least some of its interventions in the banking system. Most of these arguments hinge on the government's power to tax. Diamond and Dybvig themselves argue (1983: 413–14, 416) that private insurers would have to hold reserves to make insurance promises credible, but the government's power to tax enables it to offer credible insurance without reserves. They argue too that private agents might lack the necessary resources anyway, but the government should not, since it can always obtain them through taxation.

Anderlini (1986b: 8–9), Bryant (1980: 341) and Diamond and Dybvig (1983: 413) also argue that the government has an advantage in that it can make use of inflation to finance the cost of its bail-outs or deposit insurance but the private sector cannot. One also occasionally meets the argument that the government might not be able to hire out its 'superior technology' or that the bail-out or lender of last resort facility is some sort of public good which the private sector is (allegedly) incapable of providing.

These arguments are, however, open to question. It is not reserves as such that private insurers need to offer credible insurance but adequate wealth on which they can draw if the need arises (i.e. adequate collateral), and, as many Lloyd's names appear to do, individual insurers can offer that guarantee with few liquid reserves. The argument that individuals lack the necessary wealth anyway is open to the objection that the sheer size of modern economies makes it implausible, but it is also logically flawed because the government's own resources come from the private sector – if the private sector lacks the necessary resources, then the power to tax is of no avail, since the resources are not there to take. The inflation tax argument is also questionable. If banking were free, we would expect competition to force the banks to make their liabilities convertible, and convertibility would deprive the government of the use of an inflation tax (see, for example, Dowd 1989a: chapter 1). Since the government can use that tax only if it intervenes (e.g. by setting up a fiat currency), the very existence of the tax would seem to presuppose that it has already intervened, and so the argument would not apply to a genuine *laissez-faire* economy. There is in any case considerable evidence that inflation is a relatively inefficient form of taxation which is undesirable even if the alternative is to levy other taxes that distort economic activity (see, for example, Kimbrough 1986 or Dowd 1989a: 78–81). The remaining arguments – that the government cannot hire out its superior technology and that government must provide the bail-out facility on public good grounds – are also unconvincing in my opinion and need in any case to be developed. Even if the government has a natural monopoly in the provision of law and order, all that seems to be required to undermine the case for the government bail-out facility is that private agents have access to the government legal system to conclude contracts with each other. Nor is it obvious (at least to me) what the public good is that is being provided by a bail-out facility or why the private sector cannot provide it adequately. One last point should also be noted. The models themselves imply that the very technology that is used to justify government intervention also undermines the need for intermediation itself, and our requirement that intermediation be properly motivated is violated. If we stick strictly to the models we cannot have properly motivated financial intermediation *and* properly motivated government intervention.

BANKING INSTABILITY WITH UNCERTAIN RETURNS TO PRODUCTION

We consider now what happens if the returns to production are uncertain. Production uncertainty is not especially significant on its own, but it becomes significant if some agents have interim information about production returns on which they might act. As Jacklin (1988: 14–15) observes, production uncertainty can be of importance:

> only if there is interim information about the underlying asset returns that become available at $T = 1$. . . . If one re-examines the [earlier] arguments . . . it is clear that they do not rely on the riskless nature of R, as long as none of the uncertainty regarding R is resolved prior to trade taking place at $T = 1$. Thus, . . . the underlying asset returns are not only assumed to be uncertain, but individuals are assumed to be asymmetrically informed about the returns before trade takes place at $T = 1$.

The combination of uncertain returns and asymmetrical information makes formal analysis difficult, not surprisingly, but a few (relatively disparate) models have made some progress with the problem.[18]

One is Jacklin (1988). In his model each unit invested in $T = 0$ yields a return of 1 if the investment is liquidated in $T = 1$, and a random return of R if it is left until it matures in $T = 2$. The expected value of R exceeds unity and investors have corner preferences. Some type 2 individuals are then given private information about R in $T = 1$ which helps them to decide whether to liquidate their investments in that period. (Note that the corner preference assumption implies that private information about R is of no use to type 1s, since they would liquidate their investments anyway.) There are no restrictions against trading assets in $T = 1$, so there is no sequential service constraint. Jacklin then constructs an example where an equity contract achieves the optimal allocation, provided that the aggregate consumption shock t is nonstochastic. The equity contract is optimal because the share price fully reveals the private information about the random variable R in the absence of other shocks. However, if t is stochastic as well as R, the share price will reflect both shocks, and the equity contract no longer gives a noiseless signal about R. Jacklin demonstrates by means of an example that the equity contract can then be sub-optimal even though the Diamond–Dybvig contract cannot achieve the Diamond–Dybvig social optimum and the possibility of panics still remains. He thus gives some insight into why demand debt-type contracts have arisen that promise liquidity in $T = 1$ and a return that is fixed over a range of project outcomes, and why they have arisen instead of equity ones even though they may be more subject to runs. As he observes, demand debt arose not only to provide liquidity transformation, but also to provide 'transformation using illiquid assets with underlying values that are both *uncertain* and about which there is the *potential for great asymmetry of information* with respect to the uncertainty' (Jacklin 1988: 3). When there is a credit market at $T = 1$ demand debt is no more liquid than equity, but:

> demand debt [by which Jacklin means the Diamond–Dybvig contract] has the benefit of being relatively insensitive to informational asymmetries about the underlying portfolio values. On the other hand, demand equity is not subject to runs but is very sensitive to informational asymmetries about underlying portfolio values.
>
> (Jacklin 1988: 5)

There is, in short, a trade-off between the problems caused by the potential for bank runs which would lead one to prefer equity and the problems caused by information asymmetries which would lead one to prefer Diamond–Dybvig-type contracts instead.

More insights into these issues are provided by Jacklin and Bhattacharya (1988). They have the same production technology as Jacklin (1988) but a return of zero instead of unity if investment is liquidated in $T = 1$. (This irreversibility assumption captures the idea of a 'readily discernible cost' to early consumption. One can think of the crop being destroyed before the harvest is ripe.) Jacklin and Bhattacharya also differ from Jacklin (1988) in so far as investors are assumed to have smooth rather than corner preferences but, as in Jacklin, agents' types are revealed in $T = 1$ and some type 2s receive a signal about R later in the same period. Jacklin and Bhattacharya then show that the Diamond–Dybvig contract is subject to runs while the equity contract is not, but the value of a Diamond–Dybvig asset is unaffected by news about the underlying project return, unless the news is very bad, while the value of equity is affected by any information about the return to production. The underlying idea is that the Diamond–Dybvig contract insulates the investor against small gains or losses on production, but large losses (i.e. ones that make the intermediary insolvent) have to be passed back to him. There is therefore the same trade-off as in Jacklin (1988), and the implication is that the Diamond–Dybvig contract would be preferred where the risk of runs was relatively small (e.g. in financing low-risk projects), but the equity contract would be preferred otherwise. Unlike Diamond and Dybvig, Jacklin and Bhattacharya obtain a unique equilibrium, and they explicitly address the factors (i.e. bad interim information) that could trigger runs. Runs are now 'systematic' events triggered off by movements in economically relevant indicators (e.g. bad earnings reports). They are no longer purely random events triggered off by variables like sunspots which are in themselves economically irrelevant but which for some reason trigger off self-fulfilling expectations of a run.

While Jacklin and Bhattacharya focus on the relationship between choice of contract and the riskiness of an institution's assets when some agents are informed about the value of those assets, Chari and Jagannathan (1988) examine the implications of the converse problem of how *uninformed* agents infer private information about project values from the behaviour of other depositors who are more informed. They have a model in which some individuals may withdraw in $T = 1$ because they have private information that the future return to production will be low, while others withdraw for other reasons (e.g. liquidity needs). The uninformed consequently face a signal extraction problem in which they try to infer the private information they do not have from the size of the queue at the bank, and when they observe a long queue they are more likely to conclude that the bank is in difficulties and decide to run. A run could then harm the bank by forcing it to liquidate its assets at a loss. In their model, investments are made in $T = 0$, and returns are random but expected to be high if the investments are left until $T = 2$. The return takes one of two values: H (high) or L (low), and $H > L$. If the investment is liquidated in $T = 1$, however, the return to the bank depends on how many wish to liquidate their investment. If only a small number wish to withdraw, the return per unit deposit is one, but the return is smaller (reflecting resale losses) if a large number wish to withdraw. All agents are risk-neutral and each is endowed with one unit of the consumption good in $T = 0$. Types are revealed in $T = 1$, and the proportion of type 1s (i.e. t) is random. Type 1s care only about $T = 1$ consumption, while type 2s care about consumption in both $T = 1$ and $T = 2$. Also in $T = 1$ a random fraction α of type 2s receive (perfect) private information about prospective returns in $T = 2$, where $0 \leqslant \alpha < 1$, and no individual can predict whether he will be informed or not. The only public information in $T = 1$ is the fraction of the population who decide to liquidate their investments (i.e. the queue at the bank), but no one observes the reasons that lead others to decide to withdraw their investments. (Note, however, that there is nothing in the model to show why agents prefer to borrow and lend through an intermediary instead of dealing with each other direct.) When the 'private' information is given out in $T = 1$:

> All uninformed type-2 agents will realize that the equilibrium value of [the aggregate $T = 1$ investment] is correlated with the signal received by the informed agents and hence 'reveal', albeit imperfectly, their signal. It is important to realize that the aggregate investment could be low *either* because the value of t is high *or* because some type–2 agents have received information that prospective returns are low. It is this confounding that is crucial.
>
> (Chari and Jagannathan 1988: 753)

They then show that a unique Rational Expectations Equilibrium exists but, depending on the realizations of the stochastic variables, this equilibrium could involve a panic in which everyone withdraws even though no one receives any negative information about R. One should note, however, that the contract form is assumed, and Chari and Jagannathan fail to show why – given that there is no sequential service constraint in their model – the bank does not simply condition contractual returns on the verifiable information the informed depositors receive. The run would then be short-circuited, and the losses it could cause avoided.

Williamson (1988) provides in some ways a more satisfactory analysis. As in Diamond and Dybvig, he has agents whose random preferences generate a demand for assets that are liquid in the short term, but his agents are risk-neutral rather than risk-averse and their risk-neutrality implies that there is no risk-sharing benefit from financial intermediation. There exist primitive short-term and long-term assets, but trade in claims to these assets is hampered by the difficulties potential buyers face in distinguishing claims to 'good' assets and claims to 'bad' ones. An individual who held direct claims on the production process might then find himself unable to meet unexpected liquidity needs without having to liquidate 'good' assets at a loss that reflected the market for lemons problem in the capital market. A bank-type intermediary could, however, exploit the fact that individual liquidity shocks tend to cancel out in large numbers and issue claims that enabled individuals to invest in the underlying production process while simultaneously holding assets that could be liquidated at little loss in the short run (see also Freeman 1988). In Williamson's model, banks generate superior outcomes to unintermediated markets in some states of the world and the same outcome in others, so it always makes sense *ex ante* for agents to invest in a bank rather than invest directly themselves in the primitive assets. Banks are thus properly motivated, but should a state occur where the bank does not improve on the unintermediated outcome Williamson (unconvincingly) suggests that the bank might agree to dissolve itself and leave investors holding the underlying primitive assets, and he interprets such occurrences as bank 'failures'. His explanation is unconvincing because there is no reason in his model for the bank to dissolve rather than remain as it is, and his treatment is also unconvincing in so far as it implies that the act of bank failure *per se* is costless and, indeed, quite irrelevant. His model also suggests that bank 'failures' are only symptoms of particular states of endowments, preferences and production technology, and the failures do not cause the low output and 'bad' times that are associated with them. Outcomes in his model are always optimal, whether failures occur or not, so there is no case for government intervention to 'improve' them or counteract or prevent the failures themselves.

A final analysis of how 'noisy' indicators can lead to runs is Gorton (1985). His model has banks that finance two-period investments with deposits and equity. (Note, however, that the existence of banks and the basic forms of the deposit and equity claims are assumed rather than derived, except for the suspension clause in the deposit contract, which is discussed below.) Depositors derive utility from consumption in both periods, and they have an initial investment in $T = 0$ which they choose to invest between bank deposits and an alternative store of value. The initial amount of bank equity is chosen to equate the expected return on bank equity with the (exogenous) expected return on equity elsewhere, and the bank obtains additional funds by issuing deposits to the public. The deposit contract then offers depositors specified returns in each of the two periods provided the bank remains solvent, and it gives depositors first claim to the bank's assets if the bank defaults. Depositors also have the right to demand liquidation in $T = 1$. The return on the alternative (i.e. non-bank) asset and the return on the bank's investments are each subject to shocks in $T = 1$, and the latter shock is assumed to be private information to the bank. There is an implicit sequential service constraint by which depositors wishing to withdraw are served sequentially in the (presumably random) order in which they arrive at the bank, and the bank continues to meet demands for redemption until it runs out of assets and defaults.

If we initially assume that depositors perceive the state of the bank's investments correctly, the depositors' decision whether to withdraw or not depends on a straight comparison of the expected rates of return on the two stores of value. They will keep their deposits if the expected return on deposits is at least as high as the return on the alternative store of value, and they will liquidate them otherwise. In the latter case the bank would face a run and lose its deposits, but the outcome in either case is Pareto-optimal. If depositors are imperfectly informed about the state of the bank's investments, on the other hand, they will have to make their decisions on the basis of 'noisy' indicators of those investments, and they can make decisions that turn out to be worse than the decisions they would have made had they been better informed. Two sorts of 'mistakes' of this nature are then possible. Depositors can overestimate the value of the bank's assets and as a result mistakenly keep their deposits in the bank and earn a lower return than they would have obtained had they withdrawn their deposits. Or, alternatively, they can underestimate the value of the bank's assets and run on the bank in the mistaken belief that they could earn a higher return by withdrawing their deposits and investing them elsewhere, and in the process they bring about inefficient liquidations. The deposit contract can thus no longer be relied upon to deliver an outcome that is optimal *ex post*. Gorton then suggests that the *ex post* optimum could be achieved by inserting a suspension clause into the deposit contract. His argument is that if the 'true' state of the bank could be revealed to depositors at some verification cost – one can think of this cost as the cost of bringing in outside auditors to go over the books – the bank would make an agreement with its depositors that it could suspend on condition that it submitted to a verification, the cost of which would be borne by the bank's shareholders. (Note, however, that the assumption that shareholders are in a position to pay this cost is not trivial. The most natural interpretation of this arrangement is to think of the payment as coming out of bank capital, but then the latter must be at least as great as the verification cost.) Gorton argues that the verification–suspension clause is incentive-compatible in that the bank would have an incentive to use it only to reassure depositors who had underestimated the bank's true worth, and he suggests that this arrangement would be in the interests of both the bank and its depositors because it would protect them both against the losses they would each suffer if depositors ran while the bank was still sound. Strictly speaking, the Gorton analysis implies verification rather than suspension as such, and some additional element is needed to go from the former to the latter, but the gap can easily be filled by assuming that verification takes time to carry out. The bank then suspends while the verification is being carried out. A more serious problem is that Gorton fails to explain why the bank does not reassure depositors by posting a bond of some sort (e.g. by augmenting bank capital; see the discussion of bank capital further below). Since the shareholders know the bank is sound, they would have no reason to fear losing their investment, and augmenting bank capital has the advantage that it avoids the verification fee. Gorton therefore needs to explain why the bank opts for the apparently more expensive means of reassuring its depositors (see also Dowd 1988c).

SOME CONCLUSIONS AND A SUGGESTED WAY FORWARD

A number of points stand out from reviewing the literature. Perhaps the most obvious lesson is that relatively little of it deals with the stability of institutions that have much resemblance to real-world banks. Barring Williamson (1988) and (arguably) Jacklin, the uncertain production side of the literature fails to explain why there should be any financial intermediation at all, so any conclusions it offers on the stability of financial intermediation should be taken carefully. The Diamond–Dybvig literature (i.e. the certain-returns-to-production literature) does provide a motivation for financial intermediation, but the financial intermediaries that arise there are more like peculiar mutual funds than banks. These issues are far from semantic. As noted already, the financial institutions we do observe in the real world for the most part distinguish between creditors who hold their equity and those who hold their debt. Their equity liabilities are residual claims that also make the holders owners of the institutions in a legal sense. The debt liabilities, by contrast, promise pre-specified returns in all non-default states and first claim to the institution's assets if it defaults. When we refer to 'banks' it is these institutions we normally have in mind, and the substantive issue is that it is these institutions – whatever we may call them – that we are mostly interested in, and yet this literature has very little to say about them. The other financial intermediaries we observe are genuine mutual funds whose liabilities are equity claims on its assets, but these too are not (usually) predicted by this literature, and nowhere do we observe the peculiar mutual fund-like intermediaries that the literature does predict.[19]

Note too that, while the literature talks about 'debt' and debt-like instruments such as 'demand deposits', the instruments labelled in this way are usually not debt at all, or at least not 'debt' as defined above. The 'demand deposit' contract in much of this literature typically specifies a fixed non-default pay-off in $T = 1$, and a residual payment in $T = 2$ for those who leave their investments till then. Such an instrument may resemble debt if one looks at the $T = 1$ payment, but a real debt contract would have specified fixed payments in both $T = 1$ and $T = 2$. Again, the issue is not merely semantic. Whatever we choose to call them, the instruments I have labelled debt play an important role in real-world financial intermediation, and our theories ought to be able to predict them (and equity, for that matter). Part of the problem, one suspects, is that the literature focuses on the wrong question by asking whether a representative investor would want to hold a residual claim-type asset or one that has some 'fixity' in its pay-off which it (dubiously) identifies as 'debt'. This approach ignores the symbiotic relationship between the two types of asset – if someone is to hold debt, someone else usually has to be the residual claimant who absorbs the gains or losses to the project value and ensures that the return to the debt holder is fixed (at least outside bankruptcy) – but we then need a framework that enables us to study the simultaneous demands for both assets, and one cannot motivate such a framework if one starts off by asking which asset a representative agent will hold. We need to explain why some individuals choose to hold debt while others choose to hold equity, and it is not clear how we can provide that explanation using a framework that maintains that all agents are identical when they make their investment decisions.

These points might not matter much, perhaps, if we could be reasonably confident that any insights the literature provides about the intermediaries it generates could be safely carried over to real-world banks, but their are important differences between the two types of financial institution. The issues involved can be illustrated using an example from Dowd (1988a). Suppose we go back to the initial Diamond–Dybvig framework with corner preferences and a stochastic t. Suppose too that we ensure that an intermediary has a role to play by making an explicit isolation assumption along the lines suggested by Wallace (1989). Now introduce a new agent with K units of capital who knows in $T = 0$ that he will get utility only from consumption in $T = 2$. (One can think of this agent as someone with capital to invest who does not have to worry about short-term liquidity.) One way to invest his capital is to set up a bank. If he did so he would capitalize the bank with his endowment of capital and take in deposits from the public. The bank's capital and deposits would then be invested in the production process, and depositors would be promised fixed returns for withdrawals in both $T = 1$ and $T = 2$ as well as the option of withdrawal on demand. Denote these returns by r_1 and r_2 respectively. Suppose also that the bank would pay each depositor-type his 'optimal consumption bundle' as specified by (3), i.e. $r_1 = c_{1,1}{}^*$ and $r_2 = c_{2,2}{}^*$. Depositors would then obtain returns at least as good as they could obtain if they set up their own intermediary along the lines suggested by Diamond and Dybvig, so they would prefer the new bank to Diamond–Dybvig's intermediary. Letting E be the value of the bank when it is wound up after all deposits have been repaid, and assuming that type 2 investors do not withdraw in the first period, then it can readily be seen that

$$E = KR + [t + (1-t)R] - [tr_1 + (1-t)r_2] \tag{6}$$

The first term is the return on the investor's own capital, the second is the return on his deposits, and the third is (the negative of) his deposit liabilities. Note that $\partial E/\partial t < 0$ and E reaches its highest and lowest values respectively for $t = 0$ and $t = 1$. Assuming that he expects depositors to satisfy the self-selection constraint – and it can easily be shown that they will – our investor will expect to make a profit from the bank if t is less than the break-even level, $[R-r_2]/[r_1-1+R-r_2]$, where he would make the same profit as he would have made had he invested in the production process without a bank. He would therefore go ahead and establish the bank if he expected t to be sufficiently less than this level to compensate him for the risk he was taking by doing so.

The differences between a bank and the Diamond–Dybvig mutual fund now become apparent. The possibility of bank runs arises with the Diamond–Dybvig intermediary because each type 2 depositor is aware that he would suffer capital losses if sufficiently many others withdrew their deposits, and the prospect of these losses arises in turn because the intermediary has insufficient capital to redeem all its deposits in $T = 1$ at the rate of r_1 per deposit. If the bank had sufficient capital to meet this liability, however, the public would have no reason to fear capital losses and therefore no reason to participate in runs. The bank could provide such assurance by ensuring that its capital was adequate to cover its losses in the 'worst case scenario' when everyone withdraws in $T = 1$, i.e. by ensuring that K satisfies

$$K \geq r_1 - 1 \tag{7}$$

where $(r_1 - 1)$ is the loss the bank makes on deposits withdrawn in period 1. If this condition holds, the self-selection constraint will be satisfied, no type 2 depositor will withdraw in period 1, and there will be no bank runs. (A similar result is to be found in Eichberger and Milne 1990.) Runs arose in the Diamond–Dybvig model precisely because the zero value of K meant that this condition could not hold. The key point, therefore, is that an adequately capitalized bank can use its capital buffer to prevent runs by reassuring potentially nervous depositors, but a Diamond–Dybvig mutual fund is vulnerable to runs because it cannot provide that reassurance. Genuine banks are thus more stable than the hybrid 'mutual funds' predicted by the Diamond–Dybvig literature, and we should be careful drawing inferences about the stability of the former from the peculiar problems faced by the latter.

The question then arises how much capital is adequate. Condition (7) is only a sufficient condition to rule out runs, but it is not a necessary one, and it might well be the case in practice that a capital base that covered some but not every conceivable loss would none the less be adequate to reassure depositors. While depositors would obviously prefer as much reassurance as possible, other things being equal, a higher capital base means a lower return on bank equity, other things again equal, and a lower return on bank equity makes the equity itself harder to attract. The costs of a stronger capital position need to be taken into account, in other words, and the optimal level of capital will trade off the reassurance it provides the depositors with the cost of the capital itself. One would then expect the 'adequate' level of capital to increase with depositors' risk aversion and the riskiness of the bank's portfolio, and decrease with the return on equity elsewhere, but to the best of my knowledge there is no formal treatment yet within the post-Diamond–Dybvig banking instability literature of what determines the adequate level of capital. Ironically, the issue has been discussed for many years in the older banking literature (e.g. Peltzman 1971; Maisel 1981) and is still widely discussed in less formal literature on banking instability (e.g. Benston *et al.* 1986; Kaufman 1988a; Salsman 1990). An obvious next step would therefore be to formalize the capital adequacy problem and explore the extent to which the insights of the older and less formal literatures carry over to more formal models – and only then will we have a model of banking instability as such.

The last main point that emerges from this literature on 'banking' instability is the shakiness of the foundations on which arguments for government intervention in the financial industry are based. The uncertain production side of the literature has uncovered no welfare-improving role for government intervention, so all the arguments for intervention come from the Diamond–Dybvig literature. We then find that most of the arguments for intervention to be found in that literature are based on the premise that the government has access to technology for overcoming 'isolation' between individuals that the private sector is assumed to lack. Some would regard the idea of such governmental technological superiority as far-fetched, but even if one conceded it the first-best outcome could still be achieved in these models provided the government gave the private sector access to its own technology. The advocates of intervention would then presumably have to explain why an interventionist policy was to be preferred to the government simply hiring its technology out. And even if such an explanation was provided, the government's own technology would make financial intermediation redundant anyway by destroying the 'isolation' friction that gives rise to it. They would have to explain why their inferences about policy towards financial intermediaries should be accepted when the models they use to draw those inferences also imply that the intermediaries themselves should not exist. The other arguments for intervention that appear in this literature are questionable. The Diamond–Dybvig argument that a case for intervention might be based on the government's monopoly of the currency is open to the objection that the currency monopoly is itself the product of intervention, and the arguments for a legislated currency monopoly have been pretty much discredited (see, e.g., White 1984b, 1989, Selgin 1988, Dowd 1989a or Glasner 1989b). The proponents of intervention then have to rebut the argument that the first-best outcome is *laissez-faire* in banking *and* an end to the currency monopoly. There is, finally, the argument that policy might be required to enable firms to exploit economies of scale, but one would then need to explain why firms are not exploiting economies of scale in the first place. If it is because they are prevented by legal restrictions, as US banks are prevented by anti-branch laws, the obvious response is that the restrictions should be removed; if institutions are not prevented by legal restrictions, on the other hand, one has to explain why they are failing to pursue their own self-interest. While others are free to draw their own conclusions, it seems to me that the formal literature on banking instability has so far failed to provide any support for the government's ubiquitous involvement in the banking industry.

Part II

Historical experience

Chapter 7

Free banking in Australia

Australia experienced one of the most interesting historical experiences of free banking. Australian banking was relatively free for almost a century, from the establishment of the first banks in the second and third decades of the last century until well into the twentieth, and fully fledged central banking arrived only with the establishment of the Reserve Bank of Australia at the comparatively late date of 1959. The Australian experience of free banking is of particular interest to students of banking history because the legal framework within which banks operated was perhaps the least restrictive of any on record, and the banking system was largely free of significant government intervention until the 1890s. Australia never had 'pure' *laissez-faire* in banking, but Australian banks operated under relatively innocuous legal restrictions compared with many 'free' banks elsewhere, and the legal restrictions that did exist were frequently disregarded anyway. The comparative purity of the Australian case ought therefore to give us a reasonably fair indication of how well the theory of free banking has worked in practice.

Australian free banking is also of interest for another reason. In the early 1890s Australia experienced a banking crisis of a severity never witnessed in Australia before or since, a crisis whose severity superficially compares with that of the English crisis of 1825–6 or the banking collapses of the United States during the early 1930s. But, unlike these other crises, the Australian one occurred while banking was still in some ways quite free, and many writers have argued that the freedom of Australian banking contributed in a major way to its severity. Unrestricted competition led banks to over-extend themselves, so the argument goes, and the collapse of the land boom in the late 1880s left them exposed to a crisis that most of them lacked the resources to ride out. Had there been a monetary authority to limit competition and ensure that prudential standards were maintained, on the other hand, the banking system would not have overreached itself to the extent that it did, and the ensuing collapse ought to have been avoided. Generations of Australian economists have consequently believed that the crisis of the 1890s demonstrates that unregulated banking is inherently unstable, and have concluded that some form of government control is needed to keep this instability in check.

The Australian experience is unique in that it is the only recorded case where free banking has been associated with a major banking collapse. Free banking systems elsewhere witnessed occasional bank failures, but none ever experienced a crisis comparable with the Australian one, and the supporters of free banking need to reconcile their theory that banking *laissez-faire* is stable with the claim that the Australian banking crash indicates that it is not. Contrary to received opinion, however, the Australian experience is in fact quite consistent with the predictions of free banking theory. The depression of the 1890s was fundamentally a 'real' phenomenon driven by forces outside the bankers' control, and those forces overwhelmed the banks as well as the 'real' economy. The bank failures were also heavily influenced by government intervention, especially in Victoria, and these interventions destabilized the banking system and encouraged banks to suspend to take advantage of new laws which allowed them to reconstruct on advantageous terms. The evidence on reserve ratios and capital adequacy also provides little support for the hypothesis that the bank failures were caused by the banks' previous overexpansion. It is in any case somewhat misleading to talk of bank 'failures' in an unqualified way when virtually all these banks were subsequently able to reopen successfully. The timing of events also lends further support to the view that the primary direction of causation was from the real economy to the banking system, and the timing of the downturn is quite inconsistent with any claim that a banking 'collapse' pushed the economy into a steep depression. The crisis of 1893 was not what it might appear to be.

THE EARLY HISTORY OF MONEY AND BANKING IN AUSTRALIA

The blueprint for the first Australian colony in New South Wales in 1788 made no allowance for the provision of money or banking. Its monetary arrangements were consequently:

> almost all *ad hoc* temporary makeshifts. Foreign coins, arriving haphazardly in trade or in officers' purses and convicts' pockets, acquired local acceptability and brief legal recognition. But they did not suffice, and from the simple expedient of settling debts with promissory notes grew, in the first decade of the nineteenth century, the practice of regular issue by all and sundry of small-notes. . . .
>
> Makeshifts and *ad hoc* expedients to provide for payments between government and individuals and amongst individuals thus merged into a pattern. . . . The core of the monetary system was the Commissariat store with its Treasury bills for public and external payments, its Store receipt, its loans in kind; outside its range private local transactions were fulfilled by supplanting its Store receipts with barter and a variety of private note issues.
>
> (Butlin 1953: 4–5)

Once it had established itself the new colony began to prosper. The settlers took to farming and whaling, and by the second decade of the nineteenth century they were already exporting wool to England. The private note issues continued to prosper, and repeated attempts by Governors King, Bligh and MacQuarie to suppress them came to nothing. The first bank – the Bank of New South Wales – was set up under MacQuarie's patronage in 1817, but its note issues were small and had relatively little impact on the non-bank issuers. A number of new banks were set up in the 1820s, however – the Waterloo Company (1822), the Bank of Van Diemen's Land (1823), the Bank of Australia (1826), among others – and

> with them died at last, in the metropolitan centres but not in the country, miscellaneous issues by individuals and stores. In the country such issues were progressively pushed further and further outback as banks advanced, to be (virtually) eliminated only after a full century. What the Bank of New South Wales

had heralded they made commonplace, 'the ordinary banking business of deposit, discount and exchange'.

(Butlin 1953: 9)

These banks were all unit (i.e. one-branch) banks that operated under the English law that restricted all banks except the Bank of England to be partnerships with no more than six partners, and all partners bore unlimited liability for the debts of the bank. These banks were initially allowed to issue notes for any amount, but a domestic British ban on notes under £1 was extended to Australia in 1826.

It took some time to resolve the issue of the monetary standard. Foreign denominations circulated side by side with sterling for a number of years. One Governor (MacQuarie) introduced his own dollars – 'holey' dollars, imported dollars with a hole stamped in them – which were overvalued locally and hence circulated by virtue of Gresham's law, while another, Governor Brisbane, tried in 1822 to have the Spanish dollar made the legal unit of account and the basis of the circulating medium. This attempt was apparently well on the way to success when the UK government intervened and imposed the gold-based pound sterling as the official currency and ordered the colony to use British coins. This was the origin of the Australian pound (Butlin 1953: 8, 1961: 10). Dollars then disappeared relatively quickly in New South Wales but survived for some time in Tasmania. The value of the Australian pound was now linked to gold, but it could fluctuate by a margin that reflected the cost of shipping gold to or from England to exploit any discrepancy between its par and market values. Arbitrage therefore kept the value of the Australian pound reasonably close to par. The links between the Australian pound and gold were tightened further by the establishment of a branch of the Royal Mint at Sydney in 1855, and later on by the opening of other branches in Melbourne and Perth. The Australian mints reduced the costs of arbitrage – one could now carry out arbitrage operations without having to ship gold to or from England – and thus narrowed the range within which the value of the Australian pound could fluctuate. The result was that in the sixty years following the establishment of the mint in Sydney the value of the Australian pound was almost always within 2 per cent of sterling, and usually much closer.

THE DEVELOPMENT OF AUSTRALIAN BANKING

The transformation of the banking system

The 1830s saw a large pastoral boom – half a continent was occupied in ten years – and the inflow of large amounts of British capital. The first chartered bank – the Bank of Australasia – obtained its charter in 1835 and a 'flurry of colonial bank formations' followed in the late 1830s (Butlin 1953: 9, 10). The banking system was rapidly transformed into one that was 'for its time, mature and sophisticated':

> In place of a few localized unit banks relying on capital for loanable funds, content with a restricted business and averse to serious competition, there were a number of large banks – all the important colonial banks had greatly expanded – engaged in aggressive competition. A scramble for deposits which had pushed up deposit rates to high levels had established deposit banking as the standard practice. Competition for business as settlement spread had caused abandonment of unit for branch banking. . . . One aspect [of this transformation] was the rapid growth of a systematic foreign exchange market, primarily constituted by the English banks, outside and independent of the Commissariat.
>
> (Butlin 1953: 11)

Branching enabled banks to economize on operating costs (e.g. by holding fewer reserves per branch, and operating an inter-branch reserve market) and enabled them to provide specialist services (such as the provision of foreign exchange) at lower cost. Branch banks were also likely to have a more stable capital value, because branching enabled them to protect themselves against adverse conditions in one locality or region by diversifying their risks.

The legal framework

The chartering of the Australasia in 1835 prompted the UK Treasury to clarify its ideas on colonial banking, and these ideas were set out subsequently in the Colonial Bank Regulations of 1840. These regulations were meant to provide broad guidelines for colonial governors who were faced with petitions and bills for the granting of charters. Although they were sometimes modified in

practice, the main principles were that banknotes should be payable on demand; the personal liability of shareholders should be
limited to twice the value of subscribed capital; following a 'real
bills' view of the business of banking, banks were not allowed to
lend on land, or to deal in real estate or merchandise, except to
settle debts; there should be no notes under £1; banks should
provide regular statistics to the relevant authorities; and there were
certain restrictions on total indebtedness. The revised regulations
of 1846 also stipulated that the note issue should be limited to the
amount of paid-in capital (Butlin 1986: 89–90)

These conditions were not as restrictive as they may appear.
The note and indebtedness restrictions were seldom if ever binding
(e.g. Butlin 1986: 93). The ban on lending against land threatened
to be more restrictive, but the regulation was always accompanied
by the qualification that a bank could subsequently acquire property in settlement of a debt, and it was not too difficult to devise
ways of keeping transactions strictly within the letter of the law
while violating its intent (Butlin 1986: 94). In any case, as Pope
noted:

> Formal codes were not, however, taken very seriously. In the
> vernacular of the times, bankers drove a coach and horses
> through the hampering limitations of the legislation. The
> National Bank, almost from its inception [in 1859] lent on
> land. . . . What the National was doing so too were the others,
> land based advances possibly accounting for as much as two-
> thirds of the banks' total advances business by the 1880s.
> According to Turner '. . . the limitations [of the Acts and char-
> ters] are practically ignored, in some cases by a special adap-
> tation of the form of the entry, but frequently by an entire
> disregard of them'.
>
> (Pope 1987: 21)

The legal framework under which banks operated changed further
in the third quarter of the century. The colonies became masters
of their own banking laws as they became self-governing from
1856. (Western Australia became self-governing in 1890.) Banks
with earlier charters were still nominally subject to the previous
system of regulation, but:

> none of these [regulations] was, in practice, a serious limitation
> on a bank's freedom and the colonies soon began to diverge

from the canon basis provided by the Regulations. In the event, the only requirement that survived in more or less uniform terms was the requirement to make statistical returns.

(Butlin 1986: 92)

One change, from 1863 onwards, was the gradual amendment of colonial banking laws to make shareholders' liability for the note issue unlimited (Butlin 1986: 92–3). Tasmania also started to tax the note issue in 1863 and the other colonies followed suit:

The only purpose behind these levies was the raising of money. . . . The usual rate, two per cent, was about a half, or a little less, of what was generally accepted as the net profit on issue accruing to the banks. In time this was to make the banks dubious of the advantage of continuing note issue and readier to contemplate acceptance of government monopoly of issue.

(Butlin 1986: 94)

This period also saw the Treasury move towards eliminating the chartered banking system and the Treasury supervision that went with it (Butlin 1986: 89). Charters had been sought earlier because they were the only way to obtain the valuable privilege of limited liability, but a British Act of 1862 had allowed banks access to limited liability without the need for a special charter. (The limited liability was qualified, however, in that it did not apply to the note issue.) The Treasury then took the view that this Act provided all that was necessary, and that a special charter implied Treasury supervision and might be seen to imply some degree of government responsibility for a bank that had a charter. The Treasury therefore tended to refuse new charters and resist the renewal of existing ones.

AUSTRALIAN BANKING FROM THE 1850s TO THE 1880s

The prosperity of the golden decade of the 1850s saw a massive expansion of Australian banking:

The eight trading banks operating in Australia when gold was discovered, had grown to fifteen by the end of the fifties. At the end of 1850 there was a total of twenty-four branches (including head offices); at the end of 1860 there were 197.

(Butlin 1986: 8)

Some indication of this expansion can also be gleaned from the figures on notes, deposits and bank advances. Note issues grew from £447,000 in the first quarter of 1851 to £3,192,000 a decade later. Deposits grew from £2,932,000 to £14,583,000 over the same period, and advances grew by a comparable amount.

The next decade saw further growth in the banking system, though at a slower rate, as well as

> a flowering of fringe institutions. Most obvious were the building societies, multiplication of which was in response to the housing demand of the new population. . . . Building societies had first appeared in New South Wales in the forties, and in greater numbers in the fifties. But whereas by 1860 in Victoria the total number of mostly short-lived terminating societies had been less than twenty, in the next ten years nearly fifty were established, and the permanent type of society was more usual. Other colonies had a similar story to tell.
>
> (Butlin 1986: 67)

This period also witnessed the rapid growth of savings banks. These were started to encourage thrift, and to counter the excessive drinking and gambling which threatened to leave convict emancipists, in the famous phrase, 'poor, vicious, unmarried'. At mid-century there had been six small savings banks whose main investment was mortgages, but twenty years later their assets had grown nearly tenfold (Butlin 1986: 69). Savings banks were also encouraged by colonial governments which saw them as a means of securing cheap loans. The British model of using post offices as savings banks

> appeared to offer colonial governments . . . [which suffered] recurrent financial crises, the prospect of a steady flow of funds at moderate rates of interest, not as subject to parliamentary supervision as conventional public borrowing. This was crudely obvious in New South Wales, and not well concealed in Victoria and Queensland.
>
> (Butlin 1986: 69)

The financial system – the 'regular' (i.e. trading) banks, as well as the building societies, the savings and land banks, and other 'fringe' institutions – continued to grow until the early 1890s. All these institutions took in deposits and made advances of one sort or another, and competition for market share was fierce. The 1870s and 1880s witnessed a rapid expansion of branch banking, and institutions looked more and more to Britain to increase their deposits. Interest rates were lower in Britain than in Australia, so deposits in Australian banks were attractive to British investors and a comparatively cheap source of funds for the banks. The ratio of British to domestic deposits in Australia consequently rose from perhaps 10 per cent in the mid-1870s to 40 per cent by the eve of the depression (Pope 1989: 15–16). The relative market shares of the different types of financial institution also changed substantially over this period, with the trading banks losing ground to the fringe institutions. The trading banks' loss of market share was particularly large in the 1880s, and figures provided by Merrett (1989: 65) indicate that the trading banks' share of financial assets fell from around 90 per cent in 1883 to barely 65 per cent only a decade later. A major reason for their loss of market share was the trading banks' reluctance to participate in the land boom of the 1880s with the same enthusiasm as some of the 'fungoid' banks that mushroomed during that period on the strength of it. This conservatism was to stand them in good stead later when the boom ended and the economy went into depression.

The Australian banking system exhibited a number of distinctive features during this period:

1. The banks formed a hierarchy. By 1892 there were seven large banks with 100 branches or more spread across at least two colonies, there were five intermediate banks which tended to be concentrated in a single colony, and which had fifty to ninety-nine branches each, and there were eleven small banks which tended to be concentrated in a single region and to have fewer than fifty branches each (Schedvin 1989: 3; Merrett 1989: 73).

2. Concentration rates were very high – four banks issued about half the deposits throughout this period (Pope 1989: 29) – but no one of these banks ever looked as though it would win the others' market shares. There was therefore no tendency towards natural monopoly. The experience of Australian free banking thus matches free banking experience elsewhere (e.g. in Scotland, Canada or Switzerland) that banking exhibited economies of scale but never showed any sign of natural monopoly.

3. The note-issuing banks accepted each others' notes from a relatively early stage, and mutual acceptance seems to have facilitated the reflux mechanism whereby notes were returned to issuers, but clearing was often carried out on a bilateral basis. A (multilat-

eral) clearing house was established in Melbourne in 1867, but Sydney followed suit only at the comparatively late date of 1895. The explanation appears to be that the small number of banks involved implied that the gain from moving from bilateral to multi-lateral clearing was relatively unimportant.

4. Profit rates appear to have fallen over this period, presumably because of increased competition (Pope 1987: 7–8). Pope also notes elsewhere that bank profits do not appear to have been excessive on an opportunity cost basis, and that 'the banks' profit rate lay in the middle of the league of corporate profit earners' (1989: 10).

5. The interest rate margins – the spread between the banks' overdraft rates and their 12-month deposit rates – fell to a margin of around 4 per cent in the early 1870s and then stayed around that level (Pope 1989: 11). Boehm (1971: 211) notes that fixed deposit rates were very similar between the banks over the later part of this period (1884–94), and this evidence appears to suggest that the banks had effectively unified the Australian financial market. Note too that Australian interest rates were only about half as volatile as interest rates in the United Kingdom or the United States (Pope 1989: 24–5), and the most obvious cause of this greater interest stability would seem to have been the comparative freedom of the Australian banks from disruptive government or central bank interference.

An interesting feature of the Australian free banking system is that the note issue was never particularly important for Australian banks except in their very early years. The bank note/deposit ratio was 26.1 per cent in 1851, and fell subsequently to 7.4 per cent in 1881, 4.5 per cent in 1891 and 3.9 per cent in 1901 (Pender *et al.*, 1989: 8). These figures are well below contemporary note/deposit ratios for the United Kingdom or the United States, and seem to indicate a more mature banking system in which greater use was made of cheques and deposits. It also appears to have been generally accepted that the rapid reflux mechanism provided by the banks' clearing system made note over-issue more or less impossible, and this point was so widely accepted that it was never even controversial in Australia. The Australian attitude to competitive note issue stands in marked contrast to attitudes in countries such as the United Kingdom or the United States in the nineteenth century, where the argument that competitive banks would not over-issue notes was normally a minority view, and, indeed, a view that was considered almost completely discredited by the later part of the century.

Another remarkable feature of Australian free banking was the large number of branches that banks maintained. Branching was a significant form of non-price competition, and banks used branches to gain an edge over their competitors by distinguishing their product by means of its location (Pope 1988). The extent of Australian branching can be gauged from an article in the *Australasian Insurance and Banking Record* of 1880 which stated:

> There is . . . in England and Wales a banking office for every 12,000 persons; in Scotland, one for every 4,000; and in Ireland, one for every 11,000 of the inhabitants. Now in Victoria . . . we have a branch of a bank for every 2,760 colonists.
>
> (Quoted in Pope 1988: 2)

The corresponding figure in the United States was one for every 9,200. It has long been argued that branches were a major drain on profits. An article of 1877 in the *Record* had earlier stated that

> in a township where there is barely enough profitable business for one branch bank or banking agency, there are often two or three, each with its building and its staff of officers to maintain. . . . But when two branch managers become rival candidates for the patronage of three or four petty traders, we cannot help considering that branch business is overdone.
>
> (Quoted in Pope 1988: 3)

These claims were echoed by the chief executive of the Australasia, who at the end of the 1880s could list forty-two branches that earned less than the 5 per cent the bank was paying on its deposits (Pope 1987: 5). Such claims have also been supported by other writers such as Blainey (1958).

These claims should none the less be viewed with some suspicion. The problem is that it is not in a bank's own interest to expand its branch network to the point where it erodes its own long-run profitability, and it is no defence to say that a bank will do it if it thinks its rivals will as well. It is not rational for a firm to choose to incur losses, and this holds true regardless of whether it expects its rivals to inflict losses on themselves or not. The 'evidence' for over-branching also needs to be treated cautiously. The fact that Australia had more branches *per capita* than other countries might simply reflect their under-branching or, perhaps, the fact that Australia had a higher *per capita* real income and consequently a greater demand for financial services. The Australasia's forty-two loss-making branches may also have reflected the state of bank profitability at the time or the state of the economy as well as the bank's own policy. Branches typically made a loss to start with, but were expected to make up for it later on. A bank with a lot of relatively new branches might therefore expect a significant number of them to make temporary losses, but those losses did not necessarily mean that the branches lacked viability in the longer term. Note, lastly, that the remaining 'evidence' in favour of over-branching is merely anecdotal, and an empirical study by David Pope (1988) was unable to find any significant evidence to support it.

A final noteworthy feature of Australian banking during this period is that the banks never managed to establish a viable cartel. They repeatedly tried, but their attempts were always undermined by competitive pressures:

> The banks formed associations and collusive agreements to fix 'terms of business', more explicitly the rates to be charged on deposits, advances, bill discounts and foreign exchange. However, as the manager of the Union Bank (now ANZ) reflected, 'I do not think it has ever been believed that a strict adherence to the spirit and conditions of the [price] agreements has at any time prevailed and there is no Bank that hasn't . . . at some time or another transgressed the strict letter of it' . . . Banks cheated, agreements were ruptured and at times one of the biggest banks, the Bank of NSW (now Westpac), remained outside the agreements.
>
> (Pope 1988: 1, n. 1)

THE DEPRESSION OF THE 1890s AND THE BANK CRASH

The 1880s saw a major land boom, especially in Melbourne, and many financial institutions lent extensively against land-based assets. The boom continued into the late 1880s, when the more experienced bankers began to perceive danger and advise caution. A contemporary observer, Nathaniel Cork, later said in a lecture to the (British) Institute of Bankers,

> Many in this audience can testify that the most experienced

Australian bankers . . . emphatically discouraged this movement [i.e. jumping on the bandwagon]. They saw the danger to the depositors, the mischief to the colonies, and the fearful risk to the bank's [*sic*] concerned.

(Cork 1894: 181)

An example was the London executive secretary of the Bank of Australasia, Prideaux Selby, who warned the Bank's chief Australian executive in February 1888 that 'you Melbourne people are riding for a bad fall' (quoted in Pope 1989: 16). He had earlier warned against speculative lending on real estate, and had cautioned the Australian managers 'to be in no hurry to let out your spare funds – keep strong – profits must be sacrificed in the interests of safety' (quoted in Pope 1989: 18, n. 21.[1] These warnings were reflected in more cautious policies by a number of banks, including the big ones – the Australasia, the Union and the Bank of New South Wales – which tried to reduce their exposure to losses in the event of the property market turning down.

Concerted action followed in October 1888 when the Associated Banks of Victoria[2] raised the twelve-month deposit rate from 4 per cent to 5 per cent and announced that advances on speculative real estate were at an end. The interest rise 'abruptly halted the reckless spirit of land speculation' (Boehm 1971: 254), and the chairman of the Associated Banks was able to report by the end of the year 'that the times were acute, that the land-banks were short of funds, that the Associated Banks were slowly gaining more funds but conserving them, and that speculators were short of money' (quoted in Blainey 1958: 137). House prices started to falter, and the property companies the following year were unable to recover their deposit market share from the 'sounder' institutions despite being willing to pay 1–2 per cent more on their deposits (Boehm 1971: 256). Falling land prices led to the collapse of a number of these institutions in 1889–90. Around the same time the earlier inflows of British capital started to decline, and Australian terms of trade were already very adverse and becoming more so. The economy's momentum led real output to peak in 1891, but output declined very sharply thereafter. Blainey reports that:

Melbourne felt the scarcity of British money early in 1891. The price of property slumped, smiting the weaker building societies and land-banks. The building industry crumpled, unemployment increased and trade became dull. The cheques passing through the Melbourne clearing-house fell from £150,600,000 in the last half of 1890 to £114,300,000 in the second half of 1891.

(Blainey 1958: 141)

The year 1891 saw the first bank failures and the widespread collapse of the fringe institutions that had gambled their future on a continuing land boom. The first outright bank failure – the failure of the Bank of Van Diemen's Land – occurred in August, and the situation on the mainland rapidly deteriorated:

> Late in July the Imperial Banking Company, a Melbourne mortgage bank, collapsed, to be followed in August by two similar and related institutions. In September there was a burst of failures in Sydney of land banks and building societies. In December the centre of disaster was again Melbourne, with building societies and mortgage banks collapsing in quick succession, including the Metropolitan and Standard Banks.[3]

(Butlin 1961: 285)

Many of the building societies tried to meet the demands for withdrawals by relying on overdraft facilities with the Commercial Bank. The Commercial managed to keep them afloat for a while, but it eventually decided that it could no longer withstand the strain on its own position. It therefore called in its overdrafts in late 1891 and many societies were soon forced to close (Blainey 1958: 143).

The runs prompted – indeed, panicked – the New South Wales and Victorian governments in to rushing through emergency legislation at the end of 1891 to give beleagured institutions a chance to defer redemptions by removing the right of a single creditor to enforce liquidation. The result in New South Wales was the Joint Stock Companies Arrangement Act, 1891, which stipulated that claims could be deferred if creditors holding three-quarters of the company's liabilities agreed to it. The reconstruction scheme would then become binding on all creditors, which meant that no single creditor would (normally) have a veto over it. The Victorian legislature, by contrast, passed the Voluntary Liquidation Act, 1891, which stipulated that a company in voluntary liquidation could be wound up only if one-third of creditors demanded it, and those creditors had to have at least a third of the value of the company's liabilities. This Act was widely condemned as making it almost impossible to have a company wound up, and consequently leaving creditors more or less at the mercy of the directors.[4] (Butlin 1961: 286; Boehm 1971: 266, 301). The main effects of the Act were to harm credit in Victoria and hinder the restructuring of the financial system, and it was amended at the end of 1892 to bring it into line with the New South Wales Act.

The bank failures continued in early 1892 when the building society connections of the Federal Bank and the Commercial Bank gave rise to considerable public concern, and the Associated Banks were pressed to come up with joint action to reassure the public. (Much of the pressure came from the Federal and Commercial Banks themselves, which were members.) The result was a public statement in March in which the Associated Banks announced that they had agreed on conditions on which they would help members. (They did not announce, however, that those conditions required borrowers to provide adequate security, and this require-ment effectively nullified the support they were offering.) The announcement managed to allay public fears, none the less, and the Associated Banks remained 'unscathed for the remainder of the year, while many of their former competitors – the mushroom land-banks – were wiped away'. As Blainey continues,

> In Melbourne and Sydney forty-one land and building insti-tutions failed in the space of thirteen months, locking up £18,000,000 of deposits. In new suburbs whole streets of houses were vacant, scores of shops were shut; and in the city entire floors of new skyscrapers were tenantless.
>
> (Blainey 1958: 147)

The crisis flared up again when the Federal Bank failed in January 1893. The Federal was the smallest and weakest of the Associated Banks, and, indeed, had only been (reluctantly) admitted as an Associated Bank four months earlier. The Federal had unfortunate associations with recent building society and land company fail-ures, and these problems were reflected in a very sharp fall in its share price and a steady and substantial loss of deposits in the second half of 1892. The bank's position was hopeless,[5] and the Associated Banks' refusal to help it after a thorough investigation of its finances gave it no option but to close. The public seemed to take the news calmly at first,

> but depositors drew some obvious morals. Here was the first of

the Associated Banks to fail, and apparently no serious attempt had been made to save it; the misunderstood assurance of mutual aid of March 1892 clearly was no protection. From this time onward the withdrawal of deposits from banks believed to be weak rose to almost panic levels.

(Butlin 1961: 296)

The Commercial Bank was extremely hard hit by this loss of confidence. As noted already, the Commercial had tried to cut its losses by curtailing credit to building societies at the end of 1891, but its association with institutions that had gambled heavily in land continued to haunt it and encourage a flow of withdrawals that turned into a flood once the Federal failed. Its share price had also fallen sharply since the end of 1891. The Commercial's position became so precarious that the Victorian Treasurer pressed the Associated Banks to bail it out. The Associated Banks themselves disagreed about what should be done. The stronger banks such as the Union and the Australasia had no incentive to support the weaker ones, since their own reserve position was strong and they continued to enjoy public confidence. The Australasia, the Union and the Bank of New South Wales had all received substantial deposit inflows since late 1892 – so many deposits flowed in, in fact, that the two Melbourne banks were embarrassed by this 'sign of public confidence' (Butlin 1961: 305) – and the 'flight to quality' was to continue until the final bank failures later in May (Blainey 1958: 145, n. 1). For the weaker banks, however, an agreement was tantamount to the provision of a credit facility at interest rates generally below what they would have had to pay on the market. An agreement was thus equivalent to a transfer from the stronger banks to the weaker ones, and the stronger banks were naturally reluctant to consent to it. An initial statement was put out that the Associated Banks would support each other, but considerable political pressure had been applied, and the chief executive of the Australasia had refused to go along with the statement, which was followed soon after by a 'clarification' on 13 March that so qualified it as to render it virtually meaningless. As Butlin puts it:

The fat was really in the fire. Such an assurance . . . [meant] that the banks were not in fact prepared to give each other any guarantees at all . . . the sequence [of events] could not have been better planned to touch off panic. . . . The run on deposits

now became a panic, so far as banks believed to be tottering
were concerned. . . .

(Butlin 1961: 297)

The Commercial was faced with a run it could not meet. It applied
for assistance from the Associated Banks, but was unable, or perhaps unwilling, to satisfy the conditions required for a loan, and
it duly suspended on the weekend of 4–5 April.

When it suspended, the Commercial simultaneously announced
plans for a capital reconstruction under the terms of the recent
Victorian legislation. (There was some suspicion, indeed, that its
application for assistance had simply been a feint to provide a
justification for suspending in order to implement a reconstruction
plan that had already been decided upon.) Reconstruction involved
setting up a new bank with the same name as the old; there
were extensive calls on shareholders for more capital; and deposit
repayments were generally deferred, with existing deposit claims
being transformed into a combination of preference shares and
deposits of varying (and often long) maturities. The 'essence of
the scheme was that the bank asked for time to pay those creditors
who demanded immediate repayment, but it promised to pay them
in full, in interest and principal' (Blainey 1958: 165), and the fact
that depositors raised relatively few objections suggests that they
preferred it to any viable alternative.[6] Small depositors with £100
on current account:

> were given three £10 preference shares and a fixed-deposit
> receipt for £70 when the bank re-opened. If they were short of
> ready money they could borrow from the bank on the security
> of their fixed-deposit receipt, and within three years they were
> able to sell their preference shares at a profit and within seven
> years they received full payment for their deposit receipt. For
> eight weeks, while the bank was shut, they were seriously incon-
> venienced, but thereafter they did not suffer. . . . Reconstruction
> caused [the majority of wealthier depositors] worry but neither
> monetary loss or inconvenience. They had originally deposited
> their money for the long term in order to get a good return
> and a secure investment, and they continued to derive these
> advantages from their preference shares and fixed-deposit
> receipts. The rate of interest was higher than they had received
> before the bank crash and for some years it would be 50%
> higher than the rate offering for a new deposit in any Victorian

bank. They only suffered inconvenience if by chance they had to suddenly marshal their resources in order to meet debts or business losses. Being men of property, however, they could usually raise the money on mortgage.

(Blainey 1958: 165–6)

A curious feature of the reconstruction, and one that was later copied by other suspended banks, was the opening up by the Commercial, four days after it suspended, of trust accounts which enabled deposits and withdrawals to be made without involving any of the funds in the bank's 'old' business. These accounts undermined the banks that remained open, and there 'ensued the spectacle of depositors in banks still open, hastily withdrawing their funds to escape the threat of reconstruction and promptly depositing in a trust account in the Commercial' (Butlin 1961: 300).

The suspension of the Commercial encouraged others to follow suit. As Butlin observed:

Every surviving bank had thrust before it the great advantages of 'reconstruction': permanent accession of capital; immediate elimination of the mounting tide of deposit withdrawals; and miraculous restoration of confidence. Harassed and worried bankers . . . followed the lead of the Commercial.

(Butlin 1961: 300)

Twelve other banks suspended over April and May to gain time to reconstruct. The banks that suspended accounted for 56.2 per cent of all deposits held in March, and 61.3 per cent of all notes issued in April and May, and, while they would have accounted for smaller percentages over the next two months, these figures none the less give an idea of the order of magnitude of the suspensions (Butlin 1961: 302).

The suspensions were also prompted by government intervention. In Victoria the government imposed a five-day banking holiday from 1 May. The heads of the Union and Australasia Banks strongly opposed the holiday and ordered their banks to remain open to do whatever legal business they could. The *Australian Insurance and Banking Record* reported that the bank holiday proclamation was issued 'in the hope that the public mind might calm down, the principle being unconsciously adopted that in order to put out a fire the right thing is to shower petroleum on it'. It failed to have the desired effect. The *Record* continued:

> When Monday morning came, Melbourne was in a state of indescribable confusion and semi-panic and Collins-street presented scenes never before witnessed in the history of the colony. But when it was discovered that the Bank of Australasia and the Union Bank of Australia, ignoring the proclamation, had thrown their doors wide open . . . the excitement gradually abated.
>
> (Quoted in Boehm 1971: 307–8)

The two banks' willingness to remain open shored up public confidence in them, and the withdrawals they faced soon abated. The Bank of New South Wales reopened the next day, and also stood the storm, but the remaining banks that had closed had effectively lost public confidence and were consequently unable to reopen (Butlin 1961: 303–4). The government of New South Wales considered a similar step, but rejected it and decided instead to make banknotes temporary legal tender. The banks in New South Wales were consequently allowed to apply to have their notes made legal tender, but the major banks had no desire to apply – presumably because they felt it would signal to the market that they needed the 'support' of legal tender – and the government ended up making their issues legal tender regardless. The governments of New South Wales and Queensland also made provision for a government note issue to enable the weaker banks to meet demands for redemption.

Whatever effect these measures had, the crisis calmed down by the end of May, and the remaining suspended banks reopened again over the next three months. (The Commercial had already reopened on 6 May.) The bank suspensions hindered trade (e.g. by disrupting the circulation of cheques), and households and businesses experienced difficulties obtaining credit, but the figures for bank advances show no steep decline over this period (Boehm 1971: 214). The real economy reached its nadir in the second quarter of 1893 (Boehm 1971: 26) – annual figures indicate that real GDP in 1893 was 17 per cent lower than it had been in 1891, and the difference between the quarterly peak in 1891 and the trough in 1893 would have been even larger. Prices as measured by the GDP deflator fell by 22 per cent from 1890 to 1894 and thus implied a very sharp increase in *ex post* real interest rates.

The economy started to recover in the third quarter of 1893, but recovery was faltering and uneven, and it took nine years for real GDP to surpass its 1891 peak (Butlin 1962: table 13).

Interpreting the bank collapses

A conventional view soon grew up around the bank 'failures' of the 1890s. This interpretation of events was first put forward by Cork (1894) and Coghlan (1918), but later writers 'have fleshed out the details without altering the substance of the story' (Merrett 1989: 62). As summarized by Merrett:

> Speculation fed by the inflow of British capital in the 1880s sowed the seeds of subsequent collapse. Bankers . . . endangered the solvency of their organizations by lending against overvalued real property and shares. The inevitable end of the land boom left the banks exposed. . . . The large-scale failures among the many financial institutions more intimately connected with the property boom and the discovery of fraud by executives and directors cast a pall of suspicion over the safety of the trading banks. Pressure intensified with the closure of both the Mercantile Bank of Australia and the Federal Bank. . . . The unwillingness or inability of the Associated Banks of Victoria to mount a successful rescue operation to save members in distress further lowered public confidence. Panic sprang from the failure of the Commercial Bank. . . . Frightened depositors attacked banks willy-nilly until the crisis had run its course.
>
> (Merrett 1989: 61–2)

Merrett himself seems to opt for a similar story:

> The rapid growth of the banks' balance sheets and the spread of their branches outran the ability of some to devise adequate reporting and control mechanisms. The maturity mismatch between assets and liabilities worsened, asset quality deteriorated, and risks became increasingly concentrated. This increase in average risk in the system was not offset by any strengthening of liquidity standards or capital adequacy. Rather, the reverse occurred. Liquidity ratios declined, as did capital ratios. . . . The growing loss of confidence in particular banks was crystallized by a combination of factors into a general panic in early 1893.
>
> (Merrett 1989: 63)

One of the key issues here is the banks' liquidity, and Merrett goes on to argue that the 'inescapable conclusion is that the long decline in liquidity standards seriously undermined the banks' ability to cope with the growing problem of higher risks' (1989: 77). However, as George Selgin points out

> the facts tell a different story. Merrett (1989, p. 75) reports that the aggregate reserve ratio . . . fell from .3217 in 1872 to .2188 in 1877; but his figures for later five-year intervals show no further downward trend. . . . Even the lowest figure compares favorably to those from other banking systems, both regulated and free. It is much higher than Scottish bank reserve ratios for the mid-nineteenth century . . . and about the same as ratios for free Canadian banks in the late nineteenth century and for heavily regulated US banks today.
>
> (Selgin 1990: 26–7)

He also notes that:

> Pope's annual data, presented graphically . . . are more plainly inconsistent with [the falling reserve] hypothesis . . . in the seven years preceding the crisis . . . the average ratio of the thirteen suspended banks rose steadily from about .15 to .16. . . . Pope's reserve figures also show a minor difference only – perhaps two percentage points – between the reserve holdings of failed Australian banks and those that weathered the crisis. This also suggests that 'overexpansion' was not the root cause of the banking collapse.
>
> (Selgin 1990: 27)

The other key issue is capital adequacy. The figures given in Butlin *et al.* (1971: table 2) show a fall in the capital ratio from about 20 per cent in 1880 to 12.5 per cent in 1892, but these figures ignore the uncalled liability attached to bank shares, and a number of banks also had a contingent reserve liability which took effect if the bank went into liquidation (Merrett 1989: 82). Merrett himself estimates that this extra capital resource amounted to 'nearly 45 per cent of the conventional measure of shareholders' funds' (p. 81), which suggests that these capital ratios give a considerably understated impression of the 'true' capital adequacy of the banks. It is far from clear, however, that these capital ratios are low enough for anyone to say that the banks had grossly overreached themselves in the way the conventional view maintains. The banks did run into problems later, of course, but those problems do not themselves prove that the banks' capital policies had been reckless. The banks' capital ratio recovered after the crisis, but its subsequent rise was relatively small – it reached a maximum of around 17 per cent in 1897 – and it fell again subsequently to pass through its earlier low point in 1903. (And it is interesting to note that there was apparently no concern then with the banks' capital adequacy.) One might reply that the capital ratio ought to be interpreted in conjunction with other factors (e.g. liquidity, or some index of the quality of banks' assets), but that argument only concedes the point that the capital ratio should not be read on its own and, hence, that further evidence is needed to be able to say convincingly that 12.5 per cent was an irresponsible capital ratio in 1892 but not in 1903.[7] The claim that the banks had allowed their capital ratios to fall to reckless levels is also difficult to defend in the light of Pope's chart (1989: fig. 8) on core capital adequacy. If this hypothesis were correct, we would expect the capital ratios of failed banks to have shown a distinct downward trend in the period before they failed, we would expect a model of bank failures to show that the capital ratio had a negative and statistically significant coefficient, and we would also expect there to be a major (and growing) difference between the capital ratios of failed and non-failed banks. In fact the capital ratio of failed banks appears to rise in the two years prior to failure, and their capital ratio reaches a low point five years before failure and then recovers. Pope's logit model of the probability of failure also shows that capital adequacy has a 'correctly' signed coefficient in only one out of four cases, and even that is significant only at the 10 per cent level (1989: table 1), so there is little evidence that capital adequacy 'matters' in the way this hypothesis predicts it should. And note, finally, that the difference between the capital ratios of banks that were to fail and banks that were not is relatively small – under three percentage points, and usually considerably less – and shows no tendency to grow as the dates of the failures approach (1989: figure 8).[8]

There is no denying that some bankers made serious mistakes in the run-up to the 'crash' of 1893, but the evidence just reviewed does not prove the claim that these mistakes were the major factor behind the severity of the 'crash'. Nor does the evidence support the claim that the bank 'crash' contributed in a major way to the severity of the depression. If this claim were valid, it would be possible to isolate the channel or channels through which the crash was able to push the real economy down. Several possible channels suggest themselves, but none shows any evidence of having transmitted a major shock from the banks to the rest of the economy:

1. There may have been a major disruption to the provision of credit by the banking system along the lines suggested, for example, by Bernanke (1983). The evidence indicates, however, that, while bank advances declined from 1891 onwards, there was no detectable drop in advances that can be associated with the bank failures *per se* (Boehm 1971: 214). This first channel can therefore be ruled out.

2. There may have been a sharp monetary shock. As discussed already, there was a major restructuring of bank liabilities during suspension, and this transformation implied a large fall in liquid deposits – M3 deposits minus deposits converted by reconstruction, or 'Merrett money' – fell by a massive 46 per cent from December 1892 to June 1894 (Schedvin 1989: 5). Schedvin describes this fall as 'exceeding the United States experience of the early 1930s and far greater than any other Australian deflationary shock' (p. 5). Yet there was no major fall in aggregate monetary liabilities at the time of the crash (see Schedvin 1989: figure 1) and depositors who had their claims transformed suffered inconveniences but no major monetary losses (though see also note 6). (In the United States in the early 1930s, by contrast, depositors did suffer major losses and there was a large fall in the broader monetary aggregates.) If the fall in Merrett money was a major deflationary shock, we would also expect the shock to have been followed by a downturn in the economy. Yet the economy was already recovering in the third quarter of 1893, just after the major drop in Merrett money, and the recovery continued into 1894 – a pattern of output behaviour that would appear to be quite inconsistent with any major deflationary shock in 1893.

What, then, are we to make of the events of the 1890s? The evidence seems to support the following interpretation. The depression itself was fundamentally a 'real' phenomenon. Australian terms of trade had been falling for a long time, but the effects of these terms-of-trade changes were masked until around 1890 by large inflows of British capital (see, for example, Boehm 1971: 271). These inflows dried up in the early 1890s. Investment fell, especially in the building industry (Boehm 1971: 271, 279), and falling investment itself pushed the economy down as well as forcing it to make its long overdue response to the earlier terms-of-trade changes, and the combined effect was a very sharp downturn. A number of institutions had lent heavily and, in retrospect, unwisely, against land, but other institutions, the larger banks especially, saw the danger coming and pulled in their horns. The downturn was so severe, however, that financial institutions were bound to be seriously affected, even those that had consciously restricted their lending against land-based assets. The land banks and building societies were naturally affected most, but the banks as a whole survived quite well until 1892. One might note too that there was no indiscriminate run on financial institutions; there was instead a 'flight to quality' in which depositors withdrew funds from institutions perceived as weak to redeposit them in stronger institutions such as the big banks, and it is significant that at no time were the three big banks – the Australasia, the New South Wales and the Union – ever in serious danger. The weaker banks started to fail in early 1892, and a full-scale banking crisis blew up in early 1893, but these 'failures' owed much to government intervention. The Victorian and New South Wales governments first intervened to make it more difficult for creditors to liquidate institutions, and this rewriting of the rules encouraged banks to run for the cover of a legal suspension which would allow them time to reconstruct on relatively favourable terms. As Pope noted, 'One interpretation of the "crash" of April–May 1893 is of a rush by banks to seize the vantage ground offered by reconstruction' (1987: 29). The implication is that the failures were a product of the legal framework rather than a symptom of genuine insolvency, and it is surely significant that all – with one arguable exception – were able to reopen successfully afterwards. Nor can there be much doubt that other interventions intended to allay the crisis actually had the opposite effect. The bungling attempts of the Victorian Treasurer to press the Associated Banks into bailing out the weaker banks backfired at a critical point and needlessly undermined public confidence. The Victorian banking holiday had a similar impact. It amounted to the government bullying the banks to close, and those that obeyed found it difficult to reopen. The threat of a banking holiday in New South Wales would also have encouraged withdrawals there, and it is questionable that the legal tender measures or government note issues there or in Queensland did much to allay the panic. The bottom line, then, is that the bank 'failures' were caused primarily by a combination of 'real' factors and misguided government intervention, and the 'failures' were not what they might appear to be anyway. It is ironic that a crisis in which inept government intervention played such a major part should have become so widely regarded as a failure of 'free banking'.

This 'new view' of the bank crash avoids a number of drawbacks with the traditional interpretation. First, the conventional view emphasizes banks' reckless lending as a major contributory factor to the crash, but the evidence presented to support this view is weak. The fact that reckless lending took place does not establish that it was an important force behind the crash, and the banks' liquidity and capital ratios provide relatively little evidence that it was. Second, the conventional view fails to give sufficient emphasis to the true nature of the bank 'failures', and, more important, it underrates the extent to which those failures were a product of the legal system under which the banks operated. A bank 'failure' was usually no more than a device to reconstruct before opening again, and it seldom if ever meant that an insolvent bank was going permanently out of business. Third, the bank runs were not an indiscriminate attack on the banking system as a whole, and it is misleading to think of there being a 'systemic' crisis. Instead there was a noticeable flight to quality as deposits were transferred from the weaker banks to the stronger ones, so much so, in fact, that the stronger banks sometimes did not know what to do with the deposits they were receiving. Fourth, the standard view misses the significance of the various government interventions discussed in the previous paragraph which unwittingly aggravated the crisis. Last, and of crucial importance, if the conventional view were correct, we would expect the banks' over-expansion to have been reflected in the behaviour of real economic activity. The bank expansion would have promoted real economic activity, and we would expect the real economy to have declined once the banks' expansion had ended, or soon after. But, instead of falling, real output started to rise shortly after the bank 'crash', and there appears to be relatively little correlation between bank lending and real activity. The conventional view predicts that the gun should have been smoking, as it were, yet we can find no evidence that it had even been fired.

EPILOGUE: THE DEVELOPMENT OF CENTRAL BANKING IN AUSTRALIA

The events of the 1890s dealt a heavy blow to the reputation of the banking profession. 'The crash, and subsequent revelations of fraud and chicanery' by some bankers 'tarnished the image of bankers as responsible guardians of society's savings' (Merrett 1989: 61). After the suspended banks had reopened,

> it could appear to those who had suffered acutely that, by financial legerdemain, the banks had saved themselves ... at the expense of thousands of individuals. Suspicion of financial institutions had long been endemic in Australian thinking ... [and it appeared obvious that] in the 'nineties the banks' escape by reconstruction was made at the expense of their customers.
>
> (Butlin 1961: 302)

This view combined with an increasingly interventionist ideological climate to have a profound effect on twentieth-century politics.[9] Political parties identified the banks as a major source of economic instability and social injustice, and this view helped to undermine resistance over succeeding decades to the notion that the state should take control over the banking industry (see, for example, Schedvin 1989: 5–6). The drive to establish state control was especially strong on the political left, and state control of the financial system – and, later on, outright nationalization – became a key part of the Australian Labour Party's political platform. The poor public standing of the banks also undermined their bargaining position relative to the political authorities. The politicians could make demands on the banks in the knowledge that they could easily whip up anti-bank feeling and impose more unpleasant measures on them if they resisted. The banks were consequently cowed into submission, and the new Commonwealth government established in 1901 frequently had its way with them without having to resort to the formality of legislation.

The banking system consolidated itself considerably when the crash was over. The number of branches fell from 1,553 in 1892 to a low of 1,223 in 1896 (Butlin 1986: table 38) and a wave of mergers started in the 1890s which was to reduce the number of banks by half in the first two decades of the twentieth century (Schedvin 1989: 6). Bankers became much more conservative. Their first priority was to rebuild their strength to reassure the public of their soundness, and the need for prudential strength was reinforced by the growing competition of the public-sector savings banks, whose market share grew from 6 per cent in 1890 to over 30 per cent by 1928 (Merrett 1989: 84). The trading banks also tended to take fewer risks and give more emphasis to short-term self-liquidating investments in place of longer, more speculative ones (e.g. Merrett 1989: 83). The 'spirit of banking entrepreneurship was dead, cremated in the fire of 1893' (Schedvin 1989: 8). One other change was that the banks were now able to maintain agreements on deposit rates and foreign exchange rates and margins, and there was no longer any effective competition except for advances. Competitive banking had given way to a banking cartel operating in the government's shadow.

Section 51 of the Commonwealth constitution gave the Commonwealth the power to legislate on currency and banking, and Andrew Fisher's Labour government used it to begin the process of capturing seigniorage revenue (Fane 1988: 5). The first stage in the process was a pair of Acts passed in 1910 to give the Commonwealth a monopoly of the note issue. The Australian Bank Notes Act authorized the Commonwealth Treasurer to issue notes which would be legal tender throughout the federation but would be redeemable in gold at the Commonwealth Treasury. The Act also specified that the government was to observe a minimum gold reserve ratio of 25 per cent for amounts less than £7 million and to observe a 100 per cent reserve ratio on amounts exceeding that value, but the 100 per cent reserve ratio was abolished in an amending Act the following year (Copland 1920: 490). (The bankers strongly resisted this amendment, as they obviously feared – rightly, as it turned out – that it would pave the way for the government to inflate the currency, but they could not prevent it.) The other Act of 1910 was the Bank Notes Tax Act, which imposed an annual tax of 10 per cent on all other note issues and effectively taxed them out of existence. These measures were followed by the establishment in 1911–12 of the Commonwealth Bank as a Commonwealth-owned trading and savings bank. It was to compete with the private banks and promote a national savings bank system, but it was also to assist the government by conducting the government account and managing the national debt.

More government intervention followed after the outbreak of war in 1914. In September 1914 the Associated Banks were 'persuaded' to supply the Commonwealth government with £10 million in gold, and the banks reluctantly consented in case the government passed an order to seize all their gold instead (Fane 1988: 6). Gold was replaced by notes in inter-bank clearings at the same time (Copland 1920: 491, n. 13) and private non-bank holdings of gold were mostly expropriated (Fane 1988: 6). Gresham's law ensured that gold disappeared from circulation and the Australian pound note replaced the gold sovereign as the economy's basic unit of account. The government's augmented gold reserves enabled it to increase the note issue massively – from £9.6 million notes in June 1914 to £32.1 million notes a year later, and it then grew to £55.6 million by June 1919 (Copland 1920: table VI). The resulting increase in the monetary base represented a major contribution to the government's war finances (Fane 1988: 8), but it also fuelled a considerable increase in the broader money supply and a substantial rise in the price level (Copland 1920: table X). Though the nominal price of gold continued to be fixed at its old rate, the automatic discipline which the gold standard would have applied to this monetary expansion was aborted by the prohibition of gold exports effective in June 1915 and the government's refusal to redeem its notes even though they remained convertible *de jure* (Fane 1988: 5–6). This refusal provoked no legal challenge – presumably no one wished to appear 'unpatriotic' by demanding redemption – and the gold standard was effectively suspended.

The First World War also saw the Commonwealth Bank develop further into the role of central bank. It:

> greatly assisted the Government in financing the war, and was especially helpful in floating war loans and in establishing the enormous issue of Australian notes which the financial policy of the Government necessitated.
>
> (Copland 1920: 491)

The development of central banking continued in the 1920s. The note issue was transferred to a Notes Board by the Commonwealth Bank Act of 1920 but then transferred to the Commonwealth Bank itself by an amending Act of 1924. In addition, the amending Act reorganized the bank and gave the Secretary of the Treasury a seat on its board (Fane 1988: 9) as well as granting the bank authority to publish a rediscount rate (Schedvin 1989: 10). Fane also notes, by the way, that this last section was never proclaimed, because the banks adopted it 'freely' and made a formal proclamation unnecessary. This episode illustrates how the trading banks were willing to comply with official wishes without waiting for formal orders to do so.

Australia did not return to the gold standard until 1925, when the ban on exporting gold was lifted and Australia joined Britain in restoring the convertibility of the currency into gold. The exchange rate between the Australian and British currencies was maintained by the

> trading banks, acting as a cartel. To a limited extent one can regard the behaviour of these banks as a manifestation of official monetary policy: any attempt blatantly to flout the government's wishes might have precipitated stringent controls or nationalisation. To a large extent, however, the banks appear to have voluntarily chosen to set the exchange rate at parity, or close to parity, and were able to do so because the government kept the growth of domestic credit within [suitable] limits.
>
> (Fane 1988: 10–11)

Apart from a brief episode in 1920–1, these arrangements managed to keep the exchange rate between the Australian and British pounds reasonably stable until 1929 (Fane 1988: 10–11), but the combination of heavy government borrowing overseas, a fall in the overseas funds of the trading banks and a 60 per cent fall in export prices between 1928 and 1931 made the exchange rate increasingly difficult to defend (Fane 1988: 15). The government's response was the Commonwealth Bank Act of December 1929, which provided for the control of gold exports and the requisitioning of gold, and this Act 'marked Australia's effective departure from the gold standard' (Fane 1988: 16). These measures prompted the trading banks to agree in January 1930 to hand over two-thirds of their gold reserves to the Commonwealth Bank, and they then sold their remaining gold while they still could. The banks feared that full-scale exchange controls would follow, so they tried to placate the authorities and head off more drastic measures by agreeing in August 1930 to the 'mobilization agreement' by which they were to hand over UK£3 million each month to the Commonwealth Bank and restrict their overseas borrowing. The authorities had effectively seized the bulk of the trading banks' foreign exchange reserves and then left the banks to defend an exchange rate that was already under considerable pressure because of Australia's large current account deficit (see Fane 1988: 16–17). The banks responded with a combination of rationing sterling and raising its price, but sterling was at an even greater premium on the unofficial market and the trading banks saw their foreign exchange market share fall significantly. Their attempt at price-fixing broke down when the Bank of New South Wales broke ranks in January 1931, and the banks only recovered their market share once the price of sterling had risen to A£1.3 (Schedvin 1970; Fane 1988: 18). The price of sterling fell to A£1.25 following Britain's abandonment of the gold standard in September 1931. The Commonwealth Bank then maintained the exchange rate at this level, and the price of sterling was to remain unchanged until sterling was devalued in 1967 (Fane 1988: 18–19).

The Commonwealth Bank's role expanded further in the 1930s. Apart from taking responsibility for the exchange rate, it also assumed greater responsibility for setting interest rates and managing the financing of the government deficit. It became a key player in the determination of fiscal as well as monetary policy, and its influence on fiscal policy 'politicized banking to a remarkable degree' and created 'rising popular antagonism against the banking system as a whole' (Schedvin 1989: 10–11). Governments, especially Labour ones, were then able to portray banks:

> as uncompromising and unwilling to share in the general sacrifice, a perception that triggered underlying resentment about the use of oligopoly power and activated memories of . . . the 1890s. Even more important was the widespread belief that the banks in association with the international 'money power' were, somehow, responsible for the depression.
>
> (Schedvin 1989: 11)

The controversy led to a Royal Commission, whose report in 1937 advocated increasing the Commonwealth Bank's central banking powers still further. It recommended that the private trading banks should be required to maintain minimum deposits with the Commonwealth Bank and give it greater access to their London funds. The central bank was also to supervise banks and impose capital standards, and it was to have the power to take over weak banks. The report also recommended that the government should consider controlling the banks' profits, and it proposed the public utility model of the banking system that provided the rationale for later regulation (Schedvin 1989: 11–12). It is interesting to note how the resentment created by the central bank's own policies was channelled against the private banks and used to justify further increases in the central bank's powers, and the option of curtailing the Commonwealth Bank's powers instead does not appear to have been taken seriously.

Yet even this far-reaching regulatory regime was insufficient for the government, which used it to rationalize regulation but actually adopted far more drastic measures than the report itself had recommended. Comprehensive exchange controls were adopted in August 1939, and these were followed in November 1941 by the National Security (Banking) Regulations, introduced under the Commonwealth's defence powers. These gave the central bank the power to direct banks' advances and impose interest rates. They also gave it the power to require banks to lodge funds in Special Accounts at the Commonwealth Bank, and the interest on these funds was manipulated to control the trading banks' profits (Schedvin 1989: 13). Government control was now effectively unlimited and the public interest model was imposed 'lock, stock and barrel' (Schedvin 1989: 14) as a kind of fig leaf in order to rationalize that control. These regulations were constitutionally valid only under the defence powers, but they were enshrined none the less in a modified form in the banking legislation of 1945, and this regulatory regime continued substantially intact until the mid-1980s (Fane 1988: 21).

Two factors were therefore decisive in the twentieth-century transformation of the Australian banking system. The first was the Commonwealth government's craving for revenue:

> The history of Australian monetary policy from Federation to the Second World War can best be understood as a gradual process by which the new government established a monopoly on the ability to issue money and then expanded the revenue by inflationary finance.
>
> (Fane 1988: 1)

The establishment of the currency monopoly, the establishment of the Commonwealth Bank and the use the government made of it, the expansion of the central bank's powers, and the reluctance to set aside 'emergency' powers once emergencies had passed, were all geared to raising revenue for the government. The other decisive factor was ideological. The climate of opinion in Australia was hostile in the extreme to *laissez-faire*, and prevailing mythology blamed the banks for much of the misery of the 1890s and 1930s. The banking system was therefore an easy target for demagogues looking for convenient scapegoats. Governments stirred up anti-bank feeling and made good use of it to promote their own interests while masquerading as defenders of the broader social good. In the process they undermined the banking system further and lent additional credence to the view that the banks were letting the economy down. Government self-interest and the prevailing ideology thus reinforced each other, and there was relatively little to resist them.

Chapter 8

US banking in the 'free banking' period

> The two decades preceding the American Civil War ... witnessed something approaching a natural experiment. During those years the Federal government withdrew from the regulation of banking, a policy that was the final outcome of Andrew Jackson's war with the Second Bank of the United States. A wide range of experiments concerning entry into commercial banking were tried, from 'free' banking to 'socialized' banking. Moreover, other kinds of legislation affecting banking varied from state to state as well. While the regions of the United States differed in terms of economic structure, a common language, a common legal tradition, and, to some extent, a common culture permeated all regions. Thus the period provides excellent conditions for observing the effects of financial legislation on ... financial intermediation.
>
> (Rockoff 1975b: 160)

Banking has always occupied a unique place in American history. When the republic was founded, entry to other industries was normally free, but banking was made an exception. Those who wished to set up a bank had to obtain explicit authorization in the form of a charter, and the constitution assigned the power to grant charters to the state legislatures to use as they saw fit. A typical charter would give the shareholders some limit on their liability and place restrictions on the ratio of notes to capital. Following on from English practice, the law interpreted a 'bank' as an institution that issued notes, and this narrow interpretation implied that, while the issue of notes was quite restricted, the issue of deposits for a long time was not. (The restrictions on notes were important, none the less, in that notes were still a considerable part of the circulating medium.[1]) The controlled entry to the industry implied that charters normally involved a degree of monopoly privilege. They were therefore valuable, and state legislatures were often inclined to sell them for financial favours (e.g. cheap loans) rather than give them away. In addition, charters often restricted the bank to operating only in one county and one office – a restriction that would have propped up the value of charters, and, therefore, what they could be sold for, by restricting competition at the local level. Not surprisingly, perhaps, the state chartering process was often highly politicized and frequently controversial. The chartering of federal banks was even more so, and, although the federal government did grant banking charters, the constitutionality of its power to do so was always controversial.[2] Whether the (Second) Bank of the United States should have its charter extended on its expiry in 1836 became a key issue in national politics, and the 'war' against the bank was the dominant theme in Andrew Jackson's presidency. Jackson eventually succeeded and vetoed the Bill to re-charter the bank. The bank's charter expired and the federal government effectively withdrew from the banking industry to leave the field almost entirely to the individual states.[3]

'FREE BANKING' IN NEW YORK

New York had a particularly controversial charter system. The legislature had long been accustomed to grant charters 'as patronage to political favorites' (Holdsworth 1911: 31), and the corruption surrounding the chartering process was widely regarded as scandalous. As early as 1825 a report to the state senate recommended opening entry to the banking industry by repealing the laws against non-chartered banks. If noteholder safety was a major concern, the report suggested, the law could require non-chartered banks to deposit approved bonds with the state authorities, and these bonds could be used to repay noteholders of any banks that failed. These two features – free entry and a bond deposit condition – were to become the distinguishing characteristics of the 'free banking' laws,[4] and numerous petitions were subsequently presented to the legislature for the passage of a 'free banking' Act. The charter system meanwhile had become 'so shameless and corrupt that it could be endured no longer',[5] and a 'free banking' Act finally became law in April 1838.[6]

The New York law allowed free entry to the industry subject to a number of conditions.[7] Banks had to have at least $100,000 in capital, they were to observe a 12.5 per cent specie reserve requirement against notes, and their notes had to be redeemable on demand. Their notes were also to be secured by deposits of eligible assets with the state comptroller, and these assets included US bonds and the bonds of New York and other 'approved' states, and certain mortgages. Shareholders of 'free banks' were also allowed limited liability, and noteholders had first lien on the assets that were deposited to secure the note issue. The Act was revised in 1840, when the reserve requirement was eliminated and US bonds and the bonds of other states were removed from the list of eligible bonds – a move, incidentally, that Knox (1903: 418) says was expressly intended to promote the demand for New York bonds. A revised state constitution in 1846 also altered the 'free banking' law and made shareholders personally liable for notes up to the amount of their capital subscription ('double liability').

A large number of 'free banks' were set up immediately after the passage of the Act – Hammond (1957: 596) suggests that fifty were set up very soon after, and 120 within two years. The early years of New York 'free banking' coincided with the financial difficulties of the late 1830s and early 1840s, however, and a number of banks failed when a group of southern and western states defaulted on their debts and inflicted large losses on them (see Root 1895: 20).[8] (As an illustration, Rolnick and Weber (1985: 8) note that the seventeen banks that closed in the period from January 1841 to April 1842 held no less then 95 per cent of their asset portfolio in the form of bonds issued by defaulting states.) After this initial growth spurt, the New York banking system settled down to two decades of fairly steady expansion. From 1841 to 1861:

> the banking sector's volume of outstanding circulating notes doubled. . . . Even more dramatically, deposits at New York banks increased by more than six times as New York City became the financial center of the US economy. . . . There was also substantial growth in the total number of banking institutions, which more than doubled between 1838 and 1863, rising from 133 to 301.
>
> (King 1983: 143)

The impression of rapid growth is also borne out by Rockoff's observation that *per capita* bank money in New York grew at an annual rate of 4.41 per cent in the period from 1845 to 1860 (Rockoff 1975b: 162–3). (Rockoff notes, too, that this growth rate compares with a national average of 2.56 per cent over the same period.) The losses that noteholders suffered in the first few 'free banking' years were also substantially reduced in the later period. To quote King again:

> In the twenty year period from October 1842 through September 1862 . . . [the] average annual percentage loss was about 0.04 percent, described by a contemporary observer as being far less than the loss arising from wear, tear, and shaving of specie coins. The largest percentage loss – about one third of one percent – occurs during a period of general financial distress and sharp economic decline.
>
> (King 1983: 148)

The success of 'free banking' in New York was widely acknowledged. Rockoff (1975a: 11) describes New York 'free banking' as 'brilliantly successful', and even Knox (who is often quite hostile to 'free banking') acknowledged that 'New York in 1863 had an excellent banking system; the banks under it were sound and solvent and issued a satisfactory and safe currency' (1903: 392).

'FREE BANKING' LAWS ELSEWHERE

The New York 'free banking' law was widely imitated, and eighteen states had eventually passed versions of it by 1860. The list of eligible assets that could be used to secure the note issue almost always included the bonds of the state that passed the law, and it usually also included US bonds. The bonds of other states were often included as well, and other assets such as mortgages were sometimes allowed. These laws also required that banks should redeem their notes on demand at face value, on pain of dissolution – chartered banks were normally under the same obligation too – and they had a minimum (and sometimes a maximum[9]) capital requirement. As with earlier charters, 'free banking' laws sometimes included restrictions against investment in real property (Rockoff 1975b: 162), restrictions on branch banking, and (usually) restrictions on the maximum ratio of the note issue to bank capital. In addition, banks were often subject to usury laws[10] and a variety of restrictions on the minimum denominations of their notes.[11] And while early laws normally limited shareholders' liability to the amount of their initial investment, there was a tendency to extend their liability as time went on, and most states had 'double' liability for the shareholders of 'free' (and chartered) banks by 1860 (Klebaner 1974: 11). As we saw, already in New York there was also a gradual tendency to strengthen noteholder protection, and most states eventually gave noteholders preferred status as creditors and first lien on the assets deposited with the state authorities. Early restrictions on the note–capital ratio were also supplemented as time went by with explicit reserve requirements, and twelve states had reserve requirements of one sort or another by 1860.[12]

Apart from New York, 'free banking' laws were passed in Michigan (1837), Georgia (1838), Alabama (1849), New Jersey (1850), Illinois, Massachusetts, Ohio and Vermont (1850), Connecticut, Indiana, Tennessee and Wisconsin (1852), Florida and Louisiana (1853), Michigan again (1857), Iowa and Minnesota (1858) and Pennsylvania (1860). The spread of 'free banking' appears to have been due to a variety of factors. One was New York's clear success with it. One suspects, too, that it was not just the success of New York in achieving a stable and growing banking system that accounts for its imitation, but also the realization by state legislatures that it offered a good way to raise revenue by promoting the demand for state debt. The usefulness of 'free banking' in this regard is illustrated by the fact that the New York 'free banking' system held no less than 57 per cent of New York's state debt in 1860 (Rockoff 1975a: table 4). In a number of southern states the adoption of 'free banking' also appears to have been facilitated by the fact that the earlier controversies over banking that had been so pronounced in the 1830s and 1840s had to some extent burned themselves out by the 1850s. As the protagonists fought themselves to a standstill they gradually converged to more liberal policies as a matter of pragmatism rather than principle (see, for example, Schweikart 1987: 47). There was also considerable dissatisfaction in many states with state banking systems which either prohibited banking entirely or else implied a large degree of political control through a state bank or a politicized charter system. Dissatisfaction with the results of prohibition thus led to its replacement with 'free banking' in Iowa and Wisconsin, and dissatisfaction with the politicized process by which bank capital was allocated was a major factor behind the adoption of 'free banking' in Ohio and Tennessee. Rockoff observes that the 'sentiment for free banking was especially strong in the West' (1975a: 50) because of these sorts of difficulties, and the restrictions were felt particularly acutely in areas of new settlement where there was scope for rapid economic development (1975b: 163–4). There appears to have been a general perception that 'free banking' would promote economic and financial development, and that more restrictive systems would hold it back, and these beliefs appear to be borne out by a comparison of different states' experiences, especially in the 1850s.

We turn now to take a closer look at the various experiences of 'free banking'.

'Free banking' in Michigan (1837)

Michigan was the first state actually to pass a 'free banking' law. As in New York, there was considerable dissatisfaction with the existing 'monopoly' in banking, and a 'free banking' law was passed in March 1837, modelled on a Bill that was still before the New York legislature. Hammond (1948: 6) reports that forty banks were set up very quickly after the passage of the new law and all were in liquidation within a year, while Knox (1903: 735) reports that forty-two banks were in liquidation and only six banks – two chartered banks and four 'free banks' – still remained in operation by the end of 1839. The 'free banking' Act itself was suspended in 1838, and it was subsequently repealed in 1839 and declared unconstitutional in 1844. What had happened?

The most important factor behind the failures appears to have been a suspension law that resulted from a special legislative session in June 1837 – three months after the 'free banking' law – that authorized all banks in the state to stop specie payments. This law effectively removed the discipline against over-issue – if banks' notes are convertible, then a bank is limited in its ability to issue notes by the legal requirement that it must redeem them on demand for specie. The suspension law removed that requirement and thereby eliminated any effective check on the note issue. As Rockoff put it:

> a unique situation was set up in which a group of men could issue bank notes with practically no risk to themselves. Few free banks had been started up to this time, but now the rush to start began in earnest, and in fact, nearly all the Michigan

wildcats lived their brief lives during the period of general suspension.

(Rockoff 1975a: 95)

Far from telling us much about 'free banking' as such – recall that 'free banking' laws required that banks should maintain convertibility – the Michigan experience thus appears to tell us more about the dangers of suspension laws.[13] Yet the Michigan experience, ironically, had a profound impact on later generations' perceptions of 'free banking', and 1837 Michigan was remembered when the successes of 'free banking' in New York and other states were all but forgotten. Many of the colourful stories about 'wildcat' banking that were later regarded as the natural outcome of 'free banking' stem from episodes in late 1830s Michigan. With convertibility suspended, banks had no need to keep reserves other than to satisfy the bank commissioners, and the famous episodes of barrels of nails covered with coins and of specie being moved around the country to fool the commissioners were perhaps only to be expected.

Illinois

In 1835 the state of Illinois set up a state bank ostensibly modelled after Indiana's,[14] but the bank defaulted (as, indeed, did the state itself) in 1842, and the state constitution was subsequently amended in 1847 to ban state involvement in banking and to submit all banking legislation to referendum. A 'free banking' Act modelled on New York's was then approved in 1851 (see, for example, Hammond 1948: 5, 13–14) and 141 'free banks' were subsequently formed (Economopoulos 1988: table 1). The Illinois 'free banking' system 'escaped practically unscathed' from the crises of 1854 and 1857 (Rockoff 1975a: 113), and Economopoulos reports that it 'worked reasonably well prior to 1861' (1988: 254). He notes, too, that it outperformed three out of Rolnick and Weber's four states during this period (1988: 113). However, a potential problem was highlighted in a bank commissioners' report of 1857 which revealed that over two-thirds of Illinois banknotes were secured by bonds from the state of Missouri, and the Illinois banking system was therefore vulnerable to a fall in the price of Missouri state debt (Economopoulos 1988: 253). Relatively little was done to reduce the banking system's vulnerability to the prices of Missouri bonds, and a large number of bank failures followed when Missouri bond prices plummeted at the start of the Civil War. The prices of Missouri 6s fell from over 80 per cent of par in mid-1860 to under 40 per cent of par a year later (Rolnick and Weber 1984: figure 2). Only two banks had failed prior to 1861, with losses of only eight cents in the dollar, but eighty-nine failed in 1861 and noteholders took average losses of 33 cents per dollar (Economopoulos 1988: 254). 'Free banking' in Illinois thus had a successful run until it was undermined by the fiscal instability associated with the outbreak of the Civil War.

Wisconsin

Wisconsin's experience of 'free banking' was similar to that of Illinois. The territorial legislature was initially very hostile to banking and did what it could to prevent it,[15] and the prohibition on banking was continued under the constitution of the new state until it was reversed and a 'free banking' law passed in 1852 (Hammond 1948: 8). One hundred and forty 'free banks' were set up, and thirty-seven eventually failed (Rolnick and Weber 1983: table 2). Wisconsin's 'free banking' appears to have been relatively successful throughout the 1850s, and there were no failures until 1860–1 (Rolnick and Weber 1984: 280). The balance sheet data provided by Rolnick and Weber (1985: table 3) indicate that those Wisconsin 'free banks' that failed had secured 48.8 per cent of their note issues with the Missouri 6s that subsequently lost over half their market values in 1860–1 and inflicted such damage on the 'free banks' of Illinois, and an additional third or more of their note issue was secured by the bonds of other southern states that also fell heavily in price. The failed 'free banks' of Wisconsin were thus victim of the same fiscal instability as their Illinois counterparts.

Ohio

Ohio had a charter system until its banking system was overhauled in 1845 and a dual system established in which a state bank was established to operate beside 'independent' ones (Holdsworth 1911: 33). Branches of the state bank were obliged to contribute to a safety fund, and independent banks were subject to a bond deposit provision, but there was no automatic free entry (Rockoff 1975a:

121–2). These reforms helped develop the banking system, but there was still a feeling in 1850 that the state did not have enough banks or enough bank capital (Rockoff 1975a: 56), and this feeling led to the passage of a 'free banking' law in 1851. The 'free banking' law was apparently successful – one Ohio historian noted that 'The banks organized under the general banking laws of 1845 and 1851 were attended by a high degree of success, and furnished a currency well adapted to the business wants of the people' (Huntington 1964: 479) – and, while there were some failures, noteholder losses were trivial at most (Rockoff 1975a: 16).

Indiana

Indiana set up what was nominally a state branch bank but really a system of private chartered banks in 1834 (see Calomiris 1989a: 15).[16] Yet despite the fact that many modern historians have regarded this system as very successful, the legislature none the less chose in 1852 to pass a 'free banking' law modelled on that of New York. Ninety-four banks were established in three years and the circulation increased from $3.5 to $9.5 million (Hammond 1948: 12), and 104 'free banks' were established altogether (Rolnick and Weber 1982: table 2). Some 86 per cent of these banks closed, but only 31 per cent actually closed without paying their creditors at par (i.e. failed). Most of these failures occurred in 1854–5 (Rolnick and Weber 1983: table 5) and can be traced to the large falls in the prices of Indiana state bonds which occurred just before the failures, and which would have inflicted capital losses on the holders of Indiana bonds (see, for example, Rolnick and Weber 1984: figure 1). These failures notwithstanding, Indiana's 'free banking' appears to have been reasonably successful – Rockoff (1975a) quotes the state auditor's assessment in 1856: 'The experiment of free banking in Indiana, disastrous as it has been in some particulars, has demonstrated most conclusively the safety and wisdom of the system' (p. 22) – and there were eighteen 'free banks' still operating on the eve of the Civil War (p. 98).

Minnesota

Minnesota had an unusual experience with 'free banking'. A 'free banking' law was passed in July 1858, and sixteen 'free banks' subsequently opened (Rolnick and Weber 1982: table 2). Seven of these failed in the period from June to September 1859, and two more in the period from June 1860 to June 1861 (Rolnick and Weber 1986: 884). The cluster of failures in 1859 and the low redemption rates of these failed institutions – Rolnick and Weber (1988: 57) report an average redemption rate of only 21.25 cents in the dollar – had led many earlier writers to the conclusion that 'free banking' in Minnesota had been a failure, but Rolnick and Weber (1988) have put forward an interpretation of the Minnesota experience that suggests it was more successful than had hitherto been realized. The Minnesota law was amended in August 1858 to allow US or Minnesota bonds valued at par to be used as eligible assets, and the 'free banking' laws were passed at almost the same time as the 'five million dollar' loan Bill which provided for an issue of Minnesota state debt – the Minnesota 7s – secured *de facto* by the assets of the railroad companies whom the Bill was designed to assist (Rolnick and Weber 1988: 54–7). What was effectively private debt was thus classified as state debt, and was therefore eligible security for a note issue. Five banks were then set up which secured their note issues with Minnesota 7s, and they all failed the next summer when the railroad boom ended and the railroad companies themselves failed (Rolnick and Weber 1988: 57). (The reasons for the failure of the other Minnesota banks are not clear.)

While earlier writers interpreted these banks as 'wildcats', Rolnick and Weber suggest they should be interpreted as mutual funds whose liabilities were priced to reflect the riskiness of their assets. They emphasize that the notes of these mutual fund banks were not sold and did not trade at par (1988: 57) – and the implication is that earlier estimates of noteholder losses are inappropriate, since they were based on the assumption that the notes had been sold at par. Rolnick and Weber suggest these institutions performed a useful intermediation service – enabling ordinary people to invest in the railroads on the one hand, and providing the railroads with finance on the other – and they present compelling evidence that the public were well informed and knew the risks involved (1988: 67). The railroad banks were set up by St Paul brokers who appointed nominal owners out-of-state to protect themselves from extended liability, and the first-lien provisions of the laws were circumvented by the banks making loans to the brokers secured only by promises to repay banknotes (1988: 59). To prevent arbitrage at their expense by the public, the railroad banks refused to redeem at par the notes they sold at a discount, and they announced this policy clearly in advance (1988: 59). Noteholders had no incentive to force the issue, since they could only recover the risky assets securing the notes, minus the costs of litigation, and no one apparently tried to protest their notes. This interpretation is supported by various pieces of evidence – the timing of the railroad bank failures shortly after the failure of the railroads themselves, the discussions of the risks involved in the press, the absence of any outcry when the state government announced that it would repay the notes of failed banks at about 20 cents in the dollar, some circumstantial evidence that railroad banknotes were discounted on the market, and the fact that most other 'free banks' continued well past the summer of 1859 (Rolnick and Weber 1988: 64–70).

OTHER 'FREE BANKING' EXPERIENCE

'Free banking' experience elsewhere can be summarized more briefly. 'Free banking' laws were passed in Alabama, Florida, Georgia, Iowa, Massachusetts, Pennsylvania and Vermont, but few (and, in the case of Iowa, no) 'free banks' were ever formed under them.[17] One reason in most of these cases – Florida is an exception, Iowa a possible exception, and the Pennsylvania law was passed only in 1860 – was that charters were already easy to obtain before the Act was passed (e.g. in the New England states) or else the passage of the Act was accompanied by a more liberal chartering policy (e.g. in Alabama). An additional reason seems to have been that the constraints implied by the bond deposit requirements of the 'free banking' law sometimes bound so tightly that 'free banks' were not set up because they would have been unable to compete effectively. A case in point is Massachusetts, where the 'free banking' law was passed in 1851 but no 'free banks' were set up until 1859, despite the very considerable growth of the Massachusetts banking industry from a capital of just over $4 million in 1850 to nearly $19 million in 1857 (Knox 1903: 364; Rockoff 1975a: 125). The Massachusetts law restricted eligible assets to US, New England and New York bonds, which all sold at a substantial premium in the 1850s and yet were valued at par when used as collateral for a 'free bank' note issue. Banking entrepreneurs presumably preferred to apply for a conventional charter so they could avoid the tax on a 'free bank' implied by the difference between the high market price of eligible bonds and their par valuation by the authorities.[18]

'Free banking' laws appear to have had more impact in other states. In New Jersey a 'free banking' law was passed in 1850 and five 'free banks' had been set up by August 1852 (Rockoff 1975a: 11, 102). The original Act authorized issues of banknotes against US bonds or the bonds of selected states, but Virginia bonds were added to the list in 1852 at about the same time as Virginia was running a large fiscal deficit. Much of this debt was absorbed by the New Jersey 'free banks', and a number of them failed in 1853 when the price of Virginia debt fell and undermined their net value (Rockoff 1975a: 102–4). Dissatisfaction with the restrictiveness of the financial system in Louisiana led to the passage of a 'free banking' law in 1853 (see, for example, Schweikart 1987). Six banks were chartered under the 'free banking' law in the 1850s and there was some growth, albeit slow, in the banking industry that decade, growth being restricted, perhaps, by the 'stiff' reserve requirements that Louisiana banks had to observe (Green 1972: 201; Rockoff 1975b: 163). The Louisiana banking system was strong and solid, and in common with a number of other southern banking systems was able to avoid any suspensions in the crisis of 1857 (Pecquet 1990: 3).[19] On-going controversy in Tennessee about the siting of the branches of the state bank apparently led to the abolition of the state bank and the passage of a 'free banking' law in 1853. The number of banks rose rapidly and the industry boomed (Rockoff 1975a: 11; Schweikart 1987: 276–7). As Schweikart has observed, 'Contrary to the oft-cited assumptions of some modern historians . . . free banking in the southern states of Louisiana and Tennessee . . . produced fairly sound institutions and increased competition' (1987: 170).

We now leave the different states' experience of 'free banking' and turn to some of the broader issues raised by *antebellum* banking.

'WILDCAT BANKING'

'Wildcat banking' is a subject on which traditional histories of *antebellum* banking have placed considerable emphasis. The notion of a 'wildcat' bank is misleadingly easy to grasp – it suggests an institution that is unsound and irresponsibly run, and which probably sets out deliberately to 'rip off' the public – but it defies attempts to pin it down precisely, despite its superficial intuitive appeal. The difficulty is illustrated by Rockoff's definition – and note that earlier writers usually sidestepped the problem by avoiding definitions altogether – of a wildcat as a 'bank that issued notes in much greater volume than it could continuously redeem, and that came into being as a result of a liberal entry provision in a free banking law' (1975a: 5). It is not at all clear what this definition effectively amounts to. Most banks operate on a fractional reserve, so it is questionable whether they 'could' redeem their notes continuously anyway. But one would presumably be reluctant to say that all fractional reserve note-issuing banks in this period were 'wildcats' – to do so would concede that the notion was more or less useless – and yet it is not clear what alternative construction one can put on this clause that drives the appropriate wedge between 'wildcat' banking on the one hand and 'good' fractional reserve banking on the other. And the fact that Rockoff then ties the notion of a 'wildcat' to an institution that operates under a 'free banking' law in no way clarifies the issue – it relates 'free' and 'wildcat' banking in terms of definition, but does not tell us what 'wildcat' banking actually was. The term 'wildcat' is ultimately a colourful label, but it does not capture any well defined theoretical construct. If 'wildcat' banking exists at all, it exists, like beauty, only in the eye of the beholder.

Many observers have none the less looked at *antebellum* banking and thought they saw 'wildcats' – whatever they might be – and have insisted, furthermore, that 'wildcat' banking was an important – indeed, critical – element in the *antebellum* banking experience. These claims seem to boil down to the hypothesis that an important proportion of banks in this period were unsound in some sense, but such a hypothesis would seem to be both implausible a priori and empirically refuted. It is implausible because it fails to explain why people should choose to patronize such institutions in the first place. If the public preferred 'responsible', solid banks, then how could 'wildcat' banks attract any business when they were presumably outcompeted? The wildcat hypothesis also seems to presuppose that the banker can simply issue notes and then disappear with the proceeds. He would lose the bonds deposited with the state authorities, of course, but the hypothesis maintains that it would be worth his while if the value of those bonds fell below the value of the liabilities outstanding (see, for example, Rockoff 1974, 1975a). One difficulty here is that such behaviour is effectively fraud, and various laws already existed to prevent it.

At a more basic level, if noteholders were afraid of being ripped off, then they would have insisted on adequate security from the banker – that he had 'respectable' people on his board of directors whom they believed would be unlikely to sanction 'misbehaviour', that he should acquire a stake in the local community (e.g. by making loans to it), and so on – and the threat of losing this security undermines his incentive to disappear with his proceeds (see also Rolnick and Weber 1984: 272). And, to bring the argument full circle, it is precisely this security that gives the 'good' banker the competitive edge over the 'wildcatter'.

The wildcat hypothesis also appears to be rejected empirically. As Rolnick and Weber (1982: 14) point out, the banknote *Reporters* which warned of counterfeit and dishonoured notes would surely have said something had it been common for bankers to abscond with whatever assets they could take. They also present empirical evidence which indicates that two of the empirical predictions of the wildcat hypothesis – that wildcat banks should stay in business only a short time, and that noteholders should suffer losses when they failed – were satisfied for only 7 per cent of failed banks in their sample of failed banks from Indiana, Minnesota, New York and Wisconsin (1982: table 2). One should note, too, that the conditions which Rolnick and Weber test are only necessary conditions, and (in the absence of a well defined notion of a wildcat bank) cannot be treated as sufficient ones. Their evidence indicates, therefore, that 7 per cent is only an upper bound on the proportion of bank failures that might be explained by wildcat banking. Their claim that 'wildcatting' was relatively unimportant is also supported by the empirical work of Economopoulos on Illinois. He identified three characteristics of a 'wildcat' – that it should last less than a year, that it should be set up when there was a 'wildcat' profit to be made on the note issue, and that it should be set up in an inaccessible location – and finds that only one 'free bank' out of 141 satisfied all three conditions, and only eight even satisfied two (1988: 261).

In short, the notion of wildcat banking is entertaining but ultimately provides little understanding of *antebellum* banking. Hammond (1948: 24) was not far off the mark when he wrote that 'wildcat' banking is falsely taken as 'typical, being in accord with picturesque notions of frontier life [but that] fancy and theory have gone hand in hand to exaggerate the "wildcat" banks' importance'. And Rockoff himself wrote:

To a remarkable extent the reigning view [about wildcats] is derived from purely anecdotal evidence . . . the traditional interpretation has been influenced by a small number of stories about wild-cat banks. It is not surprising that these stories are repeated frequently, for wild-cat banking is a romantic diversion from the usual dull recitation of statistics that makes up the backbone of most banking histories . . . little quantitative evidence has been presented that wild-cat banking was sufficiently frequent and harmful to constitute a basis for condemning free banking, and . . . few theoretical arguments have been advanced to show that wild-cat banking could not have been prevented without abandoning free banking.

(Rockoff 1975a: ii)

THE CAUSES OF THE 'FREE BANK' FAILURES

Much ink has been spilt over the causes of the 'free bank' failures. Earlier writers often ascribed the failures to 'wildcatting' but, as we have just seen, the wildcat hypothesis is unsatisfactory as a theoretical explanation, and recent empirical work indicates that it is consistent with only a small proportion of the failures anyway. We therefore have to look elsewhere, and two other factors suggest themselves. One of them was the occasional tendency of state governments to intervene to suppress the convertability of bank money. As the Michigan experience of 1837 illustrated, this intervention could eliminate the check on banks' issues and open the way to major over-expansion, and, while the Michigan suspension law was perhaps the most notorious example, many other states also adopted suspension laws during the panics of the late 1830s and 1857. Such laws illustrated what Smith (1936) regards as 'probably the worst feature of the American system' – the 'extreme laxity with which the principles of bankruptcy were applied to insolvent banks'.

A second major cause of the failures was the capital losses inflicted on 'free banks' by falls in the values of the state bonds held in their asset portfolios. A bank's liabilities were basically fixed in value, so its net worth depended on it maintaining the value of its assets, and a sufficiently large fall in the value of those assets could wipe out that net worth. There is considerable evidence to link 'free bank' failures with such capital losses, and these losses, in turn, can be linked to the fiscal instability that certain states experienced at particular times. Some evidence is presented by Rolnick and Weber using data for the states of New York, Indiana, Minnesota and Wisconsin over the years 1852–63 (1982: table 3). They use Indiana bonds as a proxy for the assets held by the 'free banks' in these states, and the prices of the bonds fell 25 per cent in the second half of 1854, 20 per cent from March to October 1857, and about 20 per cent from October 1860 to August 1861 (1982: 16). The bonds therefore fell for a combined period of about two years out of the total sample period, and yet fifty-four (or 79 per cent) of the sixty-eight known 'free bank' failures in these states during the sample period occurred during these two years (1982: table 3). Rolnick and Weber present comparable results for the same states over the longer period of 1841–61 (1984: table 9) – which, in effect, means the same sample plus New York over the additional period – and found that seventy-six out of the ninety-six known failures (i.e. 79 per cent again) occurred during periods of falling bond prices (Rolnick and Weber 1984b: 288). Economopoulos provides even stronger evidence from Illinois. He takes the whole population of known 'free bank' failures – ninety-one in all – and finds that all of them occurred in periods of falling bond prices (1988: 262). The severity of these falls in bond prices and the amounts of bonds held by failed 'free banks' also lends support to the view that they contributed in a major way to the failures. Rolnick and Weber's figure 1 (1984) indicates that Indiana 5s fell about 80 per cent in value from January 1841 to April 1842, for example, and we have already noted Rolnick and Weber's observation (1985: 8) that the seventeen New York 'free banks' which closed in the first four months of 1842 held no less than 95 per cent of their asset portfolio in the form of the bonds of states which defaulted on their debts. Similarly, there were large falls in the prices of southern bonds with the onset of the Civil War – for example, Louisiana 6s fell 53 per cent , Missouri 6s 57 per cent, North Carolina 6s 56 per cent, and Virginia 6s 59 per cent – and Rolnick and Weber's 'free banks' that failed in 1860–1 secured about 84 per cent of their note issues with southern bonds that fell severely in price (Rolnick and Weber 1984: 288; 1986: 887). The history of the period also makes it clear that these bond price falls were related to fiscal factors. The falls in the prices of Indiana state bonds in the early 1840s were related to fears that Indiana would default on its debt (Rolnick and Weber 1986: 884), and the falls in the prices of southern bonds in 1860–1 were related to fears of southern repudiation on the outbreak of the Civil War. In the final analysis, the losses that put so many of the 'free banks' out of business were ultimately caused by fiscal and, at an even more basic level, by political factors.

BANKING STABILITY DURING THE *ANTEBELLUM* PERIOD

A number of issues have been raised regarding the stability of American banking during this period. A key concern has been that banking problems may have been contagious – that the difficulties of one bank or one group of banks should adversely affect public confidence in other banks. If noteholders or depositors are imperfectly informed, so the argument goes, then:

> they might have – rightly or wrongly – interpreted the redemptions and failures at some banks as evidence that their own bank was also in trouble. In this way a local shock . . . could have caused . . . a large number of bank failures and closings that were not warranted by the local shock.
>
> (Rolnick and Weber 1985: 5)

Rolnick and Weber looked for contagion using their data set for New York, Indiana, Minnesota and Wisconsin, but they found very little evidence of it. Bank failures tended to be clustered, and they found that clustered failures in one state – in New York in 1841–2, in Indiana in 1854, in Minnesota in 1859, and in Wisconsin in 1860–1 – were associated with shocks that were specific to particular groups of banks (in fact, as already noted, these banks failed because they held large amounts of particular state bonds whose prices fell dramatically). In fact they found that there was little tendency for these banking problems to spread to other states (1985: 5–8; 1986: 885–7). Rolnick and Weber also looked for evidence of intra-state contagion, and found little evidence of that, either (1986: 887, n. 7).[20]

The *antebellum* period also saw some experience with private banking 'clubs' that both helped member banks and 'regulated' them. These clubs can be viewed as attempts to reap economies external to the individual banking firm but internal to the industry, in a context where the most direct means of exploiting such economies – amalgamation – was subject to legal restrictions. Perhaps the most famous example is the Suffolk system in New England. (For more on the Suffolk system see Trivoli 1979; Mullineaux 1987; Selgin and White 1987.) In 1819 the Suffolk Bank of Boston attempted to counter the Boston circulation of out-of-town ('country') banks by buying up country banknotes at their currently discounted prices in Boston and then presenting them to their issuers for redemption. The Suffolk system gradually developed into a multilateral clearing system, membership of which involved certain obligations – members had to maintain permanent deposits at the Suffolk, and to 'behave themselves' – but also gave member banks a public signal of 'good standing' and access to credit facilities provided by the Suffolk. Most banks judged the benefits of membership to be worth the costs, and the Suffolk system gradually spread over much of New England (see, for example, Sumner 1896: 417). It 'created lasting benefits for the New England economy' (Trivoli 1979: 5) and was successful in various specific ways: it initially reduced discounts on the notes of member banks, and ultimately eliminated them, and thus helped to 'unify' the currency provided by different note issuers; it provided a cheap and effective clearing system, and ensured the rapid return of notes and cheques to their issuers; it economized on monitoring costs (instead of the public having to monitor each bank themselves, much of the monitoring was delegated to the Suffolk and the public had merely to monitor the Suffolk and take note of any expulsions from the Suffolk system); and it provided emergency loans to member banks, and was well placed to do so because it was already monitoring them. The weaknesses of the system were that the Suffolk combined the sometimes conflicting roles of club owner, club manager and club member, and the product provided by the Suffolk was more 'hierarchical' than many member banks wanted. The Suffolk's 'dictatorial' attitude provoked frequent complaints, and after earlier attempts had failed a group of banks at last succeeded in 1855 in obtaining a charter for a rival bank – the Bank for Mutual Redemption – which was to take over the Suffolk's note exchange function and offer a less hierarchical product. (It was to impose less irksome conditions on members but provide no overdraft or vetting facilities as the Suffolk did.) The Bank for Mutual Redemption finally opened in 1858 and a brief struggle ensued which ended with the withdrawal of the Suffolk from the note exchange business. The Suffolk system was replaced by that provided by the Bank for Mutual Redemption, and the new system lasted until it was destroyed by the note restrictions of the National Banking System in the 1860s.

A related institution was the clearing house association (see Timberlake 1984: 3–4). Like the Suffolk system, these institutions initially arose to economize on redemption costs. Banks would tend to take in each other's notes in the course of business, and they soon realized that it would be more convenient for bank representatives to meet at a central clearing-house than it would be to arrange a series of bilateral note exchanges. One bank would typically be assigned to administer the clearing process, and member banks would keep balances with it with which they could settle their accounts. Later on, the administration of the clearing process would be transferred to a clearing house institution established for the purpose, and the clearing house would economize on specie by issuing certificates of its own which would be used in the clearing process in place of coins. The most important clearing house association was the one in New York which was founded in 1853, and the role of the New York association soon expanded significantly during the crisis of 1857. While the banks' initial reaction to this crisis was to want to curtail their loans, the New York association arranged a co-ordinated response by which they allowed their reserve ratios to fall while the association began to issue loan certificates which were to be used to supplement specie and which were secured against clearing house assets. These certificates helped to alleviate the specie shortage and enabled lending to continue, and they were retired after the crisis had subsided. The role of the clearing house expanded further when it arranged for the issue of more loan certificates and a co-ordinated bank policy in the run-up to the Civil War (Timberlake 1984: 4–5). Unlike the system provided by the Bank for Mutual Redemption, the clearing house associations survived the National Banking legislation and continued to evolve until the crisis of 1907.

This period also saw the establishment of the first systems of state-sponsored liability insurance. Like the Suffolk–Bank for Mutual Redemption systems and the clearing house associations, these schemes are perhaps best viewed as substitute means by which banks could reap the economies of scale which legal restrictions implied they were not allowed to exploit by the more direct means of amalgamation. In this regard it is significant that southern banks faced relatively few amalgamation restrictions, and were generally comparatively large, reasonably well diversified and noticeably more stable than many of their northern counterparts. Northern banks were frequently hemmed in by amalgamation restrictions (e.g. restrictions on branching), and their greater instability was almost certainly due, in part at least, to their restricted ability to diversify risks. This instability gave rise to political pressure to protect the small banks, and some state governments responded by instituting liability insurance schemes to protect them – New York in 1829, Vermont in 1831, Indiana in 1834, Michigan in 1836, Ohio in 1845 and Iowa in 1858 (see Calomiris 1989a). The schemes fall into one of two main classes, though the particulars vary somewhat in each case. There were the New York 'safety fund' and the Vermont and Michigan systems loosely modelled on it, which Calomiris (1989a: 12) characterizes as 'complete failures' and which ultimately defaulted. Insurance premiums were fixed and there was little or no attempt to relate them to banks' risk-taking, there was little incentive for banks to monitor each other and no effective supervision (i.e. the systems created moral hazard and failed to control it) and the systems tended to attract bad-risk institutions (i.e. had a bad adverse selection problem). The other systems were 'mutual guarantee' schemes modelled after the one introduced by Indiana which Calomiris (1989a: 16) assesses as 'extraordinarily successful'. These schemes were actuarially much sounder, they provided more effective supervision and a stronger incentive for banks to monitor each other, and they were mostly managed by the banks themselves. All three were successful and lasted until the suppression of state note issues by the National Banking System.[21]

DE FACTO FREE BANKING

One feature of *antebellum* banking experience that has often been touched upon but seldom addressed in any depth is the extent to which many states experienced free or competitive banking *de facto* (as opposed to banking under a 'free banking' law). While no state ever had pure *laissez-faire* in banking, many states had banking regimes which imposed relatively lax restrictions and which thererfore gave a reasonable approximation to banking *laissez-faire*. Massachusetts provides a good example. Massachusetts operated a charter system, but charters were apparently granted relatively routinely after 1820 (Sylla 1985: 108) and the banking industry was widely regarded as competitive and successful (e.g. E. White

1990: 27). Pennsylvania also operated a charter system with a reasonably liberal chartering policy, and the Pennsylvania banking industry appears to have been at least moderately competitive and successful.[22] New York had something close to free banking after the passage of its 'free banking' law in 1838, and the success of New York banking has already been noted. Alabama also enjoyed something like free banking after the passage of its 'free banking' law in 1849 – few 'free banks' were actually chartered, but the legislature simultaneously adopted a more liberal chartering policy – and the more liberal regime of the 1850s saw the Alabama financial sector recover from its earlier decline (Schweikart 1987). Banks were theoretically prohibited in Florida from 1845 until the passage of the 'free banking' law in 1853, but unchartered banks apparently operated there with considerable success. Schweikart (1987: 170) could say that these 'private bank agencies had preempted the revised banking law and operated so effectively that no reason to welcome new banks existed', and he went on to note that 'Florida had experienced free banking for a decade before it became official' (1987: 174).[23] The south also provides other interesting examples of approximately free banking. South Carolina had chartered banks which were allowed to branch state-wide, and the South Carolina banks were sound as well as competitive. As Knox observed:

> The laws regulating banks in South Carolina gave satisfaction throughout the country, affording as they did a sound currency and ample accommodation to the people. A Bank of Charleston note was current from Maine to Texas, and even circulated in England and the Continent of Europe.
>
> (Knox 1903: 567–8)

Virginia is another example. Virginia had a system of chartered branch banks and, as in South Carolina, the banking sysem was both stable and competitive. Schweikart (1987: 126) observes that there were no failures, and consequently no noteholder losses, and he concludes that, on the eve of war, Virginia 'could look back upon a decade marked by generally wise legislation and adequate, if not notable, growth in its banking system' (1987: 275).[24] Altogether, at least seventeen states could reasonably be said to have had approximately free banking – there were probably more, but it is hard to assess the competitiveness of the banking regimes in a number of other states (see table 8.2, n.) – and it is surely

highly significant that all appear to have been at least moderately
successful and there are no obvious 'failures'.

GENERAL ASSESSMENT

The most obvious (and overwhelming) feature of US banking
experience over this period is its sheer diversity. Some idea of the
extent of the diversity can be gauged from the appendix which
lists the main features of each state's legislative regime and the
most noticeable aspects of its banking experience (as far as I could
assess them). Legislative regimes ranged from the total prohibition
of banking at one extreme to something close to free banking
towards the other, with state monopoly banks and various forms
of state charter and 'free banking' systems at points in between.
Some of the main features of these experiences are summarized in
tables 8.1–4. Table 8.1 lists the states that adopted 'free banking'
laws and gives an assessment of the outcome in each case. As the
table indicates, eighteen states adopted 'free banking' at some
point, and Michigan did twice. The first three 'free banking' laws
were passed in Michigan, New York and Georgia in 1837–8, the
fourth in Alabama in 1849 and the remainder in the period from
1850 to 1860. In seven cases – Alabama, Florida, Georgia, Iowa,
Massachusetts, Pennsylvania and Vermont – few 'free banks' if
any were ever set up. In two other cases – Connecticut and
Michigan in 1857 – I could find no real indication of the outcome.
Of the remaining ten, 'free banking' was very successful in New
York, and at least moderately successful in Illinois, Indiana, Louisiana, Minnesota (apparently, if one adopts the Rolnick and Weber
1988 mutual-fund interpretation of the railroad banks), Ohio, Tennessee and Wisconsin. A considerable number of failures occurred
in Illinois and Wisconsin around the outbreak of the Civil War,
and in New Jersey in 1853, but these failures can be traced to the
losses banks suffered on their asset portfolio and can be plausibly
attributed to government policy; the apparent disaster of Michigan
in 1837 can be largely attributed to the state-induced suspension
that quickly followed it. As far as one can tell, 'free banking'
therefore, appears to have a reasonably good record, and most of
the problems it encountered can be put down to government policies of one sort or another.[25]

If 'free banking' has a good record, free banking has an even
better one. Table 8.2 lists the states that had reasonably competi-

Table 8.1 States with 'free banking' laws

State	Date of Act	Outcome
Alabama	1849	Few 'free banks'
Connecticut	1852	Unknown
Florida	1853	Few 'free banks'
Georgia	1838	Few 'free banks'
Illinois	1851	Successful until 1861
Indiana	1852	Moderately successful
Iowa	1858	No 'free banks' established
Louisiana	1853	Moderately successful
Massachusetts	1851	Few 'free banks'
Michigan I	1837	Apparent disaster
Michigan II	1857	Unknown
Minnesota	1858	Quite successful
New Jersey	1850	Some failures
New York	1838	Very successful
Ohio	1851	Successful
Pennsylvania	1860	Few 'free banks'
Tennessee	1852	Successful
Vermont	1851	Few 'free banks'
Wisconsin	1852	Successful until 1860

Note: In addition, Kentucky, Missouri and Virginia adopted bond deposit laws but not 'free banking' laws as such (in 1850, 1858 and 1851 respectively).

tive banking regimes (i.e. *de facto* free banking or a reasonable approximation to it), the periods roughly when this occurred, and a brief assessment of the outcome. Seventeen states appear to have had *de facto* free banking over some period. All appear to have been at least reasonably successful, and four (Massachusetts, New York and North and South Carolina) were arguably very successful indeed. Unless one includes the perverse case of Michigan in 1837 – which is of questionable relevance anyway, owing to the suspension law – there were no cases in which *de facto* free banking can be said to have demonstrably 'failed'. One should also bear in mind that the table almost certainly understates the success of free banking in so far as it excludes a number of cases – New Jersey and a number of New England states, among others – where the competitiveness of the banking system could not easily be assessed but where one would be very surprised if the banking system was not both reasonably free and relatively successful. What is also striking is the extent to which the cases of 'free banking' and free banking differ. While there are some experiences that can be considered as both 'free' and free – Alabama (perhaps),

Florida, Georgia and Ohio (in part), and Illinois, Indiana, Minnesota, New York, Tennessee and Wisconsin – many belong to one category but not the other. Connecticut, Michigan, New Jersey and Vermont all had 'free banking' laws, but I have not been able to find any notable evidence that they had free banking. A number of other states (Florida, Louisiana, Maryland, Massachusetts, North and South Carolina, Pennsylvania and Virginia) had something like free banking over periods for which they had no 'free banking' laws – some of these states in fact never passed 'free banking' laws at all – and these experiences include some of the most successful cases of *de facto* free banking (e.g. the cases of Massachusetts and the Carolinas). There is thus a considerable discrepancy between the experience of 'free banking' and of free banking, and we must be careful not to confuse the two.

Table 8.2 States with (reasonably) competitive banking regimes

State	Dates	Outcome
Alabama	1849 on	Financial recovery
Florida	1843 on?	Moderately successful
Georgia	1850s?	Successful
Illinois	1851 on	Successful until 1861
Indiana	1852 on	Moderately successful
Louisiana	1853 on?	Moderately successful
Maryland	Throughout	Successful
Massachusetts	Throughout	Successful
Minnesota	1858 on	Quite successful
New York	1838 on	Very successful
North Carolina	1850s, and maybe earlier	Very successful
Ohio	1845 on	Successful
Pennsylvania	Throughout	Successful
South Carolina	Throughout?	Very successful
Tennessee	1852 on?	Successful
Virginia	Throughout?	Successful
Wisconsin	1852 on	Successful until 1860

Note: The table includes only states where one can reasonably maintain the banking system was competitive. The competitiveness of the banking systems of Connecticut, Delaware, Iowa, Kentucky, Maine, Michigan (1857), New Hampshire, New Jersey, Rhode Island and Vermont is hard to assess. Note that Michigan (1837) is omitted as a misleading case in view of the suspension law that followed.

Tables 8.3–4 examine other aspects of *antebellum* banking. Table 8.3 lists three cases where states had monopoly state banks – Illinois until 1842, Iowa for a brief period in 1858, and Missouri until 1857. Two of these experiments – Illinois and Missouri – clearly failed and the Iowa case is (perhaps not surprisingly) hard to assess. State monopoly banks thus had a poor record, and there are no cases where any (*de facto*) monopoly banks succeeded. Table 8.4 looks at the experience of those states that prohibited banking entirely – banks were banned over various periods in Arkansas, California, Florida, Iowa, Oregon, Texas and Wisconsin. The effects of the bans in California, Oregon and Wisconsin are not clear, but the prohibitions failed to achieve any sensible purpose in any of the four cases where the outcome is easily ascertainable. In Arkansas the prohibition retarded the state's financial develop-ment, in Iowa and Texas it led people to use out-of-state notes, and in Florida it led people to resort to private bankers instead. Sumner (1896: 416) notes that 'states which had no banks . . . generally had a worse currency than those which had banks', and they presumably made other banking services (e.g. loans and

Table 8.3 States with monopoly state banks

State	Period	Outcome
Illinois	Until 1842	Failure
Iowa	1858	?
Missouri	Until 1857	Failure

Note: Table excludes Indiana, which had a state monopoly bank in name only, and Michigan, which chartered a bank that 'imitated almost exactly' the Indiana bank (Sumner 1896: 330) but was already in liquidation by the end of the next year.

Table 8.4 States which prohibited banking

State	Period of prohibition	Outcome
Arkansas	1846 on[a]	Failure
Cailfornia	1849 on	?
Florida	1845–53	Failure[b]
Iowa	Until 1858	Failure
Oregon	1857 on	?
Texas	1845 on	Failure
Wisconsin	Until 1852	?

Notes
a New charters were prohibited in 1846, but the last already existing bank disappeared only in the 1850s.
b The Florida ban failed only in the sense that it failed to achieve its objectives. Private bankers actually provided Florida with a reasonably good banking system (see table 8.2).

savings facilities) more expensive to obtain. Prohibition thus failed along with monopoly banking.

In a nutshell, *antebellum* banking experience strongly suggests that liberal financial regimes were broadly successful and that state intervention by and large failed. There was also a tendency to imitate successful systems, and New York-style 'free banking' was widely copied, especially in the 1850s. By the eve of the Civil War more than half the states in the union had adopted 'free banking' in one form or another, and a number of others had liberal financial regimes even though they never passed 'free banking' laws. There was a significant improvement in banking in most states over this period – illustrated, for instance, by the growth in *per capita* bank money from $7.64 in 1840 to $14.21 in 1860 (Rockoff 1975b: 165) – and, as Smith wrote:

> The improvement that took place in American banking in the twenty years preceding the Civil War was especially noticeable in the eastern region. The banking system was by no means perfect at this period, but except for the international crisis of 1857 . . . the situation was far steadier than before. It is very probable that this improvement was not attributable to any considerable extent to State regulations relating to bond deposit guarantees for notes. In fact, the State authorities seem to have become, after a time, rather lax in the enforcement of the law . . . Much the greater weight is to be attached to the more rigid enforcement of specie payments between banks by frequent exchange of notes due in great part to the spread of the Suffolk system and to the institution of the New York clearing-house.
>
> (Smith 1936: 45–6)

The Civil War then broke out and the federal government intervened once again to pass the National Banking legislation of 1863–5 by which the bond deposit provision was adopted at the federal level and the state note issues were effectively taxed out of existence. The measures were prompted by fiscal considerations and not by any well established dissatisfaction with the existing state systems. They were also initially intended as emergency (and, therefore, transitory) measures to help finance the federal government's wartime expenditure, but the wartime regime was left substantially intact after the war ended and it survived with relatively little alteration until the Federal Reserve Act was passed in 1913. And so it happened that:

The fiscal exigencies of the Civil War checked the process of evolution and fastened upon the country the incubus of a cumbersome and unscientific banking system. But for this check it is highly probable that some such organization as the free banking system of New York . . . would have spread throughout the entire country . . .

(Holdsworth 1911: 23)

Appendix US banking experience, 1837–63

State	Legislative framework	Comments/results
Alabama	Chartered banks and state bank until 1849. 'Free banking' law passed 1849[26] and charters now granted liberally.	Chartering policy restrictive. State bank a failure. Eight chartered and two free banks set up. Financial system recovered by 1860.
Arkansas	Real estate bank and state bank chartered 1836. Constitutional amendment 1846 to prohibit further charters.	Both corrupt and eventually failures. Banking system backward. Some private banking.
California	Banking banned 1849.	—
Connecticut	Chartered banks. 'Free banking' law passed 1852.	—
Delaware	Chartered banks.	—
Florida	Charter system until 1845, when banking theoretically prohibited. 'Free banking' law passed 1853.	Evidence that private banks provided *de facto* free banking from 1843 onwards. Only two 'free banks' set up.
Georgia	Charter system with state bank ('Central Bank'). 'Free banking' law passed 1838.	Central Bank defaulted 1840. Only two 'free banks' set up. Chartering policy (apparently) liberal in 1850s. Considerable banking progress.
Illinois	Monopoly state bank until 1842. Constitution amended 1847 to ban state involvement in banking and to submit banking legislation to referendum. 'Free banking' law passed 1851.	State bank defaulted 1842. 'Free banking' very successful until large-scale failures in 1861.
Indiana	'Free banking' law was passed 1852.[27] Safety fund system throughout period.	State bank apparently successful. Substantial number of 'free banks' rapidly set up, but most went out of business by 1854. 'Free banking' apparently quite successful. Safety fund successful.
Iowa	Banking banned by 1846 constitution. Ban lifted in 1858 when a state (branch) bank was set up.[28] 'Free banking' law passed 1858. Safety fund set up 1858.	Widespread circulation of out-of-state notes during banking ban. No 'free banks' established. Safety fund apparently successful.

Kentucky	General banking law to allow bond-secured (but not 'free') banks 1850.	—
Louisiana	Charter system with branches. Banking reformed in 1842. Constitution amended 1845 to prohibit chartering and re-chartering. Constitution amended again in 1852 to allow chartering. 'Free banking' law passed 1853.	Large fall in bank capital after 1840, and banking capital starts to recover only in 1850s. Banking system in 1850s solid but grew slowly.
Maine	Charter system.	
Maryland	Charter system. General banking law passed in 1853, but this merely consolidated existing laws and the 'free banking' principle was omitted.	Charters granted liberally, so de facto free banking.
Massachusetts	Charter system. 'Free banking' law passed 1851.	Charters granted liberally, so de facto free banking. Large increase in bank capital and number of banks in 1850s. First 'free bank' formed 1859; no more than seven 'free banks' formed altogether.
Michigan	Charter system. 'Free banking' law passed March 1837, but suspended in 1838, repealed in April 1839 and declared unconstitutional in 1844. Safety fund established 1836. Bank suspension law June 1837. Constitution amended 1850 to require that banking law be submitted to referendum. New 'free banking' law 1857.	Forty banks set up in less than a year after passage of 'free banking' law, but most rapidly went into liquidation. Safety fund a failure.
Minnesota	Charter system until passage of 'free banking' law in 1858.	Sixteen 'free banks' set up. Nine 'free banks' – mostly railroad banks – failed following the failure of the railroad companies in 1859.
Mississippi	Charter system.	Flurry of charters in 1836–7. Banking system declined in 1840s and 1850s. By 1860 there were no unchartered banks left and the circulating medium consisted mostly of Tennessee banknotes.

Appendix US banking experience, 1837–63 (contd.)

State	Legislative framework	Comments/results
Missouri	State monopoly bank set up in 1837. Constitution amended 1857 to allow more banks to be chartered. Law passed to allow bank-secured banks (but not 'free banks') in 1857.	Only three banks set up by 1860. Some amount of private banking. Missouri financially underdeveloped.
New Hampshire	Charter system.	—
New Jersey	Charter system. 'Free banking' law passed in 1850. Virginia state bonds added to list of eligible bonds in 1852.	Absorption of Virginia debt by 'free banks' and 'free bank' failures in 1853.
New York	Charter system with safety fund. 'Free banking' law passed in 1838.	Flurry of 'free banks' set up shortly after passage of 'free banking' law. *De facto* failure of safety fund in 1842. 'Free banking' very successful.
North Carolina	Charter system with state bank and branching. Most activities of state bank wound down by 1860.	Banking system competitive and charters readily granted, especially in 1850s. *De facto* free banking.
Ohio	Charter system. Reform Act of 1845 set up state bank and specified that its branches must contribute to a safety fund, and allowed 'independent' banks subject to a bond deposit requirement. 'Free banking' law passed in March 1851. Constitutional amendment effective June 1851 required that banking legislation pass a referendum.	Considerable increase in bank numbers following 1845 law. Thirteen 'free banks' established in 1851–2. Laws of 1845 and 1851 apparently successful. Safety fund successful.
Oregon	Banking banned 1857.	—
Pennsylvania	Charter system. General banking law 1850. 'Free banking' law March 1860. Banks suspended November 1860.	Charters granted liberally, but bank profits quite high. Nine 'free banks' formed.
Rhode Island	Charter system.	—

South Carolina	Charter system with branching and state bank.
Tennessee	Charter system with branching. New state bank 1838.[29] 'Free banking' law 1852 and elimination of Bank of Tennessee 1857.	Banking system highly stable and successful. Apparent decline in bank numbers from 1839 to 1853. Rapid growth in banks from 1853, and considerable financial development in state banking system. Withstood crisis of 1857 easily. 'Free banking' apparently successful.[30]
Texas	Banking banned by state constitution 1845.	Private banking and circulation of out-of-state notes.[31]
Vermont	Charter system. Safety fund established 1831. 'Free banking' law passed 1851.	Safety fund a failure. Four 'free banks' set up.
Virginia	Charter system with state bank. Charter banks allowed to branch. General banking law 1837. Law passed to allow bond deposit banking 1851.[32]	Banking system strong and stable – no failures in 1837 and 1857. Thirteen banks set up under bond deposit law but had difficulty competing against the branch-banking advantages of the chartered banks. Considerable banking development throughout period.
Wisconsin	Banks banned by territory of Wisconsin.[33] New state constitution of 1848 banned any legislative authorization of banks unless ratified by referendum. 'Free banking' law passed 1852.[34]	140 'free banks' set up. Large number of failures when southern bond prices fell with onset of Civil War.

Source: Calomiris (1989a), Hammond (1948), Rockoff (1974, 1975a, b), Rolnick and Weber (1982, 1983, 1984, 1985, 1986, 1988), Knox (1903), Schweikart (1987), Sumner (1896).

Chapter 9

Money and banking: the American experience

> Even granted the market failures that we and many other economists had attributed to a strictly *laissez-faire* policy in money and banking, the course of events encouraged the view that turning to government as an alternative was a cure that was worse than the disease . . . Government failure might be worse than market failure.
>
> (Milton Friedman and Anna Schwartz 1986: 39)

The time has come for a radical revision of US monetary history. It used to be generally accepted that the banking system required extensive government involvement to protect it from its own 'inherent' instability. For a long time even economists who were otherwise sympathetic to *laissez-faire* accepted this view and believed that the banking industry was an exception to the general rule that markets work better when left alone. Those who held this view felt that it was supported by the experience of US monetary history. Everyone 'knew' that free banking before the Civil War had caused chaos, for example, and that the institution of the Federal Deposit Insurance Corporation in the 1930s had stabilized the banking system in the post-war period. But apart from leading them to feel that it was borne out by US history, the view that banking was inherently unstable also indicated what researchers could expect when they studied history, and thereby coloured their main findings. Their findings, in turn, lent support to the theoretical view that unregulated banking is unstable.

Both the theory and the historical interpretation are now under attack. Since Hayek rediscovered free banking in 1976 a great deal of work has been done which suggests that *laissez-faire* in banking ought to be highly stable and that traditional fears of its 'inherent' instability are, at the very least, much exaggerated. If free banking is stable, however, then historical experience of banking instability must be due to the absence of free banking, and one has a clear prediction to test against the historical evidence: banking instability must be due to government involvement. The prediction that free banking is stable runs against the 'stylized facts' that people have traditionally drawn from US monetary history, but the traditional interpretation of US monetary experience has itself come under attack. Work by Rockoff (1974), Rolnick and Weber (1984, 1985, 1986) and others suggests that 'free banking' in the *antebellum* period was actually quite successful, while Sylla (1972) indicated that many of the problems of the National Banking System period can be traced to legislate restrictions, and Timberlake (1984) showed how clearing house associations evolved to help private banks cope with those restrictions. Work by Benston (1986), Benston *et al.* (1986) and Kaufman (1988) and others also indicated that US banking was much more stable in the days before the FDIC than had been generally realized, and work by Kane (1985) and Calomiris (1989a, b, 1990) suggests that deposit insurance actually *de*stabilized the banking system. Recent research by Gorton (1986) and Miron (1988a, b) also suggests that the founding of the Fed destabilized the US banking system. The revision of US monetary history is only beginning, but the evidence accumulated so far appears to be consistent with what free banking theory leads us to expect, and there are no obvious discrepancies to explain. The boot is now on the other foot, as it were, and the revised historical record presents proponents of the traditional view with serious problems. If banking is inherently unstable, then why was 'free banking' not a complete disaster, and why was US banking apparently more stable before the FDIC and the Federal Reserve than it was after? And, looking further afield, if free banking is unstable, why did relatively unregulated banking appear to work so well in the past in countries like Scotland, Canada, China and Sweden, and others besides?

THE EARLY HISTORY OF MONEY AND BANKING IN THE UNITED STATES

The constitution and the money power

The constitution granted Congress very limited monetary powers: it allowed Congress only to authorize the coining of gold or silver money and to 'regulate' (i.e. specify) the dollar value of those coins. It also gave Congress authority to borrow on the credit of the United States, but this power was intended as a fiscal power rather than a monetary one (Timberlake 1990: 305). Since the constitutional settlement was based on the principle that the powers of the federal government were delegated powers, it was also reasonable to conclude that a 'strict' interpretation of Congressional powers was called for – that powers not expressly granted to Congress were prohibited to it – and that all other powers (i.e. sovereignty) remained with the people or the states[1] (see, for example, Holzer 1981: 5–7, 199–200). The very limited powers – monetary and otherwise – of the Congress were thus further hemmed in by the 'strict' interpretation of the constitution and the pre-existing rights of the people and the states.

But it was not long before Congress began to break free of these constraints and expand its powers. In 1790 controversy arose over whether Congress had authority to charter a national bank. Supporters of the proposal pointed to its fiscal and other advantages, and they managed to get the Bill passed despite the objections of opponents, who argued that the measure was unconstitutional. The opponents were sufficiently strong, none the less, to be able to block the renewal of the bank's charter when it fell due in 1811, and the charter subsequently lapsed. In 1816, however, another bank was set up – the Second Bank of the United States – and the issue of its constitutionality went to the Supreme Court in 1819. In a famous ruling Chief Justice Marshall defended the bank's constitutionality as a fiscal arm of the government by invoking the 'necessary and proper' clause (article 1, section 10) of the constitution (and supporters of the bank proceeded to use the bank's fiscal legitimacy to defend its various other actions).[2] Significantly, Marshall also defended the constitutionality of the bank by going outside the powers explicitly granted to Congress and invoking the nebulous concept of federal 'sovereignty' that was supposed to have been repudiated when the United States was founded. In so doing he legitimized the 'loose' construction of the constitution over the 'strict' one and what decided the constitutionality of federal actions was no longer whether the constitution specifically *allowed* the federal government to do what it proposed to do but whether the constitution *explicitly prohibited* it. This ruling provided the basis on which Congress for its own (i.e. political) reasons could later lay claim to a wide range of monetary powers which were not provided for in the constitution.[3] It was however to be a long time before Congress laid claim to these powers, and in the meantime the opponents of the Second Bank were able to prevent the renewal of its charter, which lapsed in 1836. For the next generation the federal government made no further attempts to charter banks or regulate banking, and banking legislation was left entirely to the states.

In the meantime, many banks were set up under the separate legal systems of different states. The procedures for setting up state banks were inherited from colonial times. To establish a bank required a charter from the legislature, and state legislatures had the right to grant charters as and when they chose. A typical charter would give the shareholders some form of limited liability (usually fixed at twice the value of subscribed capital) and placed restrictions on the ratio of notes to capital. The lack of freedom of entry in the banking industry meant that charters involved a degree of monopoly privilege – and were therefore valuable – and state legislatures normally sold them for financial favours (e.g. cheap loans). More significantly, charters usually restricted banks to operating only in the county (and sometimes the state) where they were chartered, and often restricted banks to one office only. This restriction would have helped prop up the value of charters – and, hence, what the legislature could get for them – by restricting competition at the local level. It also had two other effects that were to be highly significant.

The first effect was to weaken – and therefore destabilize – the banking system by restricting banks' freedom to branch. Restricting branching increased banks' vulnerability by limiting the scope for diversifying their risks. It also made it more difficult for a bank office to borrow, and it hindered the development of note and deposit clearing systems which would have helped discipline over-issue and maintain the value of bank money at par. Branching restrictions created a system of 'unit banks' that was to be a major – if not *the* major – source of weakness in the American banking system throughout its later history.

The second consequence was to create a powerful group with a vested interest in maintaining restrictions against bank competition. Since branch banking was a threat to the local monopoly privileges enjoyed by unit bankers, the latter had a strong incentive to lobby against branching concessions, and they were to defeat such concessions time and time again. A very damaging combination thus emerged from the early bank charters: a system of weak banks was established, together with a powerful pressure group that had an incentive to lobby against attempts to deal with the cause of their weakness. Nor did the harm stop there. The same group also had an interest in promoting measures to protect the unit banks, and the unit banking lobby could (and did) use the very weakness of unit banks to support the case for their protection. Particularly important among these protection measures in later years was the establishment of state-sponsored liability insurance schemes to discourage bank runs, but (as related below) these schemes usually had the opposite effect to that intended and weakened the banks even more.

US 'free banking'

The federal withdrawal from banking legislation in 1836 left the field entirely to the states, and a number of them then proceeded to enact 'free banking' laws. The first states were Michigan in 1837 and New York and Georgia in 1838, and over the following years many others followed suit. These laws varied from state to state, but a typical 'free banking' law had the following features:

1. Anyone could set up a 'free bank' who could raise the capital to do so, provided a minimum capital requirement was met.

2. Free bank' note issues were to be secured with holdings of specified bonds which were to be deposited with the state authorities. The usual bonds specified were state (and sometimes federal) ones.

3. The notes of 'free banks' were to be redeemable on demand, on penalty of liquidation, and note holders had first claim on the assets of a failed bank.

4. The shareholders were normally allowed some form of limited liability, usually fixed at twice the value of the capital subscribed.

The key provisions are the first two. The first established free entry into the banking system, subject only to a minimum size constraint, while the second provision promoted the demand for state debt, and hence raised the price that states could get for it. While the earlier charter system had raised revenue for the states by selling charters, the new 'free banking' system raised revenue by creating a captive market for state debt. (The charter system continued in operation, by the way, and chartered banks operated side by side with 'free' ones.)

The 'free banking' experience of different states varied considerably, but it was reasonably successful on the whole. Recent work indicates that 'free banking' was much more successful than traditional accounts indicated (see, for example, Rockoff 1974; Rolnick and Weber 1984, 1985, 1986). Noteholder losses were comparatively low, for example, and there is no evidence of bank run contagion under 'free banking' (see, for example, Rolnick and Weber 1986: 885–6). The comparative success of 'free banking' is also indicated by the way it was imitated. There was an initial spurt of 'free banking' laws in the late 1830s, and the successes of 'free banking' encouraged a number of states to switch to it in the 1850s, and more than half the states in the Union had adopted 'free banking' by the eve of the Civil War.

The question arises, none the less, why some experiences with 'free banking' were more successful than others. Part of the reason seems to lie with differences in states' legal frameworks, and 'free banking' appears to have been more successful in states where branch banking laws were more liberal.[4] Several 'free banking' experiments also failed because states undermined checks against over-issue by intervening to order the banks to suspend convertibility (e.g. Michigan, in its first 'free banking' experiment). But the main reason for the varying success of 'free banking' appears to have been the combination of the bond deposit provision and the soundness of different states' finances. The failures of 'free banks' tended to be clustered, and the evidence indicates that the clusters occurred when there were large falls in the prices of state bonds (see the Rolnick-Weber work cited earlier). These price falls destroyed much of the banks' net worth, since it undermined the value of their assets while their liabilities remained relatively stable in value. The banks would then fail so that they could pass on some of the losses to their creditors. The large falls in the price of state debt, in turn, were caused by those states' precarious fiscal positions. In apparently every case the large falls in bond prices that occurred were associated with speculation that the states in question would default on their debt. Indiana defaulted in 1841, for instance, and it was not alone. Where states' finances were sound, on the other hand, there were no major problems with 'free banking'. The evidence therefore indicates that the main cause of the falling bond prices that put most of the failed 'free banks' out of business was fiscal. *It was the combination of the bond deposit provision and the fiscal instability of some states that was the root cause of most of the 'free bank' failures*. The failures were a case of government rather than market failure.

The National Banking System

The onset of the Civil War brought the federal government back into the business of regulating banking. Within a year, large involuntary loans to the government had weakened the banks and obliged them to suspend convertibility, and the Treasury soon began to issue notes itself. (The United States was to remain on the inconvertible greenback standard until 1879.) Still searching for more funds to fight the war, the federal government decided to raise more revenue from the banks by adopting the bond deposit provision at the federal level. A new system of federal regulation – the National Banking System – was thus established as a war measures act. Apart from raising revenue, it also had the subsidiary objective of 'unifying' the currency by eliminating the variety of state banknotes, which often fluctuated in value against each other.[5] Under the new system, any group of five or more could form a note-issuing bank provided they met (quite stringent) capital standards, and provided their note issues were secured by deposits of US bonds. (The collateral requirement raised the demand for US bonds, of course, and ensured that the Treasury would get a higher price for them.) The Treasury would have first lien on the assets of a failed bank, but the Treasury also guaranteed the notes of national banks, and shareholders were to have double liability. The national banks were also to observe a 25 per cent minimum reserve ratio between their holdings of eligible reserves and their liabilities (which also increased the demand for federal debt, since federal debt counted as eligible reserves). The national banks were also to pay taxes of 1 per cent on their notes and 0.5 per cent on their deposits, and arrangements were made for state banks to switch over to national charters. As the state banks did not switch over fast enough, another Act in 1865 killed off the state banks' note issues by imposing a prohibitive tax of 10 per cent on them.

The National Banking System had a variety of serious defects:

1. It discouraged branch banking by requiring that a bank should carry on business only at the place named on its certificate of association. The unit banking lobby had won again, and the

US banking system continued to be plagued by the problems of small unit size.

2. The restrictions it imposed on the note issue seriously stunted the development of American banking, because the US economy was still at the stage where the note issue was an important source of profit for a bank, and without it many banks could not make enough profit to survive. To make matters worse, until 1875 there was also a limit on the total amount of national banknotes that could be issued, and the geographical distribution of permits severely penalized the south and west. Restrictions on the note issue operated as entry barriers, and they retarded not only the development of non-note-issuing national banks, but also the development of state banks that could no longer afford a note issue (Sylla 1972).

3. Since the bond deposit provision tied the note issue to the price (and availability) of federal government debt, the note issue was forced to contract as the federal government ran surpluses from the end of the Civil War until 1893, and because it used the surpluses to buy back its debt and bid up its price. United States debt fell from more than $2,300 million in 1866 to less then $600 million in 1892–3 (Sylla 1972: 254–5). Ironically, this constraint became increasingly effective just as the ceiling on the total note issue was being lifted, so the abolition of the ceiling had little real effect. The prices of US bonds had risen by then well above par, and as national banks could issue notes only up to 90 per cent of the par value of their bond holdings it was no longer profitable to issue notes anyway (Sylla 1972: 244).

4. Finally, the restrictions on the note issue often prevented the supply of notes responding to an increase in the demand for them (i.e. the note issue was highly inelastic). This problem was particularly acute in the spring and autumn, when seasonal factors led to increased demand for notes which legal restrictions made it difficult for the banks to satisfy. Even if the banking system could produce the notes to satisfy normal seasonal requirements, there was always the danger that something could spark off a speculative run for notes which the banking system could not meet – there was always a possibility that people might decide to run and demand notes just in case a shortage developed – and a major banking crisis might result:

A series of acute financial crises occurred in fairly quick suc-

cession – 1873, 1884, 1890, 1893, 1907. Crises occurred on most
of these occasions in London as well, but they were nothing
like as stringent. Money rates in New York rose to fantastic
heights as compared with London, and . . . there took place in
three out of the five cases (1873, 1893, and 1907) widespread
suspensions of cash payments, either partial or complete, with
currency at a premium over claims on bank accounts

(Smith 1936: 133)

In time, however, the banks gradually evolved means of handling
these problems. A clearing house system arose which provided
banks with a form of mutual guarantee which helped in part to
overcome the vulnerability which derived from restrictions against
branching (i.e. it gave banks a means of exploiting some of the
scalar economies they could have obtained by branching, had it
been allowed). Clearing houses functioned as private lenders of
last resort, though they had no legal privileges and were subject
to all the disciplines of the market. If a bank wanted a loan in a
crisis, it would apply to the clearing house and submit to examination. If its application was accepted, the clearing house made
its resources (i.e. the resources of member banks) available to it,
and sent a clear signal to the market that the bank was sound. If
the application was rejected, on the other hand, the clearing house
sent out an equally clear signal that depositors had better close
their accounts before it was too late. The clearing house signals
were credible in the market because the clearing house stood ready
to back a favourable verdict with its own resources. The result was
that sound banks were protected and unsound banks were thrown
to the wolves, and the newly purged banking system commanded
the confidence of the public. Membership rules (e.g capital
adequacy requirements, accounting procedures and rules for support operations) were determined by the member banks themselves,
and members chose to submit to these restrictions, even though they
were sometimes burdensome, because they could expect more support
from the clearing house in a crisis than non-members could.[6]

Clearing houses also helped to overcome the effects of restrictions on the note issue by issuing clearing house loan certificates
(see Timberlake 1984). These had their origin in the crisis of 1857
when the clearing banks in New York agreed to accept certificates
from their clearing association to economize on precious reserves.
The certificates contributed to the system's liquidity at the very

time when liquidity was most needed, and their role gradually expanded until they became a form of surrogate currency. The public accepted them because they were backed by the clearing house – and implicitly, therefore, by the clearing banks as a group – and there was never really any doubt that the banks as a group were sound. By the 1907 crisis hundreds of millions of dollars' worth of clearing house certificates were being issued and willingly accepted by the public, and, while there was some doubt about their legality, their usefulness was understood and the authorities decided not to prosecute. Once the public realized that they could have as much currency as they desired – even if it was surrogate currency – the 'panic' demand for currency would fall, and the additional currency would then be retired. Clearing house certificates provided the public with the reassurance that they could get whatever currency they wanted, and most people no longer had any reason to demand currency once they had that reassurance.

THE FEDERAL RESERVE

The founding of the Federal Reserve

There had been controversy over banking reform for years, but the controversy sharpened in a very definite way after the crisis of 1907. It was clear that there needed to be some facility for the issue of emergency currency, and while the usefulness of clearing house certificates was widely recognized, their dubious legality also gave rise to considerable disquiet. Congress responded with an interim measure – the Aldrich-Vreeland Act – to authorize a (legal) issue of emergency currency, and set up a National Monetary Commission to report on longer-term banking reform. Many US economists were also impressed with the way in which European central banks were (apparently) able to handle their liquidity crises, and they tended to draw the conclusion that the greater financial stability of the European economies was due to their central banks. The alternative conclusion – that the greater vulnerability of the US financial system to crisis was due to other peculiarities in the US system, such as the restrictions on branching – does not appear to have been taken seriously. The commission eventually accepted these views, and its report recommended the establishment of an American central bank – a Federal Reserve System consisting of twelve regional Reserve Banks and a Reserve

Board in Washington which would co-ordinate the policies of the different Reserve Banks. Congress accepted these recommendations and the Federal Reserve System came into operation in 1914.

The question still arises, however: *why* did Congress establish a central bank instead of abolishing the legislative restrictions which served to aggravate the crises? Part of the explanation arises from a distrust of 'private' emergency currency and a widespread feeling that the issue of emergency currency needed to be put on a more 'official' basis. Yet, as Timberlake (1984: 13) observes, the fear that clearing houses provided a dangerous form of emergency currency:

> flies in the face of the clearing house system's actual perform-ance. The most extraordinary fact associated with the several clearing house episodes between 1857 and 1907 is that the losses from all the various note issues, spurious and otherwise, *were negligible!* ... Few of the economists who analyzed clearing house operations even noted in passing this astonishing record, and none used it as an argument for continuing the system. [Own emphasis.]

One must also bear in mind that central banking was highly fashionable in contemporary intellectual circles, and American economists were fascinated with its apparent success in Europe. The American experiences with less regulated banking systems in the *antebellum* period were by now regarded as a clear failure, and virtually no one wanted to turn the clock back to the days before the National Banking System. In any case, *laissez-faire* was regarded as anachronistic, and the general climate of opinion increasingly preferred interventionist 'solutions'. Political factors also militated against trying to remove restrictions on the banks. To have relaxed the restrictions imposed by national banking legislation would have reduced the revenue the federal government could obtain from the banking system and forced Congress either to cut expenditures or find alternative sources of funding. Estab-lishing the Fed seemed to be a cheaper way – cheaper for the government – of providing the US banking system with the elastic currency it needed.

The Federal Reserve and the US banking system

The establishment of the Fed supplanted the earlier quasi-automatic mechanism for providing emergency currency with a managed system whose success depended on the managers' discretion. The new system also differed from the old in its incentive structure. The old clearing house officials were customers of the banks, and their well-being ultimately depended on their ability to satisfy their clients. On the other hand, the Federal Reserve System now had a monopoly over the provision of emergency currency, and its privileged position prevented market forces from ensuring that emergency currency would be provided as and when required. The new system thus hinged on discretion, and there were only weak incentives for Federal Reserve officials to get their discretionary decisions 'right'.

The big test came in the early 1930s. A variety of factors helped to undermine public confidence in the banking system and encourage the public to convert (commercial bank) deposits into (Federal Reserve) notes which were perceived to be safer. The Federal Reserve had been set up to deal with exactly this kind of crisis, and the solution was for the Fed to print the additional currency that the public desired to hold. Instead of providing that currency, the Fed blamed the crisis on bad bank management and was otherwise paralysed by indecision and doubt. It failed to provide the leadership which the system required and which its privileges ensured that only it could provide, and the crisis duly escalated into waves of bank failures that had catastrophic effects on real economic activity. The failure of the Fed to support the US banking system is also borne out by a counterfactual experiment carried out by Gorton (1986). He examines the impact of the Fed by predicting what would have happened had the pre-Fed regime continued in operation after 1914, and his results indicate that, while a panic would have occurred in December 1929, the 'failure and loss percentages would have been an *order of magnitude* lower' in the absence of the Fed (p. 29; my italics). This result suggests that there might have been a downturn in the early 1930s but nothing like the disaster that actually occurred. An assessment of the Fed's performance in the period before the Second World War by Miron (1989) also concludes that the Fed's impact on the economy was destabilizing. He finds that the rate of output growth and the inflation rate both became substantially more volatile, while the average rate of growth of output actually fell (pp. 290–1). His analysis also indicates that these changes cannot be dismissed as coincidental but ought to be attributed to the founding of the Fed, and these conclusions hold even if one

ignores the period of the Great Depression. This latter result indicates, therefore, that the Fed not only destabilized the US economy
in the 1930s but destabilized it throughout its early period of
operation.

Yet relatively few people at the time saw the Fed as having
failed to stem the banking crisis. Many blamed the stock market
crash or the inherent volatility of the capitalist system, and the
Fed itself pushed the line that it had done what it could, given
its decentralized decision-making structure and its own limited
and unclear powers. Congress accepted the Fed's arguments, and
the old confederated Federal Reserve structure was replaced by a
much more centralized one under a strengthened board of governors, and the Fed's regulatory powers were increased. The Fed
had turned the disasters of the 1930s to its own advantage by
persuading Congress to extend its hegemony over the American
banking system.

After a long lag the Fed's hegemony was increased still further
by the Depository Institutions Deregulation and Monetary Control
Act of 1980. Congress had set out to deregulate the financial
system, but the Fed managed to push successfully for a major
simultaneous extension to its own powers:

> Fed officials in their testimony to congressional committees
> persistently and doggedly advanced one major theme: the
> Fed had to have more power – to fight inflation, to prevent
> chaos in the financial industry from deregulation, and to act
> as an insurance institution for failing banks who might drag
> other institutions down with them. By misdirection and
> subterfuge, the Fed inveigled an unwary Congress into doing
> its bidding.
>
> (Timberlake 1985: 101)

The history of the Fed is an object lesson in public choice economics. The Fed consistently pursued its own private interests
above everything else, and it played the political game ruthlessly
to deflect the blame when things went wrong and to advance its
own prestige and power whenever it could. And as Timberlake
notes:

> Its 70-year history as a bureaucratic institution confirms the
> inability of Congress to bring it to heel. Whenever its own
> powers are at stake, the Fed exercises an intellectual ascendancy

over Congress that consistently results in an extension of Fed authority. This pattern reflects the dominance of bureaucratic expertise for which there is no solution as long as the [Fed] continues to exist.

(1986: 759)

The Federal Reserve and the development of fiat currency

When it was founded the intention was that the Fed should operate subject to the discipline of the gold standard. Yet within a year the First World War had broken out and all the major combatants had abandoned gold. The Fed was still nominally subject to the gold standard, but it now had considerable room for manoeuvre as it was the only player left in the gold standard game. The founders of the Fed had not anticipated this development, and the Fed had no clear idea what to do with the large gold flows that entered the United States during the war. In earlier days the gold inflows would have led to higher prices, but it seemed pointless to allow this to happen when none of the other major countries was on the gold standard, so the Fed tried instead to sterilize the inflows to reduce their impact on the economy, and it continued with this policy in the 1920s. An attempt was made to restore the gold standard in the 1920s, but the new gold standard collapsed in the international financial crisis of 1931. The United States also abandoned the gold standard shortly after 1933, and then returned two years later at the depreciated rate of exchange of $35 per ounce.

After the Second World War a modified gold standard was established – the gold exchange standard in which the United States pegged the price of gold at $35 per ounce and other countries pegged their currencies to the dollar. This system produced some inflation but it seemed otherwise to work tolerably well until the 1960s. The Fed was effectively trying to expand at a faster rate than was compatible with the fixed gold price, and it could continue with this policy only by running down its gold stocks. As these stocks continued to run down, the gold reserve requirements – the gold reserves the Fed was obliged to hold against reserves and notes – threatened to become binding and limit the Fed's ability to expand the money supply further. Congress responded by abolishing them, and what remained of the discipline of the gold exchange standard was eroded further. A consequence was to weaken the Fed's ability to resist the government at the very time when the Fed was coming under increasing pressure to accommodate the heavy spending of the Johnson administration. The Fed offered only limited resistance to this pressure, and the gold shortage intensified, leading to the eventual abandonment of the gold exchange system in the early 1970s. The Fed's accommodating monetary policies also produced higher inflation, and the collapse of the discipline against excessive monetary growth gave the authorities free rein to embark on a wild career of monetary expansion. What followed over the next two decades was a series of monetary binges followed by 'mornings after' in which a short-lived attempt would be made to bring inflation back down, but which would end as the temptation to expand again eventually won. As Timberlake (1986: 753) observed:

> money stocks and price level fluctuations behaved similarly to a remorseful but irresolute alcoholic and his bottle. A period of monetary drunkenness would be followed by a weeping and wailing and gnashing of teeth and a return to monetary austerity. Then rationalizations would appear: 'High interest rates are hurting the fragile economic recovery.' . . . 'We need monetary relief from _____.' (Here, the reader can furnish his favorite scapegoat policy, such as 'monetarism'.) With a happy gasp, the bottle would reappear again.

The cycle of monetary binges continues, with no sign of any end, and the authorities still resist attempts to restore monetary discipline with the same determination that a drunk resists a drying-out programme.

It is important to understand why. The inconvertible currency gives the monetary authorities enormous discretion over the monetary system, and from their point of view this discretion can be very useful. It gives them a lever they can use, for example, to try and manipulate the economy for electoral purposes. (Though whether they succeed is another matter.) Just as important, the existence of that discretion puts the authorities under very considerable political pressure to use it. If the political process grants the authorities the means to lower interest rates, for instance, those who stand to benefit from lower interest rates will apply pressure to have interest rates lowered. Had the authorities no control over interest rates, on the other hand, low interest rate lobbyists would be wasting their time and the pressure would not arise. Even if the authorities perceive the 'right' course of action and desire to pursue it, democratic processes can make virtue very costly in political terms. The authorities are effectively 'captured' by private interest groups which manipulate them (and thence their discretionary powers) for their own ends. In the old days the commitment to redeem the currency with gold or silver provided the government with a certain degree of protection against these pressures – not to mention protecting the value of the currency the private sector used – but the political process gradually undermined this guarantee and then destroyed it altogether. An automatic monetary system was thus replaced by a politicized one, and politicized systems have never been able to ensure monetary stability for long.

LIABILITY INSURANCE

The problems caused by liability insurance are a recurring issue in US monetary history. An agency is set up by the government which guarantees those who hold banknotes and/or deposits against loss in the event of bank failure, and the usual justification is that it is to protect banks against the 'danger' of a run. Liability insurance provides this protection (at least in the short run), but it also has more subtle effects. The most important of these is to create moral hazard: by removing the concern of depositors (and noteholders) for the safety of the bank it eliminates an important mechanism – the threat of a run – which would otherwise discourage bank management from taking 'excessive' risks. A bank can then take risks in the knowledge that it will reap the benefits if the risks pay off but can pass the losses to the insuring agency if they do not. Their protection against loss also means that depositors will be concerned only about the interest they are promised (and not about the risks a bank takes), so a bank that takes more risks can easily obtain more funds simply by raising its interest rates. In the process it also puts pressure on the more conservative banks to raise their interest rates, so risk-taking is rewarded while prudence is penalized. More risks are then taken, and bank safety is undermined. The moral hazard created by insurance is intensified as a bank's net worth falls. As the bank's capital value falls, managers and shareholders have less and less to lose from further risk-taking, but they still have everything to gain. This perverse incentive structure encourages ever greater risk-taking as an institution's net worth falls, and wipes out entirely any incentive to behave prudently when the capital value becomes zero or negative. If the insuring agency is to avoid large losses it is therefore important for these 'zombie' institutions to be closed down before they can do too much damage. A policy of closing down institutions that have little or nothing left to lose – an effective failure resolution policy – is essential if insurance premiums are to be kept down without busting the insurance agency.

The problem is to find some way of containing the moral hazard. One way of doing it is to discourage banks' risk-taking by charging risk-related premiums. An insurance agency can also do that by imposing capital requirements (to give shareholders something to lose) and by imposing interest rate ceilings (to restrict banks' ability to obtain funds to gamble with). To the extent that the moral hazard still remains, the insurance agency might also restrict banks' lending activities, although such measures can be counter-productive, since they also restrict banks' freedom to diversify risks. To carry out any of these functions, an insurance agency would also need to be able to monitor banks' activities, of course, and it would also have to monitor them to know when an institution had become so weak that it ought to be closed down. A 'successful' insurance scheme – one that did a reasonable job of controlling moral hazard at relatively low cost – would therefore monitor banks effectively, discourage excessive risk-taking by various means, and close down zombie institutions relatively quickly. A 'bad' scheme, on the other hand, would let moral hazard get out of control and both undermine the safety of the banking system and eventually destroy the net worth of the insurance agency itself.

Antebellum liability insurance schemes

United States experience bears these points out. The first liability insurance scheme was set up in New York in 1829, and others followed in Vermont (1831), Indiana (1834), Michigan (1836), Ohio (1845) and Iowa (1858) (Calomiris 1989a). These schemes fell into two basic types. Those in New York, Michigan and Vermont were versions of safety fund systems in which insurance payments depended on the fund's accumulated reserves, and the fact that reserves were limited (and vulnerable) meant that the insurance cover lacked credibility. These schemes also made little attempt to handle moral hazard problems – monitoring was usually carried out by state officials who had relatively little at stake, and there were few attempts to control risk-taking – and all three eventually failed. The other schemes were based on the mutual insurance principle, which made each bank liable for the others' losses. The schemes had membership rules to control risk-taking (e.g. capital adequacy) and monitoring was left to the banks. These features 'aligned the incentive and authority to regulate, and made insurance protection credible through unlimited liability among banks' (Calomiris 1990: 8). All three schemes were reasonably successful.

It is also important to note the role of the unit banking lobby in the establishment of liability insurance. As Calomiris (1990: 4–5) writes:

> it was the desire to preserve unit banking, and the political influence of unit bankers, that gave rise to the perceived need for deposit insurance, both in the antebellum period, and in the twentieth century. It was understood early on . . . that branching . . . provided an alternative stabilizer to liability insurance. But unit banks and their supporters successfully directed the movement for banking reform toward creating government insurance funds. All six antebellum states that enacted liability insurance were unit-banking states. In the antebellum branch-banking South neither government insurance, nor urban clearing houses, developed. Similarly, the eight state insurance systems created from 1908 to 1917 were all in unit-banking states.

The National Banking System put an end to the state systems of liability insurance. The main attraction of membership to many banks had been the relatively low cost of issuing notes. (The alternative was to issue notes under a 'free bank' charter, but the bond collateral requirement made that relatively expensive.) The introduction of the federal tax on state-chartered banknotes made such issues no longer worth while, and banks either gave up the note issue entirely and switched to uninsured state charters or else adopted national charters and subjected themselves to the regulations of the National Banking System. The new federal regulations thus drove out the state insurance systems and aborted any further developments in them. The state systems of note and deposit insurance were replaced by the federal government's guarantee of the notes of national banks, and the greater part of bank liabilities – deposits – were now uninsured.

Deposit insurance in the early twentieth century

State insurance made a come-back in the early years of the twentieth century. The repeated crises of the National Banking System helped to promote demands for an extension to branch banking to make banks safer. This pressure intensified in the aftermath of the 1907 crisis, but the unit banking lobby managed to fight off branching extensions and divert the political drive for safer banking into new schemes for state deposit insurance. Eight schemes were subsequently introduced in the succeeding years, as noted earlier, and all in unit banking states. These schemes failed to heed the lessons of earlier experience:

> Supervisory authority was placed in government, not member bank, hands and often its use or disuse was politically motivated. Furthermore, the number of banks insured [was] many more than in the antebellum systems (often several hundred), and this further reduced the incentive for a bank to monitor and report the misbehavior of its neighbor banks, since the payoff from detection was shared with so many, and the cost of monitoring was private.
>
> (Calomiris 1990: 9)

These schemes made little attempt, either, to control moral hazard, and there were inordinate delays in closing down insolvent institutions. Not surprisingly, all of them eventually failed.

The evidence also indicates that they destabilized state banking systems (Calomiris 1989b: 40) while their perceived political alternative, branch banking, had the opposite effect (Benston 1986: 14–7). To quote Calomiris again, states that allowed branch banking saw 'much lower failure rates – reflecting the unusually high survivability of branching banks – and responded well to the agricultural crisis [of the 1920s] by consolidating and expanding branching systems, where this was allowed' (1990: 11). Many contemporaries understood the effects of branch banking, and many states responded by relaxing the restrictions against it. From 1924 to 1939, for example, the number of states that allowed branch banking in some form doubled from eighteen to thirty-six (Calomiris 1990: 11). The push to branch banking also made itself felt at the federal level, and there was the usual conflict between unit and branch bankers. The result was a legislative compromise – the McFadden Act (1927) – which gave national banks very limited branching power but reaffirmed other restrictions against branch banking.

Federal deposit insurance

The bank collapses of the early 1930s gave renewed impetus to the view that banks were unstable because they were vulnerable to runs, and Congress responded, in the Banking Act of 1933,[7] by authorizing the establishment of a system of federal deposit insurance.[8] The new Federal Deposit Insurance Corporation came into operation the following year (followed shortly after a sister organization for the thrifts, the Federal Savings and Loan Insurance Corporation). Congress apparently recognized the potential moral hazard problems, and sought to deal with them by restricting banks' (and thrifts') permitted range of activities. It also gave the federal insurance agencies extensive regulatory powers and, as already noted, increased the supervisory powers of the Federal Reserve.

The new regulatory regime appeared to work reasonably effectively until the 1970s. It then began to unravel with a vengeance. When the Federal Reserve began to reduce monetary growth rates in the late 1970s, the soaring interest rates that accompanied the new policy undermined the net worth of the banking system and made deposit interest rate ceilings an increasingly damaging constraint to the banks. (The same factors hurt the thrifts even more.) The pressure eased as interest rates declined, but the deregulation that followed the passage of the Depository Institutions Deregulation and Monetary Control Act of 1980, and the Garn–St Germain Act of 1982, let the moral hazard genie out of his bottle. The removal of most of the earlier constraints against institutions' exploiting moral hazard had predictable results: They took more risks, and their net worth declined.

In theory the regulatory authorities might have been able to contain the damage had they intervened to close weak institutions down before they got out of hand, but they were overwhelmed by the scale of the problem, and the measures they took to stay afloat in the short term only aggravated it in the longer run. A kind of regulatory accelerator effect took over, and the regulatory apparatus that had managed to contain the moral hazard problem earlier now served instead to magnify it. Since an energetic failure resolution policy would have been expensive and depleted the insuring corporations' limited reserves, they tended to resort to foreclosure only as a last resort. They preferred instead to arrange 'mergers' – and often paid handsomely to get them – or simply overlooked problems until they could no longer be ignored. (One has to bear in mind the sheer scale of the problem they were dealing with, and their limited resources meant that they could seldom carry out more than the most cursory 'examinations'.) An energetic failure resolution policy would also have required the insurance corporations to petition Congress for more funds, and they would have then have had to acknowledge the magnitude of the problem and accept much of the blame for it. Ironically, the insurance corporations were now playing the same game *vis-à-vis* Congress and the executive that their zombie institutions were playing with them. With nothing more to lose, they were playing for time and gambling wildly with the other people's money. The insurance corporations were now the zombie institutions, and the government had no appropriate failure resolution policy for dealing with them.

There was little incentive on the part of anyone in government to blow the whistle and get to grips with the problem. Whoever did so would have had to recommend a solution to the crisis – and then take the political flak for what a resolution of the crisis would have cost. It was easier to ignore the problem and hope that someone else would pick up the poisoned chalice. The government was now acting like a zombie itself at the public expense. Losses so far accumulated amount to about half a *trillion* dollars – the scale of the thrift bail-out alone dwarfs all previous federal bail-outs put together – and losses continued to grow at a staggering rate. If ever there was a clear-cut case of government failure this was surely it. A system that had been set up to counter an (imaginary) *market* failure – to counter the inherent instability of banking under *laissez-faire* – had ended up producing *government* failure on an unprecedented scale. The ultimate irony was that the roots of the most costly public finance disaster in US history lay in the unit banking system which had been set up in the first place to raise revenue for the government.

CONCLUSION: MARKET SUCCESS, GOVERNMENT FAILURE AND THE INTERVENTIONARY RATCHET EFFECT

Three points particularly stand out in US monetary history. The first is that banking was generally successful when left in relative peace by the government. While there has never been full-blown *laissez-faire* in American banking, American experience does none the less indicate that banking under the appropriate legal framework can be quite stable without any 'support' from the government. There is nothing in US experience to suggest that *laissez-faire* in banking does not work, and much to indicate that it does. The most obvious historical example here is the experience of 'free banking' in the *antebellum* period. It is now reasonably well established that 'free banking' was much more successful than used to be appreciated, and it is any case difficult to explain why it should have been so widely copied had it been a failure. There were problems with some 'free banking' episodes, but those problems can be plausibly attributed to specific government intervention, its usual form being a combination of the bond deposit provision and the fiscal instability of some states. The experience of US banking for fifty years after the Civil War also seems to give some indication of the way in which the banking system can stabilize itself in the absence of a government-sponsored lender of last resort. Banks observed high capital ratios to preserve the confidence of their customers, and market forces penalized banks that allowed their capital value to fall too low. The clearing house system evolved during the same period to provide banks with crisis loans and to issue emergency currency during a crisis. The problems that afflicted US banking during this period can also be attributed to government intervention, this time in the form of the restrictive provisions of the National Banking Acts. Banks achieved whatever stability they did during this period despite government interference, not because of it, and this conclusion is supported by the way in which the banking system was destabilized further when the banks' own crisis management procedures were replaced by the Federal Reserve.

The second theme that stands out is government failure. Virtually all major monetary and banking problems in US history appear to have had their root cause in government interference of some sort. The major historical banking problems – banking instability before the Civil War; banking instability, recurrent financial crisis, the inelastic currency and the stunted growth of US banking after the Civil War; the banking instability of the 1920s and the banking collapses of the 1930s; the failure of historical and contemporary liability insurance schemes – can all be traced to a greater or lesser extent to government interference in banking. And the major monetary problem, inflation, can be traced – in the War of Independence, the War of 1812, the Civil War, and more recently in peacetime – to the government's refusal to submit to the fiscal discipline that sound money requires. Government interference also seems to be responsible for the major instances of general economic instability. As Milton Friedman wrote:

> In almost every instance, major instability . . . has been produced or, at the very least, greatly intensified by monetary instability. Monetary instability in its turn had generally arisen either from governmental intervention or from controversy about what governmental monetary policy should be. The failure of government to provide a stable monetary framework has thus been a major if not the major factor accounting for our really severe inflations and depressions. Perhaps the most remarkable feature of the record is the adaptability and flexibility that the private economy has so frequently shown under such extreme provocation.
>
> (Friedman 1960: 9)

It is important to stress that these government failures had a cumulative dynamic of their own. Time and again, government intervention would produce undesirable (and usually unintended) side effects. These side effects would provoke demands for further intervention, so the government would intervene yet again, and new problems would arise that seemed to require yet more intervention. Each time intervention produced more problems, and each time the preferred solution was more intervention. This interventionary ratchet effect is the central theme of American monetary history. It was driven by the interaction of the problems posed by previous government failure and a political process that was captured by powerful interest groups who manipulated it for their own ends. Not only were these groups able to channel the drive for reform into directions that left their power and privileges intact, or augmented them further, but they were also able to influence the very perception of the problems to be dealt with, and in the process they often managed to get special-interest propaganda elevated to the rank of received analysis.

Two instances of this interventionary ratchet are particularly important in US monetary history. The first is the dynamic interplay of unit banking, banking instability and liability insurance. Unit banking arose in the first place because entry into the banking industry was not free. The constitutional settlement had confirmed the right of states to control bank chartering, and states used their chartering powers to raise revenue – and more revenue could be raised if local competition was reduced by imposing branching restrictions. A powerful interest group was thus created which had a strong interest in maintaining the restrictions, and it was able again and again to block branching concessions. These restrictions severely weakened the US banking system, and the unit banking lobby was able to use the weakness of the banks to argue for protection in the form of liability insurance. It is no accident that liability insurance was usually introduced in unit banking states, and that states with branch banking seldom saw any need for it. The 'protection' was usually counterproductive, unfortunately, and it ended up destabilizing the banking system further. In the process of pushing for these measures the unit banking/liability insurance lobby also had a crucial influence on the way in which the debate was conducted, and lobbying mythology became accepted as conventional wisdom. So branching became anti-competitive, banking inherently unstable, and deposit insurance was a means of stabilizing the banking system. Muddled economics served as a smokescreen that distracted attention from the failures of earlier policies and pushed policy-makers towards the additional intervention the lobbyists wanted.

The other outstanding example of the ratchet effect is provided by the history of the Federal Reserve. The origins of the Fed lay in the instability that arose from the legal restrictions of the National Banking System. Yet rather than abolish those restrictions, or leave the banking system as it was, Congress decided instead to establish the Fed to put the issue of emergency currency on an official basis. In doing so it supplanted a system that had proved itself in practice, and divorced the integrity of the banking system from the self-interest of those responsible for protecting it. It also created a pressure group – the Federal Reserve itself – that not only had its own private interests (i.e. power and prestige) but was also uniquely placed to lobby Congress to further those interests. The new system failed in the early 1930s, but the Fed was able to divert the blame and use the opportunity created by the emergency to obtain more power. A major theme in Federal Reserve history is the way it has used its own intellectual superiority over Congress to divert legislative reforms to its own ends, and even to use the consequences of its own mistakes as an argument for an extension of its powers. For its part, the government has sometimes found the Fed a convenient scapegoat – it can blame an 'independent' Fed for raising interest rates, for example. The government also found the Fed a very convenient source of revenue, but in the process it undermined the discipline of the gold standard and paved the way for the inflation of the last twenty-five years. Thus one set of problems led to another. The instability of the National Banking System led to the Fed, and the Fed itself destabilized both the banking system and the economy, and then turned into an engine of inflation.

What is to be done? If markets work, and governments fail, then what is required is to take the government out of the monetary system. Several issues need to be addressed. The first is to find some means of guaranteeing the value of the currency. Such a guarantee was provided in the past by the gold and bimetallic standards, but there is no necessary reason why either of these in particular should be restored. We might wish to tie the value of the currency to a broader basket of goods, for example, and have an indirectly convertible commodity standard in which each dollar-denominated bank liability has a guaranteed value equal to that of a specified commodity basket but is redeemed in terms of some medium of redemption specified by the contract under which it was issued (see, for example, Yeager 1985 or Dowd 1989a: chapters 4 and 7). We then need to design a programme to take the government completely out of the banking system. The deposit insurance agencies, the Federal Reserve and any other regulatory bodies (e.g. the Comptroller of the Currency) would all be abolished and banks would be free to do as they wished, subject only to the discipline of an unregulated market place. The phasing of such a programme would need to be carefully designed, however, if it were to avoid destabilizing the banking system in the interim before the system had had time to adjust to the new regime. Many banks have come to depend on the protection of deposit insurance and a lender of last resort, and most of them would need time to prepare themselves for the new regime. One would not wish to kick the props away before the banks had had time to stop leaning on them. Congress would also have to pay off its deposit insurance debts before moving to a *laissez-faire* system, and a large number of zombie institutions that the insurance corporations are keeping open would have to be closed down, but Congress will have to take such measures in any case. Congress must complete these tasks and then withdraw entirely from the banking system.

The last problem is how to *keep* the government out of the monetary system. Here again American history is instructive. The only monetary powers the constitution gave the federal government were the power to specify the precious metal content of the dollar and the power to authorize coinage; nothing else. Yet since then the federal government has chartered its own banks, regulated the banking system, issued its own inconvertible currency, levied forced loans from the banks, rewritten legal tender laws, expropriated private holdings of gold and demonetized both the precious metals. The federal government has taken the very limited monetary power granted it by the constitution and turned it into a monetary despotism. The solution, therefore, is to eliminate altogether the limited monetary powers that the constitution grants the federal government. What is required is a constitutional amendment that provides for total separation between government and the monetary system. That such an express prohibition on government intervention in the monetary system might work is indicated by the success of the First Amendment in outlawing censorship. That amendment states, categorically, that 'Congress shall make no law ... abridging freedom of speech, or of the press.' These freedoms have been challenged many times – usually on the basis of an alleged overriding 'public interest' (i.e. government convenience) – but even sympathetic judges had to strike such measures down, as they were unable to get past the 'no law' provision. The 'free money' amendment must be equally unambiguous:

> To accomplish its purpose, that amendment cannot be a half-way measure. Either the government can possess monetary power, or it cannot – and if it cannot, the constitutional amendment must sweep clean. *The few monetary powers delegated to Congress in the Constitution must be abolished, any reserved state monetary powers must be eliminated, and an express prohibition must be erected*

against any monetary role for government. Strong medicine, perhaps, but the disease has very nearly killed the patient.

(Holzer 1981: 202; own italics)

Chapter 10

Did central banks evolve naturally?

One of the most significant developments in monetary economics in the past few years has been the resurgence of the 'free banking' school which advocates the abolition of central banks and the deregulation of the monetary system. The free bankers argue that most of our recent monetary instability has been caused, not by the defects of the particular central banking system under which we live, but by defects inherent in central banking itself, and they conclude that the only way to establish monetary stability is to abolish central banking altogether. One might have thought that such a radical position would have attracted more attention from the defenders of central banking, but they have made little systematic attempt to meet it. The one exception is Charles Goodhart, whose book *The Evolution of Central Banks* (1988) is the first major attempt since the controversy reopened by a prominent supporter of central banking to meet this challenge, and this alone makes Professor Goodhart's book a major contribution to the literature. It also deserves attention because it sets out, not merely to provide a vigorous defence of central banking against its critics, but to go on the offensive and demolish the case for free banking.

The gist of the argument for free banking is an application of the general case for free trade. Competition in the provision of 'money' is beneficial for much the same reasons that competition is beneficial in the production of any other commodity. Goodhart himself acknowledges this: 'If free trade and free competition are beneficial in other economic activities, what is so special about banking that justifies imposing special external controls, regulation, or supervision upon banks?' (1988: 13). From this he concludes, quite rightly, that 'the onus for demonstrating a case for the benefits of Central Bank (or other external agency) regulation, supervision, etc., needs to be made by the putative supervisor' (1988: 13). This is an excellent way to approach the issue, and Goodhart's arguments are both fascinating and provocative. None the less, I shall argue in this chapter that while Goodhart compels the free bankers to clarify their position, and in places to rethink it, he fails in the end to demolish it as he sets out to do, and that the *prima facie* case in favour of free banking remains substantially intact.

Goodhart covers three major theoretical issues that are central to the free banking controversy: whether sufficient information would be provided by free banks to make free banking feasible; the role of the clearing mechanism in restraining the over-issue of notes; and whether free banking or central banking is more likely to cause economic fluctuations.[1] I will discuss each of these in turn, and then discuss the historical evidence and Goodhart's interpretation of it.

I begin with the information issue.

THE ISSUE OF INFORMATION (IN) ADEQUACY

For Goodhart the most serious deficiency of free banking is that it 'depends on the existence of perfect, costless information, or at least on the availability of much greater information than is actually available' (1985: 9).[2] The essence of the information problem is 'how difficult and costly it is for users of financial services to *distinguish* between banks with more, or less, risky strategies' (1988: 59; own emphasis). There is a legitimate problem here, but as Goodhart himself readily acknowledges, such problems

> of informational inadequacy are not unique to banking, but occur quite commonly, notably in the provision of services, including other financial services. In particular, the difficulty, and cost and effort, involved in trying to distinguish between better, and worse, purveyors of a service is a common problem. It occurs, for example with the choice ... of doctors, lawyers, teachers, stockbrokers, sellers of insurance, etc., etc., as well as with bankers.

> (1988: 68)

So the questions are: what specifically makes banks 'different', and what is it about this difference that requires a central bank? In the earlier version of his book Goodhart explained this difference in the following words:

> The first key difference between banks, notably in their role as portfolio managers, and these other institutions, is that a large proportion of the assets that banks hold in their portfolios are not-marketed (in many instances not-marketable), and do not have a readily ascertainable market value. This is true to a much lesser extent with most other portfolio managers, the bulk of whose assets are restricted to marketable assets.
>
> (1985: 29)

It is not just that the real value of bank loans is often uncertain. What justifies the need for central bank support is the combination of uncertain loan values and the banks' commitment to redeem their liabilities – often on demand and without notice – at a fixed nominal value (see, for example, 1988: 85–102). Other financial firms – insurance companies, say – also have assets whose value is uncertain, but the prospect of sudden large-scale demands to redeem their liabilities is not the problem for them that it is for banks. As Goodhart continued:

> the main criteria for determining whether Central Bank services are needed is the existence of maturity transformation, though transformation of a rather special kind. *If it is much easier and quicker to transfer the liabilities of a class of financial intermediary from one such institution to another, or to a substitute form of liability, than it is to transfer the assets held by that institution, then there is a need for a lender of last resort, providing Central Banking functions.*
>
> (1985: 33; my italics)

To get this conclusion, Goodhart maintains that the maturity transformation of banks leaves them open to the danger of illiquidity – there may be a sudden demand to redeem bank liabilities which a bank may not have the resources at hand to meet – and that the illiquidity of one bank poses a danger to others because of the possibility of 'contagion'. 'Contagion' is where the observation that a bank is in difficulties leads liability holders at other banks to demand redemption. It is a serious matter, of course, because it provides a mechanism which can convert 'runs' on individual banks into a run on the banking system as a whole. Goodhart and other supporters of central banks see contagion as a problem that is inherent in any fractional reserve banking system, and they draw the conclusion that a central bank is needed to protect the banking system as its lender of last resort.

To assess Goodhart's argument, let us consider the conditions under which it would be privately rational for someone with a bank liability to demand redemption of his bank when he sees that another bank is in difficulties. The answer, presumably, is that it would be rational for him to demand redemption when he fears that it is sufficiently likely that his own bank will default on its obligation to redeem its liabilities.[3] This could happen in three different situations.

In the first, the liability holder observes that another bank has suffered a (presumably large) capital loss, from which he estimates that his own bank has suffered a sufficient fall in its net worth to make it worth his while to demand redemption 'just in case' his own bank defaults. A default by one bank may thus lead to increased demands for redemption at other banks, but it does not follow that the other banks face runs that threaten to drive them to default. Bank managements can be expected to be aware of the danger of sudden demands for redemption, and therefore they can be expected to take appropriate measures to protect themselves.[4] They would typically do so by holding an adequate capital cushion to reassure depositors (and noteholders, if any) that the bank was still sound. If the stockholders still value the bank, and the stockholders are residual claimants, then the depositors can be reasonably confident that they will suffer no losses because they have prior claim on the bank's resources. The banks can also protect themselves against unanticipated demands for redemption by holding liquid reserves which they can use to meet redemption demands, and by lining up credit facilities on which they can draw if the need arises.

One might also note that, when people demand redemption from a bank, the funds redeemed usually find their way back to the banking system. As Benston and Kaufman (1988: 9) observe, most depositors:

> if they feared the failure of their bank(s) and believed that their funds were at risk, . . . would redeposit those funds in one or more other banks believed to be safe or they would purchase safe, e.g., US Treasury, securities. In the latter situation, the seller of the securities is likely to deposit the funds in a bank. Why else would he or she have sold the safe security? In either

event, the funds would not leave the banking system and there would not be a systemic collapse.

They go on to point out that the danger to bank reserves would arise only if depositors had lost faith in all the banks in the country, and they note that this has never happened in recent years, despite some well publicized bank failures.

Second, it could be that depositors are worried about solvency of the banks in which they hold their deposits, and try to convert those deposits into the notes of a bank or banks in which they have confidence. Under *laissez-faire*, however, the unwanted deposits would be retired and the former depositors would take their funds to the note-issuing banks who would issue them the notes they wanted. The deposit banks would lose reserves and the note-issuing banks would gain them, but that in itself should pose no problem. Provided they were still considered to be sound, the deposit banks could always borrow any reserves they wanted, and the note-issuing banks would not pass up an opportunity to make a profit by lending to them. In effect, all that would happen is that the banks would convert one type of bank liability into another, and reserves would be appropriately reallocated.

A potential banking crisis would arise only if there were restrictions on the banks' freedom to meet the demand for notes. If the note issue were frozen, for example, then an increased demand for notes could not be accommodated, and a scramble for notes could easily turn into a crisis. This has happened many times in the past (e.g. in 1847, 1857 and 1866 when the UK note issue was restricted by the provisions of the 1844 Bank Charter Act). However, in this case it would be the restriction that was the problem, not the public's initial demand to retire some of their deposits. If the restriction were relaxed, the banks would be able to meet the demands of the public, and no crisis should occur.

Third, members of the public might suspect that the banks were unable to redeem their liabilities into the 'outside' redemption medium into which they were legally convertible – for example, they might fear that banks on the gold standard were about to run out of gold – and they might demand redemption just in case, and in doing so provoke a default. In this case, unlike the previous one, the banks would not be able to ward off redemption demands by printing more notes. They could, however, protect themselves in advance by inserting 'option clauses' into their banknote contracts to give them the option of deferring redemption provided they later paid compensation to those whose demands for redemption were delayed. These clauses would give banks time to obtain additional reserves (e.g. by calling in loans) which they might otherwise be unable to obtain, or be able to obtain only with difficulty. Option clauses appear to have been used with some success in Scotland until they were banned by an ill-conceived Act of Parliament in 1765.[5]

We see, then, that in each of these cases the banking system has the means of protecting itself against unanticipated demands for redemption – provided that those means are not prohibited. The failure of a bank might give rise to some demands for redemption, but under *laissez-faire* conditions it ought not to lead to a run on the system. Our discussion also suggests that we should expect contagion to arise only under conditions where legal restrictions prevent the banks protecting themselves (e.g. where the note issue is restricted, or option clauses are banned). These conclusions seem to be borne out by the available historical evidence. At the risk of oversimplifying somewhat, there were no serious problems of contagion in relatively unrestricted banking systems – like those of Scotland, Sweden and Canada in the nineteenth century, and in the United States during its so-called 'free banking' period before the Civil War (see White 1984, Jonung 1985, Schuler 1988 and Rolnick and Weber 1984 respectively) – but runs were a serious problem in more restricted banking systems such as those of nineteenth-century England and the United States after the Civil War.

THE KEY ROLE OF THE CLEARING HOUSE

The second source of controversy concerns the role of the clearing house. The clearing house plays a major role in free banking theory. Free bankers have long maintained that a well functioning clearing house would discipline individual banks which over-issued their notes, since a bank that expanded more rapidly than the rest would face an adverse clearing balance and lose reserves. To protect its reserves and remain solvent, it would eventually have to reduce its note issues. Goodhart acknowledges this argument, but dismisses it:

There are two flaws in this analysis. The first, which was

considered at some length by Smith and the earlier economists engaged in the free-banking debate, is that the clearing house mechanism tends to lead all banks to expand, or to contract, at a broadly similar rate, but does not itself determine what the resulting average rate of growth might be, nor whether it would be stable, or subject to sharp fluctuations. The second, even more serious, flaw, as it now appears in a modern context, is that neither Smith nor apparently earlier economists had considered the possibility of more thrusting banks seeking to prevent the clearing house losses that would result from rapid expansion *by making their liabilities more attractive*.

(1988: 30; own italics)

Hence he concludes that 'the market discipline imposed by a well-functioning clearing house . . . was not capable of preventing cycles and financial crises' (1988: 10–11).

Let us consider each of these points in turn. Regarding the first point, the free bankers' claim is simply that no bank could persistently expand at a faster rate than the others, because of reserve losses, and this claim is not invalidated because it does not tell us what the average growth rate should be. The average rate would be determined by public demand, but, whatever it was, a bank that persistently expanded at a faster rate would tend to lose reserves, while a bank that persistently expanded at a slower rate would tend to gain them. This first 'flaw' in the free banking position is therefore something of a straw man.

Turning to the second point, let us assume that a bank expands its notes and makes them more attractive at the same time.[6] Let us also suppose that the bank is able to make its notes sufficiently more attractive that it manages to avoid any reserve losses, and that it uses the additional notes to expand its lending. Making its notes more attractive will increase its marginal costs, and if we assume that the marginal loans the bank takes on are no better (in the appropriate sense) than previous loans, then we can say that the bank's marginal revenue will not rise. (In fact we would normally expect it to fall, but that is not necessary to the argument.) If we assume that the bank was initially maximizing its profits, then the combination of higher marginal costs and non-increasing marginal revenue implies a fall in profits, and so the bank would not expand its issues. In short, Goodhart's point that a bank *could* still expand in this way misses the main point: no bank *would* choose to, because it would reduce its profits.

That the clearing-house-discipline-is-illusory argument is flawed can be verified by approaching the issue in another way: Goodhart's arguments are at a level of generality that applies not only to banks of issue but to banks of deposit as well. Yet those arguments would be readily dismissed if they were applied to banks of deposit, because it is generally accepted that the cheque-clearing system does provide an effective check against banks that overexpand their deposits relative to their competitors – even though it does not tell us what the average rate of deposit growth actually is. It is also generally accepted that banks will *choose* not to expand their deposits beyond some point, even though they could expand them if they wished, because to expand further would be to reduce their profits. In short, it is generally accepted that the clearing system *is* an effective discipline against a bank that over-issues deposits, and the same logic applies to banks of issue as well.

BANK EXPANSION AND FLUCTUATIONS IN ECONOMIC ACTIVITY

The third issue is whether free banking would exacerbate or reduce fluctuations in economic activity. Free bankers have long argued that the operation of the clearing system under competitive conditions would reduce such fluctuations. When there are multiple banks of issue, the banks' own private interests would lead them to develop a clearing system,[7] and reserve losses through clearing would provide a more effective check against a bank that overissues. The fact that the banks accept each others' notes at par means that the public can redeem a note at any bank, and not just at the bank that issued it. This makes it easier to redeem unwanted notes, and strengthens the convertibility check against over-issue. In the words of one of the earliest free bankers, Sir Henry Parnell, in 1827, 'It is this continual demand for coin, by the banks on one another, that gives the principle of convertibility full effect, and no such thing as an excess of paper or as a depreciation of its value can take place for want of a sufficiently early and active demand for gold.'[8]

Under central banking there is, of course, only one note issuer, and so there can be no note-clearing system. This means that the most effective check against over-issue is eliminated and the only discipline on the note issue comes from direct redemption by the public.[9] It follows from this that, if there is an over-issue, it will take longer and proceed further – and cause more disruption of economic activity – before it is finally brought under control. As Parnell continued, 'If in England the power of converting paper into gold has not prevented an excess of paper, because the demand does not take place until long after the excess has taken place, this is to be attributed to the system of English banking.' This is the basis of the argument that the clearing system under free banking would reduce disruptions of economic activity.

Goodhart disputes this argument. In part, this is because he dismisses the clearing system as an effective check on over-issue. However, he goes further and argues that free banking would actually produce greater fluctuations in economic activity than central banking. He goes on to discuss approvingly the argument that

> competitive pressures would drive the banks to seek to maintain and expand market share during normal (i.e. non-crisis) periods. Moreover, during such periods of normal business the more conservative banks would lose market share. With the public often being poorly-informed ... there was no guarantee that the more conservative banks could recover during panics and bad times the market share lost ...
>
> (1988: 47–8)

In short, this competitive expansion would lead to a loss of reserves, and at some point banks would want to pull in their horns. This in turn would produce a crisis:

> Only collusive action ... would be likely to remedy a crisis situation, and this would be improbable in a free banking context ... So, the argument against free banking was that competitive pressures would generate a cyclical path of bank expansion, despite being on the Gold Standard, with boom followed by bust.
>
> (1988: 48–9)

It seems to me that this argument is open to objections similar to the earlier one against the clearing system. Individual banks have an incentive to expand up to a certain point only, and not to the point where they put themselves in danger, and it is far from clear what mechanism would induce the banks as a whole to overexpand in this way. It is not enough to argue that competition somehow forces the banks to over-expand, or to claim that there is no 'guarantee' that conservative banks can recover their market share. One has to meet the argument that a bank management can expect to gain a competitive edge over its less cautious rivals by cultivating a reputation for soundness, so as to attract their business when public confidence in them begins to falter. Admittedly, the bank would have to forgo some 'easy' profits in the short run, but the real pay-off comes later on when its rivals get into difficulties and lose public confidence, and it can capture their business.[10]

Goodhart does not meet this argument. Instead, he claims that his interpretation of competitive over-expansion is borne out in the recent LDC debt crisis:

> the recent history of the rapid expansion of international bank lending to sovereign LDCs during the 1970s, the resulting crisis, and the subsequent cessation of further voluntary lending would appear to provide an excellent example of this syndrome. Competitive behaviour seemed to force all the major banks to take part in an undue expansion of lending . . .
>
> (1988: 48)

He then dismisses the argument that banks made so many loans because they could be confident of a bail-out if the loans turned bad, and he concludes that there is 'no evidence that banks were induced to make such loans before 1982 by a belief that the IMF or their national Central Bank would absorb the loss on such loans' (1988: 49).

This is a widely accepted interpretation of the debt crisis, but it still fails to explain why the banks allowed themselves to become so over-extended. My own view is that he dismisses the most plausible argument. Given the existence of the bail-out facility, and given their expectations of how it would operate, I would argue that it was rational for the banks to take the risks they did. If the risks turned out well, they reaped the profits; if they did not, they could pass some of the losses back to the IMF or their own central banks. There was no point in a bank holding back, as it might otherwise have done, because the likelihood of a bail-out would limit its chance of capturing its rivals' market share when their loans turned bad. The existence of the bail-out facility destroyed the incentive to be prudent. The optimal strategy for any bank was therefore to take risks but stay with the herd, on the presumption that the lender(s) of last resort could not allow them all to fail. Consequently the whole herd took excessive risks, and there was no option but to bail most of them out. Professor Goodhart might still reply that he 'sees no evidence' that the banks took risks for these reasons, but one would not expect the banks to announce publicly that they were taking risks because they were counting on a bail-out, and it is not clear what other evidence we should be looking for that is obviously lacking.[11]

THE EMPIRICAL EVIDENCE ON FREE BANKING

So far we have concentrated mainly on theoretical issues. However, Goodhart's thesis that free banking is inherently unsound has a very strong empirical prediction: it predicts that free banking could not work if it were put into practice. A central part of the argument for free banking is that this prediction is refuted by the experience of relatively unregulated banking in Canada, Sweden and, most especially, Scotland, in the late eighteenth and nineteenth centuries. The Scottish system in particular was much admired for its stability, and, despite its close ties with the English financial system, it was relatively free of the periodic crises that afflicted England during the same period. The opponents of free banking have always found its success hard to explain. As long ago as the 1820s Sir Walter Scott noted the contrast between Scotland's 'practical system successful for upwards of a century' and 'the opinion of a professor of Economics, that in such circumstances she ought not by true principles to have prospered at all'.[12] John Stuart Mill discussed the success of Scottish free banking, but was apparently unable to explain it, and in the end dismissed the issue 'with the somewhat curious conclusion, that free note issuing is very good north of the Tweed, but very bad south of it'.[13] Another opponent of free banking, William Stanley Jevons, came out with the curious argument that 'if we were all Scotchmen the unlimited issue of one-pound notes would be an excellent measure' (1875: 319), and proceeded to explain that the unlimited note issue worked in Scotland only because of the superior Scottish banking system (!).

Goodhart explains the success of these experiments in free banking on the following grounds:

(1) ... it may reflect in part the greater natural strength of a branch banking system (wider diversification, etc.) as compared with a unit banking system;

(2) ... both systems became oligopolistic in form; in a smaller group of near equals competitive (and thus pro-cyclical) pressures *may* be less, though those who have studied the Scottish banking system (pre-1844) closely are sure that it exhibited high competitive pressures ...

(3) ... the final reason for the comparative success of these banking systems may reside in the improbability that under Gold Standard conditions either the Canadian or the Scottish banking systems could be said to be independent of New York and London. In both cases the Canadians and Scots could relieve pressures on their reserves in their own areas by drawing on New York and London, thereby transferring the reserve pressure to the center.

(1988: 51–2)

It seems to me that these arguments are not convincing. Point (1) tends to ignore the consideration that the growth of branch banking in Scotland and Canada was a direct *consequence* of relatively free banking rather than an alternative to it. This argument seems to be borne out by the fact that branch banking evolved from a relatively early stage in Scotland and Canada, where there were no laws against it, while a branch banking system began to develop in England only after the Bank of England's monopoly of joint-stock banking was formally abolished in 1826, and a mature branch banking system has still to evolve in the United States because of restrictions against inter-state banking. These examples seem to illustrate that branch banking tends to prosper where there is less regulation to hinder it, and this suggests that the strength of the branch banking system is an argument in favour of free banking, not an argument against it.

The second point seems to presuppose that competition is destabilizing, and we have discussed that already. In any case, as Goodhart himself readily acknowledges, the 'oligopolistic' Scottish system seemed to be highly competitive. What still needs to be explained is how the Scottish system was apparently both more competitive and more stable than the English one.

As for the third point, the tendency was for shocks to hit Scotland and Canada from the 'reserve centres' of London and New

York, and not for shocks to originate internally in those countries and force them to transfer the reserve pressures to the centre. A good example of this occurred when the Bank of England suspended specie payments in 1797. When the news reached Edinburgh the major Scottish banks temporarily suspended as well, but they soon restored their normal convertibility practices and maintained them for the rest of the Bank Restriction period. This illustrates that the Scottish banks had the strength to maintain their liquidity despite what was happening in London, and this in turn suggests, I believe, that the Scottish banks' 'dependence' on the London reserve centre may have been exaggerated.

CONCLUSIONS

There are two key issues which divide supporters of free banking and supporters of central banking. The first is whether the banking system is sufficiently 'different' from other industries to justify the monopolization of the currency supply and the regulatory framework implied by central banking. If we accept the general case for free trade, then the onus of proof is on the supporters of central banking to establish what that difference is and why it requires us to accept central banking. Goodhart acknowledges this, but in my opinion at least his arguments fail to undermine the *prima facie* case in favour of free banking. The second issue is the success of comparatively free banking in practice. If the basic argument of the central banking school is correct – that free banking is inherently unsound – then this success ought not to have occurred. What central bankers have to live with is that free banking apparently *did* work, and their attempts to reconcile that success with their own theory are unconvincing.

Having said all this, Professor Goodhart is the first modern defender of central banking to write a systematic critique of free banking and there is much of value in it. He has an excellent discussion of central banking systems as 'clubs', for example, and the eighty-page appendix on central banking systems at the end of the nineteenth century is a mine of interesting information. His arguments for central banking are imaginative and thought-provoking, and supporters of free banking would be unwise to ignore them. Indeed, while he may take this as a backhanded compliment, he does much to advance the free banking cause by pointing to potential weaknesses in it and encouraging its supporters to attend to them. All in all, *The Evolution of Central Banks* is to be highly recommended to anyone interested in the current controversy over central banking.

Chapter 11

The evolution of central banking in England, 1821–1890

The revival of interest in free banking has made it clear how important it is to re-evaluate our monetary history. One of the reasons why so many economists support state intervention in the monetary system is that they believe that history shows that monetary *laissez-faire* is inherently unstable, and that central banking evolved to counter that instability.[1] It is now becoming increasingly apparent that the first view is unsupportable, and that the relatively unregulated banking systems of the past have a good record of stability.[2] The evidence suggests, in fact, that they have a superior record to contemporary or later banking systems which were more heavily regulated. A question then arises: if monetary *laissez-faire* is not inherently unstable, it must follow that central banking could not have evolved to counter the market's inherent instability, and we are left wondering, why *did* central banking evolve?

This chapter tries to shed some light on the question by examining the growth of central banking in England between the resumption of specie payments by the Bank of England (1821) and the Baring crisis (1890). This period has been chosen because – at the risk of slight exaggeration – it marks the transition of the Bank from a 'merely' privileged institution to a recognizable central bank. It is true, of course, that in the quarter-century before 1821 – and arguably even earlier[3] – the Bank had accumulated considerable experience of central banking,[4] and it was in this period also that the theory of central banking was first developed, but these factors appear to have had comparatively little direct influence on the subsequent development of English central banking. The resumption of specie payments was intended to restore the situation of 1793, and relatively little remained after that of the Bank's earlier central banking role. At most the Bank had some ill defined public responsibility, and even that was controversial. Most of the theory of central banking was subsequently forgotten and had to be rediscovered later. In short, the modern system of central banking in England to a large extent developed *after* 1821.

Its roots, however, go back to the Bank's privileges of the late seventeenth and eighteenth centuries. These privileges gave the bank a size and security which no other institution could match, and its size and security gave its notes a competitive advantage over the notes of other banks. The Bank also pursued a policy of using its market power to discourage rival issues, and by the end of the eighteenth century it had succeeded in eliminating other London note issues. These factors in turn encouraged the other banks to use the Bank's notes as reserves, and the Restriction completed the process by which Bank of England liabilities became the principal reserve medium of the English banking system. The fact that the other banks used Bank liabilities for their reserves meant that the Bank could control their total reserves, and this control is the key factor in the Bank's subsequent development. It made the other banks dependent on the Bank – because they might need more reserves from it – and their dependence forced them to defer to it and acknowledge its hegemony. A second consequence of this dependence was that it eventually forced the Bank to accept the role of lender of last resort for the banking system. In short, *both the Bank's hegemony over the banking system and its lender of last resort function derived ultimately from the same source – the Bank's control over other banks' reserves – which in turn stemmed from the Bank's earlier privileges.*

These developments took place in an environment of periodic crisis that was caused largely by legislative restrictions on banking. Two kinds of restriction particularly stand out. Until 1826 all English banks other than the Bank of England were restricted to partnerships of six or fewer people. In an industry characterized by extensive economies of scale, this rule meant that English banks were small and undercapitalized, and very vulnerable to failure. It was in these circumstances that the Bank of England established its hegemony in London. The restrictions on joint-stock banking were relaxed in the early nineteenth century, but the banks also had to live with restrictions on the note issue, and these restrictions were tightened by the Bank Charter Act in 1844. The restrictions on the note issue made it difficult to satisfy changes in the public's demands for bank liabilities, and gave rise to the possibility of panics in which the public would clamour for more Bank notes than the Bank could provide. It is significant that in three of these crises – those of 1847, 1857 and 1866 – what caused the panic to abate was a government promise to remove the restriction and allow the Bank to issue the additional notes that the public wanted.

The early development of central banking in England is therefore easily summarized. Legislative restrictions enabled the Bank of England to establish a position of unique strength, an important feature of which was the other banks' dependence on reserves provided by the Bank. By weakening the other banks, legislative restrictions also made the banking system prone to crises, and reduced the banks' ability to handle them. When crises occurred the banks therefore had little option but to turn for assistance to the Bank of England. The Bank at length accepted the principle that it should provide that assistance, but the price it exacted was the acknowledgement of its hegemony over the monetary system. The process was complete by the time the Baring crisis occurred, and there was no further developments in British central banking until August 1914.

THE EARLY HISTORY OF THE BANK

The Bank of England was initially established in 1694 to provide the government of William III with a loan to fight Louis XIV. The circumstances in which it was founded are most instructive: three decades earlier, Charles II had had to rely on loans from London bankers, and he ran up large debts which he could not repay. His default in 1672 destroyed the government's credit for many years. As a consequence, in the 1690s, William III found it extremely difficult to raise loans, so he fell in with a scheme suggested by a Scottish financier, William Paterson, to establish a bank – the Bank of England – to lend the government money in return for the grant of certain privileges. Over the following years the Bank's charter and privileges were gradually extended in return for a series of loans to the government. 'The early history of the Bank was a series of exchanges of favours between a needy Government and an accommodating corporation' (Smith 1936: 9). Apart from periodic increases in the Bank's capital and authorized note issue, the most significant of these provisions were the monopoly of the possession of the government's balances (1697), the granting of limited liability to the shareholders (1697), the restriction of other banks in England and Wales to partnerships of no more than six partners with unlimited liability (1708; reaffirmed and strengthened in 1742) and the management of the national debt (1751) (Smith 1936: 9–10). As one historian put it:

> It is ... evident that throughout the eighteenth century and early years of the nineteenth the Bank of England's first interests were the guarding of its monopoly issuing of notes, and the strengthening of the bonds which united it to the state by taking every advantage of the financial weakness of the Treasury.
>
> (Richards 1929: 199)

The Bank made good use of its privileges to build up a large business and establish its own supremacy. 'Possessing so many advantages the Bank easily overshadowed its competitors, and, as Bagehot has stated, "it inevitably became *the* Bank in London ..." ' (Richards 1929: 200). It used its market power to induce the other London banks to abandon their note issues some time after 1772, even though the issuing of notes was normally a lucrative business and the banks retained a legal right to issue notes until 1844 (Powell 1915: 229, n. 2).[5] The elimination of the rival note issues in London shows both the extent of the Bank's power over the London banks and its willingness to use that power to further its own private interests. Promoting its own issues against those of other banks seems to have been a consistent Bank policy.[6]

At the same time as they abandoned their own issues, London banks turned to Bank of England notes to redeem their own liabilities. Part of the reason for this was that notes were less costly to store and move than gold. Also, the public would have preferred notes to gold for the same reasons, and so a bank that offered to redeem its liabilities with gold instead of Bank notes would have put itself at a competitive disadvantage. So would a bank that offered as redemption media financial instruments issued by some institution other than the Bank – without the Bank's privileges, no other institution could offer instruments that would have been as secure in a crisis. The banks were therefore driven to use the liabilities of the Bank of England as their own reserve media. This is highly significant, because the Bank of England's control over the other banks' reserves was to provide the basis on which the lender of last function was to evolve. Indeed, one could go further and say that it was to provide the basis from which the monopoly of the note issue was to develop into a modern central bank.[7]

Then came the French revolutionary war[8] and the government's attempts to finance much of its expenditure by loans from the Bank. When it had been founded the Bank was forbidden to lend to the government without the express permission of Parliament,[9] but despite this injunction the Bank had been in the habit of making loans against Treasury bills made payable at the Bank. Perhaps because it anticipated further government demands for loans, the Bank in 1793 requested the government to pass an Act of Indemnity to protect it against liability for the loans it had made in the past, and for the future loans up to a certain amount. The Prime Minister, Pitt, lost no time putting such a Bill through Parliament, but he deliberately left out the clause limiting the loans the Bank could make without parliamentary approval. Pitt:

> was now armed with the unbounded power of drawing upon the Bank; with nothing to restrain him, unless the directors should take the audacious step of dishonoring his bills. The bank was henceforth almost at his mercy, and ... he plunged into that reckless career of scattering English gold ... across Europe.
>
> (MacLeod 1896: 105).

The Bank directors repeatedly complained about Pitt's incessant demands for loans, but they dared not refuse him even though the loans threatened to push the Bank itself into failure. At last the landing of French troops in Wales in February 1797 provoked a run for gold that the Bank lacked the resources to withstand, and the Bank had no choice but to appeal to Pitt for assistance. The government responded with an Order in Council – afterwards verified by Act of Parliament – ordering the Bank to suspend specie payments. In effect, the government had driven the Bank into failure and then legalized its bankruptcy to keep it in business.[10]

There followed the long period of the Restriction (1797–1821) in which the Bank operated an inconvertible currency. The combination of legal tender,[11] the issue of small notes by the Bank[12] and, perhaps most significantly, the depreciation of the Bank's notes,[13] all helped to further the use of Bank notes (and deposits) as the principal – and only significant – reserve medium of the other banks. In effect the Bank of England became the monopoly supplier of base money, and therefore had the power to manipulate the reserves of the banking system as it pleased. Since, furthermore, the Bank was no longer subject to any commitment to redeem its liabilities for gold, it also had ultimate control over prices. The Bank's directors generally understood that their policies could have considerable influence on financial conditions, but they had much less understanding of the extent of that influence or how it should be used, and many of them believed that the Bank could do nothing to disturb prices provided it restricted its discounts to self-liquidating bills – the 'real bills' fallacy.[14] Consequently, both the Bank's policies and the real bills doctrine came in for much criticism, and the controversy gave rise to some notable contributions to monetary theory. Two contributions in particular stand out. In 1802 Henry Thornton's *Paper Credit* provided a blueprint for managing a central bank on an inconvertible standard. It also continued a detailed analysis of the lender of last resort function,[15] and a devastating attack on the real bills fallacy. Also notable was the Bullion report (1810), which made clear the Bank's responsibility for the depreciation of its notes and provided a famous and influential critique of the real bills doctrine.

The end of the Restriction period was signalled by the Resumption Act of 1819, which stipulated that the Bank should restore convertibility by 1 May 1823. In the event it actually resumed payments two years before then. An earlier Act of 1816 had specified that the issue of notes under £5 was to cease two years after the resumption of convertibility, but the Bank anticipated this deadline as well by ceasing to issue small notes on resumption (Clapham 1944: 75–6). Another Act of 1819 tried to restore the Bank's earlier degree of independence by requiring the Bank to obtain explicit parliamentary approval before lending to the government (Andrèades 1909: 241–2), and Bank notes again ceased to be legal tender (Smith 1936: 13). The Bank's legal position was now similar to what it had been in 1793.

As in 1793, many people also regarded it as having some kind of special responsibility towards a monetary system based on the gold standard, and much of the monetary theory developed in the Restriction period slipped into oblivion.[16] The only real difference from 1793 was that banks and their customers were now more used to using Bank notes to redeem their liabilities,[17] and Bank notes remained very significant in banks' reserves even though the ban on small notes forced them to accumulate coins to redeem deposits of less than £5. The greater use of Bank liabilities as reserves implied that the Bank had a more powerful 'lever' over the monetary system than it had before the wars.

THE DETERMINANTS OF BANK POLICY

Before proceeding much further it is perhaps useful to consider in more detail the objectives of Bank policy and what determined them. The Bank's policy was a response to two sorts of pressure: on the one hand, there was pressure from the shareholders for the Bank to maximize their profits, and, while the directors could – and often did – withstand a certain amount of pressure from that direction,[18] they could not defy an organized majority which was set on a definite policy. On the other hand, the Bank had a close if informal relationship with the government, and it had to take government wishes very seriously. The government would make frequent requests of the Bank, and though it was often ready to modify its requests in the light of the opinions of the Bank management, it none the less expected its requests to be obeyed. The Bank understood this, and was reluctant to flout the government openly even though the government had no formal authority over it. We have already seen how the Bank acceded to Pitt's requests in 1793–7 even though they threatened to drive the Bank into default, and eventually did.

There appear to have been several reasons for this willingness to accommodate the government. One was the government's legislative power: the government could always bring in legislation to get its way, if necessary, and it was more convenient for both sides for the Bank simply to give in. Also, the Bank could ill afford to antagonize the government, because it was dependent on it to make sure that its charter and privileges were periodically renewed, and it would always want to retain the government's goodwill in case a crisis should occur and the Bank needed help. A second source of the government's influence over the Bank was its power of patronage (i.e. its power to offer jobs and honours). Patronage worked by 'buying off' key individuals, and governments of the period used it very effectively.[19]

Pressure from shareholders and government was not the only determinant of Bank policy. One must also consider the self-interest of the directors themselves. Most members of the court earned their living working in City firms, and their principal concern would have been the well-being of their firms. As a result, they would have had some interest in ensuring that the Bank provided the market with any support it might need. Since controversy might lead to their replacement, they also had some incentive to avoid policies that would provoke adverse criticism. We shall have more to say on this issue below.

These conflicting interests and pressures produced a Bank policy that was a compromise between maximizing – or, more precisely, satisfying – profits to satisfy shareholders, keeping the government content, and occasionally supporting the market in a crisis. The relative importance of these objectives varied:

> Up to about 1825 the Bank definitely aimed at high profits for its Proprietors, and resented any imputation of public responsibility, except to keep itself in a sound position and to give a preference to the Government in making its advances. . . . At the same time, it must be admitted that the Directors were wise enough to withstand the desire, very pertinaciously expressed by some of the Proprietors, for maximum dividends and the distribution of all available profits.
>
> (Dodwell 1934: 57)

Despite conflicts with other objectives, the Bank none the less had little difficulty making a decent profit until well into the nineteenth century. The absence of real competition enabled it to make 'a comfortable income for its stockholders, without exerting itself a great deal' (Sayers 1958: 11), but this changed when rival joint-stock banks were allowed. As Sayers put it:

> in the middle decades of the nineteenth century circumstances ceased to support its profits in quite the old easy way. Though London's business, with the country's, was undergoing spectacular expansion, the staid ways of the Old Lady of Threadneedle Street were uncompetitive, and new business went rather to the rising young men of the joint-stock banks. The decisions that followed the crash of 1857 accentuated the loss of discount business . . . [and its dividends were] a doubtful satisfaction to stockholders who could see how well the shareholders in some of the new joint-stock banks were faring.
>
> (Sayers 1958: 11)

We now return to the 1820s.

THE 1825 PANIC AND THE ACTS OF 1826

In 1825 there was a major financial crisis. It occurred after a period of considerable expansion of their issues by the Bank of England and the private banks,[20] and, perhaps more significantly, after large amounts of speculative British investment in South America. The collapse of the investment boom in mid-1825 left many British financial firms in serious difficulties. The apprehension mounted in the autumn, and there were large bank failures in November. On 5 December it became known that one of the leading City finance houses – Poles & Co. – was in serious difficulties. The Bank arranged assistance, and the firm struggled on for a while. In the meantime the crisis gradually worsened. In London it reached its peak in the week from Monday 12th to Saturday 17th, when the storm 'raged with an intensity which it is impossible for me to describe' (Richards, the deputy governor, quoted in MacLeod 1896: 122). On the Monday and Tuesday the demand for cash was so great that it was said to have been impossible to convert even the best government securities into cash on any terms.[21] The public was clamouring for Bank notes and gold coins, and neither could be produced fast enough, though the printers were working overtime and the Mint was coining sovereigns furiously (Clapham 1944: 100).[22] That same week the government refused the Bank any form of assistance – the Bank would have to meet demands for redemption until it ran dry – and the Bank decided to reverse the contractionary policy it had followed since May. In the famous words of a Bank spokesman, Jeremiah Harman:

> We lent by every possible means and in modes we had never adopted before. We took in stock as security; we purchased exchequer bills, and we made advances on exchequer bills; we not only discounted outright, but we made advances on deposits of bills of exchange to an immense amount; in short, by every possible means consistent with safety of the bank; and we were not on some occasions over-nice . . . we rendered every assistance in our power.
>
> (Quoted in MacLeod 1896: 123)

The Bank's expansionary policy 'and the resultant issue of £5 million of notes, snatched the country from the brink of the cataclysm which it already overhung' (Powell 1915: 330). By the end of the Saturday the Bank had apparently run out of notes,[23] but a new batch arrived from the printers on the Sunday, and a consignment of gold arrived from France on the Monday, 17 December. That day Poles's failed, and with them some other London banks, and forty-four country banks for which Poles's were the correspondents. Despite these events, the panic in London started to abate, and, though the panic in the provinces at first got worse, the whole country had calmed down by the end of the week.

Bagehot was later to describe the panic as so tremendous that its consequences were well remembered after nearly fifty years. The Bank had come within an ace of failure,[24] and in Lord Bentinck's colourful phrase, the country had come 'within twenty-four hours of barter' (Powell 1915: 330). The 'wreckage was already frightful', and by the end of the year seventy-three leading English banks had suspended – many of them never to resume business – while the next year was a year of extraordinarily high business bankruptcies (Clapham 1944: 102, 109). The toll that it took on the participants can be gauged from another comment of Richards, the deputy governor, that after it was over 'those who had been busied in that terrible scene could recollect that they had families who had some claim upon their attention. It happened to me not to see my children for that week' (quoted in Powell 1915: 330–1).

The crisis gave rise to considerable controversy, and the government determined to legislate.[25] Two Acts resulted. The first, in March 1826, forbade banks to issue any new notes under £5, and to reissue any such notes after 5 April 1829 (Clapham 1944: 106). The banning of small notes reflected a widespread opinion that the issue of small notes had been a major contributory factor to the commercial crisis (MacLeod 1896: 126). The second Act, in May 1826, authorized the formation of joint-stock banks with the right to note issue, provided they had no office within sixty-five miles of London (Clapham 1944: 107). The court of the Bank disliked this, but could do nothing about it (Clapham 1944: 105). This Act also encouraged the Bank to set up branches in the country by giving it explicit authorization to do so.[26] The Bank proceeded to set up branches in the provinces, but it is worth noting that it took government prompting and the threat of competition to make it do so.

THE BANK CHARTER ACT, 1833

In 1832 a parliamentary committee of inquiry was set up to examine the Bank's charter, which was due to expire the next year.[27] One of the key issues in the discussions was how far the Bank should pass up profit opportunities to promote the wider interest. There seemed to be a large body of opinion that the Bank's responsibilities were greater than those of an ordinary bank, but there was no agreement as to what they were. As Fetter (1965: 152) writes, the Bank:

> was a monopoly, but it was not clear either to Government, the public, or the management and the stockholders of the Bank whether the price that it paid for that monopoly was simply the direct services rendered to Government, or whether it had a larger responsibility to the banking community, and even to the whole economy. The answers to these questions, ever present though rarely stated directly, were made increasingly complex by the shift in public opinion, gathering strength in the 1820's and reaching high tide in the 1850's, that anything savoring of monopoly, of state direction, even of action that was not directed to the maximizing of profit, was undesirable. It is no wonder that in such a situation there was no clear and consistent opinion about the Bank's responsibilities . . .

The parliamentary inquiry led to the 1833 Bank Charter Act, the main features of which were as follows:

1. The Bank's charter was renewed until 1855, with the proviso that the government had the right to suspend it after twelve years.

2. Bank notes were to become legal tender, except at the Bank itself. This measure was intended to protect the Bank's gold reserves against internal drains by making it legally possible for other banks to satisfy demands for redemption without the need to draw gold from the Bank.

3. The Act affirmed the legality throughout England and Wales of joint-stock banks that did not issue notes, i.e. the Bank's joint-stock monopoly was explicitly restricted to note-issue banking. This measure thus eliminated the uncertainty that had surrounded the legality of non-note-issuing joint-stock banks in London. The Chancellor, Lord Althorp, rejected the Bank's appeal to have its joint-stock monopoly extended to cover deposit banks (MacLeod 1896: 49).

4. At the Bank's request, bills of exchange and promissory notes with no more than three months to run were freed from the usury laws that restricted interest rates to a maximum of 5 per cent.[28] This was highly significant, because it gave the Bank free rein to use its discount rate to protect its reserve.

5. The Bank was to furnish the Exchequer with weekly returns regarding the amount of its bullion and its note circulation and deposits, and the monthly averages were to be published each quarter in the *London Gazette* (Andrèades 1909: 262; Dodwell 1934: 58). There was a gradual increase in the early nineteenth century in the amount of information the Bank was required to furnish,[29] which appears to indicate a 'growing recognition of its special position and public responsibility' (Dodwell 1934: 58).

THE PALMER RULE AND THE BANK CHARTER ACT OF 1844

The 1832 inquiry witnessed the first public explanation of a rule of thumb that the Bank claimed to have been following since 1827 (Viner 1937: 224). This was the famous 'Palmer rule', according to which the Bank sought to maintain a gold reserve ratio of one-third against the sum of its note and deposit liabilities. The other two-thirds of the Bank's assets would be its holding of securities, and the underlying idea was that outside exceptional circumstances which might require the use of Bank 'discretion', the volume of securities should be held constant. A fall in reserves would then be self-correcting: the fall in reserves would lead to a reduced money supply, lower prices, restoration of the exchanges, and an influx of gold.[30] The Bank's attempts to follow the rule were not particularly successful, however, and the rule was frequently breached in practice because the Bank was unable to 'fine-tune' its reserves or its liabilities to the degree that it seemed to require.[31]

An interesting question is why the Bank management chose to submit themselves to the discipline of something like the Palmer rule. One explanation is that they genuinely believed that the Bank's 'optimal policy' was to follow the 'right' simple rule, and at the time believed that the Palmer rule was the right one.[32] Another explanation, not entirely inconsistent with the first, is that they believed that a rule would give them some protection against criticism of their policies. To the extent that they could persuade their shareholders that the rule was 'right', they had a defence against the criticism that they should be doing more to increase profits instead; to the extent that they could persuade Parliament and the public, they had a defence against the charge of monetary mismanagement which was often levied at the Bank, and which was dangerous to the Bank because of the possibility that it might lead to legislative intervention to curtail its power or privileges.[33]

The monetary disturbances of 1836–9 and the continued controversy over the Bank's policies led to suggestions for a new rule that proponents claimed would eliminate the main source of monetary instability. This rule – the currency principle – was apparently first set out by Loyd (1837).[34] The idea was to give the Bank (or a government bank) a monopoly of the note issue, but with a 100 per cent reserve requirement, and leave the Bank in all other respects free. The currency principle was based on the notion that monetary disturbances were due to the over-issue of notes, and could be eliminated if the currency issue was made to behave as if it were purely metallic. By this stage the inadequacies of the Palmer rule were becoming obvious, and the Bank management were sensitive to the claim of the currency school that it was an inappropriate rule to follow. The management would also have been aware that the Palmer rule could provide them with little defence against criticism if they were unable to adhere to it in practice. Far from protecting them, the Palmer rule had left the Bank management open to the additional charge of incompetence in failing to meet their own stated objectives. The doctrines of the currency school seemed to offer the Bank a solution to these problems, and the Bank management soon embraced them.[35]

In January 1844 the governor and deputy governor of the Bank submitted a memorandum to the Prime Minister, Peel, that contained what were to become the major provisions of the 1844 Bank Charter Act. Peel was a supporter of the currency school,[36] and, having realized that the ideas he was moving towards were already in the minds of the Bank management, he seized on their suggestions and had little difficulty persuading the Cabinet to go along with him. The result was the Bank Charter Act, passed later in the year. The Act separated the Bank into an Issue Department, responsible for the note issue, and a Banking Department responsible for everything else. The Issue Department was obliged to observe a 100 per cent marginal reserve requirement, and the Banking Department was left free to do as it wished. In addition, the note issues of other banks were to be frozen, so that the Bank now had an effective monopoly of the English note issue.[37]

One of the most important consequences of the Act was that it encouraged the directors to believe that it freed them of any responsibility towards the rest of the banking system (Dodwell 1934: 62–3). The Bank had surrendered its freedom over the note issue in return for what many of the directors would have seen as a confirmation of its freedom over the rest of its business.[38] As Hawtrey (1938: 20) observed, 'pushed to its logical conclusion', the Act:

> meant that the Bank would no longer undertake to be the lender of last resort. It would be free, on the one hand, to refuse to discount bills beyond such limit as seemed convenient, and, on the other, to get its share of the discounting business of the market, and for that purpose to offer to discount bills at a competitive rate.

THE CRISES OF 1847, 1857 AND 1866

The critics of the currency school had always claimed that its recommendations would not prevent crisis, and it was not long before they were proved right. The disastrous potato crops of 1845 and 1846 had given rise to large exports of gold to pay for imports of corn. The Bank's gold reserves fell, and a rise of discount rate to 3½ per cent in January did nothing to stop the outflow. Bank rate was raised to 5 per cent in April, when the Banking Department's reserve had fallen to just over £2½ million. The market then panicked, the Bank rationed its discounts, and the market discount rate rose to 10 per cent or 12 per cent. At this point gold started to come into the Bank's reserve again, and the market calmed down. Later in the year, however, a series of failures led to renewed apprehension and further falls in the Bank's reserve. In October the Bank raised its discount rate to 5½ per cent and again rationed its discounts. The market panicked again, and this time some of the banks began to fail.

The City clamoured for the suspension of the 1844 Act to enable the Bank to issue extra notes. Powell (1915: 363) reports the bankers' appeal to the Chancellor, Sir Charles Wood: 'Let us have notes. We don't mean, indeed, to take the notes, because we shall not want them; only tell us that we can get them, and this will at once restore confidence.' The government held out for a while, but at last gave in. On Saturday 23 October the government informed the Bank that a Bill of Indemnity would be presented to Parliament should the Bank issue notes in excess of those allowed under the 1844 Act. As a condition the Bank was to raise discount rate to 8 per cent. The publication of the government letter the next Monday instantly abated the panic.

> The certainty that money could be got took away all desire to have it. The Bank prepared . . . additional notes, but there was no need to use them. Notes which had been hoarded under the impression that the limit fixed by the Act of 1844 would shortly be reached, and that the Bank would be unable to assist the commercial world, were brought out in a mass from their hiding places; the same thing happened with regard to gold.[39]
>
> (Andrèades 1909: 336–7)

Another crisis occurred in October 1857. It appears to have been precipitated by a crisis in the United States which provoked a series of failures among British firms with large American investments. The Bank responded by steadily increasing Bank rate and lending extensively, but its reserve fell sharply. By the evening of 12 November its reserve had fallen to only £384,144. With bankers' balances alone of over £5 million, the governor afterwards acknowledged that 'the Bank could not have kept its doors open an hour [more]' (MacLeod 1896: 161). With 'universal ruin . . . at last impending', the government sent a letter to the Bank indicating that it was prepared to present a Bill of Indemnity to release the Bank from the note restrictions of the Bank Charter Act, the relaxation to operate for as long as the discount rate was at least 10 per cent (p. 160). As in 1847, 'the public alarm was at once abated', but this time high demand for discounts continued for more than a fortnight (Andrèades 1909: 349). Unlike 1847, the Bank Charter Act was actually breached, and the Bank issued an additional £2 million of notes in excess of the 1844 limit, although the amount of these notes in circulation never reached £1 million.[40]

A third crisis occurred in 1866. A series of failures in early 1866 had produced an atmosphere of mounting alarm. Then on Wednesday 9 May a judgement was delivered to the effect that certain bills held by the great broking firm of Overend Gurney were worthless. There was already considerable public concern about Overend's, and the firm had not the resources to withstand a major run. It therefore appealed to the Bank for assistance, but was refused a loan because it could not meet the Bank's demands for security, and the firm suspended at the end of the next day (10 May). The market opened on Friday to complete panic: there was a wild rush to sell virtually anything for notes, and asset prices plummeted. As Powell later wrote, that was a day 'of tragic memory, even at the distance of half a century' (1915: 401). That evening the Chancellor announced to Parliament that, following the earlier precedents, the government would bring in a Bill to indemnify the Bank if the Bank thought it proper to exceed the note limits specified by the 1844 Act.[41]

The Chancellor's announcement had 'such an effect that the next day the crisis seemed to be at an end' (Andrèades 1909: 359). Once again, the knowledge that the Bank had the power to issue the extra notes was sufficient to abate the panic, and in the event no additional notes needed to be issued. None the less the demand for discounts continued to be considerable – the Bank made over £12 million in discounts over the next week – a number of failures occurred the week after Black Friday, and Bank rate remained at 10 per cent until early August. After that, however, the markets returned to normal and the crisis was followed by a comparatively long period of calm.[42]

It is highly significant that each of the last three panics was cured by a promise to relax the note restrictions of the Bank Charter Act. Each panic was a panic for notes – an excess demand, in other words, to convert one form of bank liability into another – and the panic abated as soon as it became clear that the notes could be obtained. At no point was the gold standard itself in danger – the danger was always that the Banking Department would default while the Issue Department remained full of gold which it could neither lend out nor issue notes against. It is therefore difficult to avoid the conclusion that, whatever the shocks that triggered off the panics, it was the note restrictions that converted those shocks into crises. The situation was somewhat different in 1825, but even then the main demand was to get rid of country bank notes, and most of those who wanted to do that would have been happy to take Bank of England notes if they could have got them. As in the crises of 1847, 1857 and 1866, it was the unwillingness to meet the demand for Bank notes that really fed the panic, and the panic subsided once people became convinced that Bank notes could be got. There is much truth in MacLeod's assessment:

> Monetary panics, in this country at least, have been invariably produced by bad banking legislation, or by bad management of the Bank of England, sometimes by both. Monetary panics are therefore . . . avoidable.
>
> (1896: 95)

BAGEHOT AND HANKEY

The 1866 crisis led to renewed controversy over the role of the Bank in financial crises. On 22 September Walter Bagehot published an article in *The Economist* in which he wrote that the Bank had used its reserves well to support the market, and that in a recent speech the governor, David Salomons, had to all intents and purposes admitted the Bank's responsibility towards the market.[43] The view that the Bank should support the market by lending freely in a crisis was accepted opinion in the City,[44] had the support of a number of leading economists,[45] and had considerable support even in the court of the Bank itself.[46]

The following year one of the Bank directors, Thomson Hankey, published a stinging attack on Bagehot's views in his book *The Principles of Banking*. He denounced the Bagehot view that the Bank had a responsibility to support the market in a crisis as the 'the most mischievous [doctrine] ever broached', and he saw no hope for sound banking till it was 'repudiated' (quoted in Clapham 1944: 284). He claimed to be reiterating the opinion of the framers of the 1844 Act, and suggested that Peel's statement that the Banking Department should be 'governed on precisely the same principles as would regulate any other body dealing with Bank of England Notes' (ibid.) could be interpreted only in this light. Hankey was supported by another bank director, George Warde Norman, who supported him because he wished to make the other banks hold greater reserves. Hankey's argument can be summarized as follows.

1. The Bank's only responsibility was to its shareholders.

2. In a crisis the Bank should bear its full share of the pressure – Timberlake (1978: 218) calls this the 'fair share' doctrine – but it had no responsibility to support the market as a whole.

3. The admission by the Bank of a responsibility to support the

market would create a moral hazard problem – the other banks would reduce their reserves in the knowledge that they could obtain support from the Bank of England and thereby increase the pressure on the Bank to provide that support in a crisis.

4. A policy of supporting the market would require someone with the discretion to authorize its use, and a clearly recognizable signal for taking action.

Bagehot countered in *The Economist*, and then in *Lombard Street* (1873). In principle, he felt that the best system – the 'natural' one – was a system of multiple reserve banks, of not altogether unequal size, but he felt that it would be pointless to propose such a system in the circumstances of the day. He therefore set himself the task of making the existing system work as well as it could, and that meant giving the Bank suitable guidelines to follow.

Bagehot recommended that in normal times (i.e. outside a panic) the Bank should seek to protect its reserves and, if necessary, augment it. More specifically, he suggested that the Bank should aim to prevent its reserve from ever falling below £11 million to £11½ million, and should take measures to protect its reserve whenever it fell below an 'apprehension minimum'; of £15 million. This recommendation implied a significant increase in the Bank's reserve[47] and, therefore, a reduction in its profits.

During a panic, however, the Bank should pursue an expansionary policy:

1. The reserve should be advanced freely and promptly, but at a high interest rate. This penalty rate would encourage gold imports, reduce precautionary balances, 'operate as a heavy fine on unreasonable timidity' and ration the scarce gold reserve. The penalty rate would also provide a test of the soundness of distressed borrowers and, provided it was kept above the market rate, it would make them go to the market before they went to the Bank.

To stop the panic, 'it is necessary . . . to diffuse the impression that though money may be dear, still money is to be had'. If people could be persuaded that they could get money, albeit at a price, then they would cease to demand money in such a mad way. The policy of lending freely was recommended not because it would guarantee the safety of the Bank and the rest of the monetary system but because it gave them the best chance of surviving it: 'The only safe plan for the Bank is the brave plan . . . This policy may not save the Bank; but if it does not, nothing will save it' (1906: 220–1).

2. In lending, the Bank should make advances on securities that would be considered good under normal conditions.

3. The Bank should support the market but not specific institutions as such. Individual institutions – even large ones – should be allowed to fail.

4. The Bank's support policy ought to be clearly announced in advance. To make loans otherwise was 'to incur the evil of making them without obtaining the advantage', since people would be inclined to run if they were in any doubt about whether the Bank would support the market. A problem with the Bank, wrote Bagehot, was that it:

'has never laid down any clearly sound policy on the subject . . . The public is never sure what policy will be adopted at the most important moment; it is not sure what amount of advance will be made, or on what security it will be made . . . until we have on this point a clear understanding with the Bank of England, both our liability for crises and our terror at crises will always be greater than they otherwise would be' (1962: 101). Bagehot went on to criticize Hankey, who 'leaves us in doubt altogether as to what will be the policy of the Bank of England in the next panic, and as to what amount of aid the public may then expect from it' (1906: 175).

Though it came to be widely accepted, there are a number of serious problems with Bagehot's analysis:

1. There was an obvious conflict between the advice to protect the reserve and the advice to lend freely.[48] Bagehot tried to resolve it by suggesting that the Bank should protect the reserve in normal times and lend in a panic, but this requires the Bank to distinguish in practice between cases of genuine panic and cases of mere market apprehension. As Rockoff (1986) observes, Bagehot's schema makes everything depend on the Bank's psychoanalysis of the market, but he gave the Bank no advice to enable it to distinguish between the two cases. This gave rise to twin dangers: on the one hand, the Bank might mistake market apprehension for real panic and lend freely, in which case its falling reserve might increase market apprehension and either provoke a panic or leave the Bank in a weakened position to deal with a panic if one should break out; on the other hand, if the Bank mistook a real panic for mere apprehension and did nothing to counter it, the panic could well intensify, and possibly get out of control.

2. It was also far from clear that Bagehot's advice would have

helped in some past crises. Rockoff (1986: 169–72) plausibly suggests that the Bank had no way of knowing when apprehension turned to real panic in 1839 and 1847, and points out that the Bank's attempts in 1857 to lend freely on Bagehot's lines were not enough to stem the panic. He goes on to suggest that only the panic of 1866 seems to fit at all easily into Bagehot's schema: 'one cannot help thinking that his theory was essentially a generalisation of this experience' and that 'despite Bagehot's jamming and pushing not all of [the earlier crises] can be made to fit into the 1866 mould' (1986: 172).

3. A common criticism of Bagehot is that the lender of last resort function he proposed would create a problem of moral hazard. If the banks can count on the support of the Bank in a crisis, they will rationally take more risks and hold fewer reserves than they would otherwise have chosen to do. This point was raised by Hankey, of course, and Bagehot did little to answer it beyond claiming that the other banks were already counting on the Bank's support anyway.

4. A fourth criticism is that Bagehot really had no solution to the problem of the Bank's inadequate reserves beyond telling the Bank that it ought to hold more.[49] He also failed to appreciate the extent to which the problem of the reserve and the problem of discount rate policy were really different aspects of the same problem (see next section), and he failed to anticipate the ultimate solution adopted by the Bank: 'a powerful Bank Rate weapon with a "thin film of gold" ' (Sayers 1958: 18).[50]

THE DEVELOPMENT OF BANK RATE POLICY

One cannot understand the development of the Bank's reserve and lender of last resort policies without also examining the more or less concurrent development of Bank rate policy. These policies were intimately linked. As Sayers (1958: 10) observed:

> Oddly enough, arguments about the need for a stronger Bank Rate policy and about the need for a bigger reserve run parallel in many of the discussions throughout this period, and there seems to have been little realization that the two lines of attack were alternatives, in the sense that a bigger reserve implied less need for a flexible Bank Rate, and more effective use of Bank Rate made a big reserve less necessary.

The policy of using discount rate to manipulate the Bank's gold reserves can be traced to the provision of the 1833 Bank Charter Act which freed the Bank from the impact of the usury laws.[51] A high Bank rate worked by attracting gold to London from abroad and from domestic circulation, and a higher Bank rate was used to protect (and augment) the Bank's reserve when it was running low. The typical scenario was where a shortage of notes would lead to country and foreign bankers drawing on their London correspondents, who in turn would draw on the discount houses in London. The discount houses would then withdraw (or borrow) from the Banking Department of the Bank, whose reserve would fall. At some point the Bank would stop and then reverse the fall in its reserve by raising its discount rate. When 'the Bank did act firmly, it got quick results because the gold reserve was in this period extremely responsive to changes in market rate' (Sayers 1958: 13). Sayers goes on to suggest three reasons for this responsiveness: (1) high rates would draw gold from the country banks, an effect which was particularly strong in the third quarter of the century; (2) London's foreign lending was large and very interest-sensitive; (3) the world's stock of gold was rising for much of this period, and London was well placed to tap it.

Bank rate was first actively used in 1839,[52] when it was raised to protect the Bank's dwindling reserve. After 1844 it was used more often, and more vigorously, but even then it was usually used with a certain reluctance. Apart from exposing the Bank to sometimes severe public criticism, the use of Bank rate was also expensive. The cost arose because the Bank sometimes felt obliged to engage in open market operations to make its Bank rate policy effective.[53] The costs arose not just because the execution of these policies used up resources (e.g. the Bank had to pay interest on funds it borrowed) but also because they created opportunities for arbitrage profits at the Bank's expense.[54] As a consequence, when the Bank's responsibility 'clearly called for' such operations, the Bank 'did bear the expense, but it did it grudgingly' (Sayers 1958: 12), and as 'the situation was often not clear . . . doubts in diagnosis too often provided the excuse for delay in action' (ibid.). Losses also arose because for a long time the Bank insisted on discounting for its regular customers at Bank rate, and as this was almost always above market rate the consequence was a steady loss of its regular discount business.[55] Because of these costs, the use of Bank rate policy and open market operations was kept to a minimum, and in normal times Bank rate tended to follow the market rate rather than the other way round (Sayers 1958: 12).

An additional influence on the Bank's discount policy was its concern that the joint-stock banks – its commercial rivals – were able to cut down their reserves by relying on the discount houses (and indirectly on the Bank) to provide them with funds if they needed them. This created a moral hazard problem and meant that the Bank was indirectly subsidizing its commercial competitors. The Bank responded to these problems by adopting the '1858 rule' by which it retreated from day-to-day operations in the discount market. In doing so the Bank effectively served notice to the discount market that it must stand on its own feet. The 1858 rule was an indication of the Bank's willingness (sometimes, at least) to sacrifice its own profits to secure other ends – in this case, to force the joint-stock banks to be more prudent. It therefore marks an important step along the Bank's development from a profit-making 'private' bank to a 'central bank' less concerned with its own profits and more concerned with 'broader' objectives relating to the banking system generally. The rule was subsequently modified in 1878 and 1883 before being abolished in June 1890.[56] By then, of course, the transition to 'central bank' was much more complete.

The history of Bank rate policy in this period can be considered as a series

> of alternating periods of stringency and ease, each usually extending over some years. In a period of stringency recurrent applications of dear money are needed to correct a persistent tendency of the reserve to fall below the prudent limit... At last the corner is turned, possibly at the cost of a financial crisis. There follows a period of ease, when the reserve grows bigger and bigger in spite of cheap money. Presently currency begins to pass into circulation again, but cheap money continues with little interruption so long as the reserve, though falling, remains above the prudent level.
>
> (Hawtrey 1938: 46)

The reserve eventually falls below the prudent level, dear money is needed again, and the cycle repeats itself.

In 1878 the Bank announced that it would discount for its regular customers at market rate, irrespective of Bank rate, and that it would always be willing to lend on approved security at a penal rate to everyone else. The effect was to put the Bank's customers on the same level as the rest of the market and protect the Bank from further loss of business. The readiness of the Bank to borrow in the market meant that the market would never get too independent of the Bank (and vice versa), but the market could now rely on the Bank's assistance (at the penal rate) at any time.

> The technique had thus attained a textbook simplicity: Bank Rate was a penal rate, not applicable to the Bank's ordinary customers; [and] the market's knowledge that the Bank would ordinarily operate at this penal rate made it ready to operate on a pretty narrow margin of funds, so that the position of the penal rate was *ordinarily* a matter of daily concern and therefore influential over market rate itself.
>
> (Sayers 1958: 16–17).[57]

THE CONSOLIDATION OF BANK POWER

One of the most interesting and least discussed issues in the late nineteenth century was how the Bank's influence over the monetary system seemed to increase, and this despite the fact that the growth of the big joint-stock banks meant that the Bank's relative financial strength – as measured by its share of the discount business, or its size relative to the big joint-stock banks – was diminishing. Even if it had contributed to it in the past, its relative financial strength was no longer particularly important to the Bank's power over the monetary system. The source of that power, as discussed earlier, was the Bank's control over the banks' redemption media, and that control was well established by the time the Bank resumed specie payments in 1821. In addition, however, the Bank had to be ready to use that power, which in practice meant it had to be willing to sacrifice its profits (e.g. by engaging in open market operations and using Bank rate). As time went by its doubts about making those sacrifices seemed to diminish, and its influence in the market increased.

It is important to stress that the Bank's influence did not rest on any legislation which specifically compelled the other banks to use Bank liabilities as their reserves. Legislation had established the basis of the Bank's power by granting the Bank its earlier privileges, but its hegemony then evolved in the environment that the legislation did so much to create. In our earlier discussion we specifically mentioned the restrictions which weakened the banking system and prevented it from protecting itself against crises. We also mentioned the role played in the Restriction period by legal tender, the Bank's power to intimidate other banks, and the depreciation of Bank notes, which called Gresham's law into operation to drive the 'good money' – i.e. gold – out of banks' reserves. The return to gold in 1821 put some gold back into banks' reserves, but it did not restore the *status quo ante bellum*. The question then arises: given that they were under no legal obligation to use Bank liabilities as reserves, why did individual banks continue to use them when the price, in effect, was their own independence?

The banks appear to have accepted the Bank's supremacy for several reasons. One of them was the extreme difficulty of finding an alternative redemption medium to the Bank's notes that the public would be willing to accept. The Bank note had the twin advantages that it was familiar and that it was issued by the most secure bank in the land. It would have been very difficult to match these advantages while Bank notes were still available, and the only way to remove them from circulation would have been to destroy the Bank itself (e.g. by organizing a collective withdrawal of deposits in the hope of making the Bank default). An attempt to do that would have risked a major crisis, however, and even if it succeeded in causing the Bank difficulties it is more than likely that the government would have intervened to support it. Also, as Fetter (1965: 270) observed:

> it would have been necessary for the London bankers to present a united front. That would have meant civil war in the City, and even those who thought that rebellion would succeed might still question whether the fruits of victory would equal the costs ... Leaders of threatened revolts rarely advertise their intentions openly, and one might expect this to be particularly true with gentlemen of the City of London. Only a little appeared in print, but what did would indicate that at various times the problem had been raised in private discussions.

The leader of a prospective *coup* would have faced an awesome task establishing a united front, and the very considerable danger that the Bank would find out what was afoot and make an example of him by launching a pre-emptive attack before he was ready. In any case, the primary responsibility of the other banks was to their shareholders, and that responsibility would have given them relatively little leeway to engage in dubious attempts to stir up a revolution. One must also bear in mind that many managements would have felt some degree of goodwill towards the Bank for supporting them in past crises, and the Bank itself hardly seemed like an overbearing tyrant. There was therefore never any real possibility of a serious challenge to the Bank.

THE BARING CRISIS[58]

In 1890 there occurred the most significant crisis since Overend Gurney. There had been a great deal of speculative British investment in Argentina, but the situation there deteriorated and gave rise to mounting anxiety about the soundness of some of the British finance houses that were involved. Against this background, on 8 November;

> the appalling intelligence was made known to the governor . . . that [the] great house [of Baring Brothers] was in the extremest danger of stopping payment, . . . and that the most energetic measures must be taken without a moment's delay to avert the catastrophe.
>
> (MacLeod 1896: 167)

The governor's response was swift and effective: he called a meeting of the managers of the leading banks and City firms, and 'persuaded' them to participate in a fund to guarantee Baring's liabilities. The Bank itself would provide for the firm's immediate obligations, and arranged for credits from Russia and France. The settlement was publicly announced and the market instantly calmed down.

The Baring affair was remarkable in a number of respects. Unlike earlier crises, it was very localized and it was resolved almost before the market knew that there was anything going on. The governor broke with precedent by refusing to raise Bank rate beyond 6 per cent, and he refused the offer of a suspension of the Bank Charter Act. He also broke with Bagehot by arranging a rescue package for a specific institution, and came up with a solution – a collective guarantee, with the other parties cajoled into participating – that Bagehot had not foreseen. In effect he abandoned all precedent – and Bagehot's advice – by arranging an intervention package to pre-empt the crisis, and he entirely succeeded. The crisis was averted, and the contributors to the guarantee fund lost nothing in the end.

The Baring episode is also very interesting in that it revealed the extent of the Bank's influence over the rest of the financial system, and the governor's readiness to use it:

> There is a City tradition that one of the joint-stock banks . . . endeavoured to evade its share in the agreement to refrain from calling in its loans . . . The matter was brought to the attention of [the governor] Mr. Lidderdale, who, with characteristic decision, sent for the manager and informed him that if the bank did not adhere loyally to the agreement he would close its account at the Bank of England and announce the fact in the evening newspapers. He is said to have given the manager an hour to make up his mind. It would be superfluous to add what the manager's decision was.
>
> (Powell 1915: 526–7)

CONCLUSION: BRITISH CENTRAL BANKING IN THE 1890s

By 1890 a distinctive system of central banking had evolved in Britain. Its origins went back to earlier centuries, but some of its key features had evolved only more recently. The developments of the previous eighty years can be summarized in three principles:

1. The Bank had a responsibility to support the market, and this responsibility was by now accepted at the Bank itself.[59] In addition, a tradition[60] had grown up on the question of how the Bank should discharge that responsibility.

2. There was no longer any doubt about the Bank's hegemony over the banking system, and the other banks had accommodated themselves to it.

3. It was more or less understood that the Bank's private interests (i.e. its profits) now had to take second place to its broader responsibilities to the monetary system.[61] Though it was never made explicit, this was the price the Bank had to pay for its supremacy.

In these respects the British system of central banking in 1890 was not dissimilar from what it is a hundred years later. However, two other principles also underlay the post-Baring regime that make that regime quite different from English central banking in the late twentieth century – the commitment to the gold standard, and the freedom of deposit banking from regulation. There is a strong case that it was these principles that made the system more stable then than it is today, but this is not the place to pursue that particular theme. In any case, how those principles were abandoned and what happened when they were is another long story – the story of the twentieth-century central banking.

Chapter 12

The evolution of central banking in England: a reply to my critics

I have often been puzzled by the uncritical devotion of the English to the Bank of England, and I am not at all surprised by the outrage provoked by my challenge to one of their favourite tribal totems. One gets a friendlier response if one suggests abolishing the government or legalizing heroin. If Leslie Pressnell was right when he observed at the conference that all true Englishmen support the Bank, then I can only point to my Irish extraction and trust that true Englishmen will understand. However, I hasten to add that I am not against the Bank only because the English are in favour of it – I oppose the Bank (in part) because I think it is damned by its own history. I did not expect my discussants to share that view, but I certainly did not expect the largely uncomprehending hostility shown in their comments, and I am frankly amazed at the gulf between what they think I wrote and what I actually did.

Let me begin with Dr Collins. His most serious problem is that the first of his two propositions summarizing my thesis – 'that central banking did *not* evolve to counter market instability' is simply *not* a correct statement of my position. As far as I know, no one really denies that central banking evolved, in part at least, to counter market instability – I certainly never have – and Collins might just as well have saved himself the bother of attacking a position that no one defends. What I do deny – and this point is crucial to my whole argument – is that central banking evolved as a response to the *inherent* instability of the (free) market. The distinction between the market as it actually was and the market as it would have been in the absence of state restrictions is crucial, and Collins ignores it even though it is quite clear in the paper [i.e. chapter 11]. Dr Collins seems to believe that the distinction does not apply to the English financial system in this period. He is certainly entitled to his opinion, but he creates serious problems for himself by refusing to acknowledge that I draw such a distinction, and he ends up attacking me for adhering to a position that I repudiated myself. In the meantime my real position remains unchallenged – that there would have been stability under *laissez-faire* – and Collins has inadvertently conceded my case by default.

His misinterpretation of my position also leads him to attribute to me a number of other claims that I have never endorsed. For example, he claims that I '[do] not acknowledge' that many interventions were 'responses to instability either as immediate measures or after a period of considered ... debate'. Yet I *do* acknowledge this point, and chapter 11 makes this acknowledgement clear (e.g. in the discussion of the 1844 Act). Similarly, he states that 'In the real, historical world there was market instability and this did provoke political response; and it did affect how the Bank of England developed as a central bank' as if I had somehow denied it. I did not.

Let me now turn to the second proposition he attributes to me – 'that legislative restrictions were major contributory factors in the liquidity crises of the mid-nineteenth century'. Unlike his previous one, this *is* a good statement of my position. But, having stated my position correctly, Collins then makes a string of claims that purport to be criticisms but actually have little bearing on it. He notes, for instance, that, apart from the six-partner rule and the note restrictions, 'the system in the early 1820s was exceptionally free from regulation'. I would not argue with this assessment, and there is nothing in the chapter to disagree with it. He also points out that the abolition of the six-partner rule 'was no magic wand' and 'did not induce an immediate transformation' in English banking, and that private banking 'remained an important sector in England and Wales for a very long time'. I would agree with all this too, but I fail to see what light it sheds on chapter 11.

Only then does he get on to more substantive issues. One is his denial of my claim that the increased demand for notes in liquidity crises should be used as (part of) an argument in favour of removing restrictions on private notes. The reason he gives is the 'opprobrium' attached to private notes in such circumstances, and he seems to agree – at the very least, he does not disagree – with the nineteenth-century interventionists who proposed to remedy the problem by establishing a note monopoly. The problem here is that Dr Collins does not ask himself *why* opprobrium was attached to private note issues but not to Bank of England issues in these situations. Collins seems to believe that this outcome was 'natural' to a 'free' market, but he simply takes this position for granted and makes no serious attempt to defend it. As far as I can see, Collins's position here is theoretically indefensible and is rejected by the experience of relatively unregulated note-issuing in countries like Scotland, Canada or Australia in the nineteenth century (see, for example, Schuler 1992; White 1984, 1990, 1991, 1992; Dowd 1992a). My own position is that the opprobrium resulted from legislative restrictions, and, therefore, that such opprobrium would not have arisen under a *laissez-faire* system. I would also point out that this claim seems to be consistent with the experiences of relatively free banking just mentioned (see also Selgin 1988 or Dowd 1989a).

Collins goes on to claim that, before 1844, 'restrictions [on non-Bank notes] were not in force, of course, but there were still bank runs in 1826, 1837 and 1839'. This claim is simply wrong. There *were* restrictions in that period – the only joint-stock bank of issue allowed to operate in the capital was the Bank of England – and the Bank had other privileges besides (e.g. the government's balances). He then reverts to making correct points of no relevance to chapter 11: 'Just as significant, there were liquidity crises after 1866 when the Bank Charter Act did not have to be suspended and the impact of its stipulations is not considered to have been important.' We both agree on this point, but I fail to see what it establishes. He concludes that 'History shows that crises arose, subsided, or were avoided during this period irrespective of whether the regulations of the 1844 Bank Charter Act were in operation.' This claim is also true, in my opinion, but no one blames all the monetary disturbances of the period on the 1844 Act alone.

One final point: Dr Collins writes that the evolution of central banking 'took place in a largely unregulated environment – one in which a *laissez-faire*, non-interventionist philosophy dominated'. A lot depends on what one means by 'largely unregulated', but I agree that the monetary system then may appear so by comparison with twentieth-century monetary systems. Regulations still remained, none the less, and they were significant. As for the dominance of *laissez-faire*, one has only to read Herbert Spencer to realize that *laissez-faire* thought was not as dominant then as many people think, and it was never dominant as regards the monetary system. The failure to accept *laissez-faire* in money and banking was an important reason why the monetary system could never quite shake itself free of state intervention, and why the English monetary system was not as stable as its less regulated counterparts elsewhere.

I also have a few comments to make on Bill Allen's assessment of chapter 11. After outlining my argument that there were two sources of regulatory restrictions on banking, Mr Allen suggests that the partnership restriction became less significant after it had been relaxed in 1826 – I could hardly disagree with this point – and then argues that he 'finds it hard to see [the partnership restriction] as a complete answer' because the 'crises did not come to an end'. My only defence is that I never took the position that is criticized. As far as I know, no one has blamed all the crises on the partnership restriction alone.

Shortly afterwards, he goes on to discuss the possibility of a loss of confidence among depositors, and makes the point that it is 'not credible that banks struggling with the consequences of a loss of confidence among their depositors could in those circumstances have issued additional notes to replace lost deposits'. Once again I can only agree. My defence – yet again – is that I never took the position criticized. What I *did* say is that there are circumstances in which excess demand for notes can lead to crises because of restrictions on supply, and it seems to me that the crises of 1847, 1857 and 1866 definitely fall into that category (as, more arguably, does that of 1825). Such situations can arise when there are restrictions on the note supply *even when there is no fundamental loss of confidence in the banks* (see also Selgin 1988).

He then accepts that 'it is not impossible to believe that restrictions on banks' note issues made the banking system somewhat less robust than it might otherwise have been'. I obviously agree with that. However, he adds that 'it requires a considerable leap in logic to get from this proposition to the quite different, and to me implausible, proposition that without the note restriction there would have been no crises at all, or very many fewer crises'. I fail to understand why Mr Allen finds the conclusion implausible. It is theoretically well grounded (see, for example, Selgin 1988, Dowd 1989a or White 1989; it is supported by the historical experience of relatively unregulated banking, such as that already mentioned; and the immediate abatement of the crises of 1847, 1857 and 1866 when it became clear that additional notes would be made available provides very strong supporting evidence for it. I emphasized this last point in the chapter but Allen ignores it.

My principal purpose in writing about the evolution of central banking in England was to show that English monetary experience in the nineteenth century was consistent with free banking theory and the lessons that free bankers have drawn from the experience of less regulated banking systems. In doing so it was important (1) to establish that there is no reason to believe that the free market would have been unstable, and (2) to establish that regulation had destabilizing effects on the banking system. My critics have failed to provide any effective challenge to these claims, and I see no reason whatever to revise them. *Hier stehe ich.*

Monetary and banking reform

Chapter 13

Stopping inflation

Inflation has ravaged the Australian economy for four decades. It has created so much uncertainty that sensible long-term planning is now virtually impossible. It has pushed up interest rates, and high interest rates in the last couple of years have devastated the business community and destroyed many businesses and jobs. Though inflation and interest rates have fallen over the past year or so, the continuation of current monetary growth rates of 6–7 per cent can only mean that they will start to rise again, and the whole cycle will then repeat itself. Inflation has also impoverished many people who lost substantial parts of their savings merely because they did not anticipate the effects that inflation would have on the assets in which they had invested. At the same time it has awarded large and often undeserved gains to those who were lucky or smart enough to load themselves up with debt that has subsequently lost its real value. This arbitrary redistribution of wealth has eroded both the security of property and the sense of fairness on which the market system depends if it is to function properly. Inflation also undermines the efficiency with which markets allocate resources. Markets start to malfunction because inflation injects noise into the signals about relative scarcities that market prices are supposed to provide. Inflation – both in Australia and abroad – has also created a climate of exchange rate uncertainty that penalizes those who engage in international trade, and makes us all worse off by restricting the international division of labour. Yet inflation provides no clearly established gains at all to set against these losses.

There is, therefore, a strong case that the elimination of inflation ought to be a major priority. However, not everyone agrees, and one continues to hear the argument that we should learn to live with inflation because reducing or eliminating it would be costly, perhaps excessively so. The usual argument is that reducing inflation would involve an increase in unemployment or a fall in output, but this argument needs to be examined carefully. Back in the 1960s Keynesians told us that the Phillips curve represented a trade-off that the government should use to find the 'right' mix of inflation and unemployment, and in practice that mix usually meant higher inflation and lower unemployment. Governments took their advice and the eventual result was soaring inflation in the early 1970s. Unemployment fell at first, but the 'gains' in unemployment that these policies produced turned out to be merely transitory, and the end result was both higher inflation and higher unemployment – a combination of misfortunes that the Keynesian theory of the Phillips curve predicted would never occur. The experience of the last twenty years has made it clear that our long-run choice is between higher inflation and lower inflation, period, and not between high inflation and high unemployment.

Some argue, none the less, that even if there is no long-run trade-off, the short-term costs of bringing inflation down are so high that we should think twice about trying to eliminate inflation outright, and this short-run Phillips curve theory still has many supporters. They argue that there is 'inertia' in the inflation process, and this inertia implies that we can bring inflation down substantially only by putting the economy through a painful and possibly quite long recession. The usual source of inertia is the sluggishness of inflationary expectations. Whatever the authorities do, it takes a while for private-sector inflationary expectations to adjust. If the government tightened its monetary policy, inflationary expectations would still remain high for a while. But if the government persisted with its new policy the private sector would eventually come to believe it and reduce its inflationary expectations, and only then would the recession begin to ease. Supporters of this view argue that this is exactly the kind of problem that governments face in practice – that there is no 'easy answer' to inflation – and point to a number of recent cases where they claim, governments have been able to disinflate only by putting the economy through a recession. A good case in point is said to be Britain in 1979–81, which went through a very severe recession when the Thatcher government tightened monetary policy in the months after it came into power in 1979.

The opposing position maintains that private-sector expectations are fundamentally rational (that is, people try to avoid mistakes in their forecasts), and if it is rational for people to change their inflationary expectations quickly, then they will do so. The key point is credibility. If a government promises to get tough on inflation but those in the private sector have no reason to believe it then they won't believe it and the government will be able to change private-sector views only by proving its determination the hard way – in other words, by demonstrating willingness to put the economy through a recession. According to this view, it was precisely because so many recent governments lacked credibility that they have had such difficulty bringing inflation down, and the UK recession of the early 1980s is a classic example. If the government has credibility, or can enact a set of measures that have credibility, then the private sector will believe it, inflationary expectations will fall, and inflation itself will fall without any significant unemployment side effects. Put another way, the traditional argument that bringing inflation down quickly would produce large amounts of unemployment in its wake is valid only on an other-things-being-equal basis. But it is not valid here, because the key factor usually held equal – inflationary expectations – adjusts very quickly to the 'right' change in policy regime, and the fall in inflationary expectations short-circuits the process that would produce the higher unemployment. The fact is that inflation can be reduced without major unemployment or lost output, *provided* the reform package is credible.

A MONETARY REFORM TO ELIMINATE INFLATION

Once the decision has been taken, there is a simple way to implement a credible monetary reform to eliminate inflation once and for all. The essential step is to redefine the Australian dollar in terms of a basket of goods which is chosen to keep prices stable. The reform would be straightforward to implement. The government would announce that the law was to be amended to state that the dollar had a value equivalent to that of a specific basket of commodities. Anyone issuing dollars (for example, the Reserve Bank of Australia) would be legally compelled to buy them back on demand with assets of the same value as the commodity basket that defined the dollar. The bank could 'buy back' its notes and deposits with financial instruments (such as shares), but which financial instruments it used for the purpose is not especially important, provided that the money issuer could not simply create those assets at will. (This stipulation is necessary to provide some discipline on the amount of currency the bank could create.) Inflation would then end because the commodity basket would have been chosen to produce a stable price level.

Inflation would also be eliminated very rapidly indeed. It would be impossible for inflation to continue once the reform had been implemented, because any 'excess money' created would be returned to the issuer before it could push prices up. (At the moment 'excess money' leads to inflation precisely because there is no mechanism to retire it from circulation.) In addition, the private sector would realize that inflation was gone – in other words, the reform would have credibility – and inflationary expectations would consequently drop rapidly to zero. This fall in inflationary expectations would then short-circuit the Phillips curve mechanism, which might otherwise have pushed the economy into recession, and so any significant side effects on unemployment should be avoided. The fall in inflationary expectations would also eliminate the inflationary premium that is currently built into interest rates, as lenders would no longer demand a premium to compensate them for inflation. Indeed, real interest rates – that is, roughly speaking, interest rates adjusted for expected inflation – would also fall. The new regime would eliminate a lot of current uncertainty about future market conditions, and thereby reduce the risk premiums that lenders currently need to induce them to lend. The fall in real and nominal interest rates would then push asset values up (in other words, increase wealth). It is true, of course, that ending inflation would inflict losses on those who had 'bet' on inflation continuing – those who took short positions on T bills, for example – but the higher asset prices that would result from the reform would imply that the losses would be more than offset by the gains.

This proposal would effectively restore a convertible currency, and lest we think that convertible currencies are somehow unusual, we should recall that they were the historical norm until the gold standard was abandoned earlier this century. Until 1914 the value of the currency was secured by its legal definition as a particular weight of gold and the right of the holder of a pound note to demand that an issuing bank should exchange it, at any time he wanted, for gold at the legally specified rate of exchange between gold and notes. (This was what the legend 'I promise to pay the bearer on demand the sum of one pound' actually meant. The pound was gold, and a 'pound note' was only a claim to a pound.) A compelling attraction of convertibility is that it disciplines the issuer of money. If ever banks issued too much currency, the public returned any 'excess' they did not want to the issuers, who were compelled to buy it back in exchange for gold. Another attraction of the gold standard was that the price level was comparatively stable (at least in the long run), because it was tied to the real value of gold. Banks stood ready to buy and sell pound notes for gold at a fixed rate of exchange, and that meant they were 'fixing' the price of gold (in terms of pound notes). Whenever the price of gold outside the banks deviated from the banks' own fixed price, there were profits to be made buying gold from the banks or selling gold to them, and the process of making these profits caused the price of gold outside the banks to return to the banks' fixed price. The price of gold therefore tended to be uniform throughout the gold standard world. And since the price of gold was fixed, the general price level could alter only when there were changes in the relative price of gold, and such changes were relatively limited. Prices did fluctuate a certain amount from year to year, but movements in the price level tended to cancel each other out over the long term, and prices in 1914 were about the same as they had been a hundred years before. Moreover, interest rates under the gold standard were by modern standards both low and comparatively stable.

The proposal advanced here is similar in many respects to the old gold standard, but there is one important difference. The price level under the gold standard was tied to the real value of gold, and so prices tended to fluctuate whenever there were changes in conditions in the gold market (for instance, there was some inflation in the 1850s following the discovery of gold in California and Australia). If the currency were tied to a wider basket of goods the price level would not fluctuate so much in respect of changes in the market conditions for any one good. A wider basket makes the price level more stable on a year-to-year basis, and we would choose the commodity basket in such a way that there would be no significant price-level changes at all. The proposed currency reform is similar to the old gold standard in that it would discipline the issue of money and ensure long-run price stability as well as low and relatively stable interest rates, but it would improve on the gold standard by delivering price stability in the short run as well.

SOME HISTORICAL PRECEDENTS

The idea that one can stabilize prices almost immediately is not some untried academic speculation. The historical evidence indicates that credible monetary reforms to restore convertible currencies can eliminate inflation very quickly indeed. Perhaps the most instructive examples occurred in Europe in the early 1920s. Hyperinflation was then rampant in much of eastern Europe, and a number of countries – Germany, Austria, Hungary and Poland – implemented radical monetary reforms which 'stopped [their] drastic inflations dead in their tracks' (Sergent 1981: 115). These reforms re-established the discipline of the gold standard, and reinforced that discipline by limiting or prohibiting the government's right to borrow from the banking system. In several cases the inflation ended virtually overnight, but in every case it was over well within a month. An earlier assessment of these experiences confirms this conclusion:

> Whoever studies the recent economic history of Europe is struck by a most surprising fact: the rapid monetary restoration of some countries where for several years paper money had continuously depreciated [i.e. inflated]. In some cases the stabilization of the exchange was not obtained by a continuous effort, prolonged over a period of years, whose effects would show themselves slowly in the progressive economic and financial restoration of the country . . . Instead, the passing from a period of tempestuous depreciation of the currency to an almost complete stabilization . . . was very sudden.
> (Bresciani-Turroni 1937: 334)

It is also interesting to note that these stabilization packages were not accompanied by the massive rises in unemployment that the traditional Phillips curve analysis would predict. Unemployment rose in Austria, but it was already rising there before the stabilization and one cannot tell whether all the post-stabilization rise in unemployment was due to the stabilization itself. There are no figures available for Hungary before price stabilization, but the absence of any substantial rise in unemployment after stabilization is certainly consistent with the view that there was no major unemployment 'after-shock' to the stabilization reform. In Poland unemployment actual fell for six months after the reform, and in Germany the stabilization was accompanied by increases in output and employment and decreases in unemployment. (Sargent 1981: chapter 3).

One sometimes meets the reaction that these experiences are 'so extreme and bizarre that they do not bear on the subject of inflation in contemporary countries' (Sargent 1981: 101). However, as Sargent continues:

> it is precisely because the events were so extreme that they are relevant. The four incidents we have studied are akin to laboratory experiments in which the elemental forces that cause and can be used to stop inflation are easiest to spot . . . these incidents are full of lessons about our own, less dramatic predicament with inflation, if only we interpret them correctly.
>
> (Sargent 1981: 101)

One might add, however, that there is one important respect in which these experiences differ from Australia's – apart from the obvious difference that their inflation was much higher. In each of the hyperinflating countries, nominal interest rates lagged far behind the prevailing rate of inflation. The real interest rate was therefore substantially negative, and the restoration of sound money implied a considerable jump in real interest rates back to positive levels. Contemporary observers saw this hike in real interest rates as a major force making for greater unemployment. In Germany, in particular, a large amount of investment had been undertaken on the basis of negative real interest rates which was no longer viable when real interest rates returned to more normal levels. A major capital restructuring had to take place after the stabilization which cost many German workers their jobs. In contemporary Australia, on the other hand, real interest rates are probably higher than their historical norm and they could be expected to fall if a price stabilization package were implemented. (Real interest rates would fall, if only because the premiums they bear for future uncertainty would be reduced. Nominal interest rates would fall even more because of the elimination of the inflation premium they currently bear.) So the principal difference between the historical hyperinflationary experience and Australia's now is that, in the former case, real interest rates rose while in Australia they would fall once the reform had been carried out.

The unemployment side effects, to the extent that there were any, would have been more severe in the historical cases than they would be in Australia. The fact that they were so small anyway gives us further reason to expect that Australia could implement a reform package like this without it producing a recession in the process.

In any case, the 1920s also saw two other episodes in which much more moderate inflation was ended by the same sort of radical monetary reform. One was the stabilization of the French franc in July 1926. France had been in crisis for some years past. French governments had been relying on anticipated reparations receipts to meet their future debts, and government finances deteriorated as it became clear in 1924 that these receipts would not materialize on the expected scale. The government consequently resorted more and more to lending from the banking system (in other words, printing money) and the franc depreciated at an accelerating rate. Then Raymond Poincaré was appointed Prime Minister in July 1926, and the franc suddenly stabilized on the foreign exchange markets. Inflation stopped equally dramatically. It was widely known that Poincaré would restore the gold standard, and the franc stabilized even before the French legislature had had time to enact his reform measures. In the following months he pursued a tight monetary policy, and the franc recovered ground against the dollar while domestic prices declined. The stabilization of the franc appeared to have no serious ill effects on output or employment, and was 'followed by several years of high prosperity' (Sargent 1981: 119). So once again prices were stabilized with few or no harmful side effects.

The other episode occurred in Czechoslovakia. When the Austro-Hungarian empire broke up at the end of the First World War the new states that emerged from it inherited the old empire's inflation – not to mention a mass of other chronic problems – but Czechoslovakia alone among them took measures to stabilize the currency before it degenerated into hyper-inflation. In February 1919 the National Assembly ordered the country's borders to be sealed and the foreign mail closed. Circulating Austro-Hungarian notes were then to be presented for stamping, and only stamped notes were to be recognized as Czech currency. Laws were also passed to limit government note circulation and prevent inflationary government finance. The effects of the reforms were clear and dramatic. The depreciation of the crown stopped, and the crown began to appreciate against gold. The initial intention had been to restore the pre-war parity of the crown against gold, but it was later decided to stabilize the crown at its current value. No figures appear to be available about unemployment, but histories of the time do not suggest that there were any major unemployment side effects.

COMMODITY STANDARD OR MONETARY TARGET?

A common objection to the kind of reform just proposed is that it is not necessary, and that much the same benefits can be achieved by the central bank adopting a monetary target that ensures that the money supply grows at a rate low enough to be compatible with stable prices. There are several basic objections to this argument. One is that the monetary target has room for error which the commodity price rule has not. The experience of monetary targeting over the last fifteen years has well illustrated the difficulties, technical and otherwise, of central banks hitting their monetary targets. Financial innovation, the variable and unpredictable lags in the time it takes policy to take effect, and the limited and often unreliable information on which the monetary authorities have to work – all undermine the effectiveness of traditional monetary targets. Monetary targets also tend to be relatively easy to discard when the state of the economy changes and the relevant authorities – the government or the central bank – come to regard them as inconvenient obstacles to monetary stimulus. It is, of course, possible to legislate a monetary (or price level) target, but some mechanism needs to be found to ensure that the central bank's performance is adequate. The problem then is that the most obvious institution to assess the bank's performance is the central bank itself, and the scheme is still open to tampering by its supposed guardians. There is also the problem that no such scheme ever implemented has delivered price stability even for a period as short as a few years. These problems undermine the credibility of the scheme and worsen the unemployment and lost output side effects of implementing it. Even if the scheme were implemented and brought inflation down, it would not be expected to last. Inflationary expectations would remain relatively high, and worse still, the monetary target would almost certainly collapse in the end.

CONCLUSION

A reform to eradicate inflation is probably the single most important economic measure the Australian government could implement, and the foundations of the economy will never be secure without it. It is essential that the private sector should have a stable and secure monetary framework within which to go about its business. A reform like this one would not only give the government a spectacular victory over inflation, but it would also reduce interest rates and probably produce higher output and lower unemployment as well. However, it requires that conventional ways of thinking be abandoned; and the authorities must be prepared to stop tinkering with the monetary system as they have been doing ever since the war ended. If the government really is serious about inflation, it must tackle the problem at its roots and commit itself to radical monetary reform. There is no alternative route to monetary stability.

Chapter 14

Does Europe need a Federal Reserve System?

Does Europe need a Federal Reserve System? During 1988 and 1989 this question went from being a completely academic one to being one of the most controversial issues of the day. In June 1988 the leaders of the European Community (EC) member governments agreed at their Hanover summit to form a committee under Jacques Delors, president of the European Commission, to investigate alternative routes to economic and monetary union and to recommend the most appropriate direction. The Delors report, submitted in April 1989, offered nothing less than a blueprint for a federal European superstate (see Delors 1989).[1] Apart from a radical centralization of fiscal powers, the report also recommended that the separate European national central banks should be merged into a new European central bank organized along Federal Reserve lines. To achieve this objective, the United Kingdom was first to join the Exchange Rate Mechanism (ERM) of the European Monetary System (EMS). The exchange rates of the EMS currencies would then be fixed irrevocably; the existing central banks would become part of a European version of the Federal Reserve system with a status much like that of the Federal Reserve banks in the United States, and the separate European currencies would be merged into one new currency.

This chapter offers a critical assessment of the proposal for a European central bank. Because the arguments for a central bank and monetary union are often run together, I will begin by looking at the costs and benefits of different forms of monetary union and will suggest that the argument for the extreme degree of monetary union implied by a common currency is dubious. Because one of the purposes of a European central bank would be to provide a common currency, these considerations indicate that the case for a European central bank is much weaker than is often appreciated. In any case, the costs and benefits of monetary union cannot be assessed in isolation, and it is especially important to establish whether or not the central bank would produce stable monetary conditions. I then investigate the likely relationship between the central bank and the EC and the impact of the EC's financial problems on central bank policy. It is very probable that substantial fiscal pressure would be brought to bear on the central bank, resulting in both higher inflation and a drive towards reregulating the European banking system. I will also consider America's experience with its Federal Reserve System. There is considerable evidence that the Fed has significantly destabilized the US economy, and there is reason to believe that a European Fed would do even worse.

There are some alternatives to a European central bank. One option is simply to continue with present EMS arrangements. While this option would leave Europe with some unnecessary monetary instability, it is none the less demonstrably superior to a European central bank. An even better alternative would be to institute a currency reform that pegged the value of the currency to a basket of real commodities, eliminating inflation once and for all. Having stabilized the currency, we could then do better still by opening up the issue of currency to free competition and by eliminating existing central banks altogether.

THE BENEFITS OF EUROPEAN MONETARY UNION

Much of the controversy over a European central bank centres on the question of monetary union. 'Monetary union' can be used to describe an arrangement where the exchange rates between different currencies are fixed, and are widely perceived to be permanently fixed, but where currencies are still distinguishable. The term can also be used to describe an arrangement where everyone uses a common currency. It is important to keep these two types of monetary union separate, because they give rise to quite different issues.

The main benefit of adopting fixed exchange rates stems from the reduction in uncertainty about future changes in exchange rates. While exchange rates are still flexible, firms that engage in international trade have to cope with fluctuations in their profit margins that arise from unforeseen changes in exchange rates.

Sometimes firms can cover themselves against these risks by engaging in futures operations, but that kind of cover is costly even where the market is relatively thick, and elsewhere the thinness of markets (for example, for cover years ahead) makes cover so expensive that firms often prefer to take the exchange rate risk instead. It is hard to quantify the benefits of the elimination of exchange rate uncertainty, but intuition suggests that they are probably quite important.[2] We must weigh the costs of a fixed rate system against these benefits. There is some controversy over what the costs might be, but the main one seems to be implied by a move away from optimal currency areas. There is a cost to tying currencies together if they belong to different optimal currency areas, but the potential loss is hard to assess because we have little idea what the optimal currency areas might be.[3] It follows, then, that it is not clear whether or not fixing European exchange rates generates a net gain.

Whether there are any net gains from then merging separate currencies is also problematic. The main benefit of adopting a common currency is the reduction in transaction costs that arise in changing from one currency to another.[4] The costs involved seem to vary from perhaps 3 per cent to 4 per cent for tourist exchanges to trivial percentages for large business transactions,[5] and one could probably get some idea of the magnitude of potential cost savings from the resources currently used up by *bureaux de change*.[6] As a rough order of magnitude, cost savings probably amount to 0.1 per cent of GNP, and we must weigh the costs of adopting a common currency against those savings. Prices, salaries, accounts and other nominal values would all have to be altered, and machines would have to be adapted to deal with the new currency. People would have to adjust to it, and these psychic costs could be more significant than any other. There is no hard evidence on these costs, but the British experience with decimalization in 1971 is instructive. Also bear in mind that decimalization changed only the constituent elements of the basic monetary unit: shillings and old pennies were replaced by 'new pence' but the pound remained untouched. Adopting a common currency would be a more radical change, because the basic unit itself would be altered. The implication, then, is that the costs would eat significantly into the gross saving to produce a very small net gain – and there might be no net gain at all.

It should be clear that the case for monetary union in either form is far from obvious. It should also be clear that the question cannot be resolved by arguing about it in the abstract, because no one has the information needed to predict confidently the relevant gains or losses. In the final analysis the only way to resolve the issue would be to create the conditions for free competition between different currencies and see what happened.[7] If the public felt that fixing exchange rates was worthwhile, it would exercise market pressure on the issuers to peg their currencies; if the public wanted a single currency as well, one would evolve from the competitive process. As Vaubel (1989: 11) observes:

> I used to believe that the desirability of European currency union was a foregone conclusion and that currency competition would merely show us the optimal path to that end. I now realise that the end itself has to be questioned and that currency competition is not only the optimum currency unification process, if currency union is desirable, but also the optimal procedure of finding out whether currency union is desirable.

THE IMPORTANCE OF PRICE STABILITY

The monetary union issue can never be resolved in isolation. What we are really interested in is the monetary environment, and monetary union is only one part of that environment. Another aspect is its stability, and one ought not to support a plan for monetary reform without first knowing that it will produce stable monetary conditions. Monetary instability must be avoided for several reasons. It injects unnecessary 'noise' into the price 'signals' on which the market mechanism relies to allocate resources properly; therefore, it leads individuals to make costly 'mistakes' they would otherwise have avoided. Monetary instability obliges people to invest time and resources trying to cover themselves against the risks to which it exposes them, and it leads them to neglect socially worthwhile long-run projects and to concentrate excessively on short-term survival. It distorts investment activities and fuels speculative 'bubbles' by encouraging people to seek out allegedly safe assets as a hedge. Monetary instability produces arbitrary gains and losses that have nothing to do with any socially worthwhile activity, that undermine the institution of private property, and that erode confidence in the integrity and fairness of the market system. Both recent and historical experience of high inflation suggests that it causes hardship and massive social and economic disruption. I expect that the cost of inflation will vastly outweigh any gains that may be obtained from European monetary integration. Although monetary union *may* be worth while *if* it comes with price stability, we would be ill advised to sacrifice price stability for mere monetary union. Price stability is the central issue, and monetary union *per se* is secondary in comparison.

Given the importance of monetary stability we might have expected the Delors report to have offered some guarantees that the new European central bank would deliver stable prices, but the report offered no reassurance on this issue. It stated only that the bank 'would be committed to the objective of price stability' (p. 18), but it made no suggestions about how the bank would achieve that objective. It reads as if the statement of intent (that the bank is expected to achieve price stability) would be sufficient to ensure that the bank *would* actually achieve it. Central bank statutes the world over are littered with similar 'commitments' to price stability, and none of them actually achieves it for long, if at all. There is no reason to expect that a new European central bank would succeed where other central banks have failed. The Delors report further undermines price stability by insisting that it is not its only objective. Monetary policy is also to be co-ordinated with national and EC fiscal policies and with general macro-economic policies as set out by the Council of Ministers, which have a wide range of differing objectives (e.g. 'balanced growth, converging standards of living, high employment and external equilibrium'; Delors 1989: 8).

It is also doubtful whether the European central bank would achieve price stability because it would have relatively limited independence from political interference. While the Delors report stated that the central bank 'should be independent of instructions from national governments and Community authorities' (p. 20) and suggested how the bank might be constituted to give it some independence, the report undermined that independence by suggesting that the bank should be held accountable to the Council of Ministers and the European Parliament. Such accountability, however, would almost inevitably make it difficult for the central bank to pursue policies of which European politicians strongly disapproved. The Delors report also undermines the central bank's independence by recommending that the Council of Ministers should have overall responsibility for macro-economic – and, presumably, monetary – policies. Whatever the bank's independence on paper, the politicians would inevitably have considerable leverage over it in practice, and the empirical evidence clearly indicates that 'the average rate of inflation is significantly lower in countries that have highly independent central banks compared with those that do not' (Bade and Parkin 1981: 33).

CENTRAL BANKS AND INFLATION

There are various reasons to expect a central bank to be more prone to inflation the less independence it has. Suppose we have a monetary authority that has a monopoly over the issue of inconvertible currency.[8] This monetary authority can be considered a combination of central bank and government, and the objectives it follows depend on the underlying objectives of governing politicians and central bankers and on the balance of power between them. The less independence the central bank has, the more weight is assigned to the interests of the politicians. The politicians are primarily interested in manipulating the economy to get re-elected and in collecting seigniorage as a disguised tax that enables them to avoid the unpopularity of more explicit forms of taxation. The central bankers do not have to face popular re-election, and they get little or no direct benefit from seigniorage, at least at the margin.

The monetary authority is self-interested, and it aims to manipulate inflation in its own interest; that is, it aims to create sufficient inflation to bring the marginal benefit that it derives from inflation down to the marginal cost that inflation imposes on it. The marginal benefit derives from the reduction in unemployment generated by unanticipated inflation and from the seigniorage that the monetary authority collects. The cost derives from the adverse criticism that inflation provokes and the erosion of the monetary authority's credibility. If the monetary authority were to produce zero inflation, then the marginal benefit of inflation would exceed the cost; thus the monetary authority would not produce price stability, and the public would not expect it to. The public would expect the inflation rate that was in the bank's own interest, so the equilibrium inflation rate would be some rate above zero. This rate will also vary with changes in the marginal costs and benefits of inflation. These changes will often be unpredictable, because many of the benefits of inflation to the monetary authority stem from it successfully surprising the private sector. Therefore, there would be not only inflation, but unpredictable inflation as well.

It should also be clear why a central bank that lacks independence will produce more inflation. The benefits of inflation accrue primarily to governing politicians rather than to central bankers, but there is no such obvious discrepancy in the distribution of the costs of inflation. The less independence a central bank has, the greater the influence of the politicians on central bank policy, and the more it will reflect their desire for relatively high inflation. The politicians' desire for high inflation also implies that a central bank that is under the thumb of its government will have less credibility with the private sector as an institution that is serious about controlling inflation, and this lack of credibility will push the equilibrium inflation rate even higher than it would otherwise be.

THE STATE OF EC FINANCES

The likelihood that the new central bank would inflate is further reinforced by the state of EC finances. The basic problem is the European Community's failure to control its expenditure. Uncontrolled expenditure growth had already pushed the Community into technical bankruptcy by 1983.[9] The 'solution' was to massage the budget and defer spending; and, as Swinbank (1988: 3) observed, 'Crisis management, and budgetary chicanery [have] prevailed ever since.'[10] In 1985 member governments tried to ease the pressure on the Community's budget by increasing its share of VAT revenue from 1 to 1.4 per cent of the notional VAT base – an increase of about 26 per cent in its resources (Koester and Terwitte 1988: 103) – but the budgetary crisis continued to mount. By 1987 even the Commission (1987: 2) was forced to admit that

> the community is . . . faced with a budgetary situation which can only be characterised as being on the brink of bankruptcy. . . . the Community has sunk into a morass of budgetary malpractices needed to conceal or postpone the real financial implications of Community policies. Thus the budgetary effect of the unprecedented build-up of agricultural stocks has been disguised by gross over-valuation of the stocks: actual budgetary deficits have been carried forward and only covered belatedly by *ad hoc* solutions; and Community commitments

have been allowed to accumulate without proper financial provisions. . . . the Community has not been equipped with the necessary means to adapt policies to the desired expenditure scenarios [that is, the Community cannot manage its budget properly].

The escalating financial crisis led the Brussels summit in February 1988 to agree on a package of measures designed to put EC finances on a firmer basis. Principal among those measures were agricultural price 'stabilizers' intended to limit intervention if EC production quotas were exceeded. The summit also agreed to grant the Community a 25 per cent increase in its revenue by agreeing to a new contribution by each member state on the basis of its GNP (Koester and Terwitte 1988: 103) – equivalent to a rise in its implicit VAT rate to 2.2 per cent. This new revenue source was 'residual finance' to provide the Community with just enough funds to balance its budget, but it was to be subject to a ceiling intended to keep EC spending under control. The spending ceiling was initially set at 1.12 per cent of Community GNP in 1988, to increase by steps to 1.2 per cent in 1992, when it would be reviewed.[11]

It is highly unlikely that these measures actually achieved anything more than a short-term respite for the EC's budgetary problems. The stabilizer mechanisms were relatively limited, and the underlying incentive to overproduce agricultural products remained intact. As one study (Field et al. 1989: 32–3) observed:

In view of the [political] pressures for [agricultural] price increases, technological changes which will increase production, and the gradual application of EC measures and prices to Spain, the Community will have difficulty keeping support expenditures within the targets set . . . there will be considerable pressure to exceed the amounts agreed on and to borrow or transfer funds supposedly allocated [elsewhere]. . . . Any assumption that . . . genuine reform has been achieved in EC agriculture, would be highly misleading.

This conclusion was echoed by Koester and Terwitte (1988: 104): 'In [the] future the CAP will cost more, not less. The decisions regarding "stabilizers" and land set-aside schemes . . . will probably have little impact.' But perhaps the main weakness of the Brussels package was that there was no means to make its theoretical limits on EC spending effective in practice. There was no mechanism by which support could be cut off or other penalties imposed if limits were exceeded. Furthermore, the Commission had no incentive to keep its costs down.

The underlying dynamic of Community finance is therefore quite clear. Member governments impose limits on EC spending, but they do not enforce them and implicitly encourage the EC to violate them. Whenever those limits were exceeded and a financial crisis ensued, as in 1983 and 1987–8, member governments did nothing to penalize those involved and to bring expenditures under control. Instead, they rewarded the Community each time by giving it substantial increases in resources that would put the crisis off for a while. Meanwhile, EC expenditure continued to escalate, and we are now presumably heading for the next crisis in a year or two. This is the fiscal context within which the proposal for a European central bank needs to be viewed.[12]

EC FINANCES AND THE EUROPEAN CENTRAL BANK

The establishment of a European central bank would give the EC a major new source of finance: the seigniorage from money creation. The amount of seigniorage that European governments currently collect varies from one country to another.[13] Some indicative figures for the early and mid-1980s are 0.1 per cent of GDP for the United Kingdom and Belgium, 0.2 per cent for Germany, 0.7 per cent for France, 2 per cent for Italy, 3.4 per cent for Greece and 4.8 per cent for Portugal (Grilli 1989: table 1). As a general rule, the higher figures are due to reserve requirements that increase the demand for the monetary base (e.g. in Portugal), but seigniorage revenues are tending to fall in these countries as their reserve requirements are phased out. If we take this factor into account, it seems reasonable to suppose that the average seigniorage revenue in the EC will settle down to perhaps 0.2–0.3 per cent of GDP. Were the European central bank to collect the same amount and pass it back to the Community, seigniorage revenue would increase the EC resource base by 17 per cent to 26 per cent.

None the less, it would be a mistake to view seigniorage as a relatively fixed addition to Community resources, comparable, for example, to the VAT revenue over which it has no direct control. The EC could always increase its seigniorage revenue by pressing the new central bank to reimpose reserve requirements to buttress the demand for monetary base, and the figures for France and Italy give some indication of how reserve requirements and other regulations can substantially increase seigniorage revenue. If reserve requirements could push up average seigniorage even to the relatively low French figure of 0.7 per cent, then seigniorage revenue would increase by a factor of two and a half and constitute an addition to total Community revenues of around 60 per cent.[14] The Community could also generate additional seigniorage by leaning on the central bank to inflate at a faster rate. Some indication of the amounts involved can perhaps be obtained from the increases in seigniorage that occurred when inflation rose substantially during the 1970s. Grilli's figures for the 1960s and 1970s indicate that decade-average seigniorage/GDP ratios rose for eight of the eleven current EC member countries (excluding Luxembourg), and the average rise was about 0.4 per cent of GDP.[15] Such a figure implies that pushing inflation back up to the levels of the 1970s would approximately double seigniorage revenue, and seigniorage would presumably increase further if inflation was pushed even higher.

These figures suggest that a European central bank would substantially increase EC resources even if it kept inflation down to current EMS levels and refrained from reimposing reserve requirements. Apart from increasing the Community's resources, a central bank would also significantly soften the budget constraint the Community faces, and that constraint is arguably far too soft already. At the moment the cost to the Community of exceeding its budget is a lot of bad publicity and a slight increase in the low probability that member governments might become sufficiently incensed to stop arguing with each other and agree to do something about it. While still allowing the Community its traditional option of increasing its resources by spending itself into a crisis and looking to member governments to bail it out, the new bank would give the Community the additional option of increasing its resources by taking subsidized loans from the central bank that could be disguised to divert criticism and the danger of outside interference. A European central bank would, therefore, be a further disincentive for the Community to rein in its spending, and it would make the establishment of rationality in EC finances even more difficult than it already promises to be.

Apart from being detrimental to European public finance, a

central bank would also be very damaging to the European financial system. For reasons already explained, the Community would be strongly tempted to finance its overspending at least in part by imposing reserve requirements and other regulations on the banking system. Taxing the banking system in this way is politically attractive because such taxes would be relatively easy to disguise; and, in any case, banks are often an easy political target because they rarely get much public sympathy. Nor is there any reason to expect that the Community would subsequently refrain from further taxes on the banking system. The very factors that led the Community to intervene the first time will encourage it to do so again, and the burden on the banks will tend to increase with time, seriously eroding the efficiency and competitiveness of the European financial system.

There is also a very real danger that the Community's search for new ways of taxing the financial system could wipe out the Euromarket as well as undermine the relative freedom on which the prosperity of Europe's financial centres depends. London would be especially vulnerable in this regard. Another disturbing feature of these interventions is that the central bank would be most unlikely to justify them as taxes, because to do so would expose it and the Community to unwelcome criticism. Instead the central bank would be likely to hide behind the smokescreen that the interventions were required for various 'prudential' purposes: to 'stabilize' the banking system, to 'protect' widows and orphans, and so forth.[16] These excuses would establish the unfortunate precedent that the European central bank *ought* to be intervening for these purposes. The justifications for the earlier interventions would then encourage the bank to develop an active 'prudential' role, and the financial system could find itself saddled with a variety of unnecessary regulations that would undermine it even further.

Potentially most disturbing of all, however, is the danger that the EC's financial problems could lead it to inflate the European currency. Inflation would be a tempting option for the Community, not only because it generates substantial rewards but also because the costs to the EC of inflation would be relatively low. Costs would be low because it would be difficult for the injured parties (that is, the public) to figure out who was responsible, and it would be relatively easy for the Commission to throw up a smokescreen that deflected the brunt of criticism.[17] Even if the Community could not avoid criticism over inflation, the costs would still be quite low, because the public lack any easy means to penalize the EC or force it to pay attention to their concerns. There are also reasons to expect that inflation might rise over time. Taxes on the banks are likely to be politically less costly than inflation, and it would be in the Community's interest to exploit the politically less damaging taxes first and only gradually increase its use of the inflation tax. In any case, there would come a point where it would become increasingly difficult to extract further resources from the financial system, and the EC would have to rely increasingly on inflation to finance its additional spending. So there is a very real possibility that the Community's financial problems may not only lead to substantial inflation but to rising inflation as well.

US EXPERIENCE WITH THE FEDERAL RESERVE SYSTEM

Since the proposed European Federal Reserve System is modelled to some extent on the US system, it makes sense to see what could be learned from the American experience. The Federal Reserve was established in 1914 to provide the US banking system with protection against the periodic crises to which it was prone.[18] During the early 1930s, however, the Fed's failure to provide that protection escalated relatively minor banking problems into waves of bank failures that had catastrophic effects on economic activity. As Friedman and Schwartz concluded (1963: 391):

> The leadership which an independent central-banking system was supposed to give the market and the ability to withstand the pressures of politics and of profit alike and to act counter to the market as a whole, these – the justification for establishing a quasi-governmental institution with broad powers – were conspicuous by their absence.

Recent work on the Fed's performance supports this assessment. Gorton (1986) examined the impact of the Fed by carrying out a counterfactual experiment to predict what would have happened if the pre-Fed regime had continued after 1914. His results indicate that, although a panic would have occurred in December 1929 the 'failure and loss percentages would have been an order of magnitude lower' (p. 29) in the absence of the Fed. This result suggests that there would have been a downturn in the early 1930s, but not the major disaster that actually occurred. Studying the period up to 1940, Miron (1989: 290–1) found that 'the variance of both the rate of growth of output and of the inflation rate increased substantially, while the average rate of growth of output fell, and real stock prices became substantially more volatile'. He suggested that these conclusions hold even if the period of the Great Depression is ignored. Miron's analysis also suggested that these changes were not merely coincidental with the founding of the Fed but could be directly attributed to it. The record of the Fed since the Second World War has not been much better. Output variability does not appear to have decreased (Romer 1986), and prices have become much less stable than they were earlier. The post-war era was also the period when the Fed shook itself free of the discipline imposed by the gold standard, and it used its new-found freedom to create an inflation unprecedented in peacetime US history which still shows no sign of ending.

The way in which the Fed has evolved since its foundation is also disturbing. It started off as a system of twelve autonomous Federal Reserve Banks, with a Federal Reserve Board as a kind of liaison committee – much like the European central bank proposed by Delors. Subsequently, however, it evolved into a system in which 'the Board in Washington is all powerful and the Federal Reserve Banks not much more than administrative units' (Timberlake 1986: 759). In the process the Fed turned into an institution

> whose every act is to enhance the power and prestige of itself and the government. Unless one can argue that what is good for the government is good for the general public, one cannot defend either the mutation of the Fed as it has occurred, or the Fed's continued existence as an all-powerful central bank. Its 70-year history as a bureaucratic institution confirms the inability of Congress to bring it to heel. Whenever its own powers are at stake, the Fed exercises an intellectual ascendancy over Congress that consistently results in an extension of Fed authority. This pattern reflects the dominance of bureaucratic expertise for which there is no solution as long as the [Fed] continues to exist.
>
> (Timberlake 1986: 759)

Disturbing as this record is, several factors imply that a European Federal Reserve System would fare even worse. The US Federal

Reserve has generally had to deal with a federal government that was in reasonably sound fiscal shape, so the pressure to inflate for fiscal reasons was usually quite limited (a factor that has undoubtedly helped to keep American inflation lower than it would otherwise have been). As I discussed earlier, however, a European Federal Reserve would have to deal with a European Community whose financial position is anything but sound, and the fiscal pressure to inflate would be intense. A European Fed would also start off with no discipline against over-issue such as that which the gold standard provided the US Fed with during its early days. This combination of fiscal pressure and the lack of any discipline against over-issue makes it all but certain that a European Fed would make the inflation record of its American counterpart look very good indeed.

SOME ALTERNATIVES TO A EUROPEAN CENTRAL BANK

Fortunately, there are superior alternatives to a European central bank. One is simply to persist with the EMS. The EMS is a currency bloc in which the member central banks agree to maintain the exchange rates of their currencies within relatively narrow bands. Should one country attempt a more expansionary monetary policy than the rest, then that country can maintain its exchange rate within the permitted bands only by running down its reserves of foreign exchange or by borrowing reserves from elsewhere. Its ability to maintain a more expansionary monetary policy is therefore necessarily limited, and the maintenance of its exchange rate in the long run requires that its monetary growth rate must be compatible with the monetary growth rate pursued by its partners in the exchange rate system. Because the more conservative central banks can keep accumulating reserves at relatively little cost or inconvenience but the more expansionary ones would eventually run out of reserves and cease to be able to maintain their exchange rates, the pressure to adjust tends to be concentrated on the expansionary central banks, which then have to curtail their monetary growth. This implies that the system's monetary policy is effectively determined by the most conservative central bank, which therefore sets the monetary growth rate and forces its partners to restrict their monetary growth to rates compatible with its own.

The most conservative central bank in the EMS is the Bundesbank, and much of its conservatism seems to stem from the combination of its mandate to secure the value of the currency and its independence from the German federal government.[19] The asymmetry of the reserve pressure between comparatively expansionary central banks and the Bundesbank 'imparts a helpful anti-inflation bias into the EMS whereby central banks that have a tough anti-inflation stance can put pressure on other, less disciplined central banks' (Currie 1989: 21). Thus the EMS mechanism allows the weaker central banks to piggyback on the Bundesbank's superior inflation record and 'borrow' its credibility. Currie (1989: 21) found that the EMS contrasts

> with the way in which a centralized, coordinated monetary policy can operate, say within a full monetary union [with a European central bank]. For then, monetary policy will be determined by committee, and the outcome will tend to reflect the average, not the best, anti-inflationary policy.

If follows that, if a central bank is to run European monetary policy, inflation would be lower with the Bundesbank in control than with a new central bank whose policies would be bound to reflect compromises between those who wanted higher inflation and those who did not.

Although the EMS still allows of occasional currency realignments, it will become increasingly difficult to accommodate realignments as remaining capital controls are lifted across the EC. If monetary policies are not consistent across the EMS countries, then markets will have no difficulty anticipating the direction of the prospective exchange rate change and market operators will discount the currency that is expected to be devalued. In order to maintain asset market equilibrium, interest rates will then rise sharply in the country whose currency is to be devalued, and interest rates will keep rising until the devaluation takes place. As controls are lifted and capital becomes more mobile even greater interest rate movements will be required to maintain asset market equilibrium, and the capital flows involved will become larger and more disruptive.[20] The relaxation of capital controls will therefore increase the pressure on the EMS to prevent exchange rate realignments altogether, and the other central banks will find their freedom of manoeuvre even more restricted than it already is. The present 'soft' EMS would tend to evolve into a 'hard' EMS in which exchange rates were fixed once and for all, and the Bundesbank's hegemony was even stronger than it already is.[21]

The drawback with this option is that we are still left with the avoidable monetary instability created by the Bundesbank itself. It is often overlooked that the Bundesbank's inflation record is good only in comparison with that of other central banks and that it is poor compared to what commodity standards have been able to achieve in the past. Perhaps the easiest way to eliminate the price instability created by the Bundesbank would be to tie one of the ERM member currencies to a general price index.[22] The issuer of the currency would be legally compelled to buy and sell its currency for some redemption medium (e.g. shares) at an exchange rate determined by the general price index, and it would be impossible for the issuer to inflate the currency further. The new inflation-proof currency would then displace the Deutschmark as the 'strong' currency in the EMS, and the Bundesbank would no longer determine EMS inflation. If they wished to maintain their EMS parities the issuers of the remaining currencies would have to abandon their inflationary rates of monetary growth, and inflation would be eliminated throughout the EMS countries. The 'hard' EMS would thus be transformed into a 'super-hard', non-inflationary EMS that was free of the Bundesbank's own inflationary proclivities. Once the values of the EMS currencies had been tied down, the next logical, and highly desirable, step would be to remove any legal restrictions against the issue of currency and to abolish the existing central banks. The issue of 'money' could then be left entirely to the free market which is best able to look after it anyway.[23]

Chapter 15

Evaluating the hard ecu

The past few years have seen monetary integration move to the top of the European political agenda. European governments committed themselves to the principle of European monetary union as long ago as the Werner report (1971), and reiterated it when the European Monetary System (EMS) was established in 1979, but these early attempts to achieve monetary union never got very far, and it is only relatively recently that the move to monetary union has acquired any real momentum. The turning point seems to have been the adoption of the single market programme in 1985. The programme called for the removal of all legislative barriers to the free movement of capital throughout the Community, and thus paved the way for the establishment of a unified European financial market. Three years after the agreement on the single market, the Community heads of government decided at a summit in Hanover to set up a committee under M. Jacques Delors, the president of the European Commission, to recommend a plan to complete the process to full economic and monetary union. The committee submitted its report in April 1989 and recommended a three-stage plan which was to culminate in a single European currency issued by a new European central bank.

While these recommendations were immediately accepted by eleven out of the twelve member governments, the UK government dissented and expressed reservations about both the single currency and the proposed European central bank. It also maintained that the last two stages of the Delors plan – those dealing with monetary union after the UK had joined the Exchange Rate Mechanism (ERM) – were vague and unpractical, and argued that more thought needed to be given to the issues before the Community committed itself to the rest of the plan. The UK government then issued its own alternative proposal in November 1989, which envisaged a competitive, evolutionary approach towards European monetary union in place of the planned, institutional approach adopted by Delors. The main point was that the countries of the Community should promote competition between their different currencies. The process of competition would then lead the stronger currencies to displace the weaker ones and eventually, perhaps, to the strongest emerging as a *de facto* common currency.

THE 'HARD ECU' PROPOSAL

In June 1990, however, the British government modified its position and suggested that what was needed was a new European currency – the 'hard ecu' – to compete against the existing European currencies and, if market forces supported it, to emerge as the common currency. As the then Chancellor (since Prime Minister), John Major, explained, the British government was still thinking in terms of monetary evolution, but its preferred evolutionary route now involved the creation of the hard ecu as a 'parallel' currency, and the Chancellor tacitly dropped the earlier emphasis on competition between existing currencies. The UK Treasury explained the government's position in is autumn *Bulletin*:

> The centrepiece of the UK proposals for progress after Stage 1 is the creation of a new institution, the European Monetary Fund (EMF). Its main function would be to act as the monetary authority [i.e. the issuer] for a new currency, the 'hard ecu' . . . [which] would be a member of the narrow band of the ERM and its exchange rate would be free to vary within that relatively small band against the other Community currencies. . . . But its distinguishing characteristic would be that it would never be allowed to devalue against any other Community currency. At times of realignment – which should become increasingly infrequent as convergence within the Community proceeds – the hard ecu would always be at least as strong as the strongest currency, whatever that happened to be.
>
> (HM Treasury 1990: 2–3).

An important feature of the new arrangements would be a repurchase requirement to limit the ability of national monetary authorities to inflate at the expense of the EMF. If the EMF was prepared to go on buying a national currency without any limit, there would be no discipline on the amount of currency the relevant national monetary authority could issue, and it could print whatever amount it wished in the knowledge that the EMF would buy it up. To prevent this behaviour, the Treasury paper suggested a repurchase requirement which would involve:

> pre-set limits on the amounts of national currencies that the EMF could hold . . . Once these limits were reached, the EMF would have to ask the monetary authority concerned to repurchase from it its national currency in return for hard ecu or some other strong currency. . . . The repurchase requirement would accordingly close the loophole in monetary discipline which would otherwise exist.
>
> (HM Treasury 1990: 5)

The main problem with the proposal is to ensure that there would be a demand for the hard ecu in the first place. The Treasury paper acknowledges that the hard ecu 'could not have any effect if it were not used' (p. 7) but suggests that people would find it attractive for several reasons. It argues that borrowers and lenders would prefer it, the latter because it would be stable in value, and the former because its hardness would result in relatively low rates of interest. The paper also argues that its 'stability in value would also make the hard ecu attractive as a means of exchange for conducting transactions within Europe' (p. 7). Intra-Community trade and travel can be expected to grow rapidly, and the hard ecu would be a 'natural vehicle for settling the transactions involved' (p. 7). Once the transaction demand for hard ecus had developed, the Community countries could then think in terms of making the hard ecu legal tender, but this would come only after it had already 'taken off' as a parallel currency, and the British proposal rejects the use of legal tender legislation to help the hard ecu at its launching.[1]

Assuming, then, that there would be sufficient demand for it, the Treasury paper went on to argue that the hard ecu would have a strong disinflationary impact. The circulation of the weaker currencies would fall as people switched over to it, and the fall in demand would put pressure on the issuers of the weaker currencies to pursue tighter monetary policies or face the prospect of devaluation. This pressure would be asymmetrical – the pressure would fall on the issuers of the weaker currencies to tighten their monetary policies, and not on the issuers of the strong currencies to pursue easier money. The hard ecu would thus 'help achieve convergence on the best inflation performance and ultimately [achieve] price stability' (p. 3). In addition, as John Major said in his June speech, 'In the very long term, if peoples and governments so chose, [the hard ecu] could develop into a single currency' (quoted in the Treasury paper, p. 8).

WOULD PEOPLE USE THE HARD ECU?

On the face of it, the British proposal may seem quite reasonable. The new currency would be (relatively) 'hard', no one would be forced to use it against their will, and it would develop into a widely used currency – perhaps even a common currency – only if market forces support it, which is to say, only if people want it. But therein lies the fundamental problem. Why should people use it? Currency users have good reason to be 'attached' to the currencies they already use. The 'old' currency is more easily recognized and people have a readier grasp of relative prices if prices are expressed in it. They also find it easier to keep accounts in the currency they are accustomed to, and currency users usually expect trading costs to be lower if they stick with the existing currency than if they switch to some other. Switching over to a new currency requires that one must make the effort to get used to dealing with it, and one has to take into account the extent to which one expects the people with whom one trades to switch over as well. These latter costs are especially important, and most individuals would be reluctant to switch currencies unless they felt that a sufficient number of their trading partners would switch with them. I may feel that the yen is a far better currency than sterling, and be prepared to familiarize myself with it, but my readiness to hold yen instead of sterling will be limited and I may decide not to hold any yen at all if I expect everyone with whom I trade to continue to use sterling. The cost of switching currencies should not be ignored, therefore, and individuals will make the switchover only if they expect the benefits to be high enough to make bearing the costs worth while. It follows, then, that the hard ecu will be used only if it promises a (sufficiently) superior quality of monetary service to that provided by existing currencies.

It is very doubtful whether this condition would be satisfied. Suppose an individual in the UK is to decide whether he wishes to hold a note of some particular value in sterling or some other currency, and he wishes to hold the note for a week. Suppose also that the sterling rate of inflation is 10 per cent a year, but the other currency does not inflate at all. If he holds the note in sterling he will make a capital loss over the week of around 0.2 per cent, and it is difficult to believe that a prospective capital loss of that magnitude would lead many such individuals to switch currencies (see also White 1987).[2] They *might*, of course, *if* they expected other individuals to switch over as well, but such an expectation would seldom, if ever, be rational. The prospect of a very large capital loss might produce such a shift in expectations, of course, and thence lead to a major currency substitution, but it seems very doubtful that a loss of 0.2 per cent would be enough to do the trick.[3] (If it would, after all, such changes should be very common events.) In any case, there are various reasons for believing that 0.2 per cent is a significant *over*estimate of the likely capital loss.

To begin with, the capital loss was taken to be the difference between the inflation rates of the two currencies. This assumption is reasonable if we are dealing with banknotes or deposits which are not interest-bearing, but it is less reasonable if we are dealing, say, with deposits that bear market rates of interest. The capital loss in this case is no longer the differential between the inflation rates, but the difference between the interest and inflation rate differentials, and we would expect this loss to be considerably less. High inflation leads to high interest rates, so the capital loss inflicted by inflation on the holder of the 'weaker' currency has to be matched against the higher nominal interest rate he receives. (Indeed, if 'real' interest rates are unaffected by inflation, the actual capital loss on interest-bearing assets will be about zero.) Note also that the average velocity of notes seems to be higher than one transfer per week, and a higher velocity implies a lower capital loss because the average holding period is lower. A capital loss of 0.2 per cent is therefore too high even for non-interest-bearing notes.

More important, an inflation rate differential of 10 per cent between sterling and any other EMS currency, including the hard ecu, would seem to be a considerable overestimate. UK inflation for 1991 and afterwards is forecast to fall well below 10 per cent, and even the hardest of the EMS currencies is still expected to have a positive inflation rate for the foreseeable future. Further- more, the exchange rate boundaries implied by the ERM make it difficult to see how any major inflation differentials could persist over the long term. The almost fixed nature of the exchange rate system gives very little scope for member governments to pursue significantly different monetary policies. A government that followed a monetary policy significantly more lax than the others would lose reserves trying to maintain its exchange rate in the required range, and a point would come where either its policy had to fall back into line or it had to devalue its currency. The government would also have to keep on devaluing each time its exchange rate became difficult to defend, and although the ERM sanctions devaluations of a one-off nature, a policy of persistent devaluation is fundamentally incompatible with membership of the ERM in the long run. In any case, there is general agreement within the EMS that devaluations should become less frequent over time, and the intention is to eliminate them altogether. Monetary policies would fully converge, and goods market arbitrage (i.e. purchasing power parity) would eliminate any significant inflation rate differentials. The capital loss discussed earlier would then fall towards zero and in the process wipe out any incentive to switch currencies. The hard ecu proposal thus runs into a major dilemma. *On the one hand, people can only be expected to switch over to it if there is some incentive to do so, and such an incentive would seem to require a substantial difference in inflation rates. However, the convergence of monetary policies within the ERM reduces such differences, and, ultimately, eliminates them altogether.*

We also need to bear in mind that for the hard ecu to gain widespread acceptance it is not enough for it to be expected to provide a superior monetary service to one or more of the weaker ERM currencies. *It must be able to outcompete the strongest currencies as well.* Even if the issuer of sterling, say, was expected to 'misbehave' badly – and to misbehave sufficiently badly to encourage a significant switch out of it – there would still be no reason to expect that people would choose to switch into the hard ecu in preference to one or other of the stronger ERM currencies. Unless we (rather implausibly) expect each of the ERM currencies to be devalued in turn – in which case the hard ecu would eventually end up having appreciated against the lot -- the hard ecu would effectively be tied to the strongest of the ERM currencies.[4] But in that case it would have more or less the same inflation rate as the currency to which it was tethered, and it is hard to see how it could be expected to outcompete it. *A parallel currency has little chance of being adopted if it is pegged to the currencies against which it is meant to compete.*[5]

The empirical evidence seems to support this pessimistic assessment of the hard ecu's chances of being adopted. Past monetary experience indicates that people do not abandon their existing currencies without a relatively strong private incentive to do so. We do not seem to observe much substitution out of a currency when inflation is low or relatively moderate, and, at a very conservative estimate, it seems to take inflation rates well in excess of 20 per cent a year – and more usually, inflation rates well over 100 per cent – to generate a major flight from a currency. Evidence that the hard ecu would be a non-starter is also provided by the failure of earlier parallel currencies to take off in Europe. Perhaps the most prominent of these is the original ecu – the basket ecu – which was established in 1979. The basket ecu is a currency unit whose value is a weighted average of the values of the EMS currencies, and it is therefore stronger than the weakest EMS currency but weaker than the strongest one. The (basket) ecu has carved out a small niche for itself in the European currency market, but its role remains distinctly limited and any hope that it would provide a parallel currency with a circulation at all comparable to those of the major EMS currencies has been disappointed.

The failure of the earlier ecu to take off in a major way does not augur well for the hard ecu, and supporters of the hard ecu need to explain why they think it would succeed where its predecessor did not. It is true that the two ecus differ – one being an average of the EMS currencies, while the other would be tied to the strongest – but it is very doubtful from what was said earlier that the hard ecu would be sufficiently stronger than the previous one to make much difference. In any case, one could argue that the earlier ecu stood a better chance of being adopted, because inflation differentials – and hence the incentives to switch over to the ecu from the weaker currencies – were greater in the early years of the EMS than they are likely to be in for the foreseeable future. If the ecu failed to take off under those relatively favourable circumstances, there would seem to be a *prima facie* case that the hard ecu should not be expected to do any better. One might also note that there are many other units of account that could have formed the basis of a parallel currency had there been the demand for a 'hard' parallel currency that the supporters of the hard ecu seem to presuppose. A parallel currency could have developed around gold, for example, or a 'hard' currency like the Swiss franc or the Deutschmark could have developed into a European parallel currency instead. The failure of a parallel currency to develop along these lines strongly suggests that the demand for it does not exist, and thus reinforces the earlier evidence that the hard ecu would not be widely adopted.[6]

OTHER PROBLEMS WITH THE HARD ECU

The determination of European monetary policy

The British government's proposal faces other problems even if there was a demand to hold hard ecus. A key issue is who would determine European monetary policy. Suppose for the sake of argument that the Deutschmark continues to be the strong currency in the ERM, and we do not expect it to be devalued. The hard ecu would then be tied to the mark at a fixed rate of exchange, and the primary task of the EMF would be to maintain this exchange rate. In the absence of capital or exchange controls – which the EMS has now phased out – the EMF would be unable to sterilize capital flows, and the obligation to maintain the exchange rate would deprive it of any room for manoeuvre to pursue its own monetary policy. Hard ecu interest rates would then be tied to German interest rates, the amount of hard ecu base money would be determined entirely by the demand to hold it, and so on. The important point, however, is that the Bundesbank would be under no comparable obligation, and it could do effectively as it pleased subject to the mark still remaining the 'hard' currency in the EMS. (The Bundesbank would be disciplined only once its currency had ceased to be the strongest currency, and the Bundesbank would then come under the discipline of the ERM constraints that are the lot of the weaker central banks in the ERM. In that case, however, the issuer of the new 'top' currency would set European monetary policy and the EMF would still be subservient.) The Bundesbank would therefore set monetary policy and the EMF would be compelled to go along with it. The hard ecu would have the status of a piggyback currency that rode on the back of the mark. Note too that this piggyback status has *nothing* to do with the size of the relative demands for hard ecus and marks. However large the demand for hard ecu relative to the demand for marks, the issuer of marks, the Bundesbank, would still call the shots because it could issue whatever amount of marks it pleased while the EMF would have no degrees of freedom at all. Even if the hard ecu did develop into a viable parallel currency, the EMF could never get control of European monetary policy. It might ride in the front car, but it would never have the driver's seat. It follows, then, that the argument that the hard ecu could produce lower inflation than the 'best' existing central bank, or that it could eliminate inflation altogether, as the Treasury paper implies, is fundamentally mistaken. Whether there is a hard ecu or not, inflation will be eliminated only if the strongest central bank chooses to eliminate it, or if someone carries out a more radical monetary reform (as suggested, for example, in Chapter 13).

The hard ecu as a common currency?

Another limitation of the hard ecu is that it could never evolve into a single common currency and, indeed, that a universal move to switch over to it could be disastrous. Suppose the hard ecu turned out to be spectacularly popular, and the users of all the weaker currencies (i.e. all except the mark) abandoned them for it. Now suppose that the holders of marks also wanted to switch to the hard ecu. (Why they should want to do so is far from clear, but they would have to if the hard ecu was to become a common currency.) The real demand to hold marks would then fall, and, unless the Bundesbank reversed its policy and started retiring its issues at least *pari passu* with the fall in real demand, the mark price level would have to rise to ensure that the demand to hold marks was in equilibrium with the supply. (Note, by the way, that one cannot count on the Bundesbank responding in this way, and the Treasury paper never even raises the issue, which suggests that such a reversal of policy by the Bundesbank is not an essential feature of the British government's proposal.) The exchange rate between the mark and the hard ecu would be fixed, so purchasing power parity would ensure that the hard ecu price level rose with the mark price level. The danger is then that the value of the mark would hyperinflate, and the hard ecu would have to hyperinflate with it. This line of reasoning also implies that the hard ecu could never become a (universal) common currency. A necessary condition for it to become a common currency is that the real demand for the existing currencies should go to zero. If we rule out the Bundesbank keeping up the value of the mark by retiring its issues sufficiently rapidly, then this condition can be satisfied only if the real value of the mark goes to zero and the mark hyperinflates. But then the hard ecu would have to hyperinflate as well, so the real demand for hard ecus would also go to zero. The hard ecu cannot become a common currency because that would require the demand for hard ecus to be positive at the same time as the demand for the other currencies was zero, and these requirements can never be simultaneously satisfied. The idea that the hard ecu could provide a common currency is thus essentially self-contradictory.

CONCLUSIONS

The main conclusions are easily summarized. The main problem with the hard ecu is that there is no reason to believe that there would be any significant demand for it. The success of the hard ecu presupposes that there exists a demand for a 'hard' parallel currency, and there is no evidence for believing that such a demand really exists. And, even if it did, such demand would be likely to manifest itself in the form of a switch towards an existing 'hard' currency like the mark instead of a switch towards the hard ecu. The hard ecu is a non-starter for the simple reason that currency users would have no incentive to switch over to it. It is then almost superfluous to add that, even if there was a demand for it, the hard ecu would always have the subordinate status of a piggy-back currency and a near universal adoption of the hard ecu could be very dangerous. It follows that it could never cure inflation itself, and it could never evolve into a common currency.

It would be a serious mistake, none the less, to conclude that the drawbacks of the hard ecu amount to an argument in favour of the common currency and European central bank proposed by Delors. The most basic criticism one can make of the hard ecu proposal is that it will make no real difference, but it is still far better than the Delors plan which is a blueprint for disaster. The plan proposes to take control over European monetary policy away from the Germans, who have a good track record on inflation, at least in comparative terms, and give control of that monetary policy to an international body most of whose members would be unlikely to share the Germans' (relative) monetary conservatism. The new central bank is also to be accountable to the European political authorities[7] who preside over a Community that lurches from one fiscal crisis to another, and yet we are asked to believe that these same authorities will respect the bank's 'independence' and resist the temptation to use the bank to keep the Community solvent. We should entrust the liquor cabinet to an alcoholic and tell him to leave the booze alone. Present European monetary arrangements are certainly unsatisfactory, but instead of playing around with grandiose plans for novel currencies and a new central bank the governments of Europe would be better advised, in my opinion, to go back to their monetary basics and get their priorities right. The major monetary problem facing Europe is not the lack of monetary union or the absence of a supra-national central bank, and what Europe needs above all is not so much a *common* currency as *sound* currency. The key problem is inflation, and there is no reason to believe that either the hard ecu or the reforms proposed by Delors would ever get to grips with it.

Chapter 16

The US banking crisis: the way out

> The fragility of real-world banking systems is not a free-market phenomenon but a consequence of legal restrictions. This does not mean that deregulation is without its dangers. Dismantling bad bank regulation is like cutting wires in a time bomb: The job is risky and has to be done . . . carefully . . . but it beats letting the thing go on ticking.
>
> (George Selgin 1989c: 456)

The United States is now in the midst of the worst financial crisis it has faced since the bank collapses of the early 1930s. Hundreds of financial institutions have failed over the last few years, and many more – most probably more than have already failed – are economically insolvent and remain open only because they are being propped up by the regulatory agencies. The two main sectors of the banking industry – the commercial banks, and the (so-called) thrift industry, which is in even worse shape – are gradually sliding towards oblivion, and the US regulatory and political authorities have so far shown themselves helpless to prevent it. To make matters worse, the deterioration of the banking industry has also left the US deposit insurance system – and, to be more precise, the government, which backstops it – with debts that already run into many hundreds of billions of dollars, and which could get much higher yet before the whole mess is sorted out. The roots of the problem are not well understood, however:

> The causes of the disaster are hidden in much controversy and misconstruction. Guided by popular notions and doctrines, most observers exonerate the legislators who built the system and the regulators who guided it . . . They deplore the partial deregulation that took place in recent years. Deregulation, they are

convinced, together with management greed and folly [are responsible]. . . . Lax supervision permitted S&L managers to squander customers' funds . . . The obvious solution, we are told, is thorough supervision and control.[1]

(Sennholz 1989: 1)

The real causes are 'clear for all to see. The American financial system was fashioned by legislators and is regulated by regulators who together created a cartel that is crumbling under the weight of its own contradictions' (Sennholz 1989: 1). Supervision and control are the problem, not the solution.

The key to understanding the problem – and the key to the solution – is to understand the role of incentives. At one level the issue is very simple. Individuals acted in the ways they did and allowed the crisis to develop because they had incentives to do so – what Kane (1990: 2) calls the incentive-breakdown hypothesis. The most perverse incentives are generated by deposit insurance which gives banks an incentive to compromise their financial health, and regulators and politicians incentives to hide the problem even though they know that doing so ultimately makes it worse. As Kane (1990: 3) says:

> For more than a decade federal officials refused to acknowledge that the thrift red ink spill had compromised the integrity of the industry supporting the deposit insurance fund . . . officials used accounting smoke and mirrors to cover up the depletion of the funds and the increasing capital shortage. This . . . promoted official self-interests, but imposed enormous costs on society. Under existing incentives in government, covering up evidence of poor regulatory performance and relaxing binding capital requirements may be seen to be a rational government response to widespread industry insolvency . . .

which, one might add, is itself caused by the regulatory structure under which institutions operate. The crisis can therefore be resolved only if these perverse incentives are put right, and that requires more than just another cosmetic rearrangement of the regulatory system as provided for, to give a recent example, by the Financial Institutions Reform, Recovery and Enforcement Act (FIRREA) of August 1989.[2] We cannot simultaneously acknowledge the damage that deposit insurance does while continuing to think that the damage can somehow be put right by (yet another) reform of the deposit insurance system which leaves its substantial features intact. In the final analysis the only way to correct the incentives that deposit insurance creates is to get rid of deposit insurance itself.

A BENCHMARK MODEL[3]

If one is to understand and cure disease, it helps first to have a clear idea of health. Imagine that we have a banking system with no government intervention, and therefore no government deposit insurance. Those who hold bank deposits want reassurance that their savings are safe – that the bank will be able to pay back their deposits as promised – and those who borrow from banks want reassurance that their bank will not get into financial difficulties which might interrupt the credit they receive. Market forces will then lead banks to reassure their customers in various ways. Banks can give depositors the right to withdraw their funds on demand, without notice. A banker who agrees to such a contract gives depositors the right to discipline him at any moment they chose by withdrawing their funds (see, for example, Kaufman 1988c; Calomiris and Kahn 1991). Such a banker will, of course, be acutely vulnerable to the potential loss of depositor confidence, and the fact that he can do little that might disturb that confidence is what reassures his customers and gives them confidence in the first place. A banker exposed to this discipline must constantly look over his shoulder to take account of how his depositors would react. Paradoxically, therefore, though a run might weaken and possibly destroy a bank should it occur *ex post*, the vulnerability to a run – the threat of a run – helps to stabilize the banking system by imposing a discipline that limits a bank's scope to 'misbehave'.

Banks can also promote confidence by opening themselves up to scrutiny in other ways. They can hire outside monitors (e.g. credit rating agencies) or take out loans or guarantees from other financial institutions (e.g. private deposit insurance) to provide signals for their financial health, and these signals will be reliable because these parties' own wealth will be at stake. For example, a credit rating agency depends for its livelihood on its reputation – its reports are valuable only because they have credibility, and if it loses its credibility it loses its business. A good report therefore carries weight, and banks will be willing to pay for reports and adopt policies that earn favourable reports which bolster customer confidence. The same principle applies to other banks or private deposit insurance agencies which extend loans or guarantees to a particular financial institution. By exposing themselves to the risk of loss they send out a credible signal to uninformed parties that the institution is sound, and thereby promote (rational) public confidence in it. A decision by a rating agency to downgrade a bank or a decision by a guarantor to cancel its cover would undermine and perhaps destroy public confidence in that institution, so the threat of such a signal is a potentially very effective discipline. The same desire to send out good signals to the public will also lead banks to develop reliable and accurate accounting conventions which allow 'good' banks to demonstrate their soundness. The managers of 'bad' banks may not like such developments but they have limited ability to prevent them without revealing why. As Catherine England (1991: 13–14) writes:

> managers of strong banks would want their depositors to maintain confidence in their financial statements [so] they would be more forthcoming in their accounting statements . . . stronger institutions would adopt more open, market-oriented accounting in an effort to prove their superiority. Banks or S&Ls that did not follow suit would be viewed suspiciously by their customers, who would demand to know what they were hiding.

But perhaps the most important way in which a bank can reassure its customers is by maintaining adequate capital. One can think of capital here as the bank's net worth – the difference between the value of the bank's assets and the value of its liabilities. One function of the bank's capital is to give the owners, the shareholders, an interest in the 'safe' management of the bank. The shareholders of a well capitalized bank have a lot to lose if the bank incurs losses, and this downside risk is an inducement for them to discourage excessive risk-taking on the part of their managers. Indeed, the fact that they are residual claimants implies, at the margin, that any losses the bank makes are passed direct to them, so there is a strong incentive to control risk-taking. The residual nature of the shareholders' claims also implies that the shareholders help to insure the claims of bank depositors – provided that the bank has sufficient capital, any losses it makes are absorbed entirely by the shareholders, and the depositors lose nothing. Bank capital provides a buffer and that absorbs losses in order to maintain the value of the bank's deposits, and depositors will lose only if the bank's losses are so large that its net worth becomes negative and the bank becomes insolvent.

The banks' capital strength – the amount of capital they maintain relative to everything else – is then determined by customer demand operating through market forces. The better capitalized a bank is, the more reassurance it provides its customers, and, other things being equal, the more attractive it will be to them. Maintaining capital has a cost, however – it means more equity relative to debt, and those who hold the additional shares need to be compensated for the risks and inconvenience of holding shares instead of deposits. While a bank that was poorly capitalized might have difficulty maintaining its market share because customers lacked confidence in its continued ability to serve them, a bank that was excessively capitalized would also have difficulty competing because it would have to pass on its higher cost of capital to customers, who might then go elsewhere. One can think of the degree of capitalization as a quality dimension of the products the bank provides. Banks compete with each other along this quality dimension, and the important point is that competition forces them to provide the reassurance that their loan and (especially) their deposit customers demand. *If bank customers want safe banks, as they presumably do, then market forces will ensure that they get them – the banks respond to market incentives, and are exactly as safe as their customers demand.*[4] It also needs to be emphasized that the market outcome is (*ex ante*) Pareto-optimal – that is to say, there is no way in which the market outcome can be rearranged to produce an alternative that the individuals involved would prefer when they make their decisions. There are no 'externalities' or other unappropriated surpluses, and the market outcome cannot feasibly be improved.[5]

THE IMPACT OF DEPOSIT INSURANCE

The US banking industry differs from this ideal one in various important ways. Financial institutions in the United States are subject to restrictions against branch banking and other forms of portfolio diversification,[6] and they are also vulnerable to the monetary volatility – interest rate volatility, especially – generated by the erratic policies of the Federal Reserve. But perhaps the most damaging departure from the benchmark is deposit insurance. If the threat of runs helps to stabilize the banking system by making it stronger, deposit insurance removes that threat and encourages them to become weak. Deposit insurance weakens the banking industry in two principle ways:

The deterioration in banks' capital

Deposit insurance undermines banks' capital adequacy. As the benchmark model indicates, market forces under *laissez-faire* conditions would compel banks to maintain standards of capital adequacy that reflected their customers' demands for bank safety. Protecting banks against runs destroys the incentive to maintain capital and leads to a substitution of public capital, reflected in the deposit insurance guarantee (or, for that matter, a lender of last resort policy), for the equity capital they would otherwise have maintained (see, for example, Peltzman 1971). With deposits already protected, a bank no longer needs capital to reassure its customers, and the marginal benefit (to it) of maintaining capital becomes minimal. And since capital is still (usually) a more costly source of funds than deposits, the (privately) optimal capital–assets ratio becomes very small. (Or, to look at it another way, the lower the capital ratio, the greater the expected yield on shareholders' funds.) A bank's rational response to deposit insurance is therefore to drive its capital ratio right down, and a weaker capital position leaves it more exposed to losses that could wipe out its net worth and drive it into economic insolvency.[7]

The empirical evidence supports the prediction that deposit insurance encourages banks to run their capital down. In the first ten years of the federal deposit insurance regime, bank capital ratios more than halved, from 14.1 per cent in 1934 to 6.2 per cent in 1945 (Salsman 1990: 56). Regulators responded by imposing minimal capital requirements, but they did little to alter the underlying incentives banks faced, and the capital deterioration continued. A study by Peltzman (1971: 20) concluded that 'banks have substituted deposit insurance for capital' and their capital allocation

> seems not to have been affected in any important way by the regulation which intends to affect it. There was no evidence that bank investment behaviour conforms to the standards set for it by the regulatory agencies, and there is strong evidence that it never has . . .

This conclusion was reiterated later by Salsman (1990: 57), who noted that the incentives provided by deposit insurance ensured that

> the long-term trend in capital adequacy would continue to deteriorate . . . [Nothing stemmed] the tide of deterioration. In 1962 the Comptroller of the Currency proposed a solution to bank capital inadequacy that 'permitted' banks to include certain types of long-term debt as 'equity'. This merely sanctioned the growing deterioration in capital adequacy without reversing it. In 1968 more formal regulations were put in place but with long-term 'leniency' periods and exceptions for banks that failed to meet minimum capital ratios. The persistence of regulators' inability to reverse the trend toward capital inadequacy seems to confirm that capital adequacy in banking deteriorates for fundamental, institutional reasons that no amount of regulation can effectively counter. Central bankers and regulators may pose as the prudent protectors of system capital adequacy but in fact it is central banking [and especially deposit insurance] that brings about its destruction.
>
> (Salsman 1990: 57)

The fall in the industry's capital position is actually worse than the figures suggest because the regulatory authorities have colluded with the industry to disguise its true financial position by various accounting subterfuges. As we have seen, in 1962 the Comptroller of the Currency allowed banks to include certain types of debt as equity, and the accounting definition of capital was broadened further in 1976 to allow goodwill and loan loss provision to count as capital (Salsman 1990: 57, 65). Later still the (relatively) lax Generally Accepted Accounting Practices (GAAP) were replaced for regulatory purposes by the Regulatory Accounting Practices (RAP), which were even laxer. Among other differences, the RAP differs from the GAAP in that they allow subordinated debentures, pledged deposits, unamortized deferred gains and, incredibly, unrecognized losses, gains or losses on future transactions, and accounting forbearances to count as capital as well (CBO 1990: 54). Not surprisingly, the RAP have been condemned as nothing more than a 'fraud and unprincipled cover-up for the insolvent' (Salsman 1990: 115). As the same writer also notes, 'This process of redefining capital represents regulatory attempts to obfuscate, not solve the problem of capital adequacy deterioration' (1990:

65). Matters are made worse still by the use of book-value accounting instead of market-value accounting to cover up losses in the market value of banks' assets. As Kaufman (1988c) writes, the use of book value accounting in banking was promoted by regulators in the 1930s to 'deliberately mask' the banks' poor financial condition. The practical difficulties with market-value accounting are fewer now than they used to be (e.g. owing to the rise of secondary markets), and the opposition to it has come less from the bankers than from the regulators themselves (Kaufman 1988c). The impact of market-value accounting can be seen from the fact that in late 1989 many banks wrote down their Latin American loans by 25 per cent, yet the same loans were trading on secondary markets at discounts of 75 per cent. Bank balance sheets were therefore overstating the value of these loans by 200 per cent, and a true valuation would have wiped out the net worth of a considerable number of the banks involved (Salsman 1990: 66). To the Latin American loan losses must also be added losses from loans to other overseas borrowers, agriculture, oil, real estate and other sectors.

Increased lending risk

Deposit insurance also encourages banks to take more lending risks. In the absence of deposit insurance banks' lending policies would be constrained by the threat that depositors would run if they felt the bank was taking too many risks. The need to preserve depositor confidence would also force a bank to maintain sufficient capital to ensure that almost all lending risk would be borne by the shareholders, who stand to lose (what is left of) their investments, or the managers, who stand to lose their jobs and reputations. Deposit insurance allows a bank to pursue a more risky lending policy by removing the threat of runs, but it also gives a bank more incentive to take risks by providing a cushion against (at least some) of the downside risk. If a bank takes risks and they pay off, it keeps the profits; if it takes risks and they fail, some (at least) of the loss its shareholders/managers would otherwise have borne is passed instead to the insurance agency. Deposit insurance thus reduces the cost (to the bank) of taking risks, and thereby encourages it to do so. The size of the incentive to take more risks depends on several factors:

If a bank is well capitalized, its shareholders would bear a considerable proportion of the downside risk, and the incentive to take additional risks may actually be quite small. If a bank is less well capitalized, however, it will face a lower downside risk and a greater incentive to take additional lending risks. In the extreme, a bank with a zero or negative net worth might face no downside risk at all, and would have nothing to lose and everything to gain from high-risk, high-return ('shoot for the moon') lending policies. The incentive to take on additional lending risks thus rises as the institution's capital position worsens, and at the limit the institution might take virtually any risk provided that there was a probability, however small, that the risk might just pay off. (And the implication, of course, is that the losses the bank makes are then passed on to its unfortunate deposit insurer.)

The incentive to take risks also depends on the structure of deposit insurance premiums. A bank that takes more risk could be made to pay higher insurance premiums, which would reduce the expected return from its risk-taking and help offset the moral hazard created by deposit insurance. The worst incentives are provided by flat-rate deposit insurance – the premium structure actually adopted by US federal deposit insurance agencies – which gives a bank free deposit insurance cover at the margin for any additional risks and therefore does nothing to counter moral hazard.

The dynamic instability of deposit insurance

A very worrying consequence of deposit insurance is the dynamic instability created by the interaction of weaker capital positions and greater risk-taking. Suppose that the banking system is initially well capitalized when we introduce deposit insurance. As already discussed, the banking system will respond over time by running down its capital and taking more risks, especially if we have flat-rate premiums. As a bank's capital position declines, the moral hazard created by deposit insurance worsens and the bank takes ever more risks. The greater risk-taking in turn makes the bank's net worth more volatile, so a given amount of capital provides less reassurance to depositors. (Or, to put it another way, a greater amount of capital is required to keep depositors' expected losses constant when the bank takes more risks.) The greater risk-taking contributes to the deterioration in the banks' effective capital adequacy, and the two factors feed on one another to bring about an accelerating depreciation in the bank's financial health that eventually culminates in the destruction of all incentive to behave prudently or control risk. A bank that started off in a reasonably healthy financial position when deposit insurance was first introduced can end up as a 'zombie' that gambles wildly because it has nothing left to lose.

The problem is aggravated even further by the absence of any reliable mechanism to close down zombie institutions before they can inflict too much damage on other parties. Before deposit insurance was introduced, institutions that were perceived to be unsound would have lost the confidence of depositors, who would have put them out of business by withdrawing their deposits – market forces would have eliminated institutions that did not come up to the level of safety and soundness that depositors demanded. Once deposit insurance is established depositors have no reason to be concerned about a bank's financial health, and they have no reason to withdraw their deposits regardless of how poor its financial position is. Deposit insurance thus destroys the only reliable mechanism there is for putting unsound institutions out of business. A zombie institution can therefore continue to operate simply by raising its deposit interest rate, if necessary, to ensure that it continues to have enough funds to meet the losses it makes from its gambling and any withdrawals it faces, and the only factor that would prevent such a game going on for ever is that there is an upper limit to the loss that the insurance agency can withstand and itself remain solvent. At some point the insurer itself goes out of business and only then does the game end. In the absence of any mechanism for closing zombie institutions down, deposit insurance becomes an institutionalized Ponzi game in which an unsound institution can keep itself afloat more or less indefinitely by running up debts which it can never repay (as noted, for example, by Kaufman (1989: 8)), and what enables the game to keep on going is that the creditors don't care because the debts are guaranteed by the federal government. Worse still, an institution can theoretically gamble on virtually any scale it likes, since there is no mechanism to control the amount of betting an individual institution can engage in. If a bank operating under *laissez-faire* conditions were to keep expanding its deposits and loans, it would run into diminishing returns on its loans and would lose customer confidence as its capital position deteriorated. There is therefore a natural limit to bank expansion under free-market conditions. When there is deposit insurance, on the other hand, an institution can expand its size to virtually any desired extent simply by offering interest rates at least as high as those available elsewhere. A bank that had already become a zombie might then be relatively unconcerned about diminishing returns on its loans and a deteriorating capital position, and depositors would have no reason to worry, so it could keep on expanding more or less as it wished. To avoid insolvency itself, the insurance agency must therefore intervene to close down problem institutions before their loss-making gets out of hand. An effective failure resolution policy is essential if the insurance agency is to preserve its own solvency (see also Kaufman 1988c).

Apart from encouraging an individual bank to embark on policies that undermine its financial health, deposit insurance undermines the banking system by allowing unsound banks to impose various burdens on their sounder brethren that undermine their health too. It discourages financial prudence by giving hand-outs to the unsound banks that the better banks are denied, and the perversity of the incentive structure is aggravated further by the latter as net contributors to the deposit insurance funds being taxed to pay for the losses of the former. Since the safety of bank deposits is no longer tied to banks' financial health, deposit insurance also eliminates the competitive advantage that well capitalized banks would have over weaker ones under *laissez-faire* conditions. While the free market rewards a bank with a good capital position by strengthening its market share, a well capitalized bank under a deposit insurance regime merely faces a higher cost of funds that brings no compensatory advantage. Deposit insurance thus transforms a strong capital position into a liability and puts well capitalized banks at a competitive disadvantage that makes it difficult for them to maintain their capital position even if they want to. Instead of promoting bank safety, as they would do under *laissez-faire*, market pressures are converted into a destructive force that undermines the banks even further. To add to which, deposit insurance also increases the interest rates that good institutions must pay on their deposits by allowing zombie institutions that would have been eliminated by the free market to remain open and bid deposit rates up. Not only do they bid for deposits that would otherwise have gone to sounder banks, but once they degenerate into Ponzi-type activities there is little limit to what they can offer. As the banking system deteriorates the zombie institutions have an ever greater influence on deposit interest rates.

These rates become increasingly divorced from any underlying economic reality and become more and more of a burden to those institutions that are still trying to attract deposits they intend to repay. To make a bad picture even worse, the pressure on 'good' institutions is aggravated yet further by the decline in lending rates, lending standards and general management practices which occurs for much the same reasons.

The role of the regulators

It is impossible to understand the banking crisis without also considering the roles of the (supposed) 'guardians' of the banking system, the regulators and politicians. These two groups play critical roles in the process of bank deterioration, and these roles can be understood only by isolating the private interests they serve. Consider first the regulators whose task it is to administer the regulatory system, which for the most part is imposed on them by the politicians – Congress and the administration – whom the regulators nominally serve, and who determine their responsibilities, remuneration and conditions of work. In the first instance the main concern of regulators is to preserve their own positions by keeping reasonably contented the only people on whom they directly depend, the politicians. Among other things, this requires that they try to provide the politicians with what the politicians want to hear and avoid issues that might provoke political intervention which is both unpredictable and (from the regulators' point of view) potentially dangerous. When intervention cannot be avoided, the regulators' best option is to do their best to hi-jack it and divert the political pressure for change into 'safe' channels or, better still, use it to further their own private or institutional ambitions (e.g. by increasing their powers or funds). Above all, they need to avoid incurring the kind of resentment which can provoke the politicians to take action directly against them. The regulators' incentive structure influences their behaviour in various ways.[8]

1. It encourages them to focus on how policies look to the politicians (and other regulators) and to hide awkward problems. This emphasis on appearances over substance puts a premium on plausible deniability and is what lies behind the corruption of accounting standards discussed earlier. Those who still believe that governments and regulators actually promote the public interest

they claim to serve might also note that this behaviour is quite inexplicable from such a viewpoint. The fact that our 'protectors' *do* act in this way indicates that such a view is empirically false and compels us to accept a public choice interpretation of their behaviour, which ought to make us wary of what they do or say.

2. It puts a premium on cosmetic short-term measures to the detriment of longer-term solutions. A regulator can usually assume that he will be in his present position for a relatively short period of time, and he tends to be rewarded for how things look during his tenure. The roof may fall in soon afterwards, but he has relatively little incentive to worry about that, provided he can put it off until he has moved on and can plausibly deny responsibility for what happens during his successor's term of office. The regulatory structure is therefore ill equipped to resolve problems with a long gestation period whose solution would impose short-term pain on the regulators who ought to be dealing with them – the developing thrift crisis in the 1980s is a case in point – even though those involved may privately recognize the need for prompt and far-reaching reform.

3. The desire to hide problems and the excessive short-termism of regulatory bodies reinforced each other to produce an extreme reluctance to close down zombie institutions during the 1980s. While regulators understood that zombie institutions needed to be closed down if they were to control their losses, it was none the less often in their own private interest to allow them to continue in operation. To take over or close down an insolvent institution involves short-term expenses which use up the insurance agency's reserves, and the insurers were reluctant to engage in many such operations as they would have exposed their financial weakness and brought forward the evil day when they would have to appeal to Congress for more funds and explain their insolvency. Apart from the prospect of having to go cap-in-hand to Congress, regulators were sometimes reluctant to close institutions down because an 'excessive' number of bank failures might expose them to adverse criticism by giving the (correct) impression that they had a problem on their hands they could not cope with. These factors meant that regulators often preferred to keep unsound institutions open even though they were aware of the long-run costs of such policies. Instead of moving swiftly to close down problem institutions before their loss-making got out of control, regulatory 'forbearance' allowed the banking system to deteriorate further and

sanctioned the degeneration of banking into a Ponzi game. Accounting standards were repeatedly watered down so that institutions could meet regulatory 'requirements', and institutions that still failed to meet them were often explicitly exempted. Forbearance was also made possible by extensive 'lender of last resort' operations, and the collateral requirements for such support sank to very low levels to enable weak institutions to qualify. A recent study of FSLIC policies found that delays in closing down insolvent institutions were the most expensive aspect of the FSLIC closure policies (Barth *et al.*, 1989), and the deterioration was reasonably predictable as well, so there was relatively little reason for the regulators to be surprised when a specific institution became insolvent (see, for example, Brewer 1988: 10).

4. The incentive structure faced by regulators leads them to promote explanations and solutions for problems which are intended principally to legitimize the regulators' role and absolve them of responsibility. Regulatory explanations for banking problems have consequently downplayed the effects of their own policies and emphasized factors such as falling oil prices, defaults on foreign loans, deregulation[9] and bad management[10] for which they could (arguably) deny responsibility. Such explanations put the blame for banking problems on external scapegoats and thereby help to legitimize regulatory policies.[11] They also divert political pressure into safe channels and reinforce the regulators' preferred 'solutions', which usually call for the bailing out or further expansion of the regulatory apparatus to deal with the instability the external factors allegedly create. More recently, regulators in the United States have also gone in for elaborate 'theories' of forbearance that provide them with an excuse for failing to close down insolvent institutions by emphasizing the (alleged) costs of closing institutions that might recover if only they were given a bit more time or assistance.

The regulatory dynamic

It is important also to understand the way in which the regulatory process deteriorates, and how that in turn contributes to the further deterioration of the banks. The regulatory system may appear to work tolerably well provided the banking system is still in (relatively) decent shape and the regulatory agencies themselves are solvent. If there are only a few problem institutions and the insurance corporations have the reserves to handle the expenses involved, the regulators can afford to take a reasonably long-term perspective in 'resolving' problem institutions and not worry too much about the effects of the resolution on their own financial position. The regulatory system can therefore appear to work quite well provided there are not many problems, but it starts to malfunction visibly when deposit insurance undermines the health of the banking system and more and more institutions fall ill. The regulators then find it increasingly difficult to handle problem banks as they used to. The cost of failed institutions put an ever greater strain on the solvency of the deposit insurance agencies, and they are increasingly pressed to look for alternative ways of handling problem institutions which will put less immediate strain on their own finances. Instead of simply taking institutions over once their financial position has reached a critical point and then spending whatever is required to sort them out, regulators become preoccupied with policies to keep the insurance agencies themselves afloat, in increasing disregard of their ultimate cost. A point comes when the insurance agency has clearly become unsound and finds itself in the same predicament as many of the institutions for which it is still theoretically responsible. Having become a zombie in its own right, it plays the same game with Congress as its own zombie institutions play with it – it covers up its own insolvency and lives on borrowed time at massive cost to its insurer (in this case Congress and ultimately the federal taxpayer). Any remaining discipline the insurance agency exerted on the institutions under its control is undermined by the agency's own insolvency and its consequent preoccupation with its own survival.

The US federal deposit agencies fit this pattern closely. The deterioration in the thrift industry put enormous strain on the FSLIC, whose reserves fell from $4.6 billion in 1985 to −$13.7 billion in 1987 (Nakamura 1990: 18), and the FSLIC resorted to ever more desperate means to keep afloat as its finances deteriorated. Apart from a greater reliance on 'forebearance' (i.e. doing nothing), it often 'resolved' problem thrifts by arranging mergers for them, with merger partners encouraged to participate by bribes in the form of knock-down prices, FSLIC (i.e. government) guarantees of problem assets, and tax breaks of various kinds. These sorts of arrangements not only minimized the strain on the FSLIC's resrves, they helped disguise the problem and passed some of the cost on to others (e.g. the Internal Revenue Service) or into the future (which didn't matter, since the FSLIC was going bust anyway). In the most notorious programme, the so-called Southwest Plan, in 1988, the FSLIC guaranteed both principal and interest to buyers of bust thrifts (with interest substantially above market rates!), gave tax write-offs that were sometimes worth more than the capital the new owners contributed, and indemnified new owners against all resulting lawsuits. In return, buyers had to put in *at most* 1.5 per cent of the total value of thrift assets with new cash, and buyers, not surprisingly, were queuing up to participate.[12] As new owners had virtually no incentive to sort out problem loans, the mergers did little or nothing to resolve the underlying problems of the industry and their main effect was to buy time for the FSLIC at monumental cost to the federal taxpayer. The FSLIC was declared insolvent by the the General Accounting Office in 1987, and despite a recapitalization (i.e. bail-out) the same year its net worth had plummeted to −$75 billion by the end of 1988 (Nakamura 1990: 18). In the end the FSLIC was abolished by the FIRREA in 1989 and its debts were taken over by other government agencies. The other federal deposit insurance agency – the FDIC – also came under mounting financial pressure as its client industry deteriorated, and it too is widely acknowledged to be economically insolvent as well.

The role of the politicians

In theory, the role of the politicians is to promote the social good by setting up and overseeing the regulatory system to protect a banking system that is (dubiously) presumed to be unable to protect itself. In practice, it was the politicians who set up the deposit insurance regime that undermined the banking industry and it was they who failed to keep the spiralling costs of deposit insurance under control. The root of the problem is not so much that the politicians are as concerned with their own private interests as anyone else, but that there is no reliable mechanism to align their interests with those of the people whom they are supposed to serve. Several factors lie behind this incentive breakdown.

The electoral process gives politicians relatively short horizons and encourages them to downgrade substantive issues and be preoccupied instead with how policies appear to their electors.[13] It also encourages them to shun awkward issues that might bring little or no electoral pay-off. Difficult policy issues are consequently distorted and frequently left unresolved for someone else to sort out. As with the regulators, there is no mechanism to encourage socially responsible behaviour, and the bottom line is often plausible deniability.

The division of political power between the administration and Congress and among different members of Congress also encourages a game of political chicken in which everyone ignores difficult issues in the hope that someone else will take responsibility (and lose political points) for resolving them. These problems are aggravated by institutional rivalries and party political differences – and, especially, by the combination of the two – which encourage politicians to leave difficult issues alone in the hope that their political opponents will blink first or otherwise come off worse in political terms. Though the house is burning down and everyone knows it, they all stand outside waiting for someone else to take responsibility for putting it out.

Politicians are often vulnerable to pressure from interested parties. The complexity of financial issues and the disparity in research support puts them at an intellectual disadvantage when dealing with their regulatory agencies, which often allows the latter to promote their own ambitions under suitable disguises. The politicans are also vulnerable to conventional political (and financial) pressure from those who gain from protectionist policies or other forms of political patronage. Particularly in the financial area, the gains from lobbying for protection are very large relative to the costs, and they are sufficiently concentrated that lobbying is much easier for those who would gain than for those who would lose. Such lobbying was particularly prominent in the thrift industry, where those who had an interest in insolvent institutions often turned to the political market place for protection:

> Large political contributions were made by the thrift industry to Congress to postpone legislative action that would increase the cost to the industry through higher deposit insurance premiums . . . reduce its independence [or] bring about the removal of managers/owners of insolvent or near insolvent institutions. Because the dollar amounts were so massive, contributions were extraordinarily large even by Washington, D.C. standards. . . . Many Congressmen . . . acted . . . to delay potentially corrective legislative and regulatory actions.[14]

(Kaufman 1989: 11)

RESOLVING THE BANKING CRISIS

Diagnosis of the problem

We now turn at last to how the crisis might be resolved. The key point is to recognize the overriding importance of incentives. The banking crisis is no accident, to be blamed on bad luck or a few bad or incompetent individuals, as many would have it, but a natural and predictable response by the main people involved to the incentives they faced. Solving the crisis therefore requires that we get those incentives right, and that means that we get rid of the government intervention that distorts incentives and rewards anti-social behaviour on the part of those concerned. If such measures are to have the maximum benefit, however, we also need to give private agents free rein and remove all artificial (i.e. legislatively created) barriers that hinder banks and leave them unduly vulnerable. The various restrictions against financial institutions' diversifying their risks – of which the best-known are the laws against branch banking and the Glass-Steagall provisions – therefore need to be swept away. Something also needs to be done to get to grips with the chronic monetary instability of the last quarter-century and the resulting havoc it has created with the banking system. But the key factor is to get the incentive struture right, and that requires that we should get rid of deposit insurance (and, for that matter, the lender of last resort). If rent control is the best way to destroy a city apart from bombing it, deposit insurance is the next best way to destroy one's banking system, and is tantamount to bribing the banking system to commit suicide. It has not only all but destroyed the banking industry in the United States,[15] but it has managed in the process to produce the biggest public finance disaster in world history and land US taxpayers with a bill that already dwarfs all previous federal bail-outs put together – and is still rising at a ferocious rate.

Extreme as this cure may sound, there is no feasible alternative. The politicians' and regulators' favourite option – leave things substantially intact behind a façade of cosmetic changes, as they did with the FIRREA – is the worst option of all, and is in any case unsustainable. Like an alcoholic who keeps on drinking to avert his hangover, putting off the reckoning only makes it worse. It was putting off the problem, after all, that converted an ordinary multi-billion dollar disaster into an unprecedented catastrophe whose cost will probably run into the trillions. Something must be done, and soon. The other non-option is to reform the deposit insurance system. If one insists on insuring deposits, then one will continue to have the lethal incentive structure that deposit insurance implies, and one cannot reverse the incentive structure and simultaneously keep the deposit insurance that creates those incentives in the first place. At best deposit insurance reform might marginally improve the system – though, if past 'reforms' are anything to go by, it is at least as likely to make it even worse – but there is little point aiming for marginal improvements at this stage. Deposit insurance needs to be abolished outright, as soon as is practicable, and anything much less ought to be ruled out of court.

The way out

The problem is to convert this general assessment of what needs to be done into an operational reform package. It seems to me that any reasonable reform must satisfy three basic principles.

A date must be set for the abolition of deposit insurance. Setting a date for ending deposit insurance would concentrate minds in the banking industry and set in motion a sequence of changes that would restore the industry to health. Those involved would have to anticipate what conditions would be like once deposit insurance had been eliminated, and then decide whether or not they wished to operate under the new regime. With no more government guarantees, institutions could no longer take customer confidence for granted, and they could earn confidence only by maintaining the standards of financial health their customers demand. The financial industry would then look very much like the benchmark model laid out earlier. As compared with their counterparts today, banks would be highly capitalized, more cautious in their lending policies and far more competitive, and no bank could expect to survive in the post-deposit insurance world whose standards fell appreciably below those of its competitors.

Once a date has been set for abolishing deposit insurance, existing institutions (and potential new entrants, like foreign banks) must decide whether or not they are willing to operate under these conditions. Their decisions would be based primarily on the cost of bringing themselves up to scratch. Healthier institutions would be more inclined to make the effort to compete, but the managers of many zombie institutions would probably calculate that the profits from operating in the new environment would not be worth the capital and other costs of bringing their institutions back to life. Those that decided to stay in business would then have to prepare themselves and make the necessary adjustments – they would have to rebuild their capital, reappraise their lending policies, and so on. Institutions that decided to continue in business must ensure that they were financially fit by the time the government guarantee was lifted and their depositors stood to lose their investments. They would be aware that their customers would be watching them, and customers who felt that their bank was not sufficiently strong would withdraw their deposits while they could still recover them in full, thanks to the government's guarantee – no rational depositor would keep deposits with unsafe banks once the deposit insurance guarantee had expired – and they would normally redeposit the funds withdrawn in 'good' banks which enjoyed their confidence. A bank's loan customers would act in a similar way. If they felt that the bank was not going to survive, they would also disengage themselves and start building relationships with other lenders, and the bank would have lost its loan business as well by the time deposit insurance was lifted.

If an institution were to decide that staying in business was not worth while, on the other hand, then it would make little effort to preserve customer confidence, since investment in confidence-building would bring it little return. The failure to make any significant effort to keep its market share would send out a clear signal to its customers – a signal all the clearer because of the very visible efforts being made by the other institutions which intended to remain in business. Depositors would then make sure that they recovered their deposits while they were still insured, loan customers would go elsewhere, and the bank would be out of business by the time deposit insurance was lifted. So, once the reform package was announced, the banks would start dividing into two groups – those that wanted to make a go of it and build themselves up, and the no-hopers that had decided to give up and go into terminal decline. Depositors and loan customers would increasingly desert the no-hopers for the good institutions, and the differences between the two groups would become more and more pronounced as the date approached when deposit insurance was to be abolished. When that date actually arrived the no-hopers would already be out of business and the banks that remained would be restored to financial health.

A question that needs to be resolved is how much advance notice to give that deposit insurance is to be abolished. Other things being equal, an early date speeds up the recovery of the banking system and helps keep down the cost to the taxpayers of resolving the crisis. On the other hand, immediate abolition of deposit insurance might be ill advised because the adjustment would be easier if the industry could prepare for it. Institutions would want time to assess the impact of the reform and decide whether they wished to remain in business, and those that continued would have many issues to resolve – they would have to decide how to rebuild their capital structure, how to adopt new loan policies, how to adjust to new accounting conventions, and so on – and these issues would all take time to sort out. For their part, their customers would also need to decide how to respond, and those whose banks were going to the wall would need time to change banks. Exactly how much notice to give is obviously a matter of some judgement, but, all things considered, it seems to me that two to three years ought to be enough to give 'good' (i.e. in this context, retrievable) banks enough time to recapitalize and the customers of bad banks enough time to adjust in a reasonably orderly fashion. In order to arrive at an appropriate timetable, we also need to be clear why we want to give the industry time to adjust. We do not want to do so in order that the industry may be fully adjusted to the new regime when the new regime takes effect – however much notice we give, the banks can never be fully adjusted, because no one can predict in all its intricate detail what life after deposit insurance will be like, and a certain amount of learning by doing cannot be avoided. The reason we want to give advance notice is to reduce certain adjustment costs. While there is nothing much we can do about 'bad' banks that are not worth retrieving – they need to be put out of business, and we therefore have to bear the costs involved – we do not want 'good' banks to be liquidated as well. The various sunk costs involved in setting the bank up, forming relationships with it, and so on, would then be unnecessarily lost. If we give little or no notice, many institutions of this sort will not yet have put out clear signals as to whether they wish to continue after deposit insurance has been abolished, and even those that do may not have had time to build up their capital adequacy to give their customers the reassurance they would demand. There will be much confusion and possibly even panic, many retrievable institutions will be unnecessarily put out of business and a lot of valuable capital written off, including a lot of unnecessary disruption to the provision of credit. Removing deposit insurance with little or no notice also forces a great deal of adjustment to take place extremely quickly. The shock involved could place a great strain on the financial system which has to absorb it – 'dispossessed' borrowers swamp credit markets at the same time, for instance – which creates costs that can be avoided if the process of abandoning bad institutions is more orderly and 'controlled', and, of course, if 'good' institutions are not unnecessarily driven out of business as well.

Congress must honour its debts. It is very important that Congress should be prepared to pay the costs of cleaning up the mess it has done so much to create. The costs certainly include the cost of compensating those with deposits at institutions that have already failed, but they also include the cost of those future failures that will occur while Congress is still holding the deposit insurance safety net under the banking industry. While Congressmen would be anxious to keep the already staggering bill from rising much further, there are two ways of trying to cut costs which they should definitely avoid.

1. Congress should not try – as it has often done in the past – to shift clean-up costs on to the 'good' banks. 'Making the banks pay' is a superficially appealing but dangerous option whose hidden costs seriously undermine the process of restoring the banking system to financial health. It taxes the very thing one most wants to promote – financial health – in order to subsidize its opposite. The system already has too many incentives for 'good' banks to turn 'bad', and imposing more taxes on the good banks to pay the bad ones would make a perverse incentive structure even worse. It would encourage banks that would otherwise be marginal to turn bad, and then they would fail and need to be cleaned up as well. In any case, the banking industry is now so weak that there are relatively few 'good' banks that could withstand much taxation, and there are very many sick institutions to be cared for. Such a large 'dependency ratio' can easily create a crippling burden on those good banks that are left, and we cannot even be sure that the tax would raise a positive net revenue once we allow for the cost of the failures it would induce. Congress

would be better-off avoiding this option and bearing the cost directly itself, up-front.

2. Congress should also avoid any temptation to try to cut costs by skimping on the safety net it provides to institutions in the transitional period before deposit insurance is actually lifted. The hidden costs here are potentially even worse than those involved in an attempt to extract more revenue from the banking system. *It is absolutely essential that confidence in the integrity of the system is maintained during the transition period, especially when the reform programme is first announced.* If there is any suspicion that deposits are not fully guaranteed, or that depositors will be otherwise penalized if their institutions fail, they will panic and withdraw their funds as quickly as they can, and the effect could be not much different from that of an announcement that deposit insurance is to be ended the day after tomorrow – a major panic, the destruction of many 'good' institutions that would otherwise have survived, and massive disruption. We want to restore appropriate incentives to the banking system, but we do not want to make the adjustment process even more difficult than it must already be. The position of the reformer is comparable to that of a circus manager who decides that his circus is no longer drawing crowds because working with a safety net has caused his acrobats to lose their skill. He decides they must dispense with the safety net and gives them a firm date in the future when it will be withdrawn. The net will remain in the meantime, and the acrobats have to decide what to do. Those who wish to can leave, and those who stay had better get some practice in. If he has any sense, the manager will give his acrobats sufficient notice to ensure that they will have the skill to survive when the day comes to remove the net, but if he fails to give them that warning he invites disaster in the form of his acrobats walking out on him or someone having an accident for which he must take responsibility. The moral is that it is not enough to get the long-run incentives right; we must get the adjustment process right as well.

The financial system must be deregulated. Vital though they are, the abolition of deposit insurance and a willingness by Congress to underwrite the costs of the adjustment process merely put right the worst of the many government-created illnesses from which the US financial system suffers. If we wish to restore the financial system to full health, these measures need to be supplemented by thorough-going liberalization. At the very minimum, a deregulation programme ought to encompass the abolition of all restrictions on branch-banking, the abolition of Glass-Steagall-type provisions, and the removal of all remaining restrictions on financial institutions' freedom to diversify their portfolios and charge the rates the market will bear. The aim should be free trade in the financial services industry. A free-trade programme would complement the abolition of deposit insurance by freeing financial institutions of legislative and regulatory barriers that artificially weaken them. It would therefore speed up the recovery process as well as promote the overall health of the banking industry. Free trade would also encourage innovation and make the industry both more efficient and more competitive. In addition, opening up the US financial market would encourage the entry of foreign banks and foreign bank capital, and the presence of strong foreign banks would stiffen competition in the US market and stimulate the adoption of successful foreign innovations by American banks.

If we apply free-market logic consistently, however, our deregulation package must go well beyond the abolition of direct legislative restrictions against branch-banking and portfolio diversification. Free-market reasoning makes the whole interventionist apparatus – the Federal Reserve and the various remaining government banking agencies – redundant at best and very costly at worst, so the only logical course is to eliminate it altogether. It is particularly important to dismantle the Federal Reserve. Despite appearances to the contrary, the underlying logic of the lender of last resort function which the Fed provides is essentially the same as the logic behind deposit insurance. Consequently it stands or falls – and therefore falls – with the argument for deposit insurance. Nor is there any need for the Fed (or any surrogate) to regulate the banking industry because banks in a competitive environment would be regulated much more effectively by the market. The Fed's banking functions would therefore be redundant, and its only other major function – the monopolistic provision of base money – is a dangerous and harmful privilege which ought to be abolished anyway. Perhaps the best course would be to reconvert the currency to a commodity standard and then repeal all laws against the (non-counterfeit) issue of banknotes or other forms of bank money. Reconverting the currency would allow other banks to issue notes and reserve money denominated in US dollars, and the Fed could then be safely dismantled. A suitably chosen commodity standard would also put an end to the monetary volatility which the Fed and the US government have created over the past thirty years. The abolition of the Fed would also help protect the banking system and the value of the currency against future government meddling by eliminating a powerful pro-interventionist lobby and putting some distance between the government and the financial system. Finally, dismantling the Fed would have the incidental though by no means trivial consequence of giving the banks a major capital boost. Though the Fed is nominally owned by its member banks, they currently have no real control over its policies and only very limited access to that part of their wealth which is tied up in the Federal Reserve system itself. The amounts involved appear to be substantial – some illustrative figures given by Salsman (1990: 139) indicate that perhaps a third of total bank capital is tied up in this way, and transferring Fed net worth back to member banks would double their capital ratios to almost 9 per cent – so dismantling the Fed would also go a long way towards giving the industry the recapitalization it badly needs.

The politics of banking reform

Working out what needs to be done is one thing, but working out how to harness the political energy to get it done is quite another. The former task is fundamentally economic, the latter primarily political. None the less, it seems to me that economists can still contribute to the latter by helping the professional politicians and political analysts who are trying to steer the right measures through the political minefield. The principal way in which economists can help is by clarifying the public debate by demolishing the self-serving 'theories' of regulators and politicians whose explanations promote their own narrow interests at the expense of the common weal. While no one denies that fraud, bad management, external factors and sheer bad luck all contributed to banking difficulties, these factors are ultimately peripheral and we should constantly warn against superficial 'explanations' that make such factors the scapegoats. We must also be on our guard against those who attempt to add 'deregulation' to the list of scapegoats and draw the conclusion that what is needed is more regulation. We cannot restore a weak banking system to health by imposing yet more regulations on it. The comforting fig leaves that politicians and regulators use to cover themselves must be pulled away, and we must never allow the public debate to lose sight of the fundamental point that responsibility for the current mess lies with the regulatory–political superstructure in general, and with deposit insurance in particular. Above everything else, we need to keep hammering away at the point that the solution – the only solution – is to abolish deposit insurance outright, and nothing less should be entertained. We must also emphasize that the abolition of deposit insurance is only emergency surgery, and if we want to restore the banking industry to full fitness it needs the kind of rigorous exercise that can come only from a programme of radical deregulation. It is not enough to criticize this or that regulation, this or that regulatory institution, or this or that individual – the underlying problem is the regulatory process itself. To use the Marxist language, we must delegitimize the whole regulatory superstructure so that we sweep the lot away.

Finally, the politicians might note that making a serious effort to sort out the mess is not necessarily political suicide. Politicians in other countries have managed to carry through worthwhile fundamental reforms without destroying themselves in the process, and some, indeed, have shown that well thought-out reform programmes can not only be pushed through but can also win elections. The experience of New Zealand is particularly instructive in this regard. According to the former Finance Minister, Roger Douglas (1990: 2), most politicians subscribe to a conventional view that 'decisive action must inevitably bring political calamity upon their governments' and they therefore avoid 'structural reform until it is forced upon them by . . . economic and social disaster'. Douglas argues forcefully that this view is mistaken. Far from depending on the avoidance of awkward issues, 'Political survival depends on making quality decisions; compromised choices lead to voter dissatisfaction; letting things drift is political suicide . . . politicians can take practicable and politically successful action to benefit the nation, without waiting until . . . disaster has forced their hand' (1990: 2). Politicians should also go the whole hog for quality decisions and not wait for a consensus to have formed before they act. Waiting for consensus usually means watering down reforms to buy off interested parties, and it can mean waiting a very long time. Politicians should go ahead regardless, and consensus will follow later. They should also avoid the temptation to slow down the pace of reform to satisfy those who claim that a slower pace would impose lower adjustment costs.

Such pleas are usually no more than a delaying tactic by those who seek to undermine the reform, and the fact is that we do not know how to fine-tune these changes anyway. In any case, as with the US banking crisis, radical reforms are often very urgent. Politicians should therefore avoid piece-by-piece reform and move forward by quantum leaps that leave opponents with little time or opportunity to mobilize and drag the programme down. Most important of all, US politicians should note that this advice is not untried armchair theorizing. It transformed the New Zealand economy from the most sclerotic, overregulated economy in the Western world into one of its least regulated and most dynamic economies – and the government that adopted it was returned at the next election in 1987 with an increased parliamentary majority:

> The moral of New Zealand's story is plain. The politicians who sought success through *ad hoc* solutions that evaded the real problems damaged the nation and destroyed their own reputation. Voters ultimately place a higher value on enhancing their medium-term prospects than on action that looks successful short-term, but only by sacrificing larger and more enduring future gains. . . . There is a deep well of realism and common sense among the ordinary people of the community. They want politicians to have guts and vision . . .

Notes

1 Introduction

1 There are a number of treatments of free banking. The interested reader might start with Dowd (1988b, 1989a), Glasner (1989b), Salsman (1990), Selgin (1988, 1990a) and White (1984b, 1989).

2 Other papers have since pursued this idea, but get apparently conflicting results. Chappell and Dowd (1988, 1991) attack the issue by presenting theoretical counter-examples of (what we believe to be) plausible economies in which convertibility on demand is dominated by an option clause. The underlying idea is based on an application of queuing theory in which the option clause enables banks to operate on lower reserves an earn higher profits which in turn benefit noteholders by reducing their expected default losses. Dowd (1991c) examines some of the criticisms of the option clause in more detail and compares option clause suspension arrangements with the alternative of legislated suspension and concludes that the former is clearly superior. He also looks at further empirical evidence on the option clause which appears to confirm the predictions of option clause theory. On the other hand, Calomiris and Kahn (1991) suggest that convertibility on demand is always optimal because of the moral hazard that suspension arrangements create, but they explicitly refrain from any criticism of earlier work on the option clause and, in fact, actually quote the *Journal of Financial Services Research* paper as an example.

3 See, for example, Glasner (1989a) Selgin (1988), Vaubel (1986) and White (1989).

4 There are also many other cases. The reader interested in following them up might start with the collection of readings in Dowd (ed.) (1992d).

5 I took particular care to include the term 'evolution' in the title to emphasize this distinction. It is important to prevent the term 'evolutionary' being used as if it were synonymous with the term 'natural' in order to prevent arguments that central banking is 'natural' *because* it evolved. Any 'natural' (i.e. market-driven) process must be evolutionary, but an evolutionary process is not necessarily

'natural', since government intervention can influence the channels into which the evolutionary process goes.

6 Their comments are printed in full in Capie and Wood (1991), but what I believe to be the major parts are also quoted in the text of chapter 12.

7 I have never understood why so many American economists who appreciate the importance of incentive structure have resisted what seemed to me to be the obvious corollary of calling for the abolition of deposit insurance. They seem simultaneously to condemn the incentives it creates while continuing to defend the principle of deposit insurance itself. I am confident that history will demonstrate that this position is fundamentally untenable. Indeed, I believe it already has.

2 Automatic stablizing mechanisms under free banking

This chapter is a slightly revised version of a paper originally published in the *Cato Journal* 7, 1988: 643–59. I should like to thank Charles Goodhart, Catherine England, Jack Gilbert, Richard Timberlake, Lawrence H. White and several anonymous referees for helpful comments.

1 This 'invisible hand' method of explaining institutional growth was pioneered by the Scottish moral philosophers of the eighteenth century and has been widely used by social scientists ever since. Menger (1892) used it to explain the development of money, for instance, and it has been used by a number of other writers to explain the evolution of the banking system. See, for example, Wesslau (1887), Meulen (1934) and Selgin and White (1987) among many others. My discussion relies heavily on these earlier studies.

2 It could be argued in this case that the law of fraud would be redundant. It would be in the interest of a mint to pay people of unquestioned probity to issue regular reports on the quality of its coins. This would allow the mint to maintain a reputation for honesty and thereby promote its business. All dishonest mints would be thus exposed and driven out of business. This is yet another example of the ability of the unrestrained private sector to police itself quite effectively.

3 Monetary history is unfortunately full of instances of this abuse of the monetary system. For example, see the *Cambridge Economic History of Europe, 5*, chapter 5.

4 It would not take the banks long to realize that it was expensive to use gold as the medium in which to settle clearing balances. They would therefore introduce a paper clearing house medium and use that instead. An historical instance of this is the development of clearing house loan certificates among the members of the New York Clearing House Association in the late nineteenth century. An excellent discussion of this is to be found in Timberlake (1984).

5 The evolution of the clearing system is explained in White (1984b) and Selgin and White (1987).

6 If the bank is unsound it should go out of business anyway. The

liquidity problem we discuss is a source for concern only when it affects sound banks.

7 There is another possible source of liquidity that we have neglected. If the economy is an open one, then gold can always be obtained from abroad. If gold can be imported reasonably cheaply and quickly, the chances of the banking system being rendered illiquid are reduced, probably very significantly. I have chosen to ignore this possibility in order to stress the extent to which the domestic economy could evolve ways of helping itself. Alternatively, one could consider the economy I analyse to be the world economy, which does not have the option of importing gold.

8 Frankly, I see no particular reason why such a situation should arise under *laissez-faire*, as distinct from central banking, but it appears to be a major concern in the literature. See, for example, Gorton (1985) and Goodhart (1985, 1988). I discuss it simply to show how a *laissez-faire* banking system could handle it.

9 Economists have paid very little attention to the potential of option clauses to deal with problems of illiquidity. The pioneer in the field is Henry Meulen (1934) whose treatment of the problem has been unduly neglected.

10 I should like to thank one of the referees for suggesting these advantages to me.

11 One would expect that competition would leave the banks facing similar thresholds. The analysis can easily be modified to allow for threshold differences.

12 Self-fulfilling expectations of bank runs have been a major source of concern in the literature. See Gorton (1986). It is therefore reassuring to know that they should not arise under free banking.

13 In general, there is no clear criterion that would allow policy-makers to select one particular rule over another. If one adopts a monetary target, for instance, should it be M1, M2 or something else? If M1 is chosen, what version of M1 should be preferred? What should the target growth rate be? And so on. For any answer one gives to these questions there is always another that is equally plausible, and one has no way of knowing which is better.

14 For a good discussion of this episode see Andreàdes (1909: chapter 4).

15 For a discussion of this see Hammond (1957).

16 Option clauses were prohibited in the United Kingdom by an Act of 1765. They appear never to have been allowed in the United States.

17 Congress was apparently aware of the danger that deposit insurance might lead banks to take more risks, but it tried to tackle the problem by restricting what it considered to be excessively risky activities. A strong case could be made out that that only made matters worse.

3 Option clauses and the stability of a *laissez-faire* monetary system

This chapter is a slightly revised version of 'Option clauses and the stability of a *laisser-faire* monetary system', *Journal of Financial Services Research* 1,

1988: 319–83. I should like to thank Dave Chappell, Alec Chrystal, Jack Gilbert, Charles Goodhart, Neil Wallace, Larry White, John Zube and an anonymous referee for their helpful comments on an earlier draft.

1 Meulen was the last in a line of 'underground' British free bankers, most of whom were active toward the end of the last century, and of whom the best known is Herbert Spencer. While some of Meulen's views seem questionable, there is no doubt that his work has not received the attention it deserves. Meulen's principal discussions of option clauses occur in his 1934 book on pp. 81–3, 87–8 and 127–32. One should note that many of the ideas in this book were published in an earlier edition, *Industrial Justice through Banking Reform* (1917) and a pamphlet, 'Banking and the Social Problem' (Wadsworth, Keighley, 1909).

One might also add that this chapter concentrates on the stabilizing properties of option clauses and does not deal with the implications of option clauses for the long-run efficiency of the economy. Meulen stressed repeatedly that option clauses helped to promote economic efficiency by promoting the replacement of gold by paper, thereby economizing on holdings of 'dead' (i.e. non-interest-bearing) specie.

2 Our task would be much easier if we assumed that banks could pay interest on their notes, since banks could then encourage people to hold OC notes simply by increasing the interest rate on them, but unfortunately there are reasons to believe that the transactions and/or accounting costs of doing so do not make it feasible. I refer the reader to White (1987).

3 There is, however, a possible counter-argument here. It is possible that a badly run bank might use the 'breathing space' provided by the exercise of the option clause to run the bank further into the ground. This is discussed on pp. 48–9 below.

4 MacLeod (1896: 18). Note that this was the maximum permissible legal rate of interest. It is not clear what effect usury laws might have had on option clauses.

4 Monetary freedom and monetary stability

This chapter is a slightly revised version of a paper of the same title originally presented to the Cato Institute conference 'Alternatives to Government Fiat Money' in Washington, D.C., in February 1989. I should like to thank Mervyn Lewis for helpful discussions on some of the issues raised in it.

1 Indeed, it is difficult to think of plausible scenarios in which *laissez-faire* money is anything *but* stable. The famous case discussed by Friedman (1960: 8) implicitly assumes that different money issues cannot be distinguished. The hyperinflation no longer takes place when this restriction is relaxed.

2 The theory of private legal systems is discussed in D. Friedman (1978), Rothbard (1978), the Tannehills (1970) and Wooldridge (1970). Historical examples of well functioning private legal systems are medieval

Celtic Ireland (Peden 1977) Viking Iceland (Miller 1990) and the nineteenth-century American West (Anderson and Hill 1979).

3 The use of coins relieved the public of the need to weigh gold and assess its fineness. Since coins bore a premium, people were willing to pay mints to coin their gold, and competition among the mints kept minting charges down.

4 To avoid unnecessarily lengthening the discussion here, I pass over the possibility that the banks may insert 'option clauses' into their deposit and note contracts to give them the right to insist on notice. For more on the option clause see the previous two chapters.

5 The banks might find that some of these functions were more efficiently carried out by their clearing house associations. For example, a clearing house association might be able to handle a loan application from a member bank more rapidly and at less cost than that bank could obtain a loan *ab initio* on the market. For more on the functions of clearing house associations see Timberlake (1984).

The term 'sound' is used to refer to an institution with a positive net worth. It is to be distinguished from a 'solvent' institution, which is an insitution that is able to honour its debts. They differ because an unsound institution may still be solvent, at least for a while. Given the penalty for default, however, no sound bank would normally choose to become insolvent.

6 We might also note that demands to convert bank liabilities into gold will also tend to be low because bank liabilities bear a 'liquidity premium' over gold. Recall that gold is no longer used as a medium of exchange.

7 Obviously the abrogation of the commitment to redeem in gold might cause *some* resentment, and a bank would not do it if it expected the loss in business it would provoke to outweigh the savings. One must bear in mind, however, that gold is no longer used for exchange purposes, and there is no obvious reason why the banks should find it worthwhile to redeem in gold when they do not find it worthwhile to redeem in any other physical commodities.

8 If the banks were to choose to peg a commodity basket, they would have to peg the price of the basket itself, and not the individual prices of the constituent goods. They could do this by pegging the price of the basket, or by pegging a price indexed to it (e.g. a consumer price index).

9 A slight caveat is that we want to stablize current prices, and the relation between current and futures prices will usually change with the interest rate. If we were to peg a futures price, therefore, we would pick a commodity whose relative futures price was sufficiently more stable than its relative spot price to compensate for the interest component. The interest component on futures commodities with short 'terms to maturity' is quite small, however. For more on the use of futures in the commodity basket see Friedman (1951: 225–6) and Barro (1979: 30–1).

10 It is interesting to observe how the role of gold changes as the system evolves. Gold originally emerges from barter as the dominant medium

of exchange and unit of account. Banks then issue liabilities denominated in gold dollars which gradually displace gold as a medium of exchange. After this the banks abandon gold as a medium of redemption and replace the gold peg. In the meantime the bank dollar has long since replaced the gold dollar as the public's unit of account. Gold then ceases to have any monetary significance whatever. Gold is significant only in an underdeveloped monetary economy.

11 Note that the benfits of 'information' are privately appropriated (at least at the margin). Information is not a 'public good' because it does not satisfy the non-rivalness and non-exludability conditions that a public good satisfies. The same can be said of 'confidence' in the banks.

12 An interesting question is why the banks did not make much use of alternative redemption media issued by the private sector. In England, at least, part of the explanation seems to have been related to restrictions on joint stock banking which meant that all banks except the Bank of England were severely undercapitalized. As a result no private financial assets could be considered 'safe' in a crisis except Bank of England debt. The banks therefore used Bank liabilities (and gold) because the public would accept nothing else.

13 The reason for this is that, since the Fed had replaced the old system of private clearing house associations, the banks did not have their old support to fall back on when the Fed failed to help them.

14 Kaufman (1987: 22) notes that the most important determinant in the Federal Savings and Loan Insurance Corporation's losses from thrift insolvency was the delay in closing down unsound institutions.

5 Is banking a natural monopoly?

Originally published in *Kyklos* 45, 1992: 379–92.

1 Despite an apparent widespread belief to the contrary, it is doubtful whether any particular policy conclusions would follow even if banking were a natural monopoly. To say that banking is a natural monopoly is to say that only one bank would survive in the competitive equilibrium, and it does not follow that natural monopoly implies a mandate to give a particular institution a legally protected monopoly of the note issue. See also Vaubel (1986).

2 The central limit theorem indicates that $f(X)$ would approach normality were the domain of X unrestricted. The fact that the domain has upper and lower bounds implies that the normality of $f(X)$ must be only approximate.

3 A caveat here – though a plausible one – is that we require $b > 2r$ if the optimal level of reserves R is to be positive (see, for example, Baltensperger 1980: 5).

4 In addition to these points, if larger banks involve larger transactions, then optimal reserves rise (with scale) to a larger extent than is predicted by equation (3). Equation (3) would then lead one to overstate the reserve-holding economies of scale (e.g. Sprenkle 1985: 507).

5 Consider two banks with liabilities of N each. Their total optimal

reserves are then $2\,b\sqrt{N}\sigma_{xi}$. If they combined to form a single bank, their optimal reserves would then be $\sqrt{2}b\sqrt{N}\sigma_{xi}$ and they would reap a reserve gain (RG) of $(2-\sqrt{2})b\sqrt{N}\sigma_{xi}$. As N increases, the marginal reserve gain $\partial RG/\partial N = [(2-\sqrt{2})/(2\sqrt{N})]\sigma_{xi}$ is always positive but diminishes as N gets larger, and approaches zero in the limit.

6 A comparable argument also needs to be noted. King (1983: 133) argues that external economies would be likely to arise if 'users of circulating notes faced coasts of ascertaining the value of particular notes. For example, an increase in the number of users of a particular note could lower the probability of meeting an individual uninformed about the value of one's note and, hence, the expected cost of trades'. Once a particular bank's notes become well known, however, the benefits from it expanding further would seem to be small, so the marginal return to scale also seems to go to zero. Once again we have economies of scale but no particular reason to expect a natural monopoly.

7 See also Selgin (1988: 151), who adds that an 'error sometimes committed in considering the natural monopoly question is to assume that the only marginal costs of currency issue are the cost of paper and ink, which do not rise significantly at the margin and may even fall. . . . This implies that banks face an inexhaustible demand for their notes, or that they will not be asked to redeem them in base money. But, where notes are convertible, this can happen only if the issuer has a monopoly of currency supply to begin with. . . . To assume the existence of a monopoly in currency supply in order to explain its "natural" occurrence obviously begs the question.'

8 One could argue with at least as much plausibility that the power to tax actually undermines confidence. 'Confidence' is ultimately about how secure people feel about their property, and the power to tax is really only a power to seize private property for whatever purposes the government wishes. One can therefore argue that, the less restrained the power to tax, the less secure will private property be, and the less confidence people will have.

9 Melvin also makes related claims in a more recent paper (1988) but, as White (1989: 103) points out, the fixed confidence costs on which his natural monopoly argument hinges are not in fact fixed at all and therefore constitute no basis for a natural monopoly. Melvin also claims that the costs of individually contracting for high-quality 'money' are prohibitive, and he concludes that money holders therefore need to pay 'protection money' to the issuer to discourage him from hyperinflating. The initial premise is theoretically questionable and empirically refuted, as noted elsewhere, but, even if it is granted, 'the comparative cheapness of government production does not follow unless it can be shown that an equally large protection premium does not have to be paid to assure quality. If the government has an uncertain tenure and therefore . . . a higher discount rate than a private firm, as Klein has noted to be the case, then the quality-assuring premium necessary for stability with government production of money would be even higher than the premium necessary with private production' (White 1989: 104). And so

the government would be less suited to providing monetary quality than the private sector.

10 Note too that empirical evidence from other industries also casts doubt on arguments for the presence of natural monopoly in banking. Many other industries have fixed costs of one sort or another, and if these factors imply a natural monopoly in banking one needs to explain why we do not observe many natural monopolies elsewhere.

6 Models of banking instability

Originally published in the *Journal of Economic Surveys* 6, 1992: 107–32 under the title 'Models of banking instability: a partial review of the literature'. The author would like to thank John Pencavel, George Selgin and three referees for comments.

1 The notion that financial intermediation must improve on an unintermediated market is the simplest and most convenient way of providing a 'proper motivation' for intermediation. One could however also add in further factors, e.g. savings in transaction or monitoring costs, but such factors are not found in the literature considered in this chapter and there is little obvious gain from bringing in the additional complications that come with them.

2 They are unconvincing not only because they attempt to discuss an industry that the models themselves predict should not exist, but also because those same models also have alternative, unintermediated outcomes which match the optimal intermediated ones, with or without government intervention. Even if the intervention improved on the intermediated *laissez-faire* outcome, one would still need to be sure that it improved on the *un*intermediated one as well, and this criterion ensures that we only deal with cases where it does.

3 To anticipate the later discussion, the text assumes that these costs must also be paid when the intermediary redeems 'deposits' in $T = 1$, and this assumption implies that runs then have 'real' production costs. The alternative assumption is that the intermediary can hand over the maturing investment without 'killing' it in the process, but this assumption would expose the intermediary to losses from arbitrage – to anticipate the later discussion again, type 2 depositors would always wish to withdraw for $c_{1,1}*$ and then hold the investment until it matured in $T = 2$ to yield them a return of $c_{1,1}*R$. The investors would then have no reason to invest in the intermediary, since they would know that it would be unable to redeem all its deposits.

4 There are various ways these costs could be modelled. The text assumes that the cost is merely the opportunity cost of the forgone return in $T = 2$ which means that the investment process is fully reversible in $T = 1$, but one might instead suppose that the investment process has some degree of irreversibility and yields only B units in $T = 1$ for each unit invested in $T = 0$, where $0 \leq B < 1$. I shall indicate where appropriate how results might be sensitive to the assumed degree of irreversibility, but one should note that irreversibility does not 'bind'

the optimal outcome provided that a costless storage technology exists and there is no aggregate uncertainty. To anticipate the later analysis, any optimum that exists when there is no irreversibility can then be attained when there is irreversibility by using the storage technology to provide for $T = 1$ withdrawals, and there is no inefficiency (relative to the no-irreversibility case) because the amount of storage required is perfectly predictable.

5 The corner preference assumption is a convenient way to motivate differences in agents' desired consumption patterns, but it can be relaxed. One could then assume that agents' preferences are 'smooth' over consumption in both periods, but that type 1 agents (unobservably) desire more consumption in period 1 (i.e. are more impatient) (as, for example, in Anderlini 1986b or Waldo 1985). Alternatively, one could assume that all agents have the same preferences but face differing (unobservable) endowments in $T = 1$ (e.g. as in Haubrich and King 1984, 1989). Results sometimes hinge on which of these specifications is chosen, but any major differences will be flagged as we go along.

6 While the text emphasizes the role of an intermediary in sharing risk, the intermediary might also help agents overcome the constraints imposed by the cost of liquidating assets before they mature. In contrast to an agent with his own portfolio, an intermediary need never liquidate capital prematurely or hold low-return storage assets for two periods because it can predict with certainty the proportions of type 1 and type 2 agents. Even risk-neutral agents would therefore prefer an intermediary contract provided there was some degree of investment irreversibility.

7 Note that agents' self-selection means that the 'full information' optimum is achieved even though their types are not observable, but this result hinges on the assumption that agents have corner preferences. If we had smooth preferences or preferences that were identical but associated with random $T = 1$ endowments, then individual agents in the 'full information' optimum would not self-select because everyone would claim to be type 1 and it would be impossible to identify the false claims. The 'full information' insurance arrangement is therefore not feasible, and the optimal feasible contract is constrained by the private information about agents' endowments (see respectively Anderlini 1986c: 160–1; Haubrich and King 1984, 1989).

8 Note also that the Diamond–Dybvig model has nothing to say about interest rate movements during a panic. However, if we assume that investment opportunities show diminishing returns, as in Waldo 1985, then runs will be associated with a rise in short-term interest rates relative to long-term ones because banks will be forced to liquidate long-term projects with ever higher marginal products (see Waldo 1985: 277).

9 An additional difficulty with the Diamond–Dybvig model is that depositors do not take the possibility of runs into account when deciding whether to invest in an intermediary or not. The problem is that if depositors have utility functions that are unbounded below, and a run entails a positive probability of zero consumption, they may never make

any deposits in the first place (Anderlini 1986b: 1–2, 1986c: 158; see also Postlewaite and Vives 1987: 485). If depositors have to decide whether to invest all or nothing in a bank, they may invest in the bank only if there is some mechanism to guarantee that a run cannot take place. If we allow them to invest only part of their endowment in a bank, then Diamond and Dybvig 1983: 409–10 suggest, and Anderlini 1986b proves, that they would still make some investment in the intermediary provided they had a low enough expected probability of a run. (See also Waldo 1985: 276.) Depositors would then be willing to take the risk of a run because the part of their endowment they keep under the mattress provides them with insurance against a run and enables them to avoid the possibility of having nothing to consume.

10 If the extraneous variables ('sunspots') governing expectations were publicly observable and had a known influence on expectations, it would also be possible to write contracts in which payments were made contingent on those variables (e.g. as in Freeman 1988: 52–4 and Bental *et al.* 1990: 3–4). Panics could then be avoided by ensuring that sunspot-contingent returns to $T = 1$ withdrawals were low enough (relative to later returns) to eliminate any incentive for type 2 agents to withdraw early. However, this contract delivers a lower expected utility than the contract in the text precisely because it lowers return to type 1 agents when sunspot counts are 'bad'. Unlike the Diamond–Dybvig contract, it eliminates runs, but the possibility of runs is costly even though runs may never occur. The assumption that the extraneous variables are publicly observable is also questionable, since the point of bringing sunspots into the picture in the first place is presumably to proxy the unobservable (and heterogeneous) factors that influence agents' expectations about each other but which one cannot easily model explicitly.

11 One should note that the criticism that alternative arrangements can also produce the social optimum does not apply when the Diamond–Dybvig preference structure is replaced by identical preferences and random endowments in $T = 1$. An optimal arrangement under these circumstances provides insurance against illiquidity and insurance against a low endowment. (This distinction between types of insurance does not arise with the other preference specifications.) A Diamond–Dybvig contract then provides an optimal trade-off between liquidity insurance and income insurance, but an equity contract is inferior because it provides no income insurance at all (Haubrich and King 1984: 8–14). Note that the Haubrich–King specification is also immune to the criticism in the next paragraph as well.

12 The suspension arrangement is explored further by Wallace (1990) and Selgin (1991). Wallace presents an example of a Diamond–Dybvig-type economy in which the pay-outs to depositors who withdraw in $T = 1$ depend in part on their place in the queue. Those who arrive late are paid less than those who arrive earlier, and this feature of the contract discourages premature withdrawals by type 2 depositors. Wallace interprets it as a 'partial' suspension of payments, in contrast to the 'full' suspension where all payments cease, and casual observation of US

banking history suggests that the distinction is an important one. Selgin motivates a similar distinction by linking the Diamond–Dybvig saving–investment scenario to a means of exchange technology.

13 Diamond and Dybvig's own description of their 'deposit insurance' scheme is difficult to follow because it fails to draw an adequate distinction between expected and realized t. This distinction is critical. If payments to depositors are made on the basis of expected t, the Diamond–Dybvig contract achieves optimality *ex ante* (provided there is some means to eliminate runs), but it achieves optimality *ex post* only if the two t values are the same. If it makes contracts based on actual t, on the other hand, the intermediary can expect to achieve both *ex ante* and *ex post* optimality, but some topping up (or retrieval) is required *ex post* unless the two t values accidentally coincide because the intermediary cannot know until the last withdrawal what the realized value of t actually was.

14 The government's tax subsidy policy is complicated by an additional factor. If those who withdraw in $T = 1$ are paid too little when they first go to the bank, there is no problem liquidating further investments to make 'top up' payments to them to bring their returns up to promised levels. If they are paid too much, on the other hand, there is a social loss because too many investments have already been liquidated, and the 'excess interruptions' of the production process cannot be undone. The only way in which these excess interruptions can be eliminated is to make initial payments conditional on the minimum possible level of t (i.e. to pay 1 for every deposit withdrawn in $T = 1$). Top-up payments could then be made if the realized value of t exceeded this minimum, but there would never be any need to retrieve overpayments (see McCulloch and Yu 1989: 7–8).

15 Even if one accepts these results at face value, the optimality of the policy interventions is extremely delicate. The optimality of the Anderlini policy hinges on the rate of return R on physical capital being deterministic, and there is no presumption of optimality when R is made stochastic instead (Anderlini 1986b: 31). The optimality of the Freeman policy, on the other hand, is contingent on very extreme assumptions about the government and the information it has. The government 'must itself calculate the bank's optimal portfolio and liabilities in the absence of moral hazard, then impose them on the bank. . . . the bank must be made to behave as if its expected tax depends on the risk of liquidation implied by its own behavior' (Freeman 1988: 63).

16 Bhattacharya and Gale (1987) and Chari (1989) suggest that reserve requirements might also be appropriate even in the absence of any government tax subsidy scheme. In their models, intermediaries are too small to diversify away individual consumption risk, so they borrow and lend on an inter-intermediary liquidity market. Intermediaries have insufficient private incentive to hold reserves, however, so the authors conclude that the *laissez-faire* outcome is inefficient and reserve requirements are needed to bring about the social optimum. This argument is open to the objection that the reserve 'externalities' can be appropriated

by the intermediaries combining to form a single firm. In these models the *laissez-faire* outcome only appears to be inefficient because intermediaries have been arbitrarily constrained to be too small, and they cease to be inefficient when they are allowed to combine. One must also emphasize that this argument for the optimality of the *laissez-faire* outcome is in no way compromised by the lack of empirical evidence that financial intermediation actually is a natural monopoly. The argument that Bhattacharya and Gale and Chari have no convincing *theoretical* case that the *laissez-faire* outcome is inferior is not rescued by the fact that their models also make an *empirically* falsified prediction about banking being a natural monopoly.

17 It is therefore hardly surprising that Diamond and Dybvig find the sequential service constraint does not 'bind' their social optimum. They obtain that result because they have implicitly assumed that the government has the means to overcome the sequential service constraint. Imposing that constraint on the private sector alone makes no difference to the socially attainable outcome if the government can overcome the constraint itself.

18 As alluded to at the start of the chapter, the closely related literature on contract design (e.g. Townsend 1979) also places much emphasis on production uncertainty and asymmetrical information, and some of this literature manages to relate contract design to financial intermediation (e.g. Diamond 1984; Williamson 1986). This literature is not considered here because it has very little to say on the instability of financial intermediaries as such. The interested reader is referred to the surveys by Harris and Raviv (1991) and Dowd (1992c).

19 One might also note in passing that the Diamond–Dybvig models also make another empirically falsified prediction – the prediction that panics are random events set off by economically irrelevant variables (such as sunspots) is contradicted by empirical evidence (e.g. Gorton 1986) that they are systematic events triggered off by observable movements in relevant economic variables.

7 Free banking in Australia

First published as chapter 3 of Kevin Dowd (ed.) *The Experience of Free Banking*, London: Routledge, 1992, pp. 48–78. I should like to thank Mervyn Lewis, David Merrett and Ray Evans for comments on an earlier draft.

1 These warnings were by no means isolated. Further examples are given in Boehm (1971: 246–7) and Merrett (1989: 67).

2 An association of the larger Melbourne-based banks.

3 These two institutions had only recently converted from being building societies, and the Metropolitan had started to issue notes only in January (Butlin 1961: 285). These institutions were two among a number that had commenced as building societies but transformed themselves into conventional banks.

4 The politicians themselves were also heavily criticized. In Victoria 'one

of the worst features of the mounting disclosures of mismanagement, chicanery, falsified accounts, and fraud, was the extent to which leading members of Parliament were involved' (Butlin 1961: 286). Boehm (1971: 266) also refers to the 'corruptness and incompetence within the Victorian Legislature' which were revealed in the passage of the Voluntary Liquidation Act.

5 There was some controversy over whether the Federal should have been rescued, but an inquiry by the Victoria Supreme Court concluded later that it was already beyond rescue (Boehm 1971: 288).

6 Some depositors did object, however, and the 'inconvenience' caused by the suspensions was in some cases a cause of considerable distress (see Gollan 1968: 37–40).

7 For what the comparison is worth, one might add that 12.5 per cent would be considered very sound in the United States today, and American banks now, like Australian banks then, have a large number of problem loans on their books. The assets of US banks now are also probably no more diversified than the assets of Australian banks a century ago, so the comparison is perhaps not as far-fetched as it may otherwise appear.

8 One might also note, by the way, that the claim that banks' risks were becoming more concentrated receives only very weak support. Pope's figure 8 indicates only a barely perceptible increase in the suspended banks' risk concentration, and the fact that the risk-pooling variable always has an insignificant coefficient in Pope's estimates (1989: 20) indicates that it had little effect on the bank failures anyway.

9 Gollan (1968) has a good account of the controversy over banking and the political background to the banking legislation.

8 US banking in the 'free banking' period

First published as chapter 11 of Kevin Dowd (ed.) *The Experience of Free Banking*, London: Routledge, 1992, pp. 206–40.

1 As an illustration, the ratio of notes to deposits was 27 per cent in New York city in 1849 (Klebaner 1974: 26).

2 The argument put forward by opponents of federal chartering was that the federal government did not have any powers not expressly granted to it, and the chartering power was among these. For more on this issue, see Dowd (1990a) and Timberlake (1990).

3 The expiration of the charter of the Bank of the United States in 1836 saw the federal role cut down to imposing restrictions on banks that had federal deposits, and even these restrictions were removed by the adoption of the Independent Treasury System in January 1847 (Rolnick and Weber 1983: 1082; see also Scheiber 1963: 212; Timberlake 1978).

4 Note that the adjective 'free' used in this context 'referred solely to freedom of entry' – the term 'automatic' would be more accurate, however, since entry was 'free' only subject to certain conditions – 'The free banking laws ended the requirement that banks obtain their charters through special legislative acts' (Rockoff 1975b: 161).

5 These were the words of New York comptroller Millard Fillmore looking back later in 1848 (quoted in Klebaner 1974: 9).
6 Knox (1903: 413–15) and E. White (1990) have detailed discussions of
   the origins of the New York 'free banking' law. See also Holdsworth
   (1911: 31).
7 Details of the New York legislation are given in Rockoff (1975a: table
   12), King (1983: 142–8), Knox (1903: 414–15) and E. White (1990: 9,
   22).
8 Arkansas, Florida, Indiana and Mississippi defaulted in 1841, and
   Illinois, Louisiana, Maryland, Michigan and Pennsylvania in 1842
   (Rolnick and Weber 1985: 6; see also Schweikart 1987).
9 Examples are Vermont and Pennsylvania, whose 'free banking' laws
   limited the capital of a 'free bank' to no more than $200,000 and $1
   million respectively (Knox 1903: 357, 459).
10 For more on usury laws see Rockoff (1975b: 169–72). These laws varied
   considerably, both in the interest ceilings they imposed and in the
   penalties imposed for violating those limits. Rockoff's discussion suggests that they probably had some impact at some times but were often
   ineffective.
11 Eugene White (1990) has a good account of the history and effects of
   denominational restrictions. Notes under $1 were banned in Ohio in
   1819, in Florida in 1828 and in Georgia in 1830, and the federal
   Treasury and a number of states attempted to discourage the use of
   notes less than $5 in the 1830s. There were also some attempts to
   impose even higher minimum denominations (e.g. Missouri banned
   notes under $20 in 1836). Denominational restrictions were sometimes
   highly controversial, and opposition to them led to the repeal of the
   New York ban on notes under $5 in 1837. They were often ineffective,
   and led to a flood of 'foreign' (i.e. out-of-state) notes (see also Klebaner
   1974: 19). Where they were effective, on the other hand, they tended
   to put banknotes out of reach of the ordinary man.
12 Reserve requirements were generally applied to chartered and not just
   to 'free' banks. Virginia was the first state to introduce one (1837), and
   other states soon followed suit. (New York's was repealed in response
   to opposition from the bankers.) While early reserve requirements stipulated reserves against the note issue, Louisiana was the first state to
   introduce a reserve requirement against deposits as well as notes (in
   1842; see Klebaner 1974: 43).
13 The argument that it was the suspension law rather than the 'free
   banking' law that was the principal factor behind the failure is also
   supported by the observation that only two of the chartered banks
   remained in operation by the end of 1839 (Knox 1903: 735). It is
   questionable, however, whether all the 'free bank' failures can be
   blamed on the suspension law alone. Rockoff (1975a: 94) states that
   many banks 'were simply frauds which operated in violation of the free
   banking law'. He also suggests (1975a: 18) that 'only a small portion
   of the notes entered circulation at par', which suggests that the mutual
   fund model of Rolnick and Weber (1988) might be appropriate, as with
   Minnesota, or that losses might have been exaggerated.

14 Banking histories often regard the Illinois bank as modelled on the Indiana one (e.g. Hammond 1948), but this interpretation of the Illinois bank is misleading – see note 16.

15 See note 33.

16 While many previous writers have admired Indiana's state monopoly bank – Holdsworth (1911: 32) comments that it 'stands out as the most striking exception to the rule of failure among state-owned banks' – the Indiana bank was a state monopoly in name only. As Calomiris (1989a) points out, the Indiana branches were 'separately owned and operated' (p. 15), and the language of state monopoly was required because the 'state constitution only provided for the chartering of a state bank and its branches' (p. 29, n. 21). The state monopoly in Indiana appeared to work because it only appeared to be a state monopoly, and the state banks of Illinois and Missouri failed because they were apparently real state monopolies.

17 'Free banking' laws were also passed in Connecticut and Michigan in 1857, but their effects are difficult to determine.

18 This claim presupposes that the bond collateral restrictions of the 'free banking' legislation were binding, but it seems reasonable to suppose that they were. As White (1986: 893) puts it, it appears that 'collateral restrictions forced banks to hold unbalanced asset portfolios overloaded with state bonds. Such portfolios exposed the banks unduly to the risk of declining state bond prices'. He notes further that 'It seems unlikely that banks would deliberately so overload themselves absent regulatory distortions of their asset-holding choices'. While this hypothesis needs more investigation, the fact that banking entrepreneurs were sometimes so slow to set up 'free banks' (e.g. in Massachusetts) would appear to provide it with some support. Further work might focus on whether 'free banks' held more than the required amounts of state bonds in their portfolios. If they did not, as White (1986: 893, n. 3) points out, then there is prima-facie evidence that the restrictions were binding; if they did, on the other hand, then the restrictions clearly were not. Assuming that the hypothesis is valid, one can properly attribute the 'free bank' failures not only to the fiscal instability that produced the bond price falls but also to the bond deposit requirements as well. It was the latter that exposed the banks to capital losses, and the former that inflicted the losses on them.

One objection also needs to be considered. King (1983: 147) disputes the claim that the bond deposit requirements were responsible for the failures and argues that 'there are natural means for any bank to undo any pure portfolio restriction. Banks should simply have as owners or creditors individuals who would otherwise hold amounts of government debt'. However, this irrelevance result does not apply when there are limitations on agents' liability (see Dowd 1989a: 149–50, n. 31). (It would be interesting to test the issue, none the less, since King's argument makes the empirical prediction that bond deposit requirements should have no impact on the prices of state bonds. I would expect such a test to find this prediction rejected.)

19 Pecquet also notes that 'This solid banking system depended upon a

unique state constitution which forbade the legislature or governor to authorize or aid specie suspension in any way' (1990: 3) – an assessment which would seem to reinforce the earlier comments about the potential harm done by suspension laws.

20 The claim that there was little or no contagion has, however, been challenged recently by Hasan and Dwyer (1988), who present some circumstantial evidence and the results of logit analysis. In their model the probability of failure depends on the value of bonds relative to capital, the remoteness of the bank's location and a dummy variable which takes the value 1 if another bank failed in that county, and 0 otherwise, and they interpret the positive sign and statistical significance of the dummy variable as evidence of contagion. This interpretation of their results is open to the objection, however, that while the dummy may pick up contagion, it will also pick up any other factor that the first two variables proxy inadequately but which is also linked with the failure of a neighbouring bank – conditions in the local economy come to mind – and these alternative explanations need to be ruled out before one can claim to have established the presence of contagion.

21 The stability of the banking industry of the period is also borne out by other indicators. Particularly important is its capital adequacy. Salsman (1990: 95) notes that 'the banking system restored its capital adequacy in the first decade of free banking from 40.5 percent in 1836 to 55.1 percent in 1842, the greatest capital adequacy level and the swiftest rise in the entire history of banking'. He also notes that there was 'no appreciable deterioration of banking capital adequacy' in the remaining 'free banking' period. Sechrest (1990: 102) also notes that capital adequacy was high, and he notes too that capital ratios became more stable towards the end of the 'free banking' era. Indicators of banking liquidity reinforce the impression of the industry's stability. Salsman's cash–deposit ratio shows a steady climb from over 42 per cent in 1836 to 54.2 per cent in 1844, and it varies thereafter between 36.2 per cent and 41.5 per cent (Salsman 1990: table 17). Sechrest's reserve ratio, on the other hand, has a value of just over 20 per cent for 1834–49, and almost 18 per cent for the period 1850–62 (1990: 100–2). Sechrest also points out that commercial paper rates were lower and less variable in the period 1850–62, which saw the large-scale switch to 'free banking', than they had been in the earlier period 1834–49 (1990: 110).

22 There is, however, some controversy over how competitive the Pennsylvania banking system actually was. Evidence in favour is suggested by casual observation and a comment by the state auditor-general in 1863 that the reason so few 'free banks' were formed was the ease with which special charters could be obtained, which, incidentally, also imposed less onerous conditions than the 'free banking' law (Knox 1903: 460). However, Rockoff (1975a: 53) suggests that Philadelphia banks enjoyed a rather high profit rate which he attributes to restrictions on entry, and he presents anecdotal evidence that Philadelphia banks were under-capitalized.

23 The experience of Florida underlines the importance of private (i.e. unchartered or unincorporated) banking in the *antebellum* United States.

Schweikart writes that 'Unaccounted currencies, especially small-note issues, played an extremely important role in the antebellum southern economy but have defied attempts at measurement ... [for example] Georgia chartered 150 'potential currency-issuing organizations' between 1810 and 1866, and more than fifteen hundred varieties of currency of this type circulated in the state ... Florida, without chartered banks of its own, relied heavily on unaccounted currencies for its circulating medium' (1987: 80). Sylla also indicates that they were a widespread and important phenomenon. He notes that though 'Quantitative information ... is scarce, ... what there is of it suggests that the private banker was considerably more important than previously thought' (1976: 181), and he presents some indicative evidence to back that claim up (e.g. how some restraining Acts were successful in 'smoking out' private bankers). Also revealing is a comment by James Gurthrie, the Treasury Secretary, who reported to the House in 1856 that the capital of private banks was more than a third of that employed in chartered banks (Sylla 1976: 184). Hammond (1948: 16) and Klebaner (1974: 12) indicate that private banking was important in the Middle West as well, and the latter observes that, by 1860, private banks in Ohio, Indiana, Illinois, Michigan and Wisconsin had more deposits than the combined liabilities of chartered banks in those states.

24 Virginia gives a good example of the difference between 'free' and free banking. It had supplemented its chartered banks with a law to allow bond deposit banking in 1851 – although this law omitted the 'free entry' principle (Rockoff 1975b: 163) – but bond deposit banks were not allowed to branch as easily as chartered ones. Aided by branch banking, Virginian banks were 'strong and stable', and there were no failures (Schweikart 1987: 126). Thirteen bond deposit banks opened soon after the 1851 law (E. White 1990: 22), but these banks had great difficulty competing against the chartered banks, which expanded their branch networks to compete with them (Schweikart 1987: 274; E. White 1990: 22).

25 Despite the fact that 'free banking' laws were often (apparently) intended to lower entry barriers, it is far from clear that they usually did. If entry barriers fell, we would expect to see the state-level output of banks grow after the passage of 'free banking' laws. Ng (1988) tests for this prediction, using data for seven 'free bank' states and finds that it is demonstrably satisfied only for New York. He concludes that 'free banking laws did not generally lower barriers to entry [or] increase competition in the banking industry' (1988: 886), and suggests that the explanation might be the conditions attached to the establishment of 'free banks' and the fact that chartered banking in some states was reasonably competitive already (1988: 887). However, Bodenhorn (1990) presents results that suggest that 'free banking' laws may have been more effective in promoting bank competition than Ng's results indicate.

The figures for bank failures and noteholder losses also suggest that these have been exaggerated by earlier historians. Rolnick and Weber (1983: 1084) find that in their four states about half the banks closed before 1863, but less than a third actually failed and did not redeem their notes as par (i.e. 15 per cent failed altogether). They also suggest that New York and Wisconsin banks were not very short-lived, and only 14 per cent failed to last a year (1983: 1086). Kahn (1985: 882) is less sanguine, however, and suggests that banks in 'free banking' states had a much shorter life expectancy than banks elsewhere. (The explanation, presumably, has to do with the combination of the bond deposit requirement and the states' fiscal instability, discussed earlier.) Estimates of losses vary somewhat – losses were very low in New York, as already mentioned, but they were sometimes higher elsewhere (see, for example, Kahn 1985: 884–5), and these losses presumably reflect the factors that caused the 'free bank' failures.

26 There is some dispute over the date of this Act: Rockoff (1975a: 127) puts it in 1849 but Schweikart (1987: 269) puts it in 1850.

27 There is also some dispute over the date of this Act: Hammond (1948: 12) and Knox (1903: 698) put it in 1853, but Rockoff (1975a: 98) and Rolnick and Weber (1984: 279) put it in 1852. I have gone along with 1852, since Rolnick and Weber claim to give the precise date the Act was passed.

28 Sumner (1896: 542) states that this bank was chartered in March 1858, but Hammond (1948: 10–11) claims it was chartered in 1857. As in note 27, I have gone along with the author who could give the precise date of the Act (Sumner).

29 It is not clear when this bank was chartered. Schweikart (1987: 182) gives 1838, but his table 12 gives a date of 1837.

30 Note, however, that Knox (1903: 655) does not concur in this assessment. He suggests it performed badly and says that wildcats 'were as plentiful as grasshoppers', but he does not spell out the evidence behind that conclusion.

31 However, Schweikart (1987: 8, 259) suggests that there was one chartered bank in operation in the 1850s.

32 The 1851 law allowed banks to be set up under a bond deposit provision, but Rockoff (1975b: 163) states that entry was not automatic. It therefore ought not to be considered a 'free banking' law in the strict sense.

33 Note, however, that the Wisconsin Marine & Fire Insurance Company carried out some banking activities, and successfully fought off legislators' attempts to stop it.

34 There is also some dispute about the date of this Act: Hammond (1948: 8) and Rockoff (1975a: 84) say it was passed in 1852, but Knox (1903: 325) says it was passed in 1855 and Sumner (1896: 451) says it was passed in 1853.

9 Money and banking: the American experience

Originally presented as the keynote address to the Durell Foundation conference 'Money and Banking: the American Experience' in Washington, D.C., in May 1990.

1 Significantly, the constitution also stripped the states of the right they

had previously enjoyed as colonies to emit 'bills of credit' (i.e. notes). The colonies had frequently abused their note issuing privileges, and the founding fathers hoped to prevent such abuses in the future. One may also note, incidentally, that if the states did not enjoy the right to issue notes they could not delegate the power to do so to the federal government. The ban on state note issues implicitly extended to the federal government as well.

2 The absurdity of these claims was forcibly pointed out by Henry Clay in the Senate. 'It is mockery,' he said, 'worse than usurpation, to establish [the bank] for a lawful object, and then extend it to other objects which are not lawful. . . . You may say to this organization, we cannot authorize you to discount – to emit paper – to regulate commerce, etc. No! Our book has no precedents of that kind. But then we can authorize you to collect the revenue, and, while occupied with that, you may do whatever else you please!' (Quoted in Timberlake 1990: 307.)

3 The federal government began to claim these powers at the start of the Civil War. Apart from the power to charter and regulate banking (which is discussed elsewhere), the federal government also claimed the power to pass legal tender laws and, eventually, to outlaw monetary contracts with gold clauses altogether. For more on the evolution of these powers see Holzer (1981).

4 For example, Calomiris (1990: 4) notes that branch banking helped promote banking stability in the *antebellum* south – an observation which implies that restrictions on branch banking would have been one factor behind instability elsewhere.

5 The multiplicity of small note-issuing banks meant that notes often circulated at a discount far away from their bank of issue. The discount arose because the notes of distant banks were often unfamiliar, and the public had difficulty assessing the reputation of the issuers. This problem seems to have resulted from branch banking restrictions: in countries where branch banking was allowed (e.g. Scotland or Canada) a small number of note-issuing banks emerged whose notes were recognized everywhere.

6 One might also note that the banks managed well anyway. For example, Benston *et al.* (1986: 52–70, 74) note how banks used to reassure the public of their soundness by observing relatively high capital ratios. The shareholders' capital was thus used as a performance bond to persuade depositors of the banks' good faith. Their evidence suggests that the public were generally reassured, and the bank failure rate was not much different from the failure rate of businesses in general.

7 The year earlier, Congress had passed the 1932 National Banking Act (the Glass-Steagall Act) separating commercial and investment banking. While later writers have until recently seen this measure as a public-spirited attempt to promote banking stability, this interpretation was heavily criticized by E. White (1983). It now appears that the Act was no more than an (another) attempt to cartelize the banking industry (see, for example, Shughart 1988).

8 This Act too was motivated by public choice considerations (i.e. private

interest). Shughart (1988) and Benston (1986, especially p. 20) give good accounts of the background to the Act.

10 Did central banks evolve naturally?

This chapter is a slightly revised version of 'Did central banks evolve naturally? A review essay of Charles Goodhart's *The Evolution of Central Banks*', *Scottish Journal of Political Economy* 37 (1), 1990: 96–104. I should like to thank Brian McCormick, Jack Gilbert, Charles Goodhart, Larry White and a referee for helpful comments on an earlier draft.

1 Goodhart also discusses a number of other issues – pyramiding in the banking industry, the banking industry as a 'club', and the problem of banking insurance, and his discussion of these issues is very interesting. I shall not get into these issues as they are less important to the free banking controversy. I would point out, however, that Goodhart's arguments against the private provision of insurance rely to a large extent on a premise that is criticized in the text of the chapter, that the banking system is inherently unstable.

2 An earlier version of Goodhart's book was issued in 1985 by the Suntory–Toyota Centre at the LSE. Where convenient, I have quoted from this earlier version, but I believe that these quotations are an accurate reflection of Professor Goodhart's more recent opinions.

3 This discussion is abbreviated from chapter 2 of my book *The State and the Monetary System* (1989a). Further details can be found there.

4 A common argument is that banks often fail to take adequate precautions, and therefore get themselves into serious difficulties. A response to this is that banks have less incentive to take precautions when they can count on being bailed out. Because central banking encourages banks to take excessive risks, it does not follow that free banking does as well. I examine these issues in more detail in the discussion of the LDC debt crisis below.

5 The theory and experience of option clauses is discussed in Dowd (1988c). One might add here that the 'flight to specie' scenario is rare historically – none of the nineteenth-century banking panics fits into that pattern, for instance.

6 There are well known problems about the feasibility of paying interest on notes – see, for example, White (1987) – and this further undermines Goodhart's argument, at least as regards making notes more attractive to hold.

7 See, for example, White (1984b: chapter 1).

8 Quoted in Smith (1936: 63).

9 In a letter Professor Goodhart points out to me that central banks were sometimes established to promote clearing systems, and he gives the example of the Reichsbank. It seems to me that one cannot deny that some central banks were given the task of organizing note-clearing, but if one accepts the argument that unrestricted banks have an incentive to evolve their own clearing system, then one needs to explain what prevented them organizing a clearing system in the first place.

10 It is interesting to note, incidentally, that Citicorp apparently used a strategy like this to build up its market share in nineteenth-century New York (see Kaufman 1987).

11 I am not denying, by the way, that free banks would make mistakes or that a free banking system would experience cycles. Bankers' mistakes were no doubt an important contributory factor to the LDC debt crisis, but one must acknowledge the role of the bail-out facility in encouraging risk-taking. As for cycles, it is one thing to suggest that there would be cycles under free banking but quite another to claim that free banking would experience more severe cycles than central banking. To demonstrate the latter claim one would have to focus on the difference in industrial structure and explain the mechanism that enables the central banking system to dampen down the cycles that free banking would experience.

12 Quoted in White (1984b), p. 23.

13 Wesslau (1887), p. xi.

11 The evolution of central banking in England, 1821–90

A slightly revised version of a paper presentation at the City University Business School conference 'Unregulated Banking: Chaos or Order?' in London in May 1989 and printed as chapter 5 in the volume of that title edited by Forrest Capie and Geoffrey E. Wood (Macmillan, 1991). I should like to thank Larry White and, most especially, Leslie Pressnell for detailed comments which have improved the chapter very considerably.

1 An example is Goodhart (1988), who emphasizes that central banking to a large extent simply evolved, but the critical issue is not the evolution *per se* so much as the role the state played in that evolution.

2 The work of Rolnick and Weber, among others, indicates that US 'free banking' before the Civil War was considerably more successful than had been appreciated. Dowd (1989a: chapter 5 provides an assessment of this experience. White (1984b) indicates that something close to free banking worked very well in Scotland until 1845, and the work of Schuler (1988), Selgin (1987a) and Jonung (1985) indicates that competitive note issue was successful in Canada, China and Sweden. Selgin (1988: 5–15) and Schuler (1989) provide overviews of these and other experiences of free banking.

3 There were instances where the Bank acted as lender of last resort even in the late eighteenth century. For more on these episodes see Lovell (1957) and Ashton (1959).

4 Indeed, since it had the responsibility of managing an inconvertible currency, the Bank was more like a modern central bank during the Restriction period than it was even in 1890.

5 The precise date at which the other banks abandoned their issues is not entirely clear. Most writers suggest the 1780s, but MacLeod (1896: 103) reports an example of a private London banknote dated April 1793.

6 The Bank apparently had a policy of refusing to accommodate those

who issued their own notes, or who used notes other than those issued by the Bank. In the 1840s, for example, it granted some country banks accommodation favours in return for their using its notes instead of their own (Powell 1915: 344).

7 It is interesting to note that Hawtrey (1962: 131) saw the source of the central bank's power not in its being a bank of issue but in its being a lender of last resort (and therefore, by implication, in its control of base money). He went on to say, 'If the essential characteristic of a central bank is its function as the lender of last resort rather than its privilege of note issue, that does not mean that the evolution of the former function has not been intimately associated with that of the latter. It is obvious that a bank which can create currency in an emergency out of nothing has a great advantage, in facing the responsibilities of the lender of last resort, over one which runs the risk of stopping payment . . .'

8 The outbreak of war in 1793 gave rise to a financial crisis. The Bank first tried to accommodate the crisis, but the directors' 'nerves could not stand the daily demand for guineas; and, for the purpose of checking the demand, they curtailed their discounts to a point never before experienced', and in the process gave the market an 'electric shock' which greatly aggravated the panic (MacLeod 1896: 100). The government then intervened to issue £5 million in Exchequer bills, and the crisis abated. (MacLeod 1896: 98–100 has a good discussion of the crisis.) This episode was highly influential in promoting the doctrine, put forward shortly after by Sir Francis Baring and Henry Thornton, and later by Bagehot, that an expansionary policy was the best way to handle a financial panic.

9 'The enormous abuses which might be perpetrated by an unscrupulous government, and the dangerous power which so potent an engine as the Bank of England would confer upon them . . . had inspired . . . a well-founded jealousy' and led to 'stringent precautions' in the 1694 Act against unauthorized lending to the government (MacLeod 1896: 104).

10 It would be wrong, however, to blame Pitt alone for the suspension. The Bank's earlier policies contributed to its crisis. As MacLeod (1896: 115) wrote, 'Never was there a more unfortunate example of monopolizing selfishness. It [the Bank] would neither establish branches of its own in the country, nor would it permit any other private company, of power and solidity, to do so, whose credit might have interposed and aided in sustaining its own. Moreover, when a failure of confidence was felt in the country notes, it refused to issue notes of its own to supply their place. The power of issuing . . . was absolutely forbidden to powerful and wealthy companies, and left in unbounded freedom to private persons – a vast number of them nothing but small shopkeepers, with no adequate capital or property to support their issues, and whose credit vanished like a puff of smoke in any public danger. The bank consequently was left alone to bear the whole brunt of the crisis, solitary and unsupported, and finally succumbed.'

11 Bank notes were treated as if they were legal tender until their

depreciation provoked Lord King in 1811 to insist on payment of his rents in gold (as he had every right to do). The response was Stanhope's Act (1811), which made Bank paper legal tender, though the government went through contortions to avoid using that term since it reminded too many people of the assignats (Clapham 1944: 31–2).

12 The Bank started to issue £5 notes in 1795, and it began to issue £1 and £2 notes at about the time it suspended. Previously, notes of less than £5 had been banned by Act of Parliament in 1777. The reasons normally given for banning them were: (a) that they were inflationary, and (b) that the poor should be protected against losses in the event that a note failed. The first argument does not apply to a specie standard, and the second implies that the poor cannot discriminate between 'good' and 'bad' banks. It also ignores the consideration that banning small notes effectively deprived the poor of many of the benefits of banking – a curious way to help them. One suspects that the real reason for banning small notes was to create an entry barrier against smaller banks. The extent of the government's concern for the poor can perhaps be gauged from the fact that the old objections to small notes were 'thrown to the winds' when it was realized that the issue of small notes would enable the Bank to lend more money to the government (Smith 1936: 12).

13 No banker would rationally redeem his liabilities with gold when he had the legal right to give out Bank notes of the same nominal value which sold at a discount against gold. The depreciation of the Bank's notes and their legal tender thus combined to call Gresham's law into operation and drive out the 'good' (i.e. undepreciated) money from other banks' reserves.

14 To some extent, however, their enunciation of the 'real bills' doctrine can be considered as an attempt to intellectualize the discount practices of the Bank, which had some degree of soundness. The practice, therefore, was perhaps sounder than the theory the directors claimed to be following. I am grateful to Leslie Pressnell and Bill Allen (in his discussants' comments) for pointing this out.

15 Thornton in many ways anticipated Bagehot's analysis of the lender of last resort issue, but his work tended to be forgotten and it had comparatively little influence on the monetary debates later in the century. For more on Thornton see Hayek (1939) and Hetzel (1987). Humphrey and Keleher (1984: 303–5) provide a good comparison of the views of Thornton and Bagehot.

16 I would suggest two possible reasons why some of the theory of the Restriction period was later overlooked. Much of it was concerned with managing an inconvertible currency and therefore had no relevance to monetary experience later in the century. A second, more tentative, reason, and one that applies particularly to Thornton, is that it allowed too much scope for central bank 'discretion' for later economists' taste. This would especially be the case with economists of the currency school, who devoted much of their effort to imposing 'rules' on the Bank of England.

17 Bank notes were now used by the public throughout England and

Wales. In the eighteenth century, with the solitary exception of Lanca-shire, Bank notes did not circulate much beyond a sixty-mile radius of Charing Cross (Richards 1934: 195).

18 They could defy their shareholders to a certain extent by dividing them or depriving them of information. As Dodwell (1934: 57) notes, 'The Directors gave no statement of accounts to the Proprietors till 1832, though suits were brought by some malcontents in the attempt to compel them to do so.' For a long time the management appeared to hide behind the ancient Bank customs of secrecy to prevent shareholders obtaining information that could be used against them.

19 The relationship between the Bank and the government was never particularly clear. The relation was complicated further by the govern-ment's insistence that the issue of notes was a state prerogative because it trespassed on the state's 'sovereign right' to issue money. Yet, at the same time as it insisted on the right to control the note issue, it acknowledged that it had no right to regulate deposits: 'The more firmly the Government stated the principle of the absolute right of the State over the note issue, the more completely it seemed to abdicate any claim to regulate, or even to ask for information about, deposits' (Fetter 1965: 224).

20 Many observers blamed the crisis on 'excessive issues' by the country banks, and this view was widely accepted afterwards. However, as our earlier discussion indicates – and Woods (1939: chapter 1) confirms – the country banks had comparatively little scope to pursue policies independent of the Bank of England. One might also note that the Bank itself was under considerable pressure from the government to engage in 'cheap money' policies during the period 1822–4, and it went along with these policies only with some reluctance.　•

21 'The extent to which the distress had reached was melancholy to the last degree. Persons of undoubted wealth were seen walking about the streets of London, not knowing whether they should be able to meet their engagements for the next day' (MacLeod 1896: 122–3).

22 MacLeod (1896: 124) quotes an eminent country banker as saying, 'when the panic came country bank paper was brought in for Bank of England paper, and therefore all that was immediately wanted was an exchange of paper'. This strongly suggests that the main demand was for notes, not for gold as such, and therefore that the crisis could have been averted or ameliorated by a more expansionary note issue on the part of the Bank.

23 An old and forgotten box of £1 notes had been utilized the previous day, with government approval, and the Bank had run out of £5 and £10 notes by Saturday evening (Clapham 1944: 100). MacLeod (1896: 123) appears to be mistaken when he suggests that the box of £1 notes was opened the next week.

24 There is a legend that the Bank at one point in the crisis actually did suspend, by refusing to cash £16,000 presented to it by a City banker (Powell 1915: 330). This story is difficult to substantiate, but even Clapham (1944: 101) freely admits that 'As between continued cash payments and a brief actual, if not statutory, suspension it was, as the

Duke said of Waterloo, "a damned nice thing – the nearest run thing you ever saw in your life".'

25 The government's determination to legislate was ominous for the Bank. The government had already modified the monopoly of the Bank of Ireland in 1821 in the aftermath of an Irish crisis the previous year, and this despite the opposition of the Bank of England. For more on the Irish banking reform see Ollerenshaw (1987: 10) and Bodenhorn (1989a). The Bank of England's privileges had also come under attack at home. In 1821 Thomas Joplin had published an influential critique of the Bank's joint-stock monopoly, and both the Prime Minister (Lord Liverpool) and the Chancellor (Robinson) were unsympathetic to the Bank's privileges. As they wrote to the Bank, 'Such privileges are out of fashion, and what expectation can they have that theirs will be renewed?' (quoted in White 1984b: 61). In retrospect, the Bank did well in 1826.

26 The Act actually said that, 'to prevent any Doubts' about the lawfulness of such action, the Bank was formally authorized to 'empower agents to carry on banking business in any place in England' (quoted in Clapham 1944: 107). There was nothing to stop the Bank setting up branches earlier except its own reluctance to do so. See also note 10.

27 The feeling in the country seems to have been against the extension of the Bank's charter, but the government struck a deal with the Bank and steered the Bill through Parliament. For more on this episode see White (1984b: 65–8) and Dowd (1989a: chapter 5).

28 What remained of the usury restrictions was finally swept away in 1854 (Clapham 1944: 224).

29 The Resumption Act of 1819 required the weekly average of notes in circulation to be provided to the Privy Council, and a quarterly figure to be published in the *London Gazette*. Later on, the 1844 Act required the Bank to publish weekly returns (Dodwell 1934: 58).

One must bear in mind the respect in which private commercial information was held in those days. As Dodwell (1934: 57) observes, the Bank 'was not willing to give more than a minimum of information about its affairs even to Parliamentary Committees; this attitude was considered correct, and the committees were not inclined to force the Bank to make unwilling disclosures'. The compelling of the Bank to provide such information is therefore difficult to account for unless one accepts that it indicates a recognition of a public responsibility by the Bank.

30 I am grateful to Leslie Pressnell for straightening out my thinking on the Palmer rule. For more on the subject see the discussion on it in the 1832 parliamentary report, reprinted in Gregory (1929: 3–6), Matthews (1954: 165–76, 166, n. 1).

31 The Bank was only beginning to learn how to use Bank rate to control the level of its reserves – see the discussion of Bank rate policy below – and it could not easily control its liabilities because they were demand-determined.

32 Horsefield (1944: 114) saw the Palmer rule as the Bank's attempt to put into practice Ricardo's (1817) theory that a 'currency which acted

in all respects like gold, whether it consisted of coins, paper, or both together' would prevent commercial crises. Previous to that, the Bank directors had believed that the right rule was the real bills fallacy. Horsefield saw these attempts to condense 'their proper policy . . . into a simple and automatic rule' as a long-running 'delusion' resulting from their desire to 'escape from the unwanted burden of monetary management' (p. 115).

33 The Bank would have been acutely aware of this danger: recall how close the Bank came to not getting its charter extended in 1833 (see note 25).

34 The roots of the currency principle can be traced to Ricardo (1817) (see note 32) and even further back to Hume (1752). Its origins are discussed in Sayers's introductory essay (1963) and Robbins (1958). Its fallacies are explained in MacLeod (1896) and Andrèades (1909: 275–7).

35 Exactly why the Bank management suggested these provisions is something of a mystery, since the 100 per cent reserve requirement considerably reduced the Bank's profit from note issuing. Some idea of the loss to the Bank can be gained from the figures on its note circulation. In September 1844 its note issue was £28,351,295 (Andrèades 1909: 290). Its fiduciary issue was £14 million, so the Bank had to hold the difference between these two figures in gold at the Banking Department. This difference – £14,351,295 – overstates the cost to the Bank in so far as the Bank would have held some gold against the note issue, but it takes no account of the likelihood that the Bank's note issue would have increased over time. It is therefore not unreasonable to consider it as a ball-park figure for the cost of the reserve requirement to the Bank. To give it some perspective, it is not far off the size of the Banking Department's average reserve. Against this cost, the 1844 Act also gave the Bank the note privileges it had been hankering for, and consolidated its position as the government's bank. It therefore seems probable that the Bank embraced the currency school because it gave the Bank an excuse to push for the privileges that the Bank really wanted, and the reserve requirement was simply the price the Bank had to pay to get it.

One might add that Peel would have liked to abolish the 'private' note issues there and then, but he allowed them to continue, to avoid the political consequences of taking on the bankers' lobby. Nevertheless, clause 25 of the Act envisaged private note issues continuing only until 1856. The bankers clung to their local note privileges even after 1856, however, and the last English private note issue (Fox Fowler & Co., of Wellington in Somerset) did not disappear until 1921. I thank Professor Pressnell for this information.

36 In the 1820s Peel was convinced that 'the root of the evil [of crises] lay in the monopoly of the Bank of England' (MacLeod 1896: 128), but by this time he had come round to the views of the currency school. He was influenced both by the arguments put forward by the currency school and by the lessons he drew from the failure of issuing banks (such as the Bath Bank in 1841). His main argument against

free banking was that competition would undermine the quality of the currency. He had apparently abandoned his own earlier arguments about the superiority of the Scottish system of banking. Peel's arguments are summarized in MacLeod (1896: 128–9) and Andrèades (1909: 285–8).

37 In the event of any note-issuing bank giving up its right to issue, the Bank was allowed to increase its own fiduciary (i.e. unbacked) issue by up to two-thirds of the amount of the lapsed note issue.

38 Note that the 1844 Act did not remove the ambiguity about the Bank's responsibility, and there were some who believed that the Bank still had a public responsibility, even though it was not defined by legislation. The Commons Committee on Commercial Distress (1847–8) 'clearly asserted that the Bank had a special public responsibility in the conduct of its banking business' (Dodwell (1934: 63). It went on to say that the Bank's unique circumstances – including its 'special and exclusive privileges' and its 'peculiar relation to the Government' – imposed on it the 'duty of a consideration of the public interest, not indeed enacted or defined by law, but which Parliament . . . has always recognised and which the Bank has never disclaimed' (quoted in Dodwell 1934: 63).

39 For more on this panic see Andrèades (1909: 331–42) or Powell (1915: 343–63).

40 For more on this episode see Andrèades (1909: 343–52); MacLeod (1896: 156–61); Powell (1915: 364–94).

41 Again, subject to the proviso that it kept Bank rate at no less than 10 per cent.

42 This period lasted till the Baring crisis, and it was disturbed only by the comparatively minor crisis occasioned by the failure of the City of Glasgow Bank in 1878. For more on the 1866 crisis see Andrèades (1909: 353–61); MacLeod (1896: 162–6) or Powell (1915: 395–410).

43 He also suggested that the Bank Charter Act should be amended, with an expansive clause to allow the Bank to issue additional emergency currency without having to rely on the government to offer it a Bill of Indemnity.

44 Note, for instance, the comment of Andrèades (1909: 326): 'the bankers have always refused to [hold more reserves], being convinced that *in case of need the Government would always intervene to save the Bank of England*' (my italics).

45 Apart from Sir Francis Baring and Thornton, who had originated the doctrine at the end of the eighteenth century, it was also supported by John Stuart Mill and was consistent with the views of the banking school, whose leader, Tooke, consistently advocated that the Bank should hold a bigger reserve, and denied that it was just a joint-stock bank like any other.

46 One reason for the support of this view within the court would have been the argument that lending expansively in a crisis gave the Bank the best chance of surviving it. A second reason would have been that financial panics gave the Bank the opportunity to make 'arbitrage profits' by buying up assets at bargain basement prices. Both these

reasons are based on the Bank's own self-interest. A third reason, mentioned earlier, is that the members of the court would have had a personal interest in ensuring that the Bank led support to the firms they worked for or did business with.

47 Pressnell argues in correspondence that Bagehot had something of a fixation about the level of reserves. Bagehot tended to overlook that a significant part of bankers' balances at the Bank was for clearing purposes, and was therefore unlikely to be removed. As far as the Bank was concerned, the serious withdrawal risk attached only to 'hot money' balances, which were only part of the deposits held at the Bank. I agree with this point, though subject to the potential qualifications discussed in note 57. Professor Pressnell also points out that two years after *Lombard Street* Bagehot retreated somewhat from his earlier position on reserves in his evidence to the Select Committee on Banks of Issue (see Pressnell 1968; St John-Stevas 1979: 104–55).

48 Bagehot himself was aware of the problem, even if he did not provide a convincing resolution of it: 'It is with serious difficulty that the same bank which keeps the ultimate reserve should also have the duty of lending in the last resort. The two functions are, in practice, inconsistent – one prescribes keeping money, and the other prescribes parting with it' (*Economist*, 1 September 1866).

49 He also failed to appreciate that any reserve rule the Bank adopted (e.g. a working minimum of £15 million) might itself have created problems as the reserve fell to the target minimum.

50 Had he appreciated the link between Bank rate policy and the reserve, Sayers suggests, he 'could scarcely have worried quite so much about the size of the reserve' (1958: 15).

51 The idea originated with Thornton's evidence to the Lords' Committee on the Bank Restriction in 1797. The theory of Bank rate was explained by Palmer to the 1832 parliamentary committee, and Hawtrey was of the opinion that the theory of Bank rate he put forward there was substantially the same as that propounded by the Cunliffe committee in 1918.

52 In fact Bank rate had been used earlier, in 1822, when the Bank was criticized for keeping it too high. This had led to open disagreement between the Bank and the government, but the Bank eventually gave in and lowered its discount rate.

53 Wood (1939: 86) and Clapham (1944) have made it clear that the Bank did engage in open market operations, albeit disguised ones, and writers earlier than them – and also Hawtrey – have tended to misunderstand the Bank's *modus operandi*.

54 In the exceptional cases where Bank rate fell below market rate (e.g. in November 1838, see Andrèades 1909: 267) the Bank faced considerable additional losses, as it would have attracted all the market demand for discounts.

55 An interesting question is why the Bank retained *any* discount business. While an ordinary market operator would not usually wish to deal with the Bank on such terms, the Bank always had at least a potential

market with the discount houses. See also the discussion of the 1858 rule.

56 I should like to thank Leslie Pressnell for this information on the 1858 rule. Note, however, that the 1858 rule only reduced the Bank's moral hazard problem; it did not eliminate it.

57 A problem that was never satisfactorily solved was the vulnerability of the British banking system to the danger of large – and especially politically motivated – withdrawals of gold from abroad. Bagehot had worried about it but had no solution. The problem was aggravated by the Bank's small reserve. In the 1860s, for instance, the Bank's reserve varied between £12 million and £24 million – considerably less than the reserves of foreign central banks like the Bank of France and later the Reichsbank – and was very small compared with the value of the Bank's demand liabilities (Hawtrey 1938: 41). An ill disposed foreign government would have had little difficulty in mounting a very serious threat to the basis of English credit: 'the inferiority of England in this respect [i.e. its low reserves] was dangerous *owing to the difficulty of rapidly attracting gold*; gold could always be obtained, but time was necessary. . . . [given how easily conspiracies could be formed] an attack on the English stock of bullion would be a most simple matter' (Andrèades 1909: 372; my italics).

58 The Baring crisis is discussed in more detail in Pressnell (1968) and Ziegler (1988).

59 'There was no formal acceptance of Bagehot's views by the Bank, and both in and out of the Bank there were those who did not like them . . . Increasingly this [opposition to Bagehot] was a minority view. From the middle 1870's, the principle was no longer in doubt, although there might, as in 1890 or 1907, be a question as to how that principle was to be put into effect. The Bank of England as a lender of last resort was . . . accepted as the foundation of monetary and banking orthodoxy' (Fetter 1965: 274–5).

60 That tradition was much more complex than the simple acceptance of any 'Bagehot principle', as Fetter seems to suggest. What was accepted was the need for central bank support, but, as the Baring crisis indicates, the kind of support the Bank gave went beyond Bagehot and contradicted him in significant ways. The widespread idea that central banks simply accepted Bagehot's advice is a myth.

61 There seems to have been considerably less concern about the Bank's profits later in the nineteenth century. As its profits did not significantly increase, one can only suppose this to have been due to the Bank and its shareholders becoming resigned to the fact that their profits now had to take second place.

12 The evolution of central banking in England: a reply to my critics

Originally written in response to the 'Comments' of my discussants, Michael Collins and William Allen, on 'The Evolution of Central Banking in England, 1821–90', presented to the City University Business School conference 'Unregulated Banking' in London in May 1989, and published as chapter 11 of the present volume. Their comments are published in Capie and Wood (1991: 197–9, 201–5).

13 Stopping inflation

First draft written in 1990, revised and reprinted in *Saving our Dollar*, published by the Australian Institute of Public Policy, Perth, W.A., in 1992. I should like to thank Chris Ulyatt and the Institute for helpful comments.

14 Does Europe need a Federal Reserve system?

Presented to the Cato–IEA conference 'Global Monetary Order: 1992 and Beyond' held in London in February 1990, and printed in the *Cato Journal* 10 (2), 1990: 423–42. The author wishes to thank Bob Ackrill for help in sorting out EC finances and Anna Schwartz and George Selgin for their comments.

1 The Delors report has been subjected to scathing criticism in the United Kingdom. See, for example, Goodhart (1989a), Wood (1989), Eltis (1989) and Dowd (1989b). For the Treasury response to it see Treasury (1989). Goodhart (1989a: 24) captured the essence of the criticism when he wrote that the report 'reads as if its authors were convinced that there is only one currently feasible strategy for the coming stages of European unification: this is a federal strategy, a Hamiltonian strategy, to transfer increasing powers to a federal centre of the United States of Europe. No alternative is even considered.'

2 Artis (1989: 5) estimated the benefits to be about 1.5 per cent of GDP, but this is little more than an informed guess. Artis (p. 18) also suggested that 'there is an irreducible incipient instability' with fixed-rate systems because there is always a positive probability they might be dissolved. He concluded that a fixed-rate system cannot eliminate all exchange rate uncertainty but a common currency can. But the subjective probability that individuals form of a future dissolution depends on the institutional structure that lies behind the monetary system, not on whether we have fixed exchange rates or a single currency. Even a common currency might be dissolved if countries subsequently withdrew from the EC, and there are historical precedents (for example, the dissolution of the common currency after the break-up of the Austro-Hungarian empire).

3 Vaubel (1989: 6) argues that there is 'no operational scientific method of measuring and comparing the costs and benefits' of a fixed-rate system. His real exchange rate criterion for optimal currency areas allows for such factors as labour immobility, diversification and fiscal integration, so these factors should not be considered as costs in addition to those covered by the theory of optimal currency areas. According to Vaubel (p. 9), 'The traditional criteria of optimum currency areas are mostly ambiguous [and] difficult to measure.' Thus 'the availability of

a comprehensive and operational measuring rod, the real exchange rate criterion, is important.' However, for Vaubel 'It is not comprehensive enough. It ignores the other cost of currency unification: the weakening of currency competition; and it does not take full account of the benefits of currency unification.'

4 Goodhart (1989b: 12) reckoned that these savings 'are of some considerable importance, but are not massive by any standards.'

5 Eltis (1989) suggested figures of 2.5–3.0 per cent for tourist exchanges and 0.5–1.0 per cent for large business transactions. The first figure understates the cost because it includes only the pecuniary cost of exchange and ignores the inconvenience cost of having to go to a *bureau de change*. The second figure seems to be an overstatement. Large business transactions are paid for by using credit instruments (e.g. cheques and credit cards), and it is not clear why carrying out such transactions across different currencies adds significantly to their cost; whether there is a single currency or not, the settling up procedures are not fundamentally different. Even so, Eltis (1989: 1) estimated that the total savings from moving from flexible rates to a single currency amount to only 1–1.5 per cent of GDP at most, a figure that is not far different from mine.

6 The resources used by *bureaux de change* overstate the relevant cost in one respect and understate it in another. They overstate it because the only *bureaux de change* activity that would be eliminated is between the currencies that are merged. They understate it because not all currency exchanges actually take place through such bureaus.

7 To the extent that the case for a central bank depends on the case for a single currency, the only way to advance the case for a central bank would be to establish free competition to indicate whether there should be a single currency (although it is well established that a single currency does not require a single issuer; see White 1984b; Selgin 1988; Dowd 1989a; Glasner 1989b). However, I certainly do not dispute Schwartz's claim in her discussant's comment that competition among currencies might involve large information costs. I would claim only that we simply do not know enough to justify imposing a single currency by fiat.

8 This discussion is based loosely on the literature stemming from Barro and Gordon (1983b). For a good evaluation of it see Blackburn (1989).

9 One might wonder how the EC could be technically bankrupt when its budget is theoretically always in balance. In practice the EC was able to maintain the fiction of a balanced budget by pushing unfunded liabilities into the future where it lacked the means to honour them.

10 The EC had many ways of disguising its true budgetary position. One was to manipulate the accounts of its Structural Adjustment Funds. Another was to overvalue agricultural stocks by valuing them at purchase prices instead of disposal prices. The EC also massaged its accounts by diverting agricultural surpluses into its stockpiles instead of exporting them. The EC has to pay the cost almost immediately if CAP surpluses are exported, but if surpluses are stored member governments pay the immediate costs and the EC pays them back later.

Although this enables CAP expenditure to be put off to another day, the 'eventual Budget costs can be horrific, . . . for throughout the storage period storage and finance costs must be paid, and when the stocks are eventually released then the Member States must be reimbursed for the "loss" in value. If intervention, rather than export, is systematically pursued for short-run gains, then the inheritance is burgeoning inter- vention stores *and* running costs' (Swinbank 1986: 2).

11 The EC also engages in a considerable amount of off-budget financing. In 1988 such financing amounted to about 25 per cent of its total budget (Commission 1989b: 10).

12 This account of Community finances gives a rather optimistic picture because it ignores certain other problems. One is the problem of outright fraud. Tiddeman indicated that from 10 per cent to 20 per cent of Community subsidies are defrauded (in Tutt 1989: 100). Another is the sheer inefficiency of the Community. See Tutt (1989: xiii).

13 The measures of seigniorage referred to below are the increases in monetary base, but increases in monetary base are not the only revenue that governments can appropriate using inflation, or even the most important ones. As Friedman and Schwartz (1986: 56) observed, decreases in the real value of outstanding government debt due to inflation are at least as important. It follows, then, that the Community could increase its seigniorage revenue considerably beyond the levels suggested in the text if it were to start issuing debt whose value was then depreciated by inflation. This consideration, of course, further magnifies the problems already highlighted.

14 The case of France is taken only for illustrative purposes, but it may well understate the potential revenue involved. We would get consider- ably higher revenues if we used Italy or Portugal as an example or if the new central bank imposed more stringent reserve requirements.

15 Again, these figures are illustrative, but the average figure of 0.4 per cent is relatively robust to how one takes the average.

16 See Selgin (1988, 1990a) and Dowd (1988b, 1989a), who both argue that intervention to stabilize the banking system has usually had just the opposite effect. As for the 'widows and orphans' argument, the single most important service the government could provide such people would be to protect the value of their investments by refraining from inflation, something that governments have singularly failed to do.

17 Vaubel (1988) argues persuasively that one of the functions of the bureaucracy is to do the 'dirty work' for elected politicians and take the blame for it. This would presumably be one of the functions of the new central bank. Such an arrangement makes sense from a public choice point of view, because it is more difficult for the public to penalize the bureaucrats than it is for them to penalize the politicians.

18 There is considerable evidence that these crises were due to the inappro- priate legal framework provided by the National Banking System. For the destabilizing effects of these and other restrictions on the US bank- ing system see Benston (1989), Dowd (1989a) and Selgin (1990a).

19 One might also add another factor: the memory of earlier twentieth- century inflation in Germany.

20 These short-term fluctuations can be very considerable. See de Cecco and Giovannini (1989: 5). There is also empirical evidence that capital controls have helped to restrain interest rate fluctuations and capital movements (Giavazzi and Spaventa 1990).

21 It seems that this German hegemony causes considerable resentment, especially in France. This resentment may help to explain why the French have been pushing for an international central bank in which German influence would be reduced. See Eltis (1989) and Goodhart (1989b).

22 Dowd (1989b) elaborates on this proposal and suggests that the United Kingdom should introduce monetary reform to stabilize prices and then announce the entry of the pound into the ERM.

15 Evaluating the hard ecu

Originally published in *The World Economy* 14, June 1991: 215–25. I should like to thank Alec Chrystal, Charles Goodhart, David Greenaway, Michele Fratianni and Chris Tame for helpful discussions on this subject, and a referee for comments on an earlier draft.

1 The British proposal thus eschews any compulsory use of the hard ecu, at least to begin with. As the Treasury paper says, 'whether it be legal tender or not is not the critical factor for the development of the hard ecu as a transactions medium. What matters is that parties to transactions find it mutually attractive for settlement' (1990: 8).

2 Focusing on mean inflation can also be motivated by consideration of price (level) risk. If individuals are concerned about price risk, then they want low price variability and hence low inflation – the *mean* inflation rate proxies the *variability* of prices.

3 This conclusion is also supported by Gros (1989) and Thygesen and Gros (1989). As the latter state, 'Experience and some simple trans-actions costs considerations suggest that inflation differentials of about 20 per cent to 30 per cent would be needed to trigger significant currency substitution' (1989: 32, n. 24). Note too that recent theoretical work by Kiyotaki and Wright (1989) and Wärneryd (1990) also suggests that the inability of individual transactors to co-ordinate a move to another currency means that a 'mildly inferior' currency can continue to be widely used even though all recognize its inferiority. The impli-cation is that a currency needs to perform very badly in order to provoke people to give it up – it seems to take a big push to trigger widespread currency substitution.

4 Note that the proposal envisages that the new currency would become a member of the narrow band of the ERM. The exchange rate *band* would therefore be fixed against the strongest ERM currency, provided the latter did not devalue, but the exchange rate itself would be free to move within this band. However, this band is sufficiently narrow – plus or minus 2.5 per cent – that the exchange rate flexibility it allows the hard ecu *via-à-vis* the currency to which it is tied makes little practical

difference, and we can consider the exchange rate as if it were more or less fixed.

5 The earlier Treasury arguments that purport to explain why the hard ecu would be used are therefore most unconvincing. The argument that borrowers would use it because hard ecu interest rates would be lower is not correct, because those interest rates would be the same as those of the strongest ERM currency. (The argument also seems to confuse real and nominal interest rates.) Nor would borrowers prefer it because it was more stable in value – it would have no more stability of value than the 'hardest' ERM currency. The argument that people would use it for exchange or as a 'vehicle currency' to carry around on their European travels is also unconvincing because there would be no logical reason to choose the hard ecu over any of the ERM currencies, including the 'hardest' one.

6 This conclusion would be reinforced if confidence in the EMF itself was less than perfect, and the track record of (other) central banks and the theoretical literature on time inconsistency gives one no reason to suppose that it would be. In addition, there is the problem that any devaluations would impose capital losses on the EMF which would presumably need subsidizing to preserve its solvency. The fact that the UK government proposals fail to deal with this problem only adds to its credibility problem.

7 I am well aware, of course, that the Delors report states that the Bank 'should be independent of instructions from national governments and Community authorities' (p. 20), but it simultaneously undermines that independence by recommending that the bank should be accountable to the European political authorities, and by giving the Council of Ministers overall responsibility for macro-economic policy.

16 The US banking crisis: the way out

Presented to the Durell Foundation conference 'Financial Fitness in the 1990s?' held at Scottsdale, Arizona, in May 1991. I should like to thank Mervyn Lewis, Richard Salsman, and Linda Ashworth and Elizabeth Racer of the Durell Foundation, for helping me with source materials.

1 As Salsman (1990, 117) observes, there is 'a great paradox in the conventional arguments "explaining" banking system deterioration. We have persistent government intervention undermining bank safety – and the charge that deregulation is the problem. We have government creating a chaotic monetary environment and rewarding imprudence – and the charge that banker mismanagement is to blame. We have government stealing and hoarding gold, cheating creditors and money holders via chronic inflating, covering up bad banking with lax 'regulatory accounting' and the charge that bankers are fraudulent and dishonest.

2 It would, I believe, be naïve to regard the Act as providing anything near a 'solution' to the banking mess. It rearranges the regulatory superstructure but does little to alter the incentive structure faced

by the individuals involved. The (generally) higher deposit insurance premiums it calls for undermine the attempts of 'good' institutions to build up their capital and worsen incentives by increasing further the already high penalties imposed on them relative to the 'bad' institutions that get bailed out. The much vaunted greater capital requirements specified in the Act are in fact 'considerably lower' than in 1980 (Kaufman 1989: 18). In any case, they are hedged about with so many loopholes that it is doubtful whether they would make much difference anyway, especially if the regulators remain true to past form and lack the will to impose them. (And note, in this context, that the Act does little to affect *their* incentives.) This regulatory discretion makes regulatory decisions more difficult and exposes the regulatory process to further political abuse. (It does not augur well, for example, how the Act itself was hi-jacked by special interest groups who inserted 'affordable housing' objectives that compromise its (alleged) main aim of promoting financial recovery.) The Act is perhaps best viewed as the authorities' latest move in the 'smoke and mirrors' game they play with the public. It involves a 'great . . . extension of the lack of accountability that got us here in the first place' and creates a 'dauntingly complicated organizational pattern' deliberately designed to confuse (Kane 1990: 6, 8). For more on the Act, see Barth and Wiest (1989), Kane (1990), Kaufman (1989) and Short (1990).

3 For more on the benchmark *laissez-faire* model see Dowd (1989a), Glasner (1989b), Salsman (1990), Selgin (1988, 1990a) and White (1984, 1989).

4 As an illustration of how safe banks might be without deposit insurance, England (1991: 13) notes that consumer finance companies in the 1980s maintained average capital ratios in the range 12.5–15.3 per cent and were not plagued by failures. Kaufman (1989) and Salsman (1990) also point out how US banks maintained much higher capital ratios before deposit insurance was introduced, and were consequently much safer. Kaufman also explains that the reason why 'runs on individual banks or groups of banks failed, with only infrequent exceptions, to lead to runs on all banks, despite the absence of an FDIC, appears to be explained by the combined effect of greater market discipline on bank management and more timely failure closure of [insolvent] banks . . . The very threat of a run served as a powerful source of market discipline' (1988c: 568). The safety of banks without deposit insurance can also be gauged from Kaufman's observation (1988c: 567) that the average loss rate to depositors in failed banks in the 1920s was only 0.2 per cent a year – a loss rate, to give it some perspective, well below any losses that depositors have suffered in recent decades from inflation.

5 Note, of course, that decisions must be made *ex ante*, before the realizations of random variables (e.g. returns on loans), and one cannot really object that outcomes could be improved if agents knew the realizations of those variables in advance. One cannot motivate government interventions by assuming that governments have privileged access to a (reliable) crystal ball.

6 The impact of anti-branching laws is explained by George Selgin

(1989c, 431), who writes that 'The smallness and lack of diversification of so many US depository institutions has made them chronically failure-prone: Unit banks in the farm belt have been over-exposed to farming losses, and Texas and Oklahoma banks have suffered for their involvement in oil-industry loans and in local real-estate development. In the Northwest, banks have relied excessively upon loans to the timber industry. Such overexposure ... reflects the fact that banks' lending opportunities are to a large extent bound by their location.' Restrictions such as these – and others, such as the usury laws and Glass-Steagall – also undermined financial institutions in other ways. Kaufman (1989: 2) writes that 'regulation forced [thrift] institutions to assume both substantial interest rate risk, by restricting them to making mostly long-term fixed-rate residential mortgage loans financed by short-term deposits and substantial credit risk, by restricting them to making mostly residential mortgages in their local markets. Thus, many were unable to diversify sufficiently either across product lines or geographically.... many studies in the 1960s and 1970s indicated [that] the industry was a time bomb waiting to go off.'

7 The fall in capital standards obviously implies that banks are perceived to be weaker, and they therefore become more vulnerable to problems of contagious lack of confidence (i.e. where depositors run on one bank because they see that another is in difficulties). Contagion thus becomes a problem precisely because intervention has rendered the banking system artificially weak, and those who argue that intervention is needed to combat contagion have got it the wrong way round. See also Dowd (1990b, 1991b) and Selgin (1990a).

8 One might also note that the career opportunities they enjoy after leaving the government service add to the perverse incentive structure faced by regulators. Sennholz (1989: 47) observes that 'Ex-regulators of S&Ls now prosper as consultants and S&L lawyers; ... [they] arrange financings, mergers, acquisitions, or reorganizations. They are involved in dozens of thrift deals amounting to billions of dollars, including federally assisted acquisitions. They may even render consulting services to the government itself. In 1988 alone, the FHLBB and the FSLIC alone, although they employ 200 in-house attorneys, paid some $100 million to outside law firms for work on liquidations, management take-overs, mergers and acquisitions.... To [many regulators] regulatory agencies are the revolving doors to fame and fortune.'

9 Many writers have assigned a large part of the blame for recent banking problems on deregulation, but it seems to me that this is overdrawn. As Salsman (1990: 114) emphasizes, regulators and legislators often resorted to 'deregulation' – and very incomplete deregulation at that – only as a salvage operation to bail themselves out. There is also a limit to what can be achieved with partial deregulations that leave intact the incentive structure that deposit insurance creates. In any case, the thrift industry was already economically insolvent before deregulation. As Catherine England (1991: 3) points out, 'Contrary to popular understanding, the thrift industry was insolvent on a market-value basis throughout the 1970s. The industry as a whole was in the red by $110

billion by 1980, before any of the deregulatory reform initiatives were passed. . . . It was the interest-rate risk [due to volatile monetary policy and vulnerability due to legal restrictions] that bankrupted the thrift industry initially.

10 Bad and/or fraudulent management is another favourite scapegoat of those who seek to play down regulatory and legislative failures, but as Kane (1990: 4–5) notes, the GAO study that is often cited to support this position merely establishes that fraud was present in three-quarters of the deeply insolvent cases examined and does not establish that fraud was the principal factor responsible. The decisive factor was lack of capital. Furthermore, he points out that deception itself is not illegal – though perhaps it should be – when validated by the GAAP or the RAP, which allow true positions to be disguised. In any case, fraud was also related to the infrequency of examination and regulators' reluctance to close institutions down (Kaufman (1989: 9). One must also be wary of blaming 'bad' management when deposit insurance gave managers strong incentives to take risks that subsequently failed to pay off.

11 One should also point out that none of these 'explanations' really gets to the heart of the matter, anyway. A 'good' banking system should be able to take shocks in its stride, and, as England (1991: 7) points out, 'vulnerability to external shocks is merely proof that the regulatory system is not working. Instead of creating an adaptable financial system able to weather economic storms, government policies have produced a network of banks unable to survive unless conditions are perfect'.

12 *The Economist*, 29 October 1988, pp. 114–20, has more details on these operations.

13 The desire to mislead the electorate also explains why Congress often prefers off-budget financing even though it is ultimately more expensive. Off-budget financing, like official obfuscation of banking statistics, is another phenomenon that refutes the 'public interest' view of government.

14 An informative but disturbing account of the way in which failed thrift owners obtained assistance from politicians is provided by Davis (1991). He notes, for instance, how Bank Board chairman Ed Gray's attempts to get to grips with problem thrifts in Texas were undermined by House Speaker Jim Wright, acting on behalf of the owners, and the FSLIC was more or less forced to keep them open against its own better judgement. Gray's attempts to sort the thrift problem out met with much hostility from a Washington establishment that did not want to know, and Davis writes that 'In the years Ed Gray spent getting doors slammed in his face, the [thrift] bailout cost ballooned beyond what the insurance fund could handle . . . By the time Gray's term as Bank Board chairman expired in June 1987, the problem had fattened . . . And Washington late in 1987 – that is, just a bit more than one year from the November 1988 election – was agreed on how to go about confronting it. It was to be carefully, skilfully ignored. [The task was to] get Ronald Reagan (who never once as president publicly mentioned the S&L mess) out of town before the roof fell in and to allow George

Bush to go before the taxpayers without having to explain how he had chaired the administration's 1984 task force on financial deregulation . . .'.

15 The banks' weakness is also underlined by their credit ratings (which in turn erode the banks' own ability to extend credit). Only one major bank has an AAA credit rating in 1989, down from fourteen in 1980 (Salsman 1990: 71). As their credit ratings fall, customers increasingly by-pass them and resort to other means of finance such as commercial paper, and many bank customers have better ratings than the banks themselves.

Bibliography

Allen, W. A. (1989) 'Discussants' Comments' on chapter 11 of the present volume, in F. Capie and G. E. Wood (eds) *Unregulated Banking: Chaos or Order?* London: Macmillan, 1991.

Anderlini, L. (1986a) 'Correctly Anticipated Bank Runs', Economic Theory Discussion Paper 95, Cambridge: Department of Applied Economics, University of Cambridge.

——(1986b) 'Central Banks and Moral Hazard', Economic Theory Discussion Paper 103, Cambridge: Department of Applied Economics, University of Cambridge.

——(1986c) 'Competitive banking in a simple model', chapter 6 of J. Edwards *et al.* (eds), *Recent Advances in Corporate Finance, Investment and Taxation*, Cambridge: Cambridge University Press.

——(1986d) 'Theoretical Modelling of Banks and Bank Runs', mimeo, Cambridge: Department of Applied Economics, University of Cambridge.

Anderson, T. L., and Hill, P. J. (1979) 'An American experiment in anarcho-capitalism: the *not* so wild, wild west', *Journal of Libertarian Studies* 3 (1): 9–29.

Andrèades, A. (1909) *History of the Bank of England, 1640–1903*, London: King, reprinted London: Frank Cass, 1966.

Artis, M. J. (1989) 'Roads to EMU', mimeo, Manchester: Department of Economics, University of Manchester.

Ashton, T. S. (1959) *Econolmic Fluctuations in England, 1700–1800*, Oxford: Clarendon.

Azariadis, C. (1981) 'Self-fulfilling prophecies', *Journal of Economic Theory* 25: 380–96.

Bade, R., and Parkin, M. (1981) 'Central Bank Laws and Monetary Policy', mimeo, London, Ont.: University of Western Ontario.

Bagehot, W. (1873) *Lombard Street: a Description of the Money Market*, revised editions London: Kegan Paul, 1906; Homewood, Ill.: Irwin, 1962.

Baltensperger, E. (1980) 'Alternative approaches to the theory of the banking firm', *Journal of Monetary Economics* 4: 1–37.

Barro, R. J. (1979) 'Money and the price level under the gold standard', *Economic Journal* 89: 13–33.

Barro, R. J., and Gordon, D. B. (1983a) 'A positive theory of monetary policy in a natural rate model', *Journal of Political Economy* 91: 589–610.

——(1983b) 'Rules, discretion, and reputation in a model of monetary policy', *Journal of Monetary Economics* 12, September: 101–21.

Barth, J. R., and Wiest, P. R. (1989) 'Consolidation and Restructuring of the US Thrift Industry under the Financial Institutions Reform, Recovery and Enforcement Act', Research Paper 89–01, Washington, D.C.: Office of Thrift Supervision, Department of the Treasury.

Barth, J. R., Bartholomew, P. R., and Labich, C. J. (1989) 'Moral Hazard and the Thrift Crisis: an Analysis of 1988 Resolutions', Research Paper 160, Washington, D.C.: Federal Home Loan Bank Board.

Benston, G. J. (1986) 'Federal regulation of banking: historical overview', chapter 1 in G. G. Kaufman and R. C. Kormendi (eds) *Deregulating Financial Services: Public Policy in Flux*, Cambridge, Mass.: Ballinger.

——(1989) 'Does Bank Regulation produce Stability? Lessons from the United States', mimeo, Atlanta, Ga.: Emory University.

Benston, G. J., and Kaufman, G. G. (1988) 'Risk and Solvency Regulation of Depository Institutions: Past Policies and Current Options', Staff Memorandum 88-1, Chicago: Federal Reserve Bank of Chicago.

Benston, G. J., Eisenbeis, R. A., Horvitz, P. M., Kane, E. J., and Kaufman, G. G. (1986) *Perspectives on Safe and Sound Banking: Past, Present and Future*, Cambridge, Mass.: MIT Press.

Bental, B., Eckstein, Z. and Peled, D. (1990) 'Competitive Banking with Confidence Crisis and International Borrowing', mimeo, Tel Aviv: Tel Aviv University.

Bernanke, B. S. (1983) 'Non-monetary effects of the financial crisis in the propagation of the Great Depression', *American Economic Review* 73: 257–6.

Bernanke, B., and Gertler, M. (1990) 'Financial fragility and economic performance', *Quarterly Journal of Economics* 105: 87–114.

Bester, H. (1985) 'Screening *vs.* rationing in credit markets with imperfect information', *American Economic Review* 57: 850–5.

Bhattacharya, S., and Gale, D. (1987) 'Preference shocks, liquidity and central bank policy', chapter 4 of W. A. Barnett and K. J. Singleton (eds) *New Approaches to Monetary Economics*, New York: Cambridge University Press.

Blackburn, K. (1989) 'Credibility and Time Consistency in Monetary Policy' mimeo, Southampton: University of Southampton.

Blainey, G. (1958) *Gold and Paper: a History of the National Bank of Australia*, Melbourne: Georgian House.

Bodenhorn, H. (1989a) 'Irish Free Banking', unpublished MS, New Brunswick, N.J.: Rutgers University, published in slightly revised form as chapter 8 of K. Dowd (ed.) *The Experience of Free Banking*, London: Routledge, 1992.

——(1989b) 'Two Episodes of Free Banking in Ireland: Scotland's Forgotten Sister', unpublished MS.

——(1990) 'Entry, Rivalry and Free Banking in Antebellum America', mimeo, New Brunswick, N.J.: Rutgers University.

Boehm, E. A. (1971) *Prosperity and Depression in Australia, 1887–97*, Oxford: Clarendon.

Bresciani-Turroni, C. (1937) *The Economics of Inflation*, London: Allen & Unwin.

Brewer, E. (1989) 'Full-blown crisis, half-measure cure', Federal Reserve Bank of Chicago *Economic Perspective*, November–December: 2–17.

Bryant, J. (1980) 'A model of reserves, bank runs and deposit insurance', *Journal of Banking and Finance* 4: 335–44.

Butlin, S. J. (1953) *Foundations of the Australian Monetary System, 1788–1851*, Melbourne: Melbourne University Press.

——(1961) *Australia and New Zealand Bank: the Bank of Australasia and the Union Bank of Australia Ltd, 1828–1951*, London: Longman.

——(1986) *The Australian Monetary System, 1851–1914*, Sydney: Ambassador Press.

Butlin, S. J., Hall, A. R., and White, R. C. (1971) *Australian Banking and Monetary Statistics, 1817–1945*, Occasional Paper 4A, Sydney: Reserve Bank of Australia.

Calomiris, C. W. (1989a) 'Deposit insurance: lessons from the record', Federal Reserve Bank of Chicago *Economic Perspectives*, May–June: 10–30.

——(1989b) 'Do "Vulnerable" Economies need Deposit Insurance? Lessons from the US Agricultural Boom and Bust of the 1920s', Working Paper 89-18, Chicago: Federal Reserve Bank of Chicago.

——(1990) 'Is deposit insurance necessary? A historical perspective', *Journal of Economic History* 50: 283–95.

Calomiris, C. W., and Hubbard, R. G. (1990) 'Firm heterogeneity, internal finance, and "credit rationing" ', *Economic Journal* 100: 90–104.

Calomiris, C. W., and Kahn, C. M. (1988) 'The Role of Demandable Debt in Structuring Optimal Banking Arrangements', mimeo, Evanston, Ill.: Northwestern University.

——(1991) 'The role of demandable debt in structuring optimal banking arrangements', *American Economic Review* 81: 497–513.

Cambridge Economic History of Europe 5, *The Economic Organization of Early Modern Europe*, Cambridge: Cambridge University Press, 1977.

Capie, F., and Wood, G. E. (eds) (1991) *Unregulated Banking: Order or Chaos?* London: Macmillan.

de Cecco, M., and Giovannini, A. (1989) 'Does Europe need its own central bank?' in M. de Cecco and A. Giovannini (eds) *A European Central Bank? Perspectives on Monetary Unification after Ten Years of the EMS*, Cambridge: Cambridge University Press.

Chant, J. (1992) 'The new theory of financial intermediation', chapter 3 of K. Dowd and M. K. Lewis (eds) *Current Issues in Financial and Monetary Economics*, London: Macmillan.

Chappell, D., and Dowd, K. (1988) 'Option Clauses and Banknote Convertibility', mimeo, Sheffield: School of Management, University of Sheffield.

——(1991) 'Is Convertibility on Demand always Optimal?', mimeo, Universities of Nottingham and Sheffield.

Chari, V. V. (1989) 'Banking without deposit insurance or bank panics:

lessons from a model of the US National Banking System', *Federal Reserve Bank of Minneapolis Quarterly Review* 13, summer: 3–19.

Chari, V. V., and Jagannathan, R. (1988), 'Banking panics, information, and rational expectations equilibrium', *Journal of Finance* 43: 749–61.

Checkland, S. G. (1975) *Scottish Banking: a History*, London and Glasgow: Collins.

Clapham, Sir J. (1970) *The Bank of England: a History* I, *1694–1797*, Cambridge: Cambridge University Press.

——(1944) *The Bank of England: a History* II, *1797–1914*, Cambridge: Cambridge University Press.

Clark, J. A. (1988), 'Economies of scale and scope at depository financial institutions: a review of the literature', *Federal Reserve Bank of Kansas City Economic Review*, September–October: 16–33.

Coghlan, T. A. (1918) *Labour and Industry in Australia*, Oxford: Oxford University Press.

Collins, M. (1991) 'Discussants' comments' on chapter 11 of the present volume in F. Capie and G. E. Wood (eds) *Unregulated Banking*, London: Macmillan.

Commission of the European Communities (1987) *Report from the Commission to the Council and Parliament on the Financing of the Community Budget*, COM (87) 101, and corrigendum, Brussels: Office of Official Publications of the European Communities.

——(1989a) *Community Public Finance: the European Budget after the 1988 Reform*, Brussels: Office of Official Publications of the European Communities.

——(1989b) *The European Community Budget*, Brussels: Office of Official Publications of the European Communities.

Congressional Budget Office (1990) *Reforming Federal Deposit Insurance*, Washington, D.C.: Congressional Budget Office.

Copland, D. B. (1920) 'Currency inflation and price movements in Australia', *Economic Journal* 30: 484–509.

Cork, N. (1894) 'The late Australian banking crisis', *Journal of the Institute of Bankers* 15 (4): 175–261.

Cowen, T., and Kroszner, R. (1988) 'The Evolution of an Unregulated Payments System', unpublished MS, Irvine, Cal.: University of California, and Cambridge, Mass.: Harvard University.

Currie, D. (1989) 'European monetary union or competing currencies: which way for monetary union in Europe?' *Economic Outlook*, October: 11–24.

Davis, L. J. (1991) 'The money pit', *Best of Business Quarterly*, spring: 82–91.

Delors, J., *et al.* (1989) *Report on Economic and Monetry Union in the European Community*, Committee for the Study of Economic and Monetary Union, mimeo, Brussels: Office of Official Publications of the European Communities.

Diamond, D. W. (1984) 'Financial intermediation and delegated monitoring'. *Review of Economic Studies* 51: 393–414.

Diamond, D. W., and Dybvig, P. H. (1983) 'Bank runs, deposit insurance, and liquidity', *Journal of Political Economy* 91: 401–19.

Dodwell, D. W. (1934) *Treasuries and Central Banks, especially in England and the United States*, London: King.

Douglas, R. (1990) 'The Principles of Successful Structural Reform', *Policy* Sydney: Centre for Independent Studies.

Dowd, K. (1988a) 'Is Government Deposit Insurance Necessary?', mimeo, Nottingham: University of Nottingham.

——(1988b) *Private Money: the Path to Monetary Stability*, Hobart Paper 112, London: Institute of Economic Affairs.

——(1988c) 'Option clauses and the stability of a laisser-faire monetary system', *Journal of Financial Services Research* 1: 319–33.

——(1989a) *The State and the Monetary System*, Hemel Hempstead: Philip Allan and New York: St Martin's Press.

——(1989b) 'How to end European Inflation: a Proposal to deal with the Controversy surrounding British Membership of the Exchange Rate Mechanism of the EMS', Bruges Group Study Paper 4, London: Bruges Group.

——(1990a) 'Money and Banking: the American Experience', Washington, D.C.: paper presented to the Durell Foundation conference 'Money and Banking: the American Experience', May; chapter 9 of the present volume.

——(1990b) 'Who needs Government Deposit Insurance?', mimeo, Nottingham: Department of Economics, University of Nottingham.

——(1991a) 'The evolution of central banking in England, 1821–90', in F. Capie and G. E. Wood (eds) *Unregulated Banking*, London: Macmillan; chapter 11 of the present volume.

——(1991b) 'Models of Banking Instability', mimeo, Nottingham: Department of Economics, University of Nottingham; chapter 6 of the present volume.

——(1991c) 'Option clauses and bank suspension', *Cato Journal* 10: 761–73.

——(1992a) 'Australian free banking', in K. Dowd (ed.) *The Experience of Free Banking*, London: Routledge; chapter 7 of the present volume.

——(1992b) 'US banking in the "free banking" period', chapter 11 of K. Dowd (ed.) *The Experience of Free Banking*, London: Routledge; chapter 8 of the present volume.

——(1992c) 'Optimal financial contracts', *Oxford Economic Papers*, April.

——(ed.) (1992d) *The Experience of Free Banking*, London: Routledge.

The Economist (1866) Editorials, 1 and 22 September.

Economopoulos, A. J. (1988) 'Illinois' free banking experience', *Journal of Money, Credit and Banking* 20: 249–64.

Edgeworth, F. Y. (1888) 'The mathematical theory of banking', *Journal of the Royal Statistical Society* 51: 113–27.

Eichberger, J., and Milne, F. (1990) 'Bank Runs and Capital Adequacy', mimeo, Canberra: Australian National University.

Eltis, W. (1989) 'The Obstacles to European Monetary Union', mimeo, London: National Economic Development Office.

Engineer, M. (1989) 'Bank runs and the suspension of deposit convertibility', *Journal of Monetary Economics* 24: 443–54.

362   Bibliography

England, C. (1988) 'Agency costs and unregulated banks: could depositors protect themselves?' *Cato Journal*: 771–97.

——(1991) 'Judging the 1991 reform effort: do US banks have a future?' Policy Anaysis 149, Washington, DC: Cato Institute.

Fane, G. (1988) 'The Development of Monetary Institutions in Australia from Federation to the Second World War', mimeo, Canberra: Australian National University.

Fetter, F. W. (1965) *Development of British Monetary Orthodoxy, 1797–1875*, Cambridge, Mass.: Harvard University Press.

Field, H., Hearn, S., and Kirby, M. G. (1989) 'The 1988 EC budget and production stabilizers: a means of containing the Common Agricultural Policy?' Discussion Paper 89.3, Canberra: Australian Bureau of Agricultural and Research Economics.

Freeman, S. (1988) 'Banking as the provision of liquidity', *Journal of Business* 61: 45–64.

Friedman, D. (1978) *The Machinery of Freedom: Guide to a Radical Capitalism*, New Rochelle, N.Y.: Arlington House.

Friedman, M. (1951) 'Commodity-reserve currency', *Journal of Political Economy* 59: 202–32.

——(1960) *A Program for Monetary Stability*, New York: Fordham University Press.

Friedman, M., and Schwartz, A. J. (1963) *A Monetary History of the United States, 1867–1960*, Princeton, N.J.: Princeton University Press.

——(1986) 'Has government any role in money?' *Journal of Monetary Economics* 17: 37–62.

Giavazzi, F., and Spaventa, L. (1990) 'The "New" EMS', Research Paper 369, London: Centre for Economic Policy.

Gilbert, R. A. (1984) 'Market structure and competition: a survey', *Journal of Money, Credit and Banking* 16: 617–45.

Glasner, D. (1989a) 'How Natural is the Government's Monopoly over Money?' Washington, D.C.: paper presented to the seventh Cato Institute monetary conference 'Alternatives to Government Fiat Money', February.

——(1989b) *Free Banking and Monetary Reform*, Cambridge and New York: Cambridge University Press.

Gollan, R. (1968) *The Commonwealth Bank of Australia: Origins and early History*, Canberra: Australian National University Press.

Goodhart, C. A. E. (1985) 'The Evolution of Central Banks: a Natural Development?' London: Suntory–Toyota International Centre for Economics and Related Disciplines, London School of Economics.

——(1988) *The Evolution of Central Banks*, Cambridge, Mass., and London: MIT Press.

——(1989a) 'The Delors report: was Lawson's reaction justifiable?' Special Paper Series 15, London: Financial Markets Group, London School of Economics.

——(1989b) 'Economic and Monetary Union (EMU) in Europe', Special Paper Series 24, London: Financial Markets Group, London School of Economics.

Gorton, G. (1985) 'Bank suspension of convertibility', *Journal of Monetary Economics* 15: 177–93.

——(1986) 'Banking Panics and Business Cycles', Working Paper 86–9, Philadelphia, Pa.: Federal Reserve Bank of Philadelphia.

Graham, W. (1886) *The One Pound Note*, Edinburgh: Thin.

Green, G. D. (1972) 'Louisiana, 1804–61', in R. Cameron (ed.) *Banking and Economic Development: some Lessons of History*, New York: Oxford University Press.

Greenfield, R. L., and Yeager, L. B. (1983) 'A *laissez-faire* approach to monetary stabiity', *Journal of Money, Credit and Banking* 15: 302–15.

Gregory, Sir T. E., (ed.) (1929) *Select Statutes, Documents and Reports relating to British Banking, 1832–1928*, London: Oxford University Press.

Grilli, V. (1989) 'Exchange rates and seigniorage', *European Economic Review* 33: 580–7.

Gross, D. (1989) 'Paradigms for the monetary union of Europe', *Journal of Common Market Studies* 27: 219–30.

Hammond, B. (1948) 'Banking in the early west: monopoly, prohibition, and *laissez-faire*', *Journal of Economic History* 8: 1–25.

——(1957) *Banks and Politics in America from the Revolution to the Civil War*, Princeton, N.J.: Princeton University Press.

Hankey, T. (1867) *The Principles of Banking*, London.

Harris, M., and Raviv, A. (1991) 'Financial Contracting Theory', mimeo, Chicago: Graduate School of Business, University of Chicago.

Hasan, I., and Dwyer, G. P. (1988) 'Contagion effects and banks closed in the free banking period', in *The Financial Services Industry in the Year 2000: Risk and Efficiency*, proceedings of a conference on 'Bank Structure and Competition', Chicago: Federal Reserve Bank of Chicago, May.

Haubrich, J. G., and King, R. G. (1984) 'Banking and Insurance', NBER Working Paper 1312, Cambridge, Mass.: National Bureau of Economic Research.

——(1990) 'Banking and insurance', *Journal of Monetary Economics* 26: 361–86.

Hawtrey, R. G. (1938) *A Century of Bank Rate*, London: Longman.

——(1962) *The Art of Central Banking*, second edition, London: Frank Cass.

Hayek, F. A. (1939) 'Introduction' to H. Thornton, *An Enquiry into the Nature and Effects of the Paper Credit of Great Britain*, 1802, ed. F. A. Hayek, New York: Rinehart.

Hetzel, R. L. (1987) 'Henry Thornton, seminal monetary theorist and father of the modern central bank', *Federal Reserve Bank of Richmond Economic Review*, July-August: 3–16.

Holdsworth, J. T. (1911) 'Lessons of state banking before the Civil War', *Proceedings of the US Academy of Political Science* 1: 210–24, reprinted in *ibid.* 30 (1971): 23–36.

Holzer, H. M. (1981) *Government's Money Monopoly: its Source and Scope, and how to Fight it*, New York: Books in Focus.

Horsefield, J. K. (1944) 'The origins of the Bank Charter Act, 1844', in T. S. Ashton and R. S. Sayers (eds) *Papers in English Monetary History*, Oxford: Clarendon, 1953.

Hume, D. (1752) 'Of money', in *Essays Moral, Political and Literary*, 1758 edition, reprinted London: Oxford University Press, 1962.

Humphrey, T. M., and Keleher, R. E. (1984) 'The lender of last resort: a historical perspective', *Cato Journal* 4: 275–318.

Huntington, C. C. (1964) *A History of Banking and Currency in Ohio before the Civil War*, Columbus, OH.: Heer.

Jacklin, C. (1987) 'Demand deposits, trading restrictions, and risk sharing', chapter 2 of E. C. Prescott and N. Wallace (eds) *Contractual Arrangements for Intertemporal Trade*, Minneapolis, Minn.: University of Minnesota Press.

——(1988) 'Demand Equity and Deposit Insurance', mimeo, Stanford, Cal.: Stanford University.

Jacklin, C., and Bhattacharya, S. (1988) 'Distinguishing panics and information-based bank runs: welfare and policy implications', *Journal of Political Economy* 96: 568–92.

Jevons, W. S. (1875) *Money and the Mechanism of Exchange*, London, reprinted New York and London: Appleton, 1921.

Jonung, L. (1985) 'The Economics of Private Money: the Experience of Private Notes in Sweden, 1831–1902', London: paper presented to the Monetary History Group, September.

Joplin, T. (1822) *An Essay on the General Principles and Present Practice of Banking in England and Scotland*, Newcastle: Walker.

Kahn, J. A. (1985) 'Another look at free banking in the United States', *American Economic Review* 75: 881–5.

Kane, E. J. (1985) *The Gathering Crisis in Federal Deposit Insurance*, Cambridge, Mass.: MIT Press.

——(1990) 'FIRREA: financial malpractice', *Durell Journal of Money and Banking* 2, May: 2–10.

Kaufman, G. G. (1987) 'The truth about bank runs', Staff Memorandum 87-3, Chicago: Federal Reserve Bank of Chicago.

——(1988a) 'Bank runs: causes, benefits and costs', *Cato Journal* 7: 559–87.

——(1988b) 'The truth about bank runs', chapter 2 of C. England and T. Huertas (eds) *The Financial Services Revolution: Policy Directions for the Future*, Boston, Mass.: Kluwer.

——(1988c) 'The truth about bank runs', *Cato Journal* 7: 559–87.

——(1989) 'The Savings and Loan Rescue of 1989: Causes and Perspective', Issues in Financial Regulation Working Paper 89-23, Chicago: Federal Reserve Bank of Chicago.

Kerr, A. W. (1918) *History of Banking in Scotland*, third edition, London: Black.

Kimbrough, K. P. (1986) 'The optimum quantity of money rule in the theory of public finance', *Journal of Monetary Economics* 18: 277–84.

Kindleberger, C. P. (1978) *Manias, Panics and Crashes: a History of Financial Crises*, New York: Basic Books.

King, R. G. (1983) 'On the economics of private money', *Journal of Monetary Economics* 12: 127–58.

Kiyotaki, N., and Wright, R. (1989) 'On money as a medium of exchange', *Journal of Political Economy* 94: 927–54.

Klebaner, B. J. (1974) *Commercial Banking in the United States: a History*, Hinsdale, Ill.: Dryden Press.

Klein, B., and Melvin, M. (1982) 'Competing international monies and international monetary arrangements', chapter 9 or M. B. Connolly (ed.) *The International Monetary System: Choices for the Future*, New York: Praeger.

Knox, J. J. (1903) *A History of Banking in the United States*, reprinted New York: Kelley, 1969.

Koester, U., and Terwitte, H. (1988) 'Breakthrough in agricultural policy or another policy failure?' *Intereconomics*, May–June: 103–9.

Lewis, M. K., and Davis, K. (1987) *Domestic and International Banking*, Oxford: Philip Allan.

Lovell, M. C. (1957) 'The role of the Bank of England as lender of last resort in the crises of the eighteenth century', *Explorations in Enterpreneurial History* 11, October: 8–21.

Loyd, S. (1837) *Further Reflections on the State of the Currency and the Action of the Bank of England*, London: Pelham Richardson.

McCulloch, J. H., and Min-Teh Yu (1989) 'Band Runs, Deposit Contracts and Government Deposit Insurance', mimeo, Columbus, OH.: Ohio State University.

MacLeod, H. D. (1896) *A History of Banking in Great Britain, with a Historic Analysis of the Principles governing Banking, Currency and Credit*, in W. G. Sumner (ed.) *A History of Banking in all the Leading Nations*, reprinted New York: Kelley, 1971.

Maisel, S. J. (1981) *Risk and Capital Adequacy in Commercial Banks*, Chicago: University of Chicago Press.

Mankiw, N. G. (1987) 'The allocation of credit and financial collapse', *Quarterly Journal of Economics* 101: 455–70.

Matthews, R. C. O. (1954) *A Study in Trade Cycle Theory: Economic Fluctuation in Great Britain, 1833–42*, Cambridge: Cambridge University Press.

Melvin, M. (1988) 'Monetary confidence, privately produced monies, and domestic and international monetary reform', in T. D. Willett (ed.) *Political Business Cycles: the Political Economy of Money, Inflation, and Unemployment*, Durham, N.C.: Duke University Press.

Menger, C. (1892) 'On the origin of money', *Economic Journal* 2: 239–55.

Merrett, D. T. (1989) 'Australian banking practice and the crisis of 1893', *Australian Economic History Review* 29: 60–85.

Meulen, H. (1934) *Free Banking: an Outline of a Policy of Individualism*, London: Macmillan.

Miller, W. I. (1990) *Blood Taking and Peacemaking: Feud Laws and Society in Saga Iceland*, Chicago: University of Chicago Press.

Miron, J. A. (1989) 'The founding of the Fed and the destabilization of the post-1914 US economy', chapter 10 of M. de Cecco and A. Giovannini (eds) *A European Central Bank?* Cambridge: Cambridge University Press.

Mullineaux, D. J. (1987) 'Competitive monies and the Suffolk system: a contractual perspective', *Southern Economic Journal* 54: 884–98.

Nakamura, L. I. (1990) 'Closing troubled financial institutions: what are the issues?' Federal Reserve Bank of Philadelphia *Business Review*, May–June: 15–24.

Ng, K. (1988) 'Free banking laws and barriers to entry in banking, 1838–60', *Journal of Economic History* 48: 877–89.

Niehans, J. (1978) *The Theory of Money*, Baltimore, Md: Johns Hopkins University Press.

Ollerenshaw, P. (1987) *Banking in Nineteenth-century Ireland*, Manchester: Manchester University Press.

Pecquet, G. M. (1990) 'The Tug-of-war over Southern Banks during the Civil War: a Property Rights Approach', Washington, D.C.: paper presented to the Durell Foundation conference 'Money and Banking: the American Experience', May.

Peden, J. R. (1977) 'Property rights in Irish Celtic law', *Journal of Libertarian Studies* 1 (2): 81–95.

Peltzman, S. (1971) 'Capital investment in commercial banking and its relationship to portfolio regulation', *Journal of Political Economy* 78: 1–26.

Pender, H., Otto, G., and Harper, I. R. (1989) 'Free Banking in Australia', mimeo, Canberra: Australian National University and Melbourne: University of Melbourne.

Pope, D. (1987) 'Bankers and Banking Business, 1860–1914', Working Papers in Economic History 85, Canberra: Australian National University.

——(1988) 'Did Australian Trading Banks benefit from Scale Economies and Branch Networks during the Nineteenth Century'?' Working Paper 111, Canberra: Australian National University.

——(1989) 'Free Banking in Australia before World War I', unpublished MS, Canberra: Australian National University.

Porter, R. C. (1961) 'A model of bank portfolio selection', *Yale Economic Essays* 1: 323–59.

Postlewaite, A., and Vives, X. (1987) 'Bank runs as an equilibrium phenomenon', *Journal of Political Economy* 95: 485–91.

Powell, E. T. (1915) *The Evolution of the Money Market, 1385–1915*, reprinted London: Frank Cass, 1966.

Pressnell, L. S. (1956) *Country Banking in the Industrial Revolution*, Oxford: Clarendon.

——(1968) 'Gold reserves, banking reserves and the Baring crisis of 1890', in C. R. Whittlesey and J. S. G. Wilson (eds) *Essays in Money and Banking*, Oxford: Clarendon.

Pyle, D. H. (1986) 'Capital regulation and deposit insurance', *Journal of Banking and Finance* 10: 189–201.

Ricardo, D. (1817) *Proposals for an Economical and Secure Currency*, London.

Richards, R. D. (1929) *The Early History of Banking in England*, London: King.

Robbins, L. C. (1958) *Robert Torrens and the Evolution of Classical Economics*, London: Macmillan.

Rockoff, H. (1974) 'The free banking era: a re-examination', *Journal of Money, Credit and Banking* 6: 141–67.

——(1975a) *The Free Banking Era: a Re-examination*, New York: Arno.

——(1975b) 'Varieties of banking and regional economic development in the United States, 1840–60', *Journal of Economic History* 35: 160–77.

——(1986) 'Walter Bagehot and the theory of central banking', in F. Capie and G. E. Wood (eds) *Financial Crises and the World Banking System*, London: Macmillan.

Rolnick, A. J., and Weber, W. E. (1982) 'Free banking, wildcat banking and shin plasters', Federal Reserve Bank of Minneapolis *Quarterly Review*, fall: 10–19.

——(1983) 'New evidence on the free banking era', *American Economic Review* 73: 1080–91.

——(1984) 'The causes of free bank failures: a detailed examination', *Journal of Monetary Economics* 14: 267–91.

——(1985) 'Banking instability and regulation in the US free banking era', Federal Reserve Bank of Minneapolis *Quaterly Review*, summer: 2–9.

——(1986) 'Inherent instability in banking: the free banking experience', *Cato Journal* 5: 877–90.

——(1988) 'Explaining the demand for free bank notes', *Journal of Monetary Economics* 21: 47–71.

Romer, C. D. (1986) 'Is the stablization of the post-war economy a figment of the data?' *American Economic Review* 76: 314–34.

Root, L. C. (1895) 'New York currency', *Sound Currency*, 1–24.

Rothbard, M. N. (1978) *For a New Liberty: the Libertarian Manifesto*, revised edition, London and New York: Collier–Macmillan.

St John-Stevas, N., (ed.) (1978) *The Collected Works of Walter Bagehot* 11, London: Economist.

Salsman, R. (1990) *Breaking the Banks: Central Banking Problems and Free Banking Solutions*. Great Barrington, Mass.: American Institute for Economic Research.

Sargent, T. J. (1981) *Rational Expectations and Inflation*, New York: Harper & Row.

Sayers, R. S. (1958) 'The development of central banking after Bagehot', in R. S. Sayers, *Central Banking after Bagehot*, Oxford: Clarendon.

——(ed.) (1963) *Economic Writings of James Pennington*, London: London School of Economics.

Schedvin, C. B. (1970) *Australia and the Great Depression*, Sydney: Sydney University Press.

Schedvin, C. V. (1989) 'The Growth of Bank Regulation in Australia', paper presented to the joint universities conference 'Regulating Commercial Banks: Australian Experience in Perspective', Melbourne: August.

Scheiber, H. N. (1963) 'The pet banks in Jacksonian politics and finance, 1833–41', *Journal of Economic History* 23: 196–214.

Schuler, K. (1988) 'The Evolution of Canadian Banking, 1867–1914', unpublished MS, Athens, GA: University of Georgia.

——(1989) 'The World History of Free Banking', unpublished MS, Athens, GA: University of Georgia.

——(1992) 'Free banking in Canada', chapter 4 of K. Dowd (ed.) *The Experience of Free Banking*, London: Routledge.

Schweikart, L. (1987) *Banking in the American South from the Age of Jackson to Reconstruction*, Baton Rouge, La., and London: Louisiana State University Press.

Sechrest, L. J. (1990) 'Free Banking: Theoretical and Historical Issues', Ph.D. thesis, Arlington: University of Texas.

Selgin, G. A. (1987a) 'Free Banking in China, 1800–1935', mimeo, Fairfax, VA.: George Mason University.

—— (1987b) 'The stability and efficiency of money supply under free banking', *Journal of Institutional and Theoretical Economics*, September: 435–56.

—— (1988) *The Theory of Free Banking: Money Supply under Competitive Note Issue*, Totowa, N.J.: Rowman & Littlefield.

—— (1989a) 'Free banking in Foochow', published as chapter 6 of K. Dowd (ed.) *The Experience of Free Banking*, London: Routledge, 1992.

—— (1989b) 'Free Banking and Monetary Stabilization', mimeo, Athens, GA.: University of Georgia.

—— (1989c) 'Legal restrictions, financial weakening, and the lender of last resort', *Cato Journal* 9: 429–59.

—— (1990) 'Banking "Manias" in Theory and History', mimeo, Athens, GA.: University of Georgia.

—— (1991) 'Bank Runs and the Suspension of Payments: Diamond and Dybvig Reconsidered', mimeo, Athens, GA: University of Georgia.

Selgin, G. A., and White, L. H. (1987) 'The evolution of a free banking system', *Economic Inquiry* 25: 439–57.

Sennholz, H. (1989) *The Savings and Loan Bail-out: Valiant Rescue or Hysterical Reaction?* Spring Mills, Pa.: Libertarian Press.

Short, E. D. (1990) 'FIRREA: Texas and the nation', *Durell Journal of Money and Banking* 2, May: 11–18.

Shughart, W. F. (1988) 'A public choice perspective on the Banking Act of 1933', chapter 5 of C. England and T. Huertas (eds) *The Financial Services Revolution*, Boston, Mass.: Kluwer.

Smith, A. (1776) *An Inquiry into the Nature and Causes of the Wealth of Nations*, ed. E. R. A. Seligman, reprinted London: Dent and New York: Dutton, 1911.

Smith, B. D. (1984) 'Private information, deposit interest rates, and the "stability" of the banking system', *Journal of Monetary Economics* 14: 293–317.

Smith, V. C. (1936) *The Rationale of Central Banking*, London: King.

Sprenkle, C. M. (1985) 'On the precautionary demand for assets', *Journal of Banking and Finance* 9: 499–516.

—— (1987) 'Liability and asset uncertainty for banks', *Journal of Banking and Finance* 11: 147–59.

Stiglitz, J. E., and Weiss, A. (1981) 'Credit rationing in markets with imperfect information', *American Economic Review* 71: 393–410.

Sumner, W. G. (1896) *A History of Banking in the United States*, in W. G. Sumner (ed.) *A History of Banking in all the Leading Nations*, reprinted Fairfield, N.J.: Kelley, 1971.

Swinbank, A. (1986) 'Cognitations on the CAP', Discussion Paper 86.3,

Reading: Department of Agricultural Economics and Management, University of Reading.

——(1988) 'Can the EEC reform the Common Agricultural Policy?', Institut Valencia d'Economia *Papers de Treball* 4.

Sylla, R. (1972) 'The United States, 1863–1913', in R. Cameron (ed.) *Banking and Economic Development: Some Lessons of History*, New York: Oxford University Press.

——(1976) 'Forgotten men of money: private bankers in early US history', *Journal of Economic History* 36: 173–88.

——(1985) 'Early American banking: the significance of the corporate form', *Business and Economic History* 14: 105–23.

Tannehill, M. and L. (1970) *The Market for Liberty*, Lansing, Mich.: published privately.

Thornton, H. (1802) *An Enquiry into the Nature and Effects of the Paper Credit of Great Britain*, ed. F. A. Hayek, New York: Rinehart, 1939.

Thygesen, N., and Gros, D. (1989) 'Concrete Steps towards Monetary Union', Discussion Paper 177, Copenhagen: Institute of Economics, University of Copenhagen.

Timberlake, R. H., Jr (1978) *The Origins of Central Banking in the United States*, Cambridge, Mass.: Harvard University Press.

——(1984) 'The central banking role of clearing house associations', *Journal of Money, Credit and Banking* 16: 1–15.

——(1985) 'Legislative construction of the Monetary Control Act of 1980', *American Economic Review* 75, Papers and Proceedings, 97–102.

——(1986) 'Institutional evolution of Federal Reserve hegemony', *Cato Journal* 5: 743–63.

——(1987) 'Private production of scrip money in the isolated community', *Journal of Money, Credit and Banking* 19: 437–47.

——(1990) 'The government's licence to create money', *Cato Journal* 9: 301–21.

Townsend, R. (1979) 'Optimal contracts and competitive markets with costly state verification', *Journal of Economic Theory* 21: 265–93.

HM Treasury (1989) 'An Evolutionary Approach towards Economic and Monetary Union', London: HM Treasury.

——(1990) *Treasury Bulletin*, autumn, London: HMSO.

Trivoli, G. (1979) *The Suffolk Bank: a Study of a Free Enterprise Clearing System*, London: Adam Smith Institute.

Tutt, N. (1989) *Europe on the Fiddle: the Common Market Scandal*, London: Helm.

Vaubel, R. (1986) 'Currency competition *v.* governmental money monopolies', *Cato Journal* 5: 927–42.

——(1988) 'The Political Economy of International Organisations in International Money and Finance', tenth Henry Thornton lecture, London: City University Business School.

——(1989) 'Currency Unification, Currency Competition and the Private ECU: some Second Thoughts', mimeo, Mannheim: Universität Mannheim.

Viner, J. (1937) *Studies in the Theory of International Trade*, London: Allen & Unwin.

Waldo, D. G. (1985) 'Bank runs, the deposit-currency ratio and the interest rate', *Journal of Monetary Economics* 15: 269–77.

Wallace, N. (1989) 'Another attempt to explain an illiquid banking system: the Diamond and Dybvig model with sequential service taken seriously', Federal Reserve Bank of Minneapolis *Quarterly Review* 12, fall: 3–16.

——(1990) 'A banking model in which partial suspension is best', Federal Reserve Bank of Minneapolis *Quarterly Review* 14, fall: 11–23.

Wärneryd, K. (1990) 'Economic Conventions: Essays in Institutional Economics', Ph.D. thesis, Stockholm: School of Economics, Stockholms Universitet.

Webb, D. C. (1986) 'Comment' on L. Anderlini, 'Competitive banking in a simple model', in J. Edwards *et al.* (eds) *Recent Advances in Corporate Finance, Investment and Taxation*, Cambridge: Cambridge University Press.

Weber, E. J. (1988) 'Currency competition in Switzerland, 1826–50', *Kyklos* 41: 459–78.

——(1992) 'Free banking in Switzerland after the liberal revolutions in the nineteenth century', chapter 10 of K. Dowd (ed.) *The Experience of Free Banking*, London: Routledge.

Wesslau, O. E. (1887) *Rational Banking versus Monopoly Banking*, London: Elliot Stock.

White, E. N. (1983) *The Regulation and Reform of the American Banking Industry*, Princeton, N.J.: Princeton University Press.

——(1990) 'Free Banking, Denominational Restrictions, and Liability Insurance', paper presented to the Durell Foundation conference 'Money and Banking: the American Experience', Washington, D.C., May.

White, L. H. (1984a) 'Competitive payments systems and the unit of account', *American Economic Review* 74: 699–712.

——(1984b) *Free Banking in Britain: Theory, Experience and Debate, 1800–45*, Cambridge: Cambridge University Press.

——(1986) 'Regulatory sources of instability in banking', *Cato Journal* 5: 891–7.

——(1987) 'Accounting for non-interest-bearing currency: a critique of the "legal restrictions" theory of money', *Journal of Money, Credit and Banking* 19: 448–56.

——(1989) *Competition and Currency: Essays on Free Banking and Money*, New York: New York University Press.

——(1990) 'Scottish banking and the "legal restrictions" theory: a closer look', *Journal of Money, Credit and Banking* 22: 527–36.

——(1991) 'Banking without a central bank: Scotland before 1844 as a "free banking" system', in F. Capie and G. E. Wood (eds) *Unregulated Banking*, London: Macmillan.

——(1992) 'Free banking in Scotland before 1844', chapter 9 of K. Dowd (ed.) *The Experience of Free Banking*, London: Routledge.

Whittick, W. A. (1896) *Value and an Invariable Standard of Value*, Philadelphia, PA.: Lippincott.

Wicksell, K. (1907) 'The influence of the rate of interest on prices', *Economic Journal* 17: 213–20.

Williamson, S. (1986) 'Costly monitoring, financial intermediation, and equilibrium credit rationing', *Journal of Monetary Economics* 18: 159–79.

——(1988) 'Liquidity, banking and bank failures', *International Economic Review* 29: 25–43.

Wood, E. (1939) *English Theories of Central Banking Control, 1819–58, with Some Account of Contemporary Procedure*, Cambridge, Mass.: Harvard University Press.

Wood, G. E. (1989) 'One Money for Europe? A Review Essay', mimeo, London: City University Business School.

Wooldridge, W. C. (1970) *Uncle Sam, the Monopoly Man*, New Rochelle, N.Y.: Arlington.

Yeager, L. B. (1985) 'Deregulation and monetary reform', *American Economic Review* 75, Papers and Proceedings, 103–7.

Ziegler, P. (1988) *The Sixth Great Power: Baring's, 1762–1929*, London: Collins.

Index